# Technological Entrepreneurism
## Enterprise Formation, Financing and Growth

**ENGINEERING MANAGEMENT SERIES**

*Series Editor:* **Dr. John A. Brandon**
    *University of Wales, Cardiff, UK*

 * *Forthcoming*

# Technological Entrepreneurism
## Enterprise Formation, Financing and Growth

**Mario W. Cardullo, P.E.**
*Virginia Polytechnic Institute and State University*
*Northern Virginia Center, USA*

**RESEARCH STUDIES PRESS LTD.**
Baldock, Hertfordshire, England

**RESEARCH STUDIES PRESS LTD.**
**15/16 Coach House Cloisters, 10 Hitchin Street, Baldock, Hertfordshire, England, SG7 6AE**

*and*

**325 Chestnut Street, Philadelphia, PA 19106**

**Marketing:**
Research Studies Press Ltd.
15/16 Coach House Cloisters, 10 Hitchin Street, Baldock, Hertfordshire, England, SG7 6AE

**Distribution:**
*NORTH AMERICA*
Taylor & Francis Inc.
47 Runway Road, Suite G, Levittown, PA 19057 - 4700, USA

*ASIA PACIFIC*
Hemisphere Publication Services
Golden Wheel Building, 41 Kallang Pudding Road #04-03, Singapore

*EUROPE & REST OF THE WORLD*
John Wiley & Sons Ltd.
Shripney Road, Bognor Regis, West Sussex, England, PO22 9SA

**Library of Congress Cataloging-in-Publication Data**
Cardullo, M. W. (Mario W.), 1935-
   Technological entrepreneurism : enterprise formation, financing
and growth / Mario W. Cardullo.
     p.  cm. -- (Engineering management series ; 5)
   Includes bibliographical references.
   ISBN 0-86380-223-0 (alk. paper)
   1. Going public (Securities) 2. New business enterprises-
-Management. 3. Entrepreneurship. 4. New products. 5. Product
management. 6. High technology industries--Management.  I. Title.
II. Series.
HG4963.C366  1999
658.4'21--dc21
                        99-14702
                        CIP

**British Library Cataloguing in Publication Data**
A catalogue record for this book is available from the British Library.

ISBN 0 86380 223 0


Printed in Great Britain by Cromwell Press Ltd, Trowbridge

*To*
*the ancestor of my wife, friend and partner*
*Karen M. Cardullo*
Sir Dudley Digges
(1583-1639)
entrepreneur, adventurer, scholar, venture capitalist and founding member of
the
Virginia Company
*and*
*the late*
Daniel Webster
who started me on the road to technological entrepreneurism
*and*
*long time friend*
William Ferguson
technological serial entrepreneur
*and*
*my new grandson*
Daniel Amadis Ortiz
future technological entrepreneur

# PREFACE

*"Better to dare great things and fail, than to live in the gray twilight that knows not victory nor defeat."*

**Theodore Roosevelt**
(1858-1919)
26th President of the United States
(1901-1909)

Technological entrepreneurism is not for the faint hearted. The rapidity of change in the technological and market spaces is such that only the prepared and agile may succeed if stochastic resonance is with them. This book presents not only the qualities of technological entrepreneurs, but also the steps that should be undertaken to bring an innovative concept through the various phases of the enterprise's life cycle to market and to increase the probability of success. Many technological entrepreneurs begin their entrepreneurial careers with a sound technical background. However, the nature of technical education leaves the new entrepreneur, in many instances, with insufficient training and expertise, in the important non-technical business elements, for building an enterprise that can be *born* or, if established, meet the vicissitudes of the highly competitive market space. While this text presents the elements of moving through the various life cycles of a technological enterprise, only life experiences in the technological market spaces can add those elements needed to help solve the *equation of success*.

As a technological entrepreneur, I have experienced the various stages of establishing, financing and growing a technological enterprise a number of times. There is an element of excitement and thrill in bringing an innovation to fruition through a new technological enterprise. It has been said that technological entrepreneurs live with an eternal *fire in the belly*. Like all *fire* there is the potential to get *burned*. However, a technological entrepreneur rarely thinks of the potential dangers in starting a new enterprise. Many believe that technological entrepreneurs start enterprises for the financial rewards, however, that is only one of the motivations. In fact, the excitement can be compared to climbing an unconquered mountain. It has been said that when mountain climbers such as George. L. Mallory[1] undertake a dangerous climb, *they climb the mountain because it is there.* It is the same thing for many technological entrepreneurs. In the late 1990s, the Internet has provided many new mountains to climb.

While the technological entrepreneur does not usually think of the many potential pitfalls that must be transversed, there are those family members in the background who may not be entrepreneurs who must also deal with the results of the undertaking. No technological entrepreneurial activity is without its highs and lows. The successful technological entrepreneur is the one who, like the mythical *Phoenix,* can rise from the ashes and begin again. Even highly successful technological entrepreneurs have careers where one or more of their endeavors may fail prior to or after achieving success. Some of the highly successful technological entrepreneurs also serve as mentors and financial angels for new enterprises.

This text is divided into three distinct sections: Part One - Characteristics of Technological Entrepreneurs; Part Two - Process of Formulating a New Technological Enterprise; and Part Three - Process of Growth and Harvest. Within these sections, the individual chapters cover the various characteristics of the entrepreneur and the phases of the enterprise. While technological entrepreneurs and their enterprises share many characteristics with non-technology based enterprises, a complex and rapidly changing competitive landscape is one of the primary differentiators. In fact, the complexity and rapidity of change is starting to influence all entrepreneurs and enterprises. Technology has become pervasive and is impacting all. Rapidly developing electronic commerce via the Internet is causing dislocations in retailing and distribution. The twenty-first century will see disintermediation and marginalization of many industries and enterprises due to technological changes. It will be through an understanding of technological enterprise development and building agile and flexible enterprises that these changes can be used to developed sustainable competitive advantages.

Like all texts, this one had the participation and support of a number of individuals. I would like to thank my publisher, Research Studies Press, Ltd.

---

[1] **Mallory, George L.**, quoted in New York Times (answering the question of why he wanted to climb Mount Everest) stated, *"because it is there"*. Unfortunately, he did not return from his attempt to climb Mount Everest.

and in particular Guy Robinson, Publishing Editor and Mrs. Veronica Wallace, retired Managing Director and Dr. John A. Brandon, Series Editor for all the encouragement over the two years it took to prepare this text. I would also like to thank my students in the 1998 Class of the Master's of Science in Science and Technological Commercialisation Degree at the $IC^2$ Institute of University of Texas at Austin for their suggestions during my course in *Financing New Ventures*. My internal editors also deserve much of the credit for helping to make this text readable. My loving wife Karen Mandeville Cardullo not only served to edit this text but lived and shared several of my technological entrepreneurial experiences. My wife is a loving and supporting spouse, tolerant of the many vicissitudes of living with a technological entrepreneur and author, and as such deserves much credit. John May, Managing Partner of New Advantage Partners and Director of the Private Investor Network deserves credit for his assistance on the financing chapters. I will be forever grateful to Dr. C. Howard Robins, Jr., for his unswerving support and dedication to reading and making editorial suggestions. I look forward to their support and assistance on my next project, i.e., a case studies text covering the various phases discussed in this book with cases from the United States, European Union and Asia.

We are about to enter a new millennium; we are likely to see an acceleration in the growth of technology and technological entrepreneurism.

Mario W. Cardullo

*Alexandria, Virginia,*
*United States of America*
*April, 1999*

# CONTENTS

## CHAPTER 4
### Enterprise Technological Market Planning

**CHAPTER 5**
**Enterprise Formation**

# PART ONE

# CHARACTERISTICS OF TECHNOLOGICAL ENTREPRENEURS

CHAPTER 1

# Nature of Technological Entrepreneurism

> *"The general is the bulwark of the state: if the bulwark is strong at all points, the state will be strong; if the bulwark is defective, the state will be weak."*
> **Sun Tzu**
> *The Art of War, 500B.C.*

## 1. INTRODUCTION
### 1.1 Historical Perspective

Humanity has always possessed individuals with entrepreneurial spirit. Early hunters sought to find resources for themselves and the members of their group. Some dared to search over the next hill for additional game and plants when those in their own region expired. There was always one or more of the group with the inquisitiveness to move forward although not all members of early human groups had that internal drive.

When humanity discovered tool making, a new stage arose, i.e., the early technological entrepreneurs would make tools for others and trade them for food or other resources or services. Again not all members of the group possessed the requisite desire or abilities. In fact, some of those that formed this early entrepreneurial activity may have failed in a way that cost them and maybe their group their very existence. Today fewer than 1 in 60 and as low as 1 in 100 reach successful embeddment in their intended environment (Cardullo 1996, pp. 282).

Early humans also tried many concepts before arriving at the point where a new tool or process resulted in a leap in productivity. It has been shown (Kauffman 1995) that all-successful organisms, i.e., organizations[1], move in

---

[1] An organization is similar to an organism since it is composed of many individual entities working together for similar ends.

many paths before finally moving along those paths that offer the least resistance and lead to success. Successful organisms and technology are not significantly different (Kauffman 1995, pp. 191):

> *"Here (technological evolution) human artificers make fundamental inventions. Here, too, one witnesses, time after time, an early explosion of diverse forms as the human tinkers try out the plethora of new possibilities opened up by the basic innovation."*

Taking a historical perspective, the entrepreneurial landscape can be characterized as:

| Early Human Development | Entrepreneurial Landscape |
|---|---|
| Hunters | Entrepreneurs |
| Gatherers | Investment Community |
| Farmers | Professional Managers |

Like all societies, all elements are required if the community is to survive and grow. The early hunters took the largest risks and reaped the greatest rewards if successful. The gatherers took a lower risk but sometimes gathered poisonous berries, while the farmers took the least risk, but usually achieved a lower albeit consistent yield.

The term *entrepreneur* dates from about 1709 (Braudel 1979, pp. 670). Say[2] (Drucker 1985, pp. 277) gave an early definition of an entrepreneur as the individual who:

> *"...shifts economic resources out of an area of lower and into an area of higher productivity and greater yield."*

According to Say, the entrepreneur upsets and disorganizes economic stability. Say believed that an entrepreneur brought together factors of production in a way that created new wealth. A modern example is the impact on mainframe computing by Bill Gates and his company Microsoft®.

In the first half of the twentieth century, Schumpeter[3] wrote extensively on entrepreneurism and its impact on the economy (Drucker 1985, pp. 13).

---

[2] **Say, Jean-Baptiste** (1767-1832), early French economist who developed the economic principle that supply creates its own demand, known as **Say's Law of Markets**.

[3] **Schumpeter, Joseph Alois** (1883-1950), Austrian-American economist and social theorist, achieved prominence for his theories about the importance of the entrepreneur in

The thesis of Schumpeter was that the innovating entrepreneur caused dynamic disequilibrium in an economy. Throughout the twentieth century, we have seen this repeatedly. Schumpeter (Schumpeter 1936) considered the entrepreneur to be a *creative destructor*. Schumpeter saw the entrepreneur as an innovator who created disequilibrium by taking innovation to commercialization and embeddment in an environment where it did not exist previously.

The entrepreneur is not always the inventor. Take the case of chemical bleaching, which was invented by Berthollet[4] in France in 1785, but was commercialized by Tennant[5] in England in 1799 (Jay 1967, pp. 117). It was entrepreneurs like Tennant who seized upon the scientific discoveries from the Age of Enlightenment and turned them into an industrial revolution. Tennant is truly an example of Schumpeter's creative destructor who changed the socio-economic environment and forged the world that formed the basis for the start of the twentieth century.

In 1857, the Brothers Péreire[6] (Drucker 1985, pp. 25) formed in France first entrepreneurial bank. This was followed by the formation, in 1870, in Germany by Georg von Siemens of the Deutsche Bank[7] and the J. P. Morgan Bank in New York. These banks were formed to invest in new entrepreneurial enterprises and then resell the shares of these enterprises in the open market. These merchant bankers were the predecessors of today's venture capitalists (See Chapter 6 – Initial Enterprise Financing).

Throughout history, entrepreneurs have formed élites. The traditional entrepreneurial élites, which were associated with the heavy engineering industries of the *First Industrial Revolution*, were committed to

---

business, emphasizing the entrepreneur's role in stimulating investment and innovation, thereby causing *creative destruction*.

[4] **Berthollet, Claude Louis, Comte** (1749-1822), French chemist, who made contributions to several fields of chemistry including the bleaching process for cloth and paper.

[5] Bleaching powder, a solid combination of chlorine and slaked lime, was introduced in 1799 into the market by the Scottish chemist **Charles Tennant**, who then produced it in a large quantity to bleach cloth and paper.

[6] The **Péreire brothers** founded the first great investment bank in France, i.e., Crédit Mobilier.

[7] The Deutsche Bank was licensed by King William I of Prussia on March 10, 1870, and began operation in Berlin on April 9. Branches were opened in Bremen in 1871, in Hamburg, Shanghai, and Yokohama in 1872, and in London in 1873. By the end of the nineteenth century it had absorbed a number of other German banks and multiplied its capital about tenfold, under its managing director **Georg von Siemens**.

protectionism and to using cartel-like arrangements to provide high domestic prices (Clark and Staunton 1989, pp. 147). The twentieth century saw the rise of new entrepreneurial élites associated with science-based industries. Initially, this group came from chemical, electrical and automotive industries. During the last decades of the twentieth century, information technology ("IT") entrepreneurs, such as Bill Gates, Michael Dell, Steve Jobs and others, have dominated this group.

This has been called the entrepreneurial age (Bygrave 1997, pp. 1). This may be seen in the area of information technology where the growth of entrepreneurial technological enterprises is an everyday newspaper headline. The growth of the Internet has been largely based on the drive of individual entrepreneurs like Steve Case and investors like James Kimsey of America Online (See Chapter 2 – Technological Entrepreneurs), James Barksdale of Netscape Communication and others of similar ilk. These entrepreneurs, indeed, have been the creative destructors of Schumpeter, changing the technological landscape and spawning entire new industries.

The Internet[8] began in the 1960s as a U.S. Department of Defense project to provide secure communications. It was not until the 1990s that the growth of personal computers ("PCs"), another example of technological entrepreneurism, coupled with the development of a graphical user interface ("GUI") by Timothy Bernes-Lee of CERN, the European Particle Physics Laboratory, formed the World Wide Web ("WWW"). This user interface, which incorporated text, graphics, sound and video, was the basis for the entrepreneurial growth that followed. This growth has established a new term in the technological entrepreneurial lexicon: netpreneur. The Potomac KnowledgeWay[9] defines this as:

> *"1) An entrepreneur; 2) that creates innovative content, software, or communication products and/or services; 3) that are for about, or delivered over digital networks – today, the Internet."*

---

[8] The Internet had its origin in program called ARPANET (Advanced Research Projects Agency Network), established in 1969 to provide a secure and survivable communications network for organizations engaged in defense-related research.

[9] The Potomac KnowledgeWay Project was established in United States by the Morino Institute, a non-profit foundation, which focused attention on using the Internet and technology for societal good (See Chapter 2 – Technological Entrepreneurs.)

Entrepreneurs have the ability to see what Grove (Grove 1996, pp. 30) notes as a 10X change and take advantage of this strategic inflection point to implement a strategic vision. Throughout human history, entrepreneurs have seized the initiative to change the economic landscape, be it Alexander Graham Bell[10] and the invention and commercialization of the telephone or Bill Gates and the concept of a friendly user interface, i.e., Windows®.

These individuals face the challenge of convincing their associates and ultimately customers that their vision is indeed the vision that will not only service, but also assist to bring new economic productivity to market.

## 1.2 General Entrepreneurism
### 1.2.1 The Entrepreneur

According to Mintzberg and Quinn (Mintzberg and Quinn 1991), entrepreneurship is associated with the creation of a strategic vision usually associated with new concepts. Schumpeter emphasized the social leadership role of the entrepreneur through the willingness to take bold steps into the unknown and to make commitments that may not meet the criteria in standard decision processes (Rosenberg 1994, pp. 66).

Schumpeter's model of the entrepreneur consists of an individual who:

- Is the source of innovation activity.
- Causes or amplifies market disequilibrium by pushing the market out of its equilibrium state, e.g., Andy Grove, Chairman of Intel Corporation with the development and popularization of large scale microprocessors.
- Is the source of economic growth.
- Serves as the guidepost for advanced analysis of innovation and diffusion (Goodman and Lawless 1994, pp. 165).

A number of authors take the position that entrepreneurs have behavioral drives which cause them to adopt irrational positions and to take risks. This leads to more radical innovation rather than incremental improvements. However, Drucker (Drucker 1985, pp. 139) disagrees with this popular belief that entrepreneurs take reckless risks. In his opinion, successful entrepreneurs take calculated risks.

---

[10] **Bell, Alexander Graham** (1847-1922), an American inventor and teacher of the deaf, most famous for his invention and commercialization of the telephone.

Schumpeter also proposed that entrepreneurial functions become rationalized or bureaucratized, e.g., the formation of intrapreneurship, as the enterprise grows, i.e., more steps are required to achieve *bold steps* (Schumpeter 1936, pp. 132). However, such rationalization in the use of multifunctional teams (Cardullo 1996, pp. 128) does not lead to the *"obsolescence of entrepreneurial function"* (Schumpeter 1936, pp. 134) as exemplified by the rapid development of new technological entrepreneurial enterprises on the Internet.

### 1.2.2 Entrepreneurial Internal Characteristics

The internal characteristics, which influence the entrepreneurial process, are those directly associated with entrepreneurs and their ability to seize opportunities or, as eloquently stated by the Roman poet and satirist Horace,:

*"Seize the day; put no trust in the morrow."*

Horace (65 – 8 B.C.), *Epistles*

These characteristics can be divided into:

- Personal characteristics of the entrepreneur (See Section 2.0 of this Chapter, General Characteristics of Entrepreneurs).
- Organizational characteristics of the enterprise, consisting of elements brought together by the entrepreneur (See Chapter 5 – Enterprise Formation).
- Sociological characteristics associated with the entrepreneur such as interpersonal relationships (See Sections 2.0 and 3.0 of this Chapter).

### 1.2.3 Processes

The processes are those activities which the entrepreneur undertakes to move from vision to realization of that vision. These processes and events are independent of the type of enterprise and include:

- Innovation, the process of the introduction of something new, such as a new idea, method, or device.
- Triggering event(s) or discontinuity, i.e., event(s), small or large, which cause the entrepreneur to seek to take advantage of the situation (See Chapter 3 – Technological and Enterprise Strategic Planning).
- Enterprise formation, i.e., the establishment of an enterprise by the entrepreneur to realize the

entrepreneurial vision (See Part II – Process of Formulating a New Technological Enterprise).

- Enterprise growth, i.e., the process of building, managing and growing the enterprise into an organization with economic value built upon the entrepreneurial vision and spirit (See Part III – Process of Growth and Harvest).

Figure 1.1 shows a model of the general entrepreneurial process.

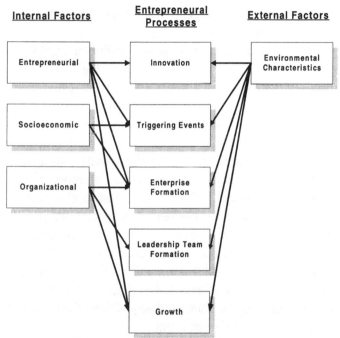

**Fig. 1.1** General Entrepreneurial Model (Adapted from Moore 1986)

As Figure 1.1 indicates, the general entrepreneurial model consists of:

- Internal characteristics associated directly with the entrepreneur.
- Processes for moving from innovation to enterprise formation and growth.
- External or environmental factors which are not under the direct control of the entrepreneur.

## 1.2.4 Environmental Factors

The environmental factors are those factors that are not directly under the control of the entrepreneur. However, these factors may respond to actions of the entrepreneur. These factors can be divided into:

- Market factors, such as customer's needs, competitive factors, and economic conditions.
- External stakeholders, such as investors, bankers, venture capitalists, and suppliers.
- Internal stakeholders, such as employees and members of the leadership team (See Chapter 5 – Enterprise Formation).
- Resources, such as availability of capital, human and inanimate resources (See Part II – Process of Formulating a New Technological Enterprise).
- Legal and regulatory factors, such as governmental policies and regulations, laws, including intellectual property (See Chapter 8 – Next Entrepreneurial Step).

The introduction of a new entrepreneurial activity into a market will, if successful, foster the formation of competitive entrepreneurial activities. When Ray Kroc[11], the founder of McDonald's fast food restaurant franchise system, proved that the fast food business was successful, imitators such as Hardee's and Wendy's soon followed. These competitors changed the market for McDonald's and not necessarily in a negative manner. The entrepreneurial spirit of Bill Gates spawned not only competitors, but also impacted the financial markets and led to legal interdiction by the U.S. Department of Justice, e.g., the attempted acquisition of Intuit by Microsoft® that was stopped by the U.S. Government.

Figure 1.2 shows a revised entrepreneurial model depicting the presence of the environmental factors in the complex entrepreneurial process. In this complex process, small changes can have major impact on the ability of the entrepreneur to achieve his/her original vision.

---

[11] **Kroc, Raymond Albert** (1902 – 1984), an American restauranteur and a pioneer of the fast-food industry with his worldwide McDonald's enterprise.

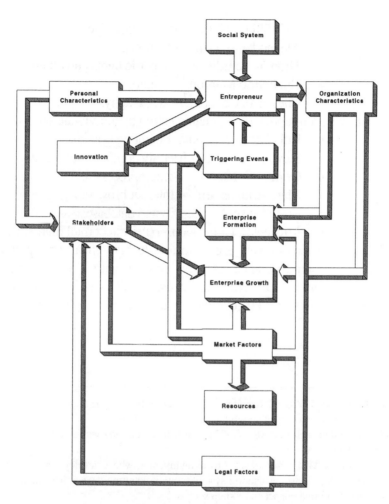

**Fig. 1.2** Interactive Model of Entrepreneurism

## 1.3 Technological Entrepreneurism

The model of technological entrepreneurism has changed over the last two hundred years. This model has moved from inventor/entrepreneurs to innovator/entrepreneurs. The inventor/entrepreneurs were characterized by individuals such as (Martin 1994, pp. 287):

- Alfred B. Nobel[12] – dynamite.
- Carl P. G. von Linde[13] – liquid air distillation.

---

[12] **Nobel, Alfred Bernhard** (1833-96), a Swedish chemist, inventor, and philanthropist who established the Nobel Prizes.

- Sir William H. Perkin[14] – aniline dyes.
- Alexander G. Bell – telephone.
- Thomas A. Edison[15] – electric lights and others.
- Guglielmo Marconi[16] – radio.
- Chester F. Carlson[17] – xerography.

The innovator/entrepreneur are characterized by individuals such as:

- Bill Gates – computer operating systems.
- Steve Jobs[18] – user friendly computer interface.
- Gordon E. Moore[19] – microprocessors.
- Marc Andreessen[20] – Internet browsers.
- Larry Ellison[21] – distributed databases.
- Michael S. Dell[22] – computer direct mail marketing.

While the inventors still are forming technological entrepreneurial enterprises, the preponderance of new market entries come from the innovator/entrepreneurs. In many instances, inventors fail in achieving the financial success even if their invention eventually is a major technological leader.

---

[13] **Linde, Carl Paul Gottfried von** (1842-1934), a German engineer and Professor who in 1895 discovered the process of liquefying air in large quantities.

[14] **Perkin, Sir William Henry** (1838-1907), a British chemist, known for the development of the first synthetic dyes.

[15] **Edison, Thomas Alva** (1847-1931), American inventor, whose development of a practical electric light bulb, electric generating system, sound-recording device, and motion picture projector had profound impact on modern society.

[16] **Marconi, Guglielmo, Marchese** (1874-1937), an Italian electrical engineer and Nobel laureate, the inventor of the first practical radio system.

[17] **Carlson, Chester F.**. (1906-68), an American physicist and inventor, who in 1934 began to experiment with electrostatics to make copies of printed material.

[18] **Jobs, Steven**, an American computer executive and one of the founders of Apple Computer.

[19] **Moore, Gordon E.,** an American engineer who foundered Intel Corporation and developed the concept of *Moore's Law* which states that the number of components doubles every 18 months and the price halves in a similar period.

[20] **Andreessen, Marc,** an American computer engineer who developed one of the first Internet browsers and then commercialized it through the Netscape Corporation.

[21] **Ellison, Larry**, an American computer executive and founder, Oracle Corporation, the world's second largest software company in 1997.

[22] **Dell, Michael S.,** a computer marketing executive, who as a young college student established a mail order computer enterprise.

### 1.3.1 American Technological Entrepreneurism

A technological entrepreneur is different to other types of entrepreneurs. This difference stems from the extedigencies of technology, i.e., rapid changes with major uncertainties. This usually requires knowledge of the technology which forms the basis of the entrepreneurial enterprise. Many entrepreneurs establish non-technical enterprises due to changes in their own financial state or in the hope of establishing an enterprise which will provide income and financial security. While these conditions may also exist for technological entrepreneurs, these individuals are driven by a technological vision. The drive of Michael Dell of Dell Computers, Michael Saylor of MicroStrategy Inc., Raul Fernandez of Proxicom, Inc., or Gordon Moore, one of the founders of Intel, can be considered to be the belief that a particular technology product, process or service is a strategic inflection point or a 10X change – Schumpeter's creative destruction (See Chapter 2 – Technological Entrepreneurs). This vision, coupled with the ability of rapid response, is the principal difference between general and technological entrepreneurism. These technological entrepreneurs can, in general, grasp major technological changes and adjust to meet them. In 1993, Bill Gates, the Chairman of Microsoft® Corporation, did not seem to believe that the Internet was significant. However, as he saw the significant growth of the Internet in 1994 and 1995, he totally changed the strategic direction of a multi-billion dollar enterprise in the course of approximately six months. Bill Gates also repeated this process with the proposal for the development of network PCs[23] ("NPCs").

The ability to rapidly make major strategic changes in a relatively short time is an important attribute of technological entrepreneurs. While Moore's model (Moore 1986) of the entrepreneurial process has one triggering point, in the technological entrepreneurial process there may be a continuous number of triggering points. This continuum causes the technological entrepreneur to continually respond and even change strategic direction.

A technological enterprise may be established to provide one type of technological product, process or service and then find a quick change is needed to adapt to changed market conditions. An example of this is in the information technology ("IT") market that served the U.S. Department of Defense ("DOD"). In the 1990s, DOD reduced its reliance upon contract

---

[23] Computers with limited computing capability based on distributed applets using JAVA™ or a modification of this computer language.

14

services, like many segments of the U.S. Government. Many technology companies serving this sector were faced with reduced or reducing revenue prospects. At the same time the use of the Internet and multimedia was increasing. Many of these technology companies, both large and small, migrated their business models toward this new growing commercial market segment.

Flexibility and rapidity of response, coupled with a strong customer focus, is the sine qua non of technological entrepreneurism. The technological entrepreneurism process is driven by rapid changes in the technology sector. It is not unusual that a technological entrepreneur sees the vision, which was used to establish the enterprise, completely overcome by events. Steve Case, Chief Executive Officer and James Kimsey, the Chairman Emeritus of America Online, established the company to provide online services through a proprietary communication network and user interface to the consumers prior to the growth and popularization of the Internet and the establishment of the World Wide Web ("WWW") graphical user interface ("GUI") market. The original concept behind America Online was a private communication network system. With the growth of the Internet, through the use of a graphical browser and a standardized communication system (HTML[24] and TCP/IP[25]), the business model which formed the basis of America Online lost its significance. The flexibility of Steve Case to change the enterprise business model eventually led America Online to become the major supplier of Internet services by 1998.

Technological entrepreneurism in the late 1990s was also driven by the phenomenal success of entrepreneurs like James Clark, the founder of Netscape Communications who saw the shares he owned become valued at $566 million after the first day of trading on the NASDAQ[26] (Collins 1996). Similarly, the 24 year old Chief Technology Officer ("CTO"), Marc Andreessen[27] of Netscape Communications was suddenly worth $58

---

[24] HTML = hypertext mark-up language, used to design graphical browser pages for the World Wide Web.

[25] TCP/IP = Transmission Control Protocol/ Internet Protocol used for Internet communications.

[26] Acronym for National Association of Securities Dealers Automated Quotations, American market for over-the-counter (OTC) securities. It is a subsidiary of the National Association of Securities Dealers (NASD) and is monitored by the Securities and Exchange Commission.

[27] **Marc Andreessen** was formally the project leader at the University of Illinois Computer Center that developed MOSAIC one of the first successful browsers for Internet.

million. This wealth came from the initial public offering ("IPO") of stock (See Chapter 8 – Next Entrepreneurial Step). In the mid and late 1990s, as the United States stock market increased to record levels, as measured by the various stock market indexes such as the Dow-Jones Industrial Average or the NASDAQ, private technology enterprises decided to raise capital by selling equity interests to the public. In 1995 $8.4 billion was raised by technology enterprises, more than in any previous year in U.S. history (Collins 1996).

Technological enterprises prosper in a constantly changing environment of novelty and innovation which endows many of them with spectacular growth trajectories (Bahrami and Evans 1996 ). While technological enterprises experience a high failure rate, technological regions, such as Silicon Valley in California continue to prosper and grow. Thus failure of a technological enterprise usually fosters the formation of others, directly or indirectly. Bahrami and Evans (Bahrami and Evans 1996) cite the example in the computer disk controller industry of the failure of Xebec, which had a positive impact on the growth of Cirrus Logic. Bahrami and Evans call this flexible re-cycling within the technological entrepreneurial process. Figure 1.3 is an example of this flexible re-cycling process.

The technological entrepreneurial process is not frustrated by the typical stigma associated with organizational failure. The failure rate more than likely causes increased experimentation and sector growth. The high failure rate among technological entrepreneurial enterprises does have a sobering impact on the surviving entrepreneurs. Large successful entrepreneurial firms such as Microsoft® learn to become agile giants (Financial 1992 ).

Entrepreneurial technological enterprises can be characterized by how they were formed. One method is through spin-offs[28], similar to those shown in Figure 1.3. This type of entrepreneurial activity is significant in the formation of technological enterprises and can be subdivided into:

- Direct Spin-off – Members of the entrepreneurial firm come from the same *parent* organization
- Hybrid Spin-off – Members come from different *parents* but have similar interests.

Scientists form an enterprise to commercialize their discoveries, e.g., Marconi was a twentieth century scientist who foundered the radio industry

---

[28] Spin-off is a new enterprise that is derived from existing company, usually in the same technological or market space.

with his invention of wireless telephony. Hobbyists are a source of technological entrepreneurism that proved successful for the formation of enterprises such as Apple Computer, Lotus Corporation and UUNET Communications (See Chapter 2 - Technological Entrepreneurs). Corporations serve for the formation of enterprise groups, and are known as intrapreneurism, within an existing corporation. These entrepreneurial groups are sometime spun out of the establishing enterprise at a later date.

Venture Capital ("VC") funds sometimes also find entrepreneurs with concepts for new technological products, processes or services and form new enterprises with these individuals. Venture capital investment groups sometimes seek the basis for the new entrepreneurial ventures within University research organizations, a source of a great deal of technological innovation.

Repeat entrepreneurs are another source of new technological enterprises. An example is Alan Shugart who left Shugart Associates and co-foundered Seagate Technology with another Shugart co-founder Finis Conner in 1979 (Bahrami and Evans 1996). In 1985, Finis Conner left Seagate Technology and foundered Conner Peripherals that was one of the fastest-growing enterprises in the United States in the late 1980s and early 1990s.

Re-starts constitute another form of technological entrepreneurism. In this form, the technological enterprise consists of typical ventures that are either acquired by larger firms or are venture-backed startups with business models that need re-engineering under new leadership teams. These technological firms can rise like the Phoenix[29] from the ashes of a failing parent or business model.

Table 1.1 shows the spin-offs resulting from the invention of the transistor at Bell Laboratories in 1945 (CVM 1970; Hamilton and Humelstein 1997). Many of these entrepreneurial enterprises did not survive. However, this explosive growth is one of the likely causes for the growth in the number of devices per silicon die, which has been referred to as Moore's Law (Schaller 1997) and is shown in Figure 1.4.

---

[29] The Phoenix was a legendary bird which lived for 500 years, burned itself to ashes on a pyre, and then rose alive from the ashes to live another 500 years.

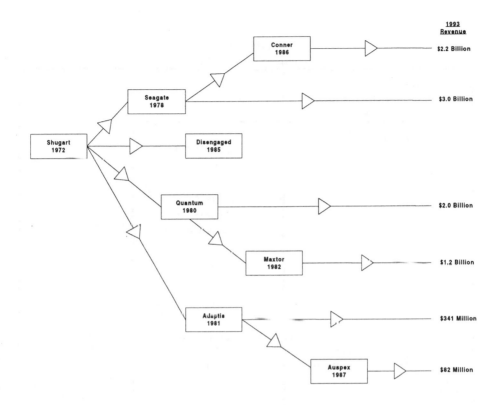

**Fig. 1.3** Spin-offs in Computer Disk Drive Industry (Bahrami and Evans 1996, ®
1996 IEEE. Reprinted by permission. )

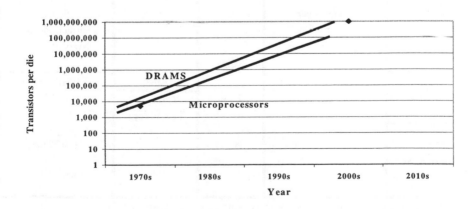

**Fig. 1.4** Moore's Law for Semiconductor Density Growth

**Table 1.1**
Transistor Spin-off Chain

| Year | | | | |
|------|------|------|------|------|
| 1945 | **Bell Laboratories** Shockley Transistor | | | |
| 1957 | **Fairchild** | **Fairchild** | | |
| 1959 | | Rheam Semiconductor | | |
| 1960 | | Electroglas | | |
| 1961 | | RCK Teledyne Anlico Signetics | | |
| 1962 | | Molestro | | |
| 1964 | | EMB | | |
| 1966 | | Semprex Diepeven Bayfield Electronics | | |
| 1967 | | **National Semiconductor** | | **National Semiconductor** |
| 1968 | **Computer Microtechnology** | **Intel** Four Phase | | Micro-Mark |
| 1969 | | AMD | | Communication Transistor |
| 1972 | | | | |
| 1973 | **Synertek** | | | |
| 1974 | | **Zilog** | | |
| 1979 | CLSI Technology | | | |
| 1981 | | | **SEEQ** | Lineor Technology |
| 1983 | Wafer Scale Integration | | | Sierra Semiconductor SDA Systems |
| 1984 | | Xilinx | | |
| 1985 | | | Atnel | **Cirrus Logic** |
| 1986 | | Synaptics | **Chips & Technology** | |
| 1989 | | | S3 | Neo Magic |
| 1993 | | | | |
| 1994 | | | 3Dfx | Planet Web |
| 1995 | | | | |

(Based on data contained in CVM 1970; Hamilton and Humelstein 1997)

### 1.3.2 European Technological Entrepreneurism

The European Union ("EU") has been cited by Andy Grove, Chairman of Intel Corporation, as having a *technology deficit* (Guissani 1997 ). European technology companies and business leaders in 1997 appeared to be desperate for new business and management models, which would be capable of helping to improve their economies in the globalized technology market. While technological entrepreneurial firms typically experience growth exceeding 50 percent in the U.S., EU innovative enterprises have been growing at 15 to 20 percent (Economist 1996 ). One of the factors that may have held back EU technological entrepreneurism is the cultural response to failure. In many instances, failed EU entrepreneurs find it impossible to obtain any financial backing for new entrepreneurial ventures. While technology entrepreneurs are not usually penalized for failing in the United States, the cultural response is the opposite in the EU. It is the cultural aspects of reduced risk taking coupled with penalization for failure which have been the greatest impediments to technological entrepreneurism in the EU.

In the EU, entrepreneurism means different things than in the United States. EU attitudes, particularly in Germany, differ substantially from those in the United States (Drucker 1985, pp. 25). The term entrepreneur for Germans, *Unternehmer*, means the boss who owns the enterprise and differentiates the professional manager from the hired hands. The United Kingdom (UK) identifies entrepreneurship with new small businesses while Germany identifies it with power and property.

Considering this cultural difference, the EU, especially nations with attitudes similar to those that Drucker attributes to Germany, may not provide a stimulating arena for new technological enterprises which by nature are more team oriented and sharing.

However, some technological entrepreneurs have succeeded in the EU, if not to the extent of those in the U.S. An example is Lars Windhorst of Germany. At the age of 14, Lars Windhorst began to import computer components from China (Economist 1996 ). By the age of 18, Lars Windhorst had built a business with revenues of DM180 million.

While Lars Windhorst is an example of a successful European technological entrepreneur, he is one of a small minority within the EU. The EU's tax structure is such that new ventures need large cash flows in their formative years, and meeting governmental regulations is time consuming and expensive. It has also been cited that the EU lacks a total venture system or food chain for entrepreneurs (Economist 1996 ). In the United States venture capital firms have also provided advice to new entrepreneurs about managing fast-growing enterprises.

### 1.3.3 Asian Technological Entrepreneurism

Asian technological entrepreneurism differs between Japan and most of the other Asian nations. In Japan, small technological enterprises have had a difficult time obtaining market share due to the preponderance of *Keiretsu*[30] and large technological enterprises like Sony, Toshiba, NEC and others. This started to change (Sugawara 1996) when Japan's ministries such as the Ministry of International Trade and Industry ("MITI") adopted a new industrial policy promoting entrepreneurs. These ministries helped to set-up a stock market similar to NASDAQ to raise capital for start-ups and allowed U.S. style stock options for managers. The old industrial alliances characterized by *Keiretsu* also started to be willing to form partnership arrangements with new technological enterprises (Sugawara 1996 ).

However, Japanese culture is still unduly burdened with a bureaucratic style that forms an impediment to technological entrepreneurism. For example, in November 1995, MITI introduced its stock option, which insisted that only enterprises that met strict criteria could participate (Sugawara 1996 ). This bureaucratic type of approach imposes barriers to entrepreneurial development, especially in the rapidly changing technological arena.

In other Asian nations, such as Malaysia, the climate for technological entrepreneurism is considered more nurturing. On May 17, 1997, Prime Minister Mahathir Mahamad launched Cyberjaya[31,] a high-tech city[32] that forms the basis for the development of technological enterprises (Ayman 1997 ). Similar steps by many of the Southeast Asian nations show a positive attitude toward technology.

While these large facilities are not entrepreneurial in themselves, they are serviced by many small and growing technological entrepreneurial

---

[30] Keiretsu is a system by which groups of Japanese companies obtain a competitive edge by managing the risks of manufacturing, distribution, and sales through extensive cross-holding of company stocks, including having long-range strategies aimed at garnering market share without regard to short-term profit, and control over retail prices.

[31] *Cyberjaya* means cyber-success in the Malay language.

[32] The city was wired totally with high capacity fibre optic lines capable of carrying large quantity of data.

enterprises.    Thus, Malaysia's aggressive support of technology and progressive attitude toward promoting large technology facilities encourages technology transfer to local entrepreneurs.  Such a technology policy led to the technological success of Singapore.  The City of Penang in Malaysia has more than 700 factories in five industrial parks covering 5,850 acres.  This includes major technology companies such as Dell Computer Corporation's $20 million plant, Acer Computers plant for monitor and keyboard manufacturing, an Intel manufacturing and test center for its Pentium series of processors, and a Motorola Inc plant for some of its telecommunication products (Reuters 1997).  However, the Asian financial crisis of 1997 and 1998 did cause some retrenchment in these plans until the financial climate improved.

In India, availability of high quality technical labor and a natural entrepreneurial spirit has led to the formation of numerous technological enterprises, primarily in computer programming.  Numerous technology enterprises worldwide are using Indian programmers to develop new products.  This is accomplished not only through the availability of highly trained personnel but also using high-speed communication systems.

### 1.3.4  Israeli Technological Entrepreneurism

While Israel is geographically near Europe, its technological entrepreneurism is more closely related to that of the United States.  In 1996, 19 primarily technological Israeli companies issued initial public offerings in the United States (Marcus and Mehta 1997).  Israel, with 58 companies had in 1997 the third-largest presence on NASDAQ after the United States and Canada.  In the 1994-1997 time-period, Israel had 800 technology start-up enterprises with military technology comprising the majority of the technological products (Marcus and Mehta 1997).

## 2.    GENERAL CHARACTERISTICS OF ENTREPRENEURS

Numerous studies have been conducted of the characteristics of entrepreneurs (Hisrick and Peters 1995).  Figure 1.5 is a model of general entrepreneurial characteristics.  An important characteristic is entrepreneurial *ego*, which includes *locus of control, independence, achievement needs* and *risk taking*.

**Locus of Control** – Entrepreneurs are calculated risk takers who believe in themselves.  They view themselves as individuals who take control of the situation instead of waiting for the environment to deliver results.

**Independence** – The need to control is accompanied by the need for independence. This is based on the fact that the entrepreneur believes that only they have the *right* answer.

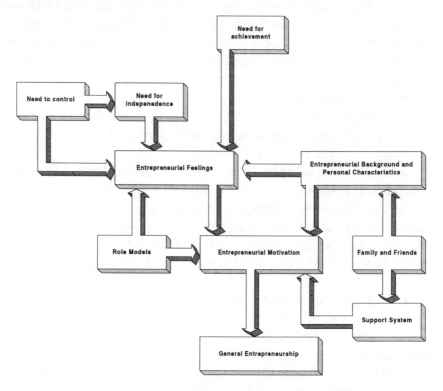

**Fig. 1. 5** Model of General Entrepreneurial Characteristics

**Achievement Needs** – An entrepreneur has a strong need to achieve. Accepting individual responsibility for solving problems, setting goals, and achieving those goals through his/her own efforts is part of the achievement needs of an entrepreneur. So is moderate risk taking as a function of skill, i.e., entrepreneurs are not general *gamblers* but *gamblers in themselves,* which requires forecasting the results of decisions or task accomplishments.

**Risk Taking** – This characteristic has always been attributed to entrepreneurs. Innovation by its nature involves taking risks. Drucker (Drucker 1985, pp. 139) disagrees with this generalization and believes that entrepreneurs are **not** *risk-takers*. This is defended by the proposition that entrepreneurs define the risks they have to take and minimize them as much as possible. He believes entrepreneurs are *calculated* risk-takers. The degree of this calculated risk-taking varies with each individual. Some entrepreneurs proceed with small amounts of information while others seek a greater degree of certainty. Entrepreneurs are not *risk-focused* but *opportunity-focused.* However, by nature, entrepreneurism is enterprise establishment under uncertainty. While more information will provide increased knowledge and possibly reduced risk, no amount will eliminate uncertainty. Also, the time required obtaining the additional information increases cost and might even totally preclude enterprise establishment. There is a balance that must be achieved between the need for additional information for decision making and increased effectiveness and reduced risk and increased cost. Figure 1.6 is an example of this trade-off.

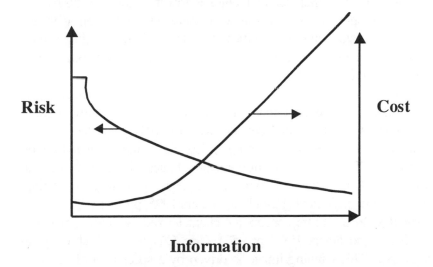

**Risk**                                               **Cost**

**Information**

**Fig. 1.6** Tradeoff Between Information Cost and Risk

The entrepreneur's background and personal characteristics are important characteristics. Entrepreneurs are future oriented since they think ahead in their decision-making (Roberts 1991, pp. 44 ). The formative years of the entrepreneur appear strongly linked to their success (Hisrick and Peters 1995, pp. 55 ). The factors influencing the entrepreneur include *birth order, parent's occupation, parental values, parental achievement attitude, education, personal values, age, motivation, role models,* and *support system.*

**Birth Order** – There is some disagreement as to the effect of birth order (Hisrick and Peters 1995, pp. 55 ). First-born children tend to be more entrepreneurially oriented, presumably because their achievement-oriented parents can set higher standards and be more affectionate than with several children (Roberts 1991, pp. 49). This is not an important characteristic for technological entrepreneurs.

**Parents Occupation** – There is strong evidence that entrepreneurs tend to have a self-employed or entrepreneurial parent or parents (Hisrick and Peters 1995, pp. 56).

**Parental Values** – As indicated by religious orientation, entrepreneurism is strongly associated with parental values (Roberts 1991, pp. 49 ). This is associated with the *achievement ethic* of certain groups, such as those of Jewish and Asian heritage.

**Parental Achievement Attitude** – Studies reported by Roberts (Roberts 1991, pp. 49) indicate that parental attitude toward achievement has an impact on developing entrepreneurial characteristics. Children who are encouraged to master various activities, e.g., trying hard for themselves, being active and energetic, making their own friends and being competitive, have higher entrepreneurial scores on psychological tests.

**Education** – Another factor influencing individual entrepreneurship is the level of education of the entrepreneur. Education was found important in the upbringing of a future entrepreneur (Roberts 1991, pp. 49). A good educational level and continual learning assists the entrepreneur in dealing with problems. The studies of entrepreneurs indicated that they had an educational need in areas of finance, strategic planning, marketing, distribution, and management (Hisrick and Peters 1995, pp. 56).

**Personal Values** – Entrepreneurs are characterized as having a *winning image* (Hisrick and Peters 1995, pp. 57), (See Chapter 2 –Technological Entrepreneurs). This winning image is driven by a special set of attitudes about the management and business processes. Table 1.2 shows some of the variations between managers and entrepreneurs. Entrepreneurs appear to have a Myers-Briggs[33] type indicator ("MBTI") characterized by ENTP, i.e., extroverted ("E"), intuitive ("N"), thinking orientated ("T"), and perceiving ("P") (Roberts 1991, pp. 86).

---

[33] The Myers-Briggs type indicator measures individuals according to typology developed by Carl Jung. **Carl Jung** (1875 - 1961) was a Swiss psychologist and psychiatrist who founded analytical psychology. Jung proposed and developed the concepts of the extroverted and introverted personality, archetypes, and the collective unconscious.

**Table 1.2**
Variation between Managers and Entrepreneurs

| Element | Entrepreneurs | Managers |
|---|---|---|
| Nature of Enterprise | Expansive | Conservative to mildly expansive |
| Opportunism | Opportunistic | Cautionary |
| Institution | Flexible | Maintains status quo |
| Individuality | Self assured | Seeks consensus |
| Planning | Some but with time constraints | Tends to over-plan |
| Predictability | Unpredictable | Predictable |
| Rationality | May seem over responsive | Needs more information than most entrepreneurs |

**Age** – There is a difference between the age of the entrepreneur reflected by experience and the chronological age of the entrepreneur. Entrepreneurial experience is one of the best predictors of success (Hisrick and Peters 1995, pp. 57 ). The age at which most entrepreneurs initiate their entrepreneurial careers is between 22 and 55[34]. Roberts (Roberts 1991, pp. 65) reports that his study showed an age range between 23 and 69 with an overall median of 37 for technological entrepreneurs. The work experience or experiential age of the entrepreneur is a strong indicator in the growth and eventual success of a new enterprise. Managerial experience is important; the need for experience increases as the complexity of the new enterprise increases. Both Roberts (Roberts 1991) and Hisrick and Peters (Hisrick and Peters 1995) report that for most entrepreneurs their most significant enterprise was not their first. In fact, successful entrepreneurs often were not totally successful in their first venture. This learning nature of the entrepreneur and the ability to continually re-invent themselves is one of the principal driving forces of economic growth. The ability to not judge an entrepreneur solely on the basis of the first enterprise differentiates the United States from the EU.

**Motivation** – Motivation of entrepreneurs varies significantly. Some are motivated due to changing personal conditions such as the need to simply earn a living, others with dissatisfaction with their current position. However, the need to *be one's own boss* or independence is the most

---

[34] This author began his first entrepreneurial enterprise at the age of 12 and continues to this day to be an entrepreneur.

significant motivating factor for entrepreneurs (Hisrick and Peters 1995, pp. 58 ).

**Role Models** – Entrepreneurs have entrepreneurial parents or role models. These role models can range from actual parents to a successful entrepreneur who has been brought to the attention of the embryonic entrepreneur. Thus exposure to entrepreneurial cultures or communities is likely to raise the entrepreneurial quotient of a community, i.e., increase the number of entrepreneurs. An excellent example of this is the south region of San Francisco in California known as *Silicon Valley*. This region associated with Stanford University has spawned many of the successful technological entrepreneurs in the United States.

**Support System** – Like any other organism, entrepreneurs cannot easily survive without a supporting environment. This supporting environment can range from an encouraging personal family environment to a structured entrepreneurial incubator program similar to those established at many universities. The support system of entrepreneurs can be characterized as both moral and professional. Entrepreneurs need a social context in which to operate. The entrepreneur seeks to establish connections early in the enterprise formation process. These connections can be described by the factors of *density* and *certainty* (Hisrick and Peters 1995, pp. 59 ). *Density* is the extensiveness of relationships between two or more individuals. The strength of the ties between members of the network is dependent on frequency, level and reciprocity of the relationships. The greater the strength the more durable the entrepreneur's network. *Centrality* is the distance to all other individuals and the total number of individuals in the network.

## 3. DISTINGUISHING CHARACTERISTICS OF TECHNOLOGICAL ENTREPRENEURS

Dr. Edward B. Roberts of the Sloan School of Management of the Massachusetts Institute of Technology ("MIT") (Roberts 1991) presents a detailed empirical study of the characteristics of technological entrepreneurs. It is important to state that technological entrepreneurs are indeed different from general entrepreneurs. Table 1.3 summarizes these differences.

All entrepreneurs generally share similar characteristics. However, the principal differences seem to be associated with the following factors:

- Achievement.
- Birth Order.
- Education.

### 3.1 Achievement

Roberts (Roberts 1991, pp. 87) showed that technological entrepreneurs have a need to achieve. This need to achieve leads technological entrepreneurs to take moderate as opposed to high or low risks. Neither low nor high-risk activities are believed helpful as achievement oriented strategies because of the ease or high probability of failure. The technological entrepreneur, probably due to a deeper understanding of technology coupled with techniques gained over an average of 13 years of professional experience, is more capable of judging risks then the general entrepreneur.

### 3.2 Birth Order

Hisrick and Peters (Hisrick and Peters 1995) and Roberts (Roberts 1991) describe the different impact of birth order on general and technological entrepreneurs, respectively. Although many technological entrepreneurs are *first born sons* it was found that there were a similar portion among their employed technical associates (Roberts 1991, pp. 340). In a reported national study (Hisrick and Peters 1995, pp. 55) of 408 female entrepreneurs 50 percent were found to be first born. However, it was also reported that in many other studies the first born effect has not been present or only weakly demonstrated.

### 3.3 Education

Both Hisrick and Peters (Hisrick and Peters 1995) and Roberts (Roberts 1991) indicated that, in general, entrepreneurs are college educated. Studies have shown that 40 percent of entrepreneurs surveyed had more than a high school education (Roberts 1991, pp. 60). Roberts also found that the entrepreneurs who had been spun-off from MIT laboratories were primarily educated with a least a technical college degree and most had a masters degree. This may be biased by the fact that to be employed in an MIT laboratory a college degree would have been a primary requirement.

28

**Table 1.3**
Characteristic Differences Between General and Technological Entrepreneurs

| Characteristic | Technological (Roberts 1991) | General (Hisrick and Peters 1995; Roberts 1991) |
|---|---|---|
| Achievement | Moderate feedback | Higher – Need to make things happen |
| Affiliation | Low | Unknown |
| Age when first enterprise formed | Range 23 to 69, median 37 | Range 25 to 35 |
| Birth order | No first born effect | First born effect |
| Control | Unknown | Desire to be in control |
| Critical events | New invention, process or service such as Internet and the drive of Netpreneurs | Unknown |
| Education | Technical education usually with a graduate degree, 40 percent of the general sample had higher than high school education. | College educated |
| Family background | Related to religious values | Unknown |
| Family size | No relationship | Unknown |
| Fathers occupation | Professional or manager who in general were self employed | Self employed |
| Goal orientation | Sharing a wide range various goals | Highly goal oriented |
| Marital status | 75 percent married, most with children | Unknown |
| Motivation | Strong motivation to succeed with a wide range of particular goals | Strong motivation to succeed with a wide range of particular goals |
| Personality | ENTP | ENTP |
| Power to control | High | High |
| Religious orientation | Protestant or Jewish | Unknown |
| Work experience | Very important with 13 years average work experience | Very important |
| Risk taking | Takes calculated risks | Tends to be a risk taker |

## 4 SUCCESSFUL TECHNOLOGICAL ENTREPRENEURIAL CHARACTERISTICS

Successful technological entrepreneurs have been shown to depend largely upon the entrepreneur's expertise (Reuber and Fischer 1994 ). The experience was found not to be as important as the expertise of the entrepreneur. Reuber and Fischer (Reuber and Fischer 1994) suggest that experience measures are an inadequate surrogate for expertise. What is important is not the experience of the technological entrepreneur but what the entrepreneur has learned from the experience.

Successful technological entrepreneurs have been found to (Bhide 1994):

- Handle analytical tasks in stages, i.e., *eating the elephant one slice at a time.*
- Solve problems rapidly as they appear, i.e., *if it's not broken don't fix it.*
- Evangelical investigator, i.e., research and sell at the same time – *beta sites.*
- Be smartly arrogant – an entrepreneur's willingness to act on sketchy plans and inconclusive data, i.e., *shoot from the hip*, is often sustained by an almost arrogant self-confidence.

## 5  TECHNOLOGICAL ENTREPRENEURIAL PROFILE

No profile of a technological entrepreneur will be totally correct. Based upon the variety of research that has been cited in this chapter, the average entrepreneur appears to have the following characteristics:

General Characteristics (those shared by all entrepreneurs)

- Age at which the first entrepreneurial venture is initiated is in the mid-thirties.
- The father of the entrepreneur is usually a self-employed professional, i.e., entrepreneurs stimulate progeny.
- Very goal oriented.
- A need to control outcomes, need for power – n-Pow[35].
- Has a strong motivation to succeed with a wide range of particular motivations.
- In terms of personality, as measured by the Myers-Briggs type indicator, the average entrepreneur can be described as having a ENTP personality, i.e., an extrovert ("E"), very intuitive ("N"), thinking oriented ("T"), and perceiving-oriented ("P").
- The experience of the entrepreneur is very important to the success of a new enterprise.

---

[35]Thematic Apperception Test ("T.A.T") test score for power is high. T.A.T. is a psychological coding based on verbal interpretations of fuzzy sketches to determine motivation behind the entrepreneur's behavior.

- The education and expertise of most entrepreneurs includes usually at least one college degree.

Technological Characteristics (additional characteristics of technological entrepreneurs)

- Technological entrepreneurs usually have a technical degree and may have a master's degree.
- The technological entrepreneur is a moderate calculated risk taker.
- Rather than resolve all issues at once, the technological entrepreneur does only enough research to justify the next action or investment.
- As soon as any problems or risks develop, technological entrepreneurs begin developing solutions.
- The technological entrepreneur has a moderate need for achievement, power and a low need for affiliation.
- Technological entrepreneurs in general are highly oriented toward independence and search to overcome challenges with less concern for financial rewards than the general population of entrepreneurs.

The technological entrepreneur is different to the average general entrepreneur primarily in his/her attitude to develop a new concept or expand upon a technological opportunity.

## REFERENCES

Ayman, Syed. 1997. Malaysia to launch futuristic Cybercity: Reuters Ltd.

Bahrami, Hema, and Stuart Evans. 1996. Flexible Re-Cycling and High Technology Entrepreneurship. *IEEE Engineering Management Review* 24 (2):64-80.

Bhide, Amar. 1994. How Entrepreneurs Craft Strategies That Work. *IEEE Engineering Management Review* 22 (4):52-59.

Braudel, Fernand. 1979. *The Wheels of Commerce: Civilization and Capitalism 15th - 18th Century - Volume 2*. Translated by Reynolds, S. 2 vols. Vol. 2. New York, NY: Harper and Row, Publishers.

Bygrave, William D. 1997. The Entrepreneurial Process. In *The portable MBA in Entrepreneurship*, edited by W. D. Bygrave. New York, NY: John Wiley & Sons.

Cardullo, Mario W. 1996. *Introduction to Managing Technology*. Edited by J. A. Brandon. First ed. 5 vols. Vol. 4, *Engineering Management Series*. Baldock, Hertfordshire, England: Research Studies Press Ltd.

Clark, Peter, and Neil Staunton. 1989. *Innovation in Technology and Organization*. London, England: Routledge.

Collins, James. 1996. Winners. *Time Magazine*, 96/2/19, 43-47.

CVM. 1970. The Fairchildren. Milwaukee, WI: Center for Venture Management.

Drucker, Peter F. 1985. *Innovation and Entrepreneurship: Practice and Principles.* New York, NY: Harper and Row, Publishers.

Economist. 1996. Small beginnings. *The Economist,* 96/11/23, 13-15.

Financial. 1992. Newcomers Snipping at Their Heels. *Financial Times,* 92/6/18, 16.

Goodman, Richard A., and Michael W. Lawless. 1994. *Technology and Strategy: Conceptual Models and Diagnostics.* New York, NY: Oxford University Press.

Grove, Andrew S. 1996. *Only the Paranoid Survive: How to Exploit the Crisis Points that Challenge Every Company and Career.* New York, NY: Currency Doubleday.

Guissani, Bruno. 1997. Eurobytes: Europeans Tour Silicon Valley, Looking for Clues to Success. CyberTimes: New York Times.

Hamilton, Joan O'C, and Linda Humelstein. 1997. A Wellspring Called Stanford. *Business Week,* 97/8/25, 82-84.

Hisrick, Robert D., and Michael P. Peters. 1995. *Entrepreneurship: Starting, Developing, and Managing a New Enterprise.* Chicago, IL: Irwin.

Jay, Anthony. 1967. *Management and Machiavelli: An Inquiry into the Politics of Corporate Life.* New York, NY: Holt, Rinehart and Winston.

Kauffman, Stuart. 1995. *At Home in the Universe: The Search for Laws of Self-Organization and Complexity.* New York, NY: Oxford University Press.

Marcus, Amy Dockster, and Stephani N. Mehta. 1997. Israel's High-Technology Push Stumbles; IPOs are Delayed. *The Wall Street Interactive Edition,* 97/6/10, http://interactive5.wsj.com/edition/current/articles/SB865898885733545500.htm.

Martin, Michael J. C. 1994. *Managing Innovation and Entrepreneurship in Technology - Based Firms.* Edited by D. F. Kocaoglu, *Engineering and Technology Management.* New York, NY: John Wiley and Sons.

Mintzberg, Henry, and James Quinn. 1991. *The Strategy Process: Concepts, Contexts, Cases.* Second ed. Englewood Cliffs, N.J.: Prentice Hall.

Moore, Carol. 1986. Understanding Entrepreneurial Behavior. Paper read at Forty-Six Annual Meeting of the Academy of Management, at Chicago, IL.

Reuber, A. Rebecca, and Eileen M. Fischer. 1994. Entrepreneurs' Experience, Expertise, and the Performance of Technology-Based Firms. *IEEE Transactions on Engineering Management* 41 (4):365-374.

Reuters. 1997. Sci-Tech News: Malaysia's Expects to Keep Electronic Firms: Reuters Ltd.

Roberts, Edward B. 1991. *Entrepreneurs in High Technology: Lessons from MIT and Beyond.* New York, NY: Oxford University Press.

Rosenberg, Nathan. 1994. *Exploring the black box: Technology, economics, and history.* Cambridge, England: Cambridge University Press.

Schaller, Robert R. 1997. Moore's Law: past, present, and future. *IEEE Spectrum,* 97/6, 53-59.

Schumpeter, Joseph A. 1936. *The Theory of Economic Development.* Cambridge, MA: Harvard University Press.

Sugawara, Sandra. 1996. Upstart Start-ups: Japan's Once Shunned Entrepreneurs Gain Respect, Incentives for Creating Jobs. *The Washington Post,* 96/7/28, H01.

## DISCUSSION QUESTIONS

1. Using a technical concept, such as the invention of the transistor, prepare a chart showing the relevant entrepreneurial ventures that have been developed.
2. Discuss the differences between entrepreneurial ventures in early history, middle ages, age of enlightenment, Industrial Revolution and the early and late twentieth century. What do you believe will characterize entrepreneurial development in the twenty-first century?
3. Using data available from various media, give examples of U.S., EU, and Asian technological entrepreneurs.
4. Choose a technological entrepreneur who you are familiar with or about whom you can obtain biographical data and prepare a detailed profile based upon what you have read in this chapter.
5. Prepare profiles of the entrepreneurs who have established MCI-Worldcom, America Online, Yahoo! and Amazon.com.

CHAPTER 2

# Technological Entrepreneurs

> *"Veni, vidi, vici"*
> *("I came, I saw, I conquered.")*
> **Gaius Julius Caesar**
> Dispatch to Senate of Rome
> after the Battle of Zela, First
> Century B.C.

## 1.  INTRODUCTION

There are various ways to view technological entrepreneurs. Some entrepreneurs not only become exceedingly wealthy, the Crasssus[1] of their day, but they also change the direction of human development. Thomas Alva Edison is a case in point. Edison was a true technological entrepreneur and the pre-eminent inventor who changed the course of human history. Other entrepreneurs achieved fleeting fortune and fame by accelerating an existing trend; an example is Steve Jobs, one of the founders of Apple Computer Company who did popularize personal computers ("PCs"). Other technological entrepreneurs achieve wealth and then quietly disappear from the headlines, such as Paul Allen the co-founder of Microsoft® Corporation. Finally, some technological entrepreneurs never achieve notoriety or wealth, but their technological contributions change the course of human development. It is not the intent of this chapter to present biographies, but to highlight the driving forces of technological entrepreneurs.

Success can be measured in many ways: notoriety, fortune or societal contribution. William Shockley[2] and his associates spawned an economy not just a new enterprise when they discovered the transistor and then formed Shockley Transistor Corporation, also known as Shockley Laboratories, to commercialize the invention. These inventor entrepreneurs also made

---

[1] **Crassus, Marcus Licinius** (115-53 B.C.), rich, Roman financier and politician and financial backer of Julius Caesar.

[2] **Shockley, William Bradford** (1910-89), American physicist, Nobel laureate, and co-inventor of the transistor.

possible a totally new world that is still influencing society. Shockley and his associates' discovery, which was honored by a Nobel Prize in 1956 for physics, and the subsequent commercialization of the transistor, was indeed a *strategic inflection point* (Grove 1996).

The technological entrepreneur does not initiate a new enterprise solely to achieve financial success; financial success is not a *prima facie* reason for enterprise formation in many instances (See Chapter 1 – Nature of Technological Entrepreneurism). The technological entrepreneur is in general seeking to accomplish or take advantage of a *strategic inflection point*, i.e., a change in an industry's direction or, in some instances, the course of human development, e.g., Alexander G. Bell and Thomas A. Edison. Sometimes, as in the case of William Shockley and his associates, the enterprise arises from the commercialization of a scientific discovery.

Entrepreneurs, especially technological entrepreneurs, are highly successful in capitalizing on new concepts. These highly motivated individuals also are very tenacious and do not fear failure. An example is the case of Scott Spencer and Ken Husch the founders of Mensana Diagnostics Corporation in Newark, Delaware (Silver 1997). Spencer and Husch's enterprise was established to develop expert computer systems to manage chronic pain cases for insurance companies. The founders' experience and expertise were based upon the disability insurance industry. The enterprise was started in 1994, but the founders did not obtain sufficient capital to develop their concept until 1996, when they raised $1.25 million in venture funding (Silver 1997)

Entrepreneurs tend to be more prone to *delusion* and *opportunism* than managers in more traditional roles (Busenitz and Barney 1997). The term delusion may be related to the entrepreneur's system of beliefs concerning judgement. These characteristics are likely to be very important in the starting of a new technological venture. The internal belief of the entrepreneur in his/her ability to succeed is vital if the enterprise is to have any chance of success. The opportunistic nature of entrepreneurs is very evident when analyzing the development of the Internet. In 1984, Sandy Lerner and Leonard Bosack developed a router[3] that became the basis of Cisco Systems Inc. Over a period of time, the enterprise grew at a reasonable rate. However, as the growth of the Internet started to increase exponentially,

---

[3] A router is an intermediary device on a communications network that expedites message delivery and is indispensable to the operation of Internet systems.

so did the revenues of Cisco Systems Inc., which by 1996 exceeded $4 billion (Morino 1997).

Also exemplifying this opportunism is Robert Nelson, founder of Cross Media of Washington, D.C. Nelson used the capabilities of the Internet to develop the technology in 1996 to allow travelers to call their e-mail[4] and have it automatically read to them (Morino 1997). Many technological entrepreneurs, similar to Nelson, formed new enterprises in the late 1990s based on using or developing computer software products to take advantage of the Internet for sources of information and electronic commerce.

However, while a strong individual belief system and an opportunistic nature are important, expertise is vital for the ultimate success of a technological entrepreneurial venture. The level of a technological entrepreneur's expertise was shown strongly associated with performance of the enterprise, though expertise and experience are not always positive (Reuber and Fischer 1994). There is a significant negative correlation between start-up experience and research and development ("R&D") expertise. There was also found significant and negative correlation between enterprise start-up experience and expertise with back office functions of office procedures, automation and computerization and inventory control and purchasing. Individuals who have extensive administration experience and expertise may have had less of an opportunity to be involved in the start-up of a new venture. Thus the more experience and expertise an entrepreneur has in technological start-up, the less time he/she will have had to develop the administrative skills involved in operating a mature enterprise. The researchers, i.e., Reuber and Fischer, were surprised by the finding that there were the fewer significant correlations between expertise and experience for entrepreneurs with prior management experience. This was surprising since the venture capitalists (See Chapter 6 – Initial Enterprise Financing) appear to value prior management experience heavily when making investment decisions. An example of this is the significant signing bonus, salary and funding of a new telecommunication venture to attract the former president of AT&T, Alex J. Mandl(Starzynski 1997a).

It appears that expertise in strategic planning, developing business plans, globalization, financing and strategic alliance formation is more important for enterprise growth than expertise in back office functions, which are more beneficial in a more mature enterprise. The research findings also indicate

---

[4]E-mail or electronic mail refers to messages sent and received electronically via telecommunication links such as the Internet.

that new technology formation or start-up experience is valuable and is an important learning process in itself. Thus, new enterprises started with executives with little or no start-up experience are less likely to meet expectations. This can be seen in several of the cases discussed in this chapter.

Successful technology regions such as Silicon Valley[5] have spawned many of the technological entrepreneurs in the United States. The management and financial culture of these regions have been the principal reasons for the growth of technological entrepreneurism in the United States.

## 1.1 Historical Perspective

One of the early groups of technological entrepreneurs originated in Phoenicia[6] on the coast of the Mediterranean. In approximately 1000 B.C., an unnamed Phoenician developed the process for extracting purple dye from the secretion of the Murex sea snail, known as Tyrian purple[7]. This dye became so popular that it was reserved for royalty, i.e. *those born to the purple.* However, since intellectual property laws were non-existent, the only way the Phoenicians could maintain a monopoly was by adopting a *trade secrets* approach. Another example of the maintenance of entrepreneurial market dominance by trade secrets is the development of porcelain in China in the second century of the Common Era[8]. The Chinese maintained a virtual monopoly for over 1,500 years until Count Ehrehfried von Tschiruhaus and J. F. Böttger discovered in 1708 a method of manufacturing true hard paste porcelain (Hellemans and Bunch 1991).

Technological entrepreneurs have also been produced from other entrepreneurial ventures. James Watt[9], the inventor of the steam engine, was an example of Schumpeter's *creative destructor*, who not only started a new industry, but also formed an enterprise out of which other entrepreneurs

---

[5] The region of California southwest of San Francisco Bay, otherwise known as the Santa Clara Valley, roughly extending from Palo Alto to San Jose.

[6] Phoenicia was an ancient maritime country of city-states along the eastern Mediterranean Sea in present-day Syria and Lebanon.

[7] Tyrian purple was a dye of great importance in antiquity; it was obtained from a secretion of a sea snail (*Murex brandaris*) common in the Mediterranean. This dye has never been produced synthetically on a commercial basis.

[8] The period coinciding with the Christian era.

[9] **Watt, James** (1736-1819) Scottish engineer and inventor who invented modern condensing steam engine (1765, patented 1769) in which the exhaust steam from cylinder is condensed in separate chamber (condenser).

emerged. James Watt was one of the first to couple scientific research to technological invention and development (Cardwell 1995, pp. 181). One of the important features of James Watt's career was his close association with University of Glasgow where he was mathematical-instrument maker and came into contact with the scientific discoveries of Joseph Black[10].

John Roebuck[11], a leading English entrepreneur of the eighteenth century, was played a significant role in the career of James Watt (Cardwell 1995, pp. 149). In 1746, Roebuck and Garbeth developed a method of manufacturing sulfuric acid, which became the basis for bleaching cotton materials. James Watt developed a partnership with John Roebuck. However, this first venture failed when Roebuck became bankrupt. This did not deter James Watt, who then formed a partnership with Matthew Boulton[12] in 1775 in Cornwall, England (Cardwell 1995, pp. 162). Boulton and Watt learned about installing and improving steam engines in their joint venture. In 1786, Boulton and Watt opened the Albion Flour Mill in London, England. The mill used two of Watt's new steam engines. Technically the mill was a great success and ushered in the Industrial Revolution. However, it became a financial disaster when it burned down in 1791 long before its capital debt had been repaid (Cardwell 1995, pp. 168). Boulton and Watt's reputations attracted a number of young men to work for and learn from them. One of these young men was William Murdock[13] who commercialized the concept of gas lighting. The concept of gas lighting using coal gas had been the idea of Phillipe Lebon, a Frenchman, and F. A. Winzer, a German (Cardwell 1995, pp. 216). Thus, the invention and commercialization by Watt had a cascading impact on society. This cascading impact of technological entrepreneurism is the one of the *engines* that has driven the growth of modern society.

## 1.2 Spin-offs from Institutions

As in the case of James Watt, academic institutions have played a significant role in the development of technological entrepreneurism. A case in point is Stanford University located south of the city of San Francisco in California.

---

[10] **Black, Joseph** (1728-1799), Scottish chemist who taught at University of Glasgow and evolved the theory of latent heat; measured latent heat of steam; founded doctrine of specific heats.

[11] **Roebuck, John** (1718-1794), English physician and inventor.

[12] **Boulton, Matthew** (1728-1809), English inventor, manufacturer and engineer.

[13] **Murdock, William** (1754-1839), Scottish engineer and inventor who developed a method of distilling coal gas for lighting purposes.

In 1938 a Stanford professor of electrical engineering, Fredrick E. Terman, who later became Dean of Engineering, started the process of the development of Silicon Valley in California by lending two of his former students, David Packard and William Hewlett $538 to produce an audio oscillator (Reinhardt, Hamilton, and Himelstein 1997). This was the start of the highly successful enterprise known as the Hewlett Packard Corporation. Dean Terman, at the end of World War II discerned that the United States Government was poised to invest in science and technology. His vision, which he lived to see fulfilled, was to build a highly successful technological community centered on Stanford University.

Stanford University has spawned many technological enterprises such as Silicon Graphics, Cisco Systems, and Sun Microsystems. These enterprises, in a cascading fashion, have given birth to other technological enterprises.

The Massachusetts Institute of Technology ("MIT") in Cambridge, Massachusetts has also been a source of technological entrepreneurism. Similar to Stanford University, MIT and its professors, such as Stark Draper, have fostered technological entrepreneurs. Stark Draper was the Director of MIT's Instrument Laboratory in the 1950s (Roberts 1991, pp. 40). Professor Draper encouraged entrepreneurial spin-offs from his laboratory. Other MIT laboratory directors followed Stark Draper's path and helped to establish the Route 128 technological corridor outside of Boston, Massachusetts. Many universities throughout the United States and in England have established industrial science parks and technological entrepreneurial incubator programs. In many instances, entrepreneurial university activities have been the basis of entire new industries.

## 1.3 Technological Regions

While the presence of academic institutions in a region is a necessary condition for the establishment of a technological culture, which fosters entrepreneurism, it is not sufficient in terms of the development of technological regional entrepreneurship. Other elements are needed to develop a technological region such as Silicon Valley in California and Route 128 in Massachusetts. These elements are shown in Figure 2.1 and result in a culture characterized by tolerance of failure, learning, innovation, rapid response, competition, entrepreneurial exit, reward sharing, seeking market dominance and the willingness to acquire technology (Sager 1997).

**Tolerance of Failure** – A culture rewards entrepreneurial risks and does not penalize failure. This element is missing in many other cultures such as Japan, Germany and France.

**Learning** – In a technological culture failing is also not only not stigmatized but is a learning experience. Thus, the investment community provides capital to technological entrepreneurs who have failed. Jean-Louis Gassée founder of Be Inc. has stated (Sager 1997): *"It's hard to learn when you succeed."*

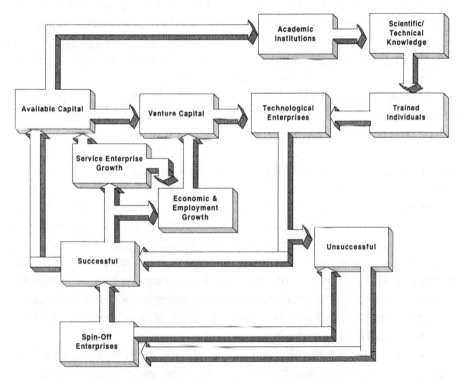

**Fig. 2.1**     Development of Technological Entrepreneurial Regions

**Innovative** – A culture that allows the growth of innovative concepts is an important element. Many new technological enterprises have been successfully financed (See Chapter 6 – Initial Enterprise Financing) with minimal business plans or without detailed market research for enterprises based on innovative projects.

**Rapid Response** – In a region such as Silicon Valley or Route 128, not only are speed and reduced product life cycles important, but also important

40

is the ability to rapidly adjust to a changing and chaotic environment. This ability requires:

- Multifunctional teams.
- Learning environment.
- Rapid communications.
- Delegation of authority to teams.
- Collaborative environment.

**Competition** – A highly competitive environment, internally and externally, is an important element. This, however, can result in the enterprise being self-competitive in some instances. In many instances, a technological entrepreneurial enterprise will cease development of an existing concept due to development of a new competitive concept within the enterprise. This practice is known as *eating your young*.

**Entrepreneurial Exit** – While the desired technological entrepreneurial characteristics (See Chapter 1 – Nature of Technological Entrepreneurism) foster enterprise start-up, these characteristics can be an impediment to an enterprise which matures (Reuber and Fischer 1994). This culture results in many instances of technological entrepreneurs founding a number of successive enterprises.

**Reward Sharing** – A major difference between many regional technological entrepreneurial cultures is in the use of compensation systems that reward achievement throughout the enterprise. Liberal stock options and vesting[14] programs such as those at Microsoft® Corporation and Intel Corporation have helped to make many of their employees millionaires and some even billionaires. Such reward sharing systems not only help to attract the most highly qualified, but also aid in retaining them in a highly competitive and tight job market.

**Seeking Market Dominance** – This cultural element seeks to capture market share and maintain it, even if it requires unusual practices such as giving a portion of a product away. This concept develops markets by dividing a product along system lines. An example is a client/server[15] environment where the client, i.e., the portion with the higher user

---

[14] The right to buy equity in the enterprise at some predetermined price.

[15] Client/server architecture is an arrangement used on local area networks that makes use of distributed intelligence to treat both the server and the individual workstations as intelligent, programmable devices, thus exploiting the full computing power of each. Splitting the processing of an application between two distinct components, a front-end client and a back-end server, is the basic concept that accomplishes this.

population, is used to capture market share while the server portion captures the economic rents. In some instances, entrepreneurs in the Internet market have used the approach of freely distributing the initial version of their product or service to capture market share and establish a brand name. The extensive promotional activities in the 1990s of America OnLine ("AOL"), which provided free access for a number of hours and thus achieved a significant market share and brand presence, is an example of this practice.

**Willingness to Acquire Technology** – Rapid technological change implies that technology life cycles are compressed. In an innovative culture with numerous entrepreneurial participants, external acquisition of technology may prove more beneficial than internal development. In a number of instances mature technological enterprises, such as Microsoft® Corporation, Cisco System Inc. and others, bought or invested in new technological ventures to obtain new innovative technologies. Some of the mature technological enterprises such as Intel Corporation set up venture capital funds for this purpose (Sager 1997).

These cultural elements when combined with those shown in Figure 2.1 provide the ability for technological economic growth through entrepreneurism.

### 1.4    Entrepreneurs from Academia

While academic institutions are a core element of a technological region due to knowledge generation, they are also a source of technological entrepreneurs. In an academic environment, faculties are the essential element in the knowledge creation process (Allen and Norling 1991, pp. 85). An example is a British born, Oxford educated scientist, Timothy Bernes-Lee, the developer of the World Wide Web ("WWW"). In 1990, while at CERN, Bernes-Lee developed the graphic user concept now known as the WWW. However, instead of founding a new enterprise he left this to other former academics such as James Clark. Professor Bernes-Lee was content with remaining an academic and serving as the Director of the World Wide Web Consortium at the MIT Laboratory for Computer Science in Cambridge, Massachusetts. In 1982, James Clark an assistant professor at Stanford University, with six others started Silicon Graphics (Hamilton and Humelstein 1997).

Not only academics, but also graduate students have become technological entrepreneurs. In 1994, two Stanford University engineering graduate doctoral students, David Fhilo and Jerry Yang started Yahoo! Inc.

in a campus trailer (Hamilton and Humelstein 1997). In 1996, Yahoo! Inc. issued a highly successful initial public offering (See Chapter 8 – Next Entrepreneurial Step) and Fhilo and Yang immediately were worth $100 million based upon their ownership interests. In turn, to show their appreciation to Stanford University, they endowed a professorship in the engineering school with a gift of $2 million.

Similar technological entrepreneurial activities have taken place at many of the academic institutions, including MIT, Virginia Polytechnic Institute and State University, Georgia Institute of Technology, and others. A number of successful start-ups may be initiated by researchers but many are not able to continue as the chief decision-maker ("CDM") once the enterprise enters maturity (Reuber and Fischer 1994).

## 1.5 Continuous Entrepreneurs

Many successful entrepreneurs achieve significant economic rewards early in their entrepreneurial careers. David Fhilo and Jerry Yang, previously discussed, are excellent examples. When the achievement of financial reward is accompanied by exit from the enterprise, the entrepreneurs usually find themselves with significant resources and the desire to continue the technological entrepreneurial process. This continual technological entrepreneurial process takes place even if the initial enterprise fails or is only marginally successful. The entrepreneurial activity of Andrew Busey, founder and Chief Technology Officer ("CTO") of ICHAT, a provider of interactive, real time chat communication products to WWW users and corporate Intranets[16], is an example of this continuous process. By 1997, when Andrew Busey was 26 years old, he had founded three technology enterprises (Willis 1997).

Not only do the founders tend to continuously initiate new technology enterprises, but also the former employees are similarly energized. Jamie Hamilton was an employee of Freeloader Inc., an Internet enterprise which was sold in 1997 for $38 million after a relatively short time in business (Hilzenrath 1997). Freeloader Inc. had been started by former America OnLine employees who sold their stock option interests and used these funds and their expertise to set-up this venture. Jamie Hamilton, who was 30 years

---

[16] An Intranet is a network designed for information processing within a company or organization and is so called because it usually employs Web pages for information dissemination and applications associated with the Internet, such as Web browsers.

of age when the company was sold, then proceeded to invest his portion of the proceeds from the sale of Freeloader Inc. into a new venture, Torso Inc.

## 1.6    Female Technological Entrepreneurs

Roberts (Roberts 1991, pp. 41) reported that his research study in 1976 found only one technology enterprise founded by women, i.e., Margaret Hamilton and Saydean Zeldin who started Higher Order Software Inc. Fewer women than men in the 1990s were pursuing college degrees in technical fields such as computer science. In 1984, 37.1 percent of computer science bachelor's degrees in the United States were awarded to women. This decreased to 28.4 percent by 1995.

Research shows that while both male and female entrepreneurs generally possessed similar characteristics (See Chapter 1 – Nature of Technological Entrepreneurism), female entrepreneurs tended to possess very different motivations, business skill levels, and occupational backgrounds to male entrepreneurs (Hisrick and Peters 1995, pp. 62). Their studies found that female entrepreneurs tend to be more motivated by the need for achievement arising from job frustration in not being allowed to perform and grow at the level at which they are capable. This managerial growth barrier has been termed the *glass ceiling*. The *glass ceiling* was a reality in 1996 in the technology sector (Geppart 1996). In 1996, less than ten percent of engineers in the United States were female; worldwide the percentage was considerably less. However, much less than ten percent of the CEOs of technological companies were women in 1996. The *glass ceiling* in this sector is fostering the growth of female technological enterprises.

In general, male and female entrepreneurs differ in terms of the nature of the enterprise initiated (Hisrick and Peters 1995, pp. 64). Women were found to be more likely to start an enterprise in a service sector, while men were more likely to establish a manufacturing, construction or technological enterprise. An example is Carol Walcoff, the CEO and principal owner of Walcoff and Associates Inc., a government service contractor in Falls Church, Virginia. Ms. Walcoff started this successful technology service company after leaving the Mitre Corporation, a government established contractor. The company was founded based on providing service contracting for government agencies. In the 1990s, the enterprise started to diversify into the commercial Internet sector.

In Silicon Valley, the world's primary technological center, in 1997 there was only one woman CEO at a major technological enterprise, Carol Bartz, the CEO of Autodesk Inc. (Hamm 1997). Female entrepreneurs have started new technological enterprises in Silicon Valley. Kim Polese, a former product manager at Sun Microsystems Inc., founded Marimba Inc., a *push*[17] technology enterprise in 1996. Marimba Inc. received substantial venture capital backing for their *Java*[18] based technology. However, technology enterprises either founded or operated by women did not obtain a large share of available venture financing. In 1991 to 1996, female technological entrepreneurs only obtained 1.6 percent of the $33.5 billion invested by venture capitalists.

In 1983, Katherine Clark, at the time a programmer with Blue Cross/Blue Shield, a medical group insurer, and a male associate founded Landmark Systems Inc. Katherine Clarke is an example of a highly successful female technological entrepreneur. Clark and her associate developed an innovative performance management software application for the Blue Cross/Blue Shield. In 1983, they negotiated for the rights to this software that became the basis of their company. When Landmark Systems Inc. was founded, both technology entrepreneurs had only high school degrees and little business experience (Technology 1996). By 1996, Clark's enterprise had grown to 230 professionals with annual revenues of $45 million and had become a worldwide leader in computer mainframe performance software. Landmark Systems Inc. had a highly successful initial public offering in the summer of 1998, making Ms. Clark and other founders multimillionaires.

## 1.7 Entrepreneurial Immigrants

Immigrants to the United States have not only brought themselves and their families, but also their talents. This immigration movement was in a number of instances motivated by the lack of technological opportunities in the immigrants' native countries. There were 1,500 Asian American owned technology enterprises in Silicon Valley in 1997 (Engardio and Burrows 1997).

In 1997, it was estimated that one-third of the engineers in the United States were not native to the U.S. (Engardio and Burrows 1997). Many of these engineers have become technological entrepreneurs, including Andrew

---

[17] Push technology sends data or a program from a server to a client at the instigation of the server.

[18] Java is an object-oriented programming language, developed by Sun Microsystems, Inc. and was designed to be platform-neutral (meaning that it could be run on any platform).

S. Grove (Hungary), Chairman of Intel Corporation; Eric Benhamou (Algeria), CEO of 3COM Corporation; S. Atiq Raza (Pakistan), founder and CEO of NexGen Inc. and many others. S. Atiq Raza, the founder of NexGen, a microprocessor design company, sold his enterprise in 1996 to Advanced Micro Devices Inc. for $620 million.

Yuji Ide worked for 15 years for Toshiba Corporation in Japan (Engardio and Burrows 1997). Ide had been a contributor to over 100 patents including the first digital camera. In 1995 Ide left Japan and immigrated to Silicon Valley in California. In California, he started a technological enterprise, Pixera Corporation. Yuji Ide obtained a great deal of the $11.6 million in venture financing to form his new enterprise from the Toshiba Corporation.

Technological entrepreneurs born outside of the U.S.A. were starting many new enterprises in 1997 and obtaining significant financing through specially targeted funds. Venture capital funds such as Sequoia Capital and Alpine Technology Venture, were started primarily to invest in immigrated technology enterprises.

In 1996, Peter Kang, the son of Korean immigrants and Gene Na, a 22 year old Vietnamese immigrant who came to the United States as an eleven month old child, started an Internet enterprise named Kioken (Napoli 1997). By 1997, Kioken had become a small well-known web design enterprise based in *Silicon Alley* [19] and created *Fire Magazine,* a web based magazine. Kang and Na used this enterprise to form an alliance with Kang-Lee Advertising, an Asian advertising accounts company (Napoli 1997) and started to obtain Asian clients for their innovative web designs.

Trained engineers worldwide also have become major technological entrepreneurs. Allen Salmasi was born in Tehran, Iran in 1954 and by 1971 had immigrated to Los Angles, California (Schine and Barrett 1996). Salmasi came from a highly successful Iranian family. His father and uncle owned a very large construction business in Iran. With the fall of the Shah of Iran a substantial portion of the family wealth was lost (Schine and Barrett 1996). In 1977, Allen Salmasi received a Bachelor of Science degree with majors in electrical engineering and management economics from Purdue University. This was followed by a Master of Science degree in engineering from Purdue University in 1979 and a Master of Science degree in applied mathematics in 1983 from the University of Southern California (Schine and Barrett 1996). In 1984, Salmasi founded Omninet Corporation to track truck

---

[19] Silicon Alley is the name given to the concentration of enterprises in lower Manhattan Island ( New York City) who specialize in the Internet.

movements by satellite. Also in 1984, Salmasi's father and several associates relocated to Los Angles, California from Iran and invested initially $14 million and later an additional $9 million into Omninet. Omninet applied concepts that Salmasi had helped to develop while employed from 1979 to 1984 by the National Aeronautics and Space Administration ("NASA") and the Jet Propulsion Laboratory of the California Institute of Technology. Four years later, in 1988, Allen Salmasi and his family sold Omninet to another technology start-up Qualcomm for a 47 percent interest in the new venture. By 1995, when Allen Salmasi left Qualcomm, more than half of the company's $387 million in annual revenue came from the satellite truck tracking service (Schine and Barrett 1996).

After leaving Qualcomm, Salmasi started NextWave Telecom Inc. in 1995. The objective of NextWave Telecom was to establish a wireless network to compete against AT&T and Sprint Corporation. In 1996, NextWave Telecom agreed to pay $4.7 billion for Federal Communication Commission ("FCC") licenses to provide digital wireless telephone service to 110 million potential customers. Enterprises of the nature of NextWave Telecom require multi-billion dollar investments and are not always successful, but it is the technological entrepreneurs such as Allen Salmasi who have made technological growth a reality.

## 1.8 Young and Old Entrepreneurs

The age at which technological entrepreneurs establish their initial enterprise varies between 23 to 69 according to the studies of Roberts (Roberts 1991, pp. 65), with an overall median of 37 years. Table 2.1 shows the data from various studies conducted by Roberts (Roberts 1991, pp. 65) and reported by Hisrick and Peters (Hisrick and Peters 1995, pp. 57-58).

Geoffrey Allen founded Source Digital Systems Inc. in 1990 at the age of 19. Source Digital Systems provided digital video editing services and delivery solutions for full-motion digital video over networks, and developed interactive multimedia products. By 1995, Allen's enterprise had annual revenues exceeding $7 million. Allen then established Axicom in Vienna, Virginia to manufacture digital video servers (Roach 1997).

Some technological entrepreneurs start companies while still in their mid-teens. Nexgen Solutions Inc. of Washington, D.C. is one such enterprise (Roach 1997). In 1988, Edward Howlette founded Nexgen Solutions at the age of 18, based on a patent he had obtained. The company he founded specialized in various software for use in a client-server environment. By 1995, Nexgen Solutions had annual revenues of more than $2 million and employed 25 professionals (Roach 1997).

**Table 2.1**
Technological Entrepreneurial Ages

| Organization | Age Range | Median |
|---|---|---|
| MIT Laboratory Spin-offs | 24 – 64 | 33 – 36 |
| Technology Enterprise Spin-offs | 25 – 54 | 39 |
| Information Technology Spin-offs | 24 – 51 | 37 |
| New Technology Ventures | 26 – 52 | 39 |
| Venture Capital Investments | 23 – 69 | 39 |
| Technical and Non-technical Entrepreneurs | 22 – 55 | No data |
| Male Entrepreneurs | 25 – 35 | No data |
| Female Entrepreneurs | 35 – 45 | No data |

(Based on data contained in Hisrick and Peters 1995; Roberts 1991, pp. 65)

The technological entrepreneurial careers similar to both Howlette and Allen are not unusual and many individuals start their careers at young ages either through contact with role models or through personal interest in a technology. Other entrepreneurs such as Robert Bemer start entrepreneurial careers at a much later age. Robert Bemer, founded BMR Software Inc. in Dallas, Texas at the age of 77 (Ouellette and Scheier 1997). Bemer had completed a career with a number of large technology enterprises including IBM, Univac, Rand Corporation and General Electric Company. In the early years of his career, Bemer had help to create Cobol[20], an early business computer language, and had developed various computer language standards.

As the year 2000 approaches, computer professionals have recognized that many legacy computer programs that had been written earlier contained only a two-digit field for the year in order to reduce storage and memory requirements. It was assumed that by the start of the twenty-first century these programs would have been replaced. By the year 2000, these older legacy computer programs would give erroneous year results, i.e., in the year 2000 non-corrected legacy software could incorrectly assume the year was 1900! This problem appeared to have significant impacts and could be costly to correct. Robert Bemer, seeing an opportunity, established his new

---

[20]Common Business-Oriented Language (COBOL) is an English-like compiled programming language developed between 1959 and 1961 for primarily business applications typically run on mainframes.

48

technological enterprise to market a product that could correct the problem caused by older software programs using the Cobol language which he had helped to develop.

Another example is Robert L. Uffen, a professor emeritus in microbiology from Michigan State University who at 60 years of age with his wife Ellen Uffen, a former professor of english literature, and Guy Orgambide, a French professor of microbiology, age 36, established SciCentral.com site in 1997. By 1999, SciCentral.com had become the dominant science and technology Internet portal. The enterprise then implemented an electronic commerce strategy.

## 2.    UNITED STATES TECHNOLOGICAL ENTREPRENEURS

The technological entrepreneurs of the United States can be classified in numerous ways. No technology starts *de novo*, i.e., spontaneously. All technological innovations have a technological heritage. The technical *parents* and *grandparents* of a technological innovation are the outputs of various enterprises (public, private and academic). These public, private and academic enterprises in many instances, in their way, serve as the progenitors of new technological enterprises.

These incubators of technological entrepreneurism have both academic centers and resources where technological enterprises tend to cluster. Established and new technological enterprises tend to cluster in regions to take advantage of pools of highly skilled workers and the collection of technology resources (AEA 1997). In the United States these regions include: *Silicon Valley* in California; *Route 128* in Massachusetts; *Research Triangle* in North Carolina; *Silicon Hills* in Austin, Texas; the technology corridor of Redmond, Bellevue, and Kirkland in Washington State; *Silicon Forest* in Oregon; *Netplex* in the Washington, D.C. – Northern Virginia metropolitan area; and *Silicon Alley* in New York City. These regions have had major impacts on the economy of the United States. Table 2.2 shows the impact of technology on regional economies in 1995.

**Table 2.2**
Impact of Technology in the United States
(1995)

| State | Employment | Technology Average Wage | Merchandise Technology Exports ($ Billion) |
|---|---|---|---|
| California | 669,349 | $55,160 | 58.8 |
| Texas | 313,460 | No data | 29.4 |
| New York | 295,649 | $51,766 | 14.4 |
| Massachusetts | 190,036 | $52,999 | 10.2 |
| Illinois | 189,062 | No data | 13.6 |
| Florida | 175,709 | No data | 9.8 |
| New Jersey | 164,929 | $55,970 | No data |
| Pennsylvania | 145,531 | No data | 5.9 |
| Virginia | 126,810 | $49,668 | No data |
| Ohio | 119,343 | No data | 7.1 |

(Based on data contained in AEA 1997)

## 2.1 Silicon Valley Entrepreneurial Incubator

Silicon Valley, a 50-mile corridor in California, has become the *sine qua non* of technological entrepreneurism in the world. This region south of the city of San Francisco, by the 1990s, had become the major center of technological activity in the United States.

The statistics for Silicon Valley are impressive (Week 1997):

- In 1997, more than 33 percent of the 100 largest technology enterprises in the United States were contained in Silicon Valley.
- Real wages in 1996 grew by 5.1 percent versus the U.S. average of less than one percent.
- In 1996, more than 50,000 new jobs were created.
- In 1997, it contained eleven percent of the technology positions in the United States, but only one percent of the population.
- In 1997, over 60 percent of its manufacturing was technology based versus nine percent for the United States.
- In 1997, the average wage was 55 percent more than the average for the United States.
- In 1996, the academic institutions produced 2,268 advanced engineering degrees, the highest number in the United States.

The *Information Revolution* was the major driving force for the development of Silicon Valley. The computer and semiconductor industries of Silicon Valley accounted for 45 percent of the industrial growth in the 1993 – 1997 period.

The culture of Silicon Valley evolved in a manner which promoted the development of new technology enterprises (Saxenian 1996, pp. 38 - 39). These cultural elements include (Sager 1997; Saxenian 1996):

- **Freedom to fail** – This encourages all levels of management to try new ideas.
- **Acceptance of rapid change** – This develops corporate cultures that can more easily make major revisions in their business model and cannibalize their existing products before competitors challenge their market share.
- **Entrepreneurial exit** – Few entrepreneurs remain with their enterprise into maturity. This exit usually occurs as the enterprise approaches $1 billion in revenue.
- **Enterprise wide compensation** – Entrepreneurial and mature enterprises compensate and incentivize their employees at all levels, based on enterprise success. This includes compensation packages, e.g., stock options at all employee levels.
- **Agile systems** – This includes rapid building of a customer base through incentivization such as free beta copies of software and initial products. This allows for comments and development of brand recognition.
- **Investing in the young enterprises** – Successful enterprises maintain technological lead by investing in new technological entrepreneurial ventures. This allows many mature enterprises such as the Intel Corporation to gain access to new technical developments with lower research and development investments.

The phenomenal success of entrepreneurial enterprises such as Yahoo!, Netscape Communications, and others is based on the culture that had developed in Silicon Valley over a long period of time. These phenomenally successful technological entrepreneurial enterprises started with Hewlett-Packard in the 1930s and developed thereafter. Subsequent successful mature enterprises include Intel Corporation, Sun Microsystems Inc., Cisco Systems Inc. each of which has spawned a number of other technological entrepreneurial ventures that, in turn, have and will spawn additional enterprises. This cascading effect does have some limitations. These limitations include:

- Availability of physical space for new enterprises.
- Availability of trained technical workers.
- Economic factors which can accelerate growth in costs.

However, while many other areas of the United States and other nations have tried to duplicate the technological entrepreneurial success of Silicon Valley, few if any have succeeded to a similar degree. The essential element that has been difficult to clone is the exuberant entrepreneurial culture and spirit that exists in Silicon Valley.

### 2.1.1 Spin-offs from Stanford University

The initial nucleation point for entrepreneurial activity in Silicon Valley has and continues to be Stanford University. Stanford University's entrepreneurial spirit began when a young electrical engineering professor, Fredrick E. Terman encouraged and provided the initial funds for two of his former students, William Hewlett and David Packard (Saxenian 1996, pp. 20). Professor Terman's belief that a strong and encouraging academic entrepreneurial culture would drive technological developments was the basis for the initial enterprises surrounding Stanford University that became known as Silicon Valley. Figure 2.2 illustrates some of the technological enterprises that have been spawned from Stanford University.

Stanford University's record in spawning technological entrepreneurs has been substantial. While many universities in the United States have seen their alumni move after graduating, many Stanford University engineering graduates stayed in Silicon Valley and joined or formed new technological entrepreneurial enterprises. Between 1960 and 1990, technology enterprises started by graduates of Stanford University created 250,000 jobs (Hamilton and Humelstein 1997).

Figure 2.2 depicts a multigenerational *begetting* of technology enterprises from firms started by Stanford University graduates. Not only did Stanford University contribute graduates, its academic faculty also had symbiotic relationships with many of those technological enterprises either as consultants, members of boards of directors or entrepreneurial participants.

52

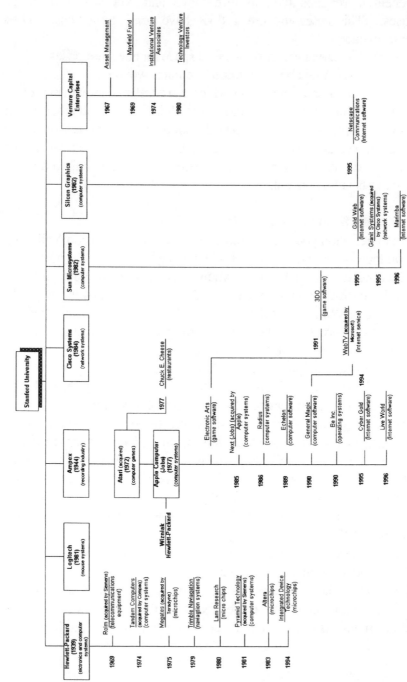

**Fig. 2.2** Some of the Spin-offs from Stanford University

Former professors, such as James H. Clark started Silicon Graphics Inc. and used the financial resources from his share of the company to form Netscape Communications with James Barksdale and Marc Andreessen. There has been a continuing cross-fertilization between the academic faculty of Stanford University and technology enterprises. This is exemplified by John Hennessy, who in the early 1980s was deeply involved in the research of the RISC[21] computer processor. Taking an academic sabbatical, he obtained venture capital and formed MIPS Computer Systems Inc. (Hamilton and Humelstein 1997). In 1985 Hennessy returned to Stanford University and eventually became dean of engineering.

### 2.1.2 Spin-offs from Fairchild and Xerox

Existing technology enterprises can be technological parents of new entrepreneurial enterprises. Fairchild Semiconductor Company and the Xerox Palo Alto Research Center ("PARC") exemplify this begetting of new technological enterprises.

**Fairchild Semiconductor Company**

In 1945, William B. Shockley, Walter H. Brattain, and John Bardeen invented the transistor while working at Bell Laboratories[22] which at that time was the principal research laboratory of American Telephone and Telegraph Company ("AT&T".) In 1955, Dr. Shockley returned to Palo Alto, California where he was raised. He and other technological entrepreneurs formed Shockley Transistor Corporation to capitalize on his invention (Saxenian 1996, pp. 25). In 1957, eight members of Shockley Transistor Corporation, who became known as *the traitorous eight*, left to establish Fairchild Semiconductor Company. The eight founders were: Gordon Moore, Sheldon Roberts, Eugene Kleiner, Robert Noyce, Victor Grinich, Julius Black, Jean Hoerni and Jay Last. William Shockley had recruited these eight from various research facilities on the East Coast of the United States. However, due to Dr. Shockley's erratic management style these eight engineers and scientists became disgruntled and left the company.

---

[21]Reduced Instruction Set Computing (RISC) is a microprocessor design, which focuses on rapid and efficient processing of a relatively small set of simple instructions that comprises most of the instructions a computer decodes and executes.
[22]After the break-up of AT&T, Bell Laboratories became a subsidiary of Lucent Technologies Inc.

They formed Fairchild Semiconductor Company to develop and manufacture silicon semiconductors. Fairchild Semiconductor Company and its founders in turn became the basis of the West Coast semiconductor industry. The Fairchild Semiconductor Company was the first company to manufacture integrated circuits. It helped to initiate the semiconductor industry and from it, over three dozen computer microprocessor enterprises were founded. Many of these companies did not survive, others, were merged and others such as Intel Corporation, garnered the major market share of the microprocessor industry.

The funding for the eight founders of Fairchild Semiconductor Company came from a New York City financier, Sherman Fairchild. However, Sherman Fairchild contributed to the defection of many of the founders due to his propensity for micromanaging the enterprise from his New York City office while the core of the enterprise was in Silicon Valley, California (Patterson 1997). The individual founders of Fairchild Semiconductor Company and others from the company went on to form their own technological enterprises based on their activities at the company. Some of these included:

- Research and Development – Intel Corporation with Robert Noyce and Gordon Moore.
- Manufacturing – National Semiconductor Corporation with Charles Sporch.
- Sales and Marketing – Advances Semiconductor Devices Inc. with W. J. Sanders III.
- Finance – Sequoia Capital.

One of the first children of Fairchild Semiconductor Company was Signetics Inc., which was formed by a number of technical professionals from the company, including David Allison, David Jones, Lionel Kattner, Mark Weissenstein and several others (Hamilton and Humelstein 1997). Phillips Semiconductor eventually acquired Signetics Inc. Phillips Semiconductor in turn, spawned Cirrus Logic Inc. in 1985 when Michael Hockworth, Kamran Elahian and others left the company. In 1993, Kamran Elahian and Prakach Agarwal left Cirrus Logic Inc. to form NeoMagic Inc. By 1996, Kamran Elahian had formed Planet Web Inc.

By 1959, Robert Noyce, one of the founders of Fairchild Semiconductor Company had filed a patent for the first integrated silicon circuit, which became the basis of microprocessors. In July 1968, Robert Noyce and Gordon Moore left Fairchild Semiconductor Company and formed Intel

Corporation. Intel Corporation was formed to develop and manufacture large-scale integrated ("LSI")[23] semiconductor products. Initially Intel Corporation was devoted to the development and manufacture of semiconductor memories.

Gordon E. Moore, a *giant* of the semiconductor industry, graduated from the University of California at Berkeley in 1950 with a Bachelor of Science in chemistry. In 1954, Moore received a Ph.D. in chemistry and physics from the California Institute of Technology. William Shockley recruited Dr. Moore from the Applied Physics Laboratory at John Hopkins University in 1953 where he was conducting basic research in chemical physics (IEEE 1997).

The Intel Corporation has also served as a major *parent* of new technological entrepreneurial ventures. This process is illustrated by the formation of Seeq Technology Inc. in 1981 when Gordon Campbell and George Perlegos left Intel Corporation. In turn, Gordon Campbell, Dado Banatao and two others left Seeq Technology Inc. to form Chips and Technologies Inc. in 1985. In some instances, as in the case of Chips and Technologies Inc., the Intel Corporation later acquired its own *grandchild*. In 1989, Dado Banatao and Ron Yara left Chips and Technologies Inc. to form S3 Inc. The other founder of Chips and Technologies Inc., Gordon Campbell, and another employee, Scott Sellers, left the company to establish 3Dfx Inc. in 1994. Among the other technology, enterprises founded by former members of Intel Corporation is Zilog Inc. in 1974 which in turn, spawned Xilinx Corporation in 1984 and Synaptics Inc. in 1986.

Another child of the Fairchild Semiconductor Company is National Semiconductor Corporation. In 1967, Charles Sporch, one of the founders of Fairchild Semiconductor Company left to form the National Semiconductor Corporation. Charles Sporch served as the CEO of National Semiconductor Corporation for 24 years and built the company into a major developer and manufacturer of analog and digital components. National Semiconductor Corporation also served as the basis of new technological entrepreneurial enterprises. In 1981, two employees of National Semiconductor Corporation, Robert Swanson and Robert Dolkin, formed Linear Technology Corporation. Sierra Semiconductor Corporation in 1983 was formed by James Diller and SDA Systems Corporation was formed by James Solomar, both members of National Semiconductor Corporation.

---

[23]LSI stands for large scale integrated chip describing the concentration of between 100 and 5000 circuit or more elements on a single chip.

The *children* of Fairchild Semiconductor Company (See Table 1.1, pp. 16) have been extremely productive and have established the basis for the phenomenal growth of the new *information age*. However, it must be remembered the original *nucleation point* was Dr. William Shockley, who brought together the critical *intellectual and entrepreneurial mass* when he formed Shockley Transistor Corporation.

## Xerox Corporation Palo Alto Research Center

Technological enterprises, such as Xerox Corporation and Fairchild Semiconductor Company, have been the entrepreneurial incubators that have fueled the growth of technology. While the *parent* enterprise may not have employed a direct strategy in formulating these new entrepreneurial enterprises, their culture while sometimes precluding the commercialization conceived within them encouraged innovation. For example, in 1970 the Xerox Corporation created the Palo Alto Research Center ("PARC") with the hope of this research laboratory becoming the *architect of the information age* (Patterson 1997; Saxenian 1996). PARC has produced many of the technology concepts that have stimulated the growth of the personal computer ("PC") industry. The technologies conceived by PARC include:

- Graphical User Interface ("GUI") which was the basis for the Apple Computer's Macintosh and Microsoft® Corporation's Windows operating systems.
- Laser printers.
- Desktop publishing – Two former PARC staff members founded Adobe Systems Inc. based on the PostScript[24] printer language.
- Ethernet[25] Local Area Network ("LAN") – Invented by Robert Metcalf a former PARC scientist and founder of 3Com Corporation. By 1997, 3Com Corporation had become a $6 billion enterprise (Patterson 1997).
- Object-oriented programming language (smalltalk).

However, Xerox Corporation itself did not prosper from the commercialization of the innovative technologies developed by PARC's staff due to reticence to enter non-copier markets. Many technological

---

[24] PostScript is a page-description language that offers flexible font capability and high-quality graphics.

[25] Ethernet developed by Xerox in 1976 was originally for linking minicomputers at the Palo Alto Research Center that is now an IEEE 802.3 standard for networks.

enterprises when they reach maturity fail to recognize internal developments that can serve as the basis of future growth.

### 2.1.3 Entrepreneurs of the 1990s

The 1990s have been a period of phenomenal growth in technological entrepreneurism. A great deal of this entrepreneurism has been coupled to the growth in the use of the client/server computer paradigm and the Internet. Many of these new technological enterprises are located in Silicon Valley. The financial successes of these enterprises have served as a positive feedback to encourage other technological entrepreneurs and the financial community. A great deal of the wealth of these technological entrepreneurs comes from initial public offerings ("IPO") (See Chapter 8 – Next Entreprencurial Step) which, in the 1990s, have experienced an unprecedented boom. In 1995, $8.4 billion was invested in IPOs. This rapid rise in valuation of new technological enterprises fueled additional growth.

The ideal objective of IPOs is to reward dynamic entrepreneurs. In the culture of Silicon Valley and similarly, successful technology regions, the beneficiaries of IPOs usually also include many employees, including secretaries who have been granted stock options. These stock options are granted because many of the new technology entrepreneurs cannot afford to pay high salaries or generous benefits.

An example of this is Marc Andreessen, one of the founders of Netscape Communications Corporation. Marc Andreessen was raised in Wisconsin where his father had been a salesman and his mother worked for Lands End, a mail order seller of outdoor clothing. Marc Andreessen, while an undergraduate student at the University of Illinois at Urbana-Champaign, worked to develop an Internet browser that would facilitate navigating the World Wide Web. In this position, his responsibility was to write software for three-dimensional scientific visualization. In this position as a programmer, he was paid $6.85 per hour (Collins 1996). This work resulted in the Internet browser named *Mosaic* that was given away by the University to encourage its use. Another more mature technological entrepreneur, James Clark, a former Stanford University professor, who had founded Silicon Graphics Inc. and built it into a major supplier of workstations, became very interested in the *Mosaic* browser and, in particular in Marc Andreessen one of its developers. In 1994, James Clark contacted Marc Andreessen via E-mail and arranged to meet. The result of that meeting was the formation of Netscape Communications Corporation. The initial capital required for the formation of this new technological enterprise came from James Clark. On August 9, 1995, Netscape Communications Corporation issued an IPO. Originally, the IPO was to be issued at an opening price of $28 per share, but instead opened at $71 per share. This produced an initial paper wealth of $58 million for Marc Andreessen who was 23 years of age at the time of the IPO.

Not all the new technology enterprises in Silicon Valley are computer related. In the late 1980s, Paul Turner and Stephen W. Simons formed RockShox Inc. RockShox Inc, based in San Jose, California, was established to manufacture high-value bicycle components such as front-suspension forks used in mountain bicycles. Paul Turner, at the time, worked for Honda Research and Development North America Inc. and Stephen Simons operated a small motorcycle-parts business (Armstrong 1997). Both had been childhood friends. Turner was dissatisfied with how bicycles handled difficult terrain and devised oil filled front-end shock absorbers for bicycles. Through development of their product and brand through creative advertising, RockShox Inc. became an industry leader and by March of 1997, the sales of RockShox Inc. had risen to $106 million annually with a 27 percent growth rate. In September 1996, RockShox Inc. issued an IPO, however, unlike computer stocks the price did not initially substantially fluctuate above its $15 per share offering price (Armstrong 1997).

Some technological entrepreneurs formulate new enterprises based on the potential of the technology. William McKiernan, the President and Chief Executive Officer ("CEO") of CyberSource Corporation met his partner John Pettit through the Internet (Clancy 1997). CyberSource Corporation was established in San Jose, California to develop a WWW site where buyers could purchase and download software from developers including the major software suppliers like Microsoft® Corporation, Symantic Corporation and Lotus Development Corporation. CyberSource Corporation developed an Internet commerce service that offered *turnkey* transaction-processing services for electronic-commerce services. The strategic differentiator that William McKiernan introduced was viable computer architecture for electronic distribution (Clancy 1997). It has been noted that one of the best skills of McKiernan is his ability to bring together diverse individuals into a multifunctional team. John Pettit had the contacts to assist in this team building process.

CyberSource Corporation also had the critical capability of seizing on new product opportunities. The concept for Internet Commerce Services

Inc., a subsidiary of the CyberSource Corporation, was not part of the original business plan (Clancy 1997). McKiernan and his team developed the concept for this subsidiary in two months to meet perceived market needs. Initially McKiernan invested the capital for the formation of CyberSource Corporation with several others, total funds amounting to $1 million (See Chapter 6 – Initial Enterprise Financing). As the enterprise required more capital, it turned to venture capitalists such as The Paul Allen[26] Group, Unterberg Harris and Batterson Venture Partners.

## 2.2 Eastern Technological Entrepreneurs

Technological entrepreneurism is not solely confined to Silicon Valley in California. In fact, many regions of the United States have similar centers of technological entrepreneurism. In the eastern portion of the United States, these include: Route 128 in Massachusetts; the Research Triangle in the Raleigh, Durham and Chapel Hill area of North Carolina; and Northern Virginia. As in the case of Silicon Valley, other regions have had nucleation points from which new technological enterprises have been established.

### 2.2.1 Spin-offs from Massachusetts Institute of Technology

The Massachusetts Institute of Technology ("MIT") has served as a technological entrepreneurial formation source similar to Stanford University. The entrepreneurial activity focused at MIT started in the early 1930s. Academic faculty, laboratory staff or graduates of MIT spawned many of the early technological enterprises. Many of the early technological entrepreneurs in the Boston, Massachusetts area were members of the faculty of MIT who seized technological opportunities. One of these early technological children of MIT was EG&G Inc., which was founded by three individuals with links to MIT (Roberts 1991, pp. 3 - 4). EG&G Inc. was formed by Kenneth J. Germeshausen, who formed a consulting partnership with his professor, Harold E. Edgerton in 1931. In 1933, another MIT graduate, Herbert Grier, joined Edgerton and Germeshausen. The partnership entered an agreement with MIT to use their facilities and equipment for work on high-speed motion picture techniques using the stroboscopic photography technique developed by Edgerton. After World War II, the three partners formed EG&G Inc. in 1947 with each partner

---

[26] **Paul Allen** is the second largest shareholder in Microsoft® Corporation that he founded with Bill Gates.

investing $5,000 (Roberts 1991, pp. 4). The enterprise grew significantly and by 1990, the annual revenue exceeded $1.5 billion.

Kenneth H. Olsen, another MIT graduate, joined Professor Jay W. Forrester's[27] MIT Digital Computer Laboratory group in July 1950 as a research associate (Roberts 1991, pp. 6). While working at this laboratory, Olsen learned to appreciate Professor Forrester's operational abilities and those of IBM where he served as MIT's on-site liaison in Poughkeepsie, New York. In 1957, Olsen and Harlan Anderson, another MIT engineer, evolved the concept of a new computer enterprise which became Digital Equipment Corporation ("DEC"). At the time of the founding of this enterprise, Olsen was 31 and Anderson was 28 years old.

RSA Data Security Inc. was founded in 1982 by three mathematicians, Ronald Rivest, Adi Shamir and Leonard Adelmar, who had developed the concept of public key encryption[28] while at MIT (Clark 1996). Realizing their lack of business acumen, the founders hired D. James Bidzos, a Florida marketing executive, to manage the enterprise. In ten years, Bidzos built RSA Data Security Inc. into an enterprise with revenues exceeding $200 million annually. Mr. Bidzos is a Greek born entrepreneur who, while not a technologist himself, was able to bring entrepreneurial skills to an enterprise established by technologists. In many instances, technological entrepreneurs have failed due to a lack of understanding of fundamental business principals. Many entrepreneurial technological enterprises such UUNet, Yahoo!, and Netscape Communications, were able to achieve sustainable growth due to professional managers who were brought into the enterprise to serve as the CEOs.

### 2.2.2 Netpreneurs

The Northern Virginia region of the Commonwealth of Virginia, adjacent to the Washington, D.C., developed many new entrepreneurial enterprises as the result of the rapid growth of the Internet, and by the mid-1990s became the center of the *information highway* for the United States. By 1996 there were more than 1,300 technology businesses in the Northern Virginia region, employing 155,000 people (Cardullo 1996). More than 50 to 60 percent of

---

[27] **Forrester, Jay Wright**, a U.S. electrical engineer and management expert who invented the random-access magnetic core memory.

[28] Public key encryption is an asymmetric early scheme that uses a pair of keys for the encryption of information. The public key encrypts data, and a corresponding secret key decrypts it.

all Internet traffic worldwide traversed this region in 1996. Ten of the major worldwide Internet providers were based in Northern Virginia and a total of 61 Internet access providers were located in the Washington Metropolitan Region in 1996. Due to this concentration, *The Washington Technology Journal* named this region *Netplex*. Although the technology enterprises in the Northern Virginia region comprised only four percent of the total enterprises in the region (Stough, Rigyle, and Kulkarni 1997), these technology enterprises directly produced 24 percent of the private sector employment and 29 percent of the earnings of the region. Stough et al (Stough, Rigyle, and Kulkarni 1997) found that each technology sector position in Northern Virginia generated one additional position in another sector. The growth of the Internet in this region is shown in Table 2.3 (Based on data contained in Henry 1997).

**Table 2.3**
Significant Internet Events in Netplex During the 1990s

| | |
|---|---|
| **1991** | The National Research and Education Network is established by the U.S. High Performance Computing Act |
| **1992** | Internet Society is established in Reston, Virginia |
| **1993** | InterNIC is created by the National Science Foundation<br>The White House establishes a WWW site |
| **1994** | *Intellectual Property and National Information Infrastructure* is issued by the Clinton Administration addressing Internet policy issues including copyright |
| **1995** | NSF Net returns back to a research network<br>MCI, PsiNet, UUNet, Sprint and ANS/AOL, all based in Netplex, become suppliers on the Internet *backbone* communications<br>InterNIC, a former subsidiary of SAIC, registers Internet domain names<br>America Online ("AOL"), CompuServe and Prodigy provide Internet acess to their subscribers |
| **1996** | Telecommunication companies request the U.S. Congress to ban Internet telephone technology<br>InterNIC suspends 9,272 domain name listings of those who have not paid domain name fees.<br>AOL has 19 hours outage that calls into question the capacity constraints of online service providers |
| **1997** | America Online had 8.5 million subscribers and users of the Internet out of approximately 20 million users of the Internet in the U.S.A.<br>WorldCom parent of UUNet buys CompuServe and sells subscriber base to AOL and acquires AOL network capabilities |

(Based on data contained in Henry 1997)

Mario Morino, a highly successful technological entrepreneur in the Northern Virginia region, was the driving force behind the *Netpreneur* (See Chapter 1 – Nature of Technological Entrepreneurism) to foster new technological entrepreneurs based on the Internet. Mario Morino began his career as a computer programmer in the 1960s at General Motors in Euclid, Ohio before he graduated from Case Western Reserve University (Higgins 1995). In 1973, Morino co-founded Morino Associates with William Witzel, each making an initial investment of $600. After a number of years of expansion, merger, and acquisitions, the enterprise became Legent Corporation. By 1995, Legent Corporation became one of the ten largest software companies in the world (Higgins 1995). In 1992, Mario Morino retired with a personal fortune of more than $80 million, making him one of the wealthiest 100 individuals in the Commonwealth of Virginia. His wealth further increased in 1995, when Computer Associates International Inc. acquired Legent Corporation in one of the largest computer software acquisitions up to that time.

In 1993, Mario Morino and his wife Dana founded the Marino Foundation, a private organization funded solely by his family. The foundation funded the Morino Institute in Reston, Virginia that in turn founded the Potomac KnowledgeWay Project. The centerpiece of this project is the Netpreneur Program to foster new technological entrepreneurism based on the Internet. While Morino has been given credit for stimulating technology growth in Northern Virginia (Henry 1997), there were many other relevant factors, including the growth of the Internet itself and the end of the *Cold War*. With the end of the *Cold War*, many of the technology enterprises located in the Washington Metropolitan region sought to enter the commercial technology market and provided much of the technology growth.

Not all technological entrepreneurs begin as technologists, some come from very diverse backgrounds and circumstances. James V. Kimsey, one of the founders of America Online Inc. is a case in point. Kimsey was raised in middle class family. His father had been in the U.S. Army, had fought in the Boxer Rebellion in China in the early 1900s and married late in life. James Kimsey graduated from the U.S. Military Academy at West Point, New York. He served with the U.S. Army airborne rangers, rising to the rank of Major. After serving on two combat tours of duty in Vietnam, Kimsey resigned to enter the security business. With $2,000, James Kimsey bought a building in central Washington, D.C. where he opened a trendy singles bar named the *Exchange* with a working stock market ticker tap machine. In turn Kimsey and his associates opened successively three other trendy single bars in Washington, D.C. The last bar and restaurant, known as *Bullfeathers on the Hill*, brought Kimsey over $1.5 million when it was sold.

After the sale of his last bar, James Kimsey went on a rafting vacation with his son in Colorado with Frank Caufield, a friend who had also gone to West Point. Caufield asked Kimsey to join him in CVC a company in McLean, Virginia which was trying to sell a computer game service over telephone lines to access early computer users. CVC had been started by William F. Von Meister, an early Northern Virginia technological entrepreneur (Swisher 1998, pp. 9). Kimsey and a number of his associates who had participated with him in the bar industry invested in CVC and formed, in May 24, 1985, Quantum Computer Services Inc after a series of financial reversals had caused Von Meister to leave CVC (Swisher 1998, pp. 46). Stephen (Steve) McConnell Case from Pizza Hut Corporation had been hired by Von Meister in 1984. Steve Case and Kimsey changed the business model and renamed the enterprise America Online. In 1993, James Kimsey turned over the CEO title to Stephen Case. Kimsey took the title of Chairman of the Board Emeritus and managed his investments and other interests, including an orphanage he founded in Vietnam in the mid-1960s.

William N. Melton, by 1997, had spent 20 years as a technological entrepreneur in the computer and telecommunication industries. Melton is typical of technological entrepreneurs who initiate an enterprise, but leave once it reaches maturity to start-up another technology enterprise. In 1971, Melton founded Real-Share Inc. a database and telecommunications company. This enterprise pioneered the use of minicomputers, voice response systems and distributed nodes in the financial industry. William Melton's academic background is not technical. Melton received a master's degree in Asian studies and Chinese philosophy. The association of Real-Share Inc. with the financial industry led Melton to see the need for automated credit card transaction terminals and data processing services for the retail industry. In 1981, in order to meet this need, William Melton founded VeriFone Corporation. Hewlett-Packard Corporation acquired this enterprise in 1997. In 1991, Melton founded Transaction Network Systems Inc. to provide customized data networks for financial institutions. By 1997, the enterprise, which had a highly successful initial public offering in 1994, was handling more than three million financial transactions daily.

Melton's entrepreneurial activity with both VeriFone and Transaction Network Systems, providing digital credit card authorization terminals and processing in many of the retail stores across the United States, indicated to Melton a *strategic inflection point.* This *10X* change (Grove 1996) represents a switch in the way people use money, i.e., from bank teller windows to retail electronic transactions. This change, coupled with the growth of the Internet, led Melton to start a new technological enterprise, named Cyber Cash Inc. Cyber Cash Inc. was established to create a secure Internet payment system. In 1996, the company launched Cyber Coin, a micro-payment service that allowed users to make cash payments for small purchases over the Internet (Henry 1997).

The Internet built the fortune of Richard L. Adams, Jr., the founder of UUNet Inc., a major provider of Internet communication services. Adams had been interested in computers since high school in Cleveland, Ohio, and received both bachelor and masters degrees in computer science from Purdue University. In 1982, Adams came to the Northern Virginia region to work for Science Applications International Corporation ("SAIC"), a government contractor. After a management disagreement with SAIC, Adams left and joined the Center for Seismic Studies, another U.S. Department of Defense contractor. At this company, Adams started to use the U.S. Government provided network known as ARPANET, the predecessor to Internet. This led Adams to attend meetings of Usenix Association, a professional group working with Unix[29] software. Adams noticed that many of the members of the association wanted to have access to ARPANET, which was a communication link between the U.S. Government and university computers. The major constraint at the time was the access communication costs. In 1987, Adams and the association established UUNet[30] as a tax-exempt non-profit company with the association providing $250,000 in start-up capital. Within a year UUNet had returned the original capital and had an annual revenue of $1 million. The enterprise was operated on an all-volunteer basis (Swisher 1996). By 1989, Adams left his position at the Center for Seismic Studies to manage UUNet from his home on a full time basis with four employees. In 1990, due to complaints from other Internet service providers regarding UUNet's tax-exempt status, Adams switched the enterprise to a for-profit corporation (See Chapter 5 – Enterprise Formation).

---

[29] A multi-user, multitasking-operating system originally developed by Ken Thompson and Dennis Ritchie at AT&T Bell Laboratories in 1969 for use on minicomputers.

[30] UUNet stands for Unix to Unix network.

Stochastic resonance[31] also plays a part in technological entrepreneurial success. In 1992, Adams was introduced to Mitch Kapor, the founder of Lotus Development Corporation. Mitch Kapor invested several hundred thousand dollars in UUNet. Adams had to be convinced to accept this investment since his objective was to build a service company which was *home-grown* and not a corporation (Swisher 1996). At this time, the Internet was growing exponentially. Through Kapor, UUNet obtained approximately $12 million in venture capital in 1993 and 1994 from Menlo Ventures, Accel Partners, New Enterprise Associates and Hancock Venture Partners (Swisher 1996). This funding allowed Adams and UUNet to resist the first attempt by MFS Inc., a communication enterprise, to acquire the enterprise. This also eventually resulted in Adams equity interest being reduced from 98 percent to 15 percent. The venture capitalist also insisted that Adams hire a professional management team and he became the Chief Technology Officer ("CTO"). However, the management team of UUNet that were hired by the venture capitalists and Adams became combatants. Hiring John Sidgmore solved this difficulty. Sidgmore had spent 14 years of his career at General Electric Information Services before starting and then selling a telephone software company. Sidgmore shifted the focus of UUNet from individual subscribers to corporate clients and to building a worldwide communication network. This eventually led to UUNet forming an alliance with Microsoft® Corporation, who acquired a 17 percent interest in the enterprise (Swisher 1996), and to a highly successful initial public offering. This in turn resulted in UUNet being acquired by MFS Inc. and both companies being merged into WorldCom Inc., a major telecommunication company. The market value of UUNet increased from its initial public offering in May 1995 to over $50 billion when the final merger with WorldCom Inc. was achieved in mid-1996. When UUNet was acquired and then merged into WorldCom Inc., Richard Adams became very wealthy, with a net worth in 1996 of over $300 million.

Raul J. Fernandez, young *Netpreneur* of Cuban immigrant heritage, is an example of how the Internet has stimulated technological entrepreneurism. Fernandez's father immigrated to the United States from Cuba when Fidel Castro became the leader of Cuba in the late 1950s, and his mother was an immigrant from Ecuador (Starzynski 1997c). Raul Fernandez graduated from the University of Maryland with a Bachelor of Science degree in

---

[31] Stochastic resonance is when a number of probabilistic events interact with each other resulting in amplification of the outcomes, either negatively or positively.

Economics in 1990. Fernandez attended the university while employed as the legislative assistant to Congressman Jack Kemp, the 1996 Republican vice-presidential candidate. After graduation, Raul Fernandez was employed as Director of Emerging Technologies at Digicon Inc., a U.S. government contractor. In 1991, Fernandez and three engineers left Digicon Inc. to form Proxima[32] Inc., which in 1996 changed its name to Proxicom Inc. This enterprise was established to provide integrated systems Internet solutions. By 1996, the revenue of Proxicom Inc. had grown to $10 million annually and in mid-1996, Mario Marino and Jack Kemp joined the board of directors of the company. By November 1996, Proxicom had completed a private placement of $5.3 million with General Atlantic Partners, at the time one of the world's largest venture capital funding organizations for technology and software companies. The revenue of Proxicom, Inc. exceeded $50 million annually in 1998 and the company was posed for an Initial Pubic Offering ("IPO") until the IPO *window* closed (See Chapter 8 - Next Entrepreneurial Step).

One of the new breed of technological entrepreneurs is Michael J. Saylor, the founder and Chief Executive Officer of MicroStrategy Inc. of Vienna, Virginia. Saylor started MicroStrategy in 1989 at the age of 24, with another MIT classmate, Sanju Bansal, to create data storage systems and data-mining[33] tools (Starzynski 1997b). The initial start-up capital of $100,000 came from a grant from DuPont Corporation. Michael Saylor had joined DuPont after graduating from MIT (Herring 1997). While at DuPont, Saylor worked on in-house market-simulation computer applications. This project developed into the concept that Saylor used to establish MicroStrategy and its Decision Support Software[34] ("DSS") product family. MicroStrategy soon after being established, obtained a $10 million contract from McDonald's Corporation to develop a customer data-mining application. The software that MicroStrategy Inc. developed allowed companies to *drill-down* into their databases and make highly specific queries. By 1997, MicroStrategy Inc. employed over 400 staff, with revenues of approximately $40 to $50 million annually. Saylor considered himself a philosopher who

---

[32] Proxima is the Spanish word for next. The company changed its name due to a trademark dispute with a similarly named company.

[33] Data mining is the process of identifying commercially useful patterns or relationships in databases or other computer repositories using advanced statistical computer programs.

[34] DSS is a set of computer programs and related data designed to help with analysis and decision making.

wanted to change the world. He kept a miniature replica of Rodin's *The Thinker* on his credenza to inspire him (Starzynski 1997b). MicroStrategy Inc. was profitable since it was established, with revenue growth of more than 100 percent annually. To encourage enterprise staff loyalty and retention, Saylor maintained a policy of offering employees stock options. MicroStrategy, Inc. had a highly successful IPO in June of 1998 which raised Michael Saylor's net worth in terms of his stock to over one billion dollars (See Chapter 8 - Next Entrepreneurial Step).

## 2.3    Fabulously Wealthy Technological Entrepreneurs

The rapid technological growth in the last decades of the twentieth century has created phenomenal wealth for some technological entrepreneurs. This has created some of the wealthiest people in the world, e.g., Bill Gates, in 1997 the second richest individual in the world in terms of assets based on his ownership in Microsoft® Corporation. Stories of phenomenal riches have fostered other technological entrepreneurs to develop new enterprises based upon innovative technologies. This positive feedback cascading model has not only provided great wealth for many individuals but has greatly increased the productivity of much of the world's economy. We can not uncouple technological derived wealth from the development of new innovative concepts; each feeds upon the other.

### 2.3.1    William Gates and Paul Allen – Microsoft® Corporation

William ("Bill") Gates, III and, Paul G. Allen, founders of Microsoft® Corporation, represent the pinnacle of what technological entrepreneurs want to achieve. This achievement is not in terms of their immense wealth but in the development of entire new industries with their concepts and products. Indeed both individuals are Schumpeter's *creative destructors* (See Chapter 1 - Nature of Technological Entrepreneurism).

Bill Gates and Paul Allen were high school friends with an interest in computers. Henry Ford and Bill Gates have been compared in both their impact and character (Stross 1996, pp. 6 - 7). Bill Gates was born in 1955 into a successful middle class family in Seattle, Washington. His father was a lawyer and his mother a teacher. His story is now part of business legend.

Bill Gates attended a private school at Lakeside School in the suburbs of Seattle, Washington where he met Paul Allen (Gates, Myhrvold, and Rinearson 1995, pp. 11). He wrote his first computer program in 1968, at the age of thirteen, with Paul Allen who was sixteen. In 1972, Bill Gates and

Paul Allen were stimulated by the announcement from the Intel Corporation of the 8008 microprocessor (Gates, Myhrvold, and Rinearson 1995, pp. 13). Both Gates and Allen formed their first entrepreneurial enterprise Traf-O-Data Inc. to process traffic-volume tapes. However, this venture failed when no customers wanted to buy the 8008 based processor computer system (Gates, Myhrvold, and Rinearson 1995, pp. 14). In 1973, Bill Gates entered Harvard College and Paul Allen joined Gates in Boston, Massachusetts where he became a programmer at the Honeywell Corporation. Not discouraged by their failure with their first entrepreneurial venture, Gates and Allen bought an Altair[35] 8800 computer in 1974 for $397 as a kit (Gates, Myhrvold, and Rinearson 1995, pp. 16) with no keyboard and no display. They *seized the day* and this was the genius of Gates and Allen. Both Gates and Allen used their experience in developing the BASIC[36] computer language to write software for the Altair. The program for the Altair was called *Microsoft*. BASIC was a simple computer language developed at Dartmouth College in 1964 for mainframe and minicomputers. *Microsoft* was based on a publicly available version of the language and adapted to Micro Instrumentation Telemetry Systems Inc. ("MITS") computer's Altair PC (Cusumano and Selby 1995, pp. 136). This lesson of taking an existing product and improving upon it is one of the main factors in Microsoft® Corporation's highly successful strategy.

In the spring of 1975, Allen left his job as a programmer and Gates left Harvard College and together they started Microsoft® Corporation. They moved to Albuquerque, New Mexico to be near to where the Altair was manufactured by MITS. MITS, a small entrepreneurial venture, was the first company to sell an inexpensive personal computer (Gates, Myhrvold, and Rinearson 1995, pp. 41). With the advent in 1977 of personal computers built by Apple Computer, Commodore Corporation, and Radio Shack, Microsoft® Corporation's BASIC compiler[37] became a standard. Microsoft® Corporation's strategy was to sell licenses for their software when the personal computers were sold by these companies (Gates, Myhrvold, and

---

[35] The Altair 8800 was a small computer introduced in 1974 by Micro Instrumentation Telemetry Systems of New Mexico and sold primarily in kit form. The Altair was based on the 8-bit Intel 8080 microprocessor, and had 256 bytes of random access memory.

[36] BASIC is an acronym for Beginner's All-purpose Symbolic Instruction Code, a high-level programming language developed in the mid-1960s by John Kemeny and Thomas Kurtz at Dartmouth College.

[37] A compiler is a computer program that translates all the source code of a program written in a high-level language like BASIC into object code prior to execution of the program.

Rinearson 1995, pp. 41). By January 1979, Gates and Allen moved Microsoft® Corporation to a suburb of Seattle, Washington with twelve employees (Gates, Myhrvold, and Rinearson 1995, pp. 43). By 1979, half of Microsoft® Corporation's revenue of $2.4 million annually was coming from Japan (Cusumano and Selby 1995, pp. 3; Gates, Myhrvold, and Rinearson 1995, pp. 41) primarily through a Japanese company ASCII. In total, the contract with ASCII of Japan produced more than $150 million in revenue. It also resulted in Bill Gates and Kayuhiko ("Kay") Miski, the president of ASCII, designing one of the first laptop computers in 1982, which was manufactured by Kyoceia Corporation and sold by Radio Shack as the Model 100 (Gates, Myhrvold, and Rinearson 1995, pp. 42).

To help operate Microsoft® Corporation, Bill Gates asked a classmate from Harvard College, Stephen Ballmer, to join him. Ballmer, after graduating from Harvard College, had been a product manager for Proctor and Gamble Corporation in Cincinnati, Ohio and then entered Stanford University Business School (Gates, Myhrvold, and Rinearson 1995, pp. 43). To encourage Ballmer to join Microsoft® Corporation and to leave Stanford University, Gates offered him a share in the ownership of the enterprise. This ownership share made Ballmer a multi-billionaire by 1997. In 1998, Ballmer became the President of the Microsoft® Corporation.

While Microsoft® Corporation was developing its market for BASIC, the company did not intend to develop an operating system for computers. In 1980, Bill Gates' mother, who was a member of the Board of Directors of United Way Inc. was at a meeting in Alexandria, Virginia. Also at the meeting was another board member, the President of IBM. The relationship between Mrs. Gates and the President of IBM, coupled with IBM's respect for the highly successful BASIC software, led IBM to send two staff members to meet with Bill Gates in the summer of 1980.

IBM was in the process of developing a personal computer based on the Intel Corporation 16-bit 8088 microprocessor. This project had been conceived by William Lowe and managed to completion by Donald Estridge, two members of IBM (Gates, Myhrvold, and Rinearson 1995, pp. 48). However, because Microsoft® Corporation did not have an operating system they could license. Bill Gates directed the two IBM emissaries to Digital Research Inc., in Grove, California. Gary Kildall, the President of Digital Research Inc. had the CP/M[38] operating system which was used in

---

[38] CP/M is the acronym for Control Program/Monitor that was a line of operating systems from Digital Research, Inc., for microcomputers based on Intel microprocessors.

over 100 brands of early computers from those produced by Xerox Corporation to those from Victor Graphics (Raymond 1997). When IBM was not able to achieve closure with Kildall and Digital Research Inc. the IBM executives returned to Microsoft® Corporation, where Bill Gates informed them he could obtain an operating system. He purchased the license with the rights to another company's Disk Operating System ("DOS") for $50,000. Gates also hired Timothy Paterson who had helped to develop DOS (Gates, Myhrvold, and Rinearson 1995, pp. 48). To achieve market dominance, Microsoft® Corporation sold their MS-DOS software for $60 per copy versus UCSD Pascal P-System[39] at $450 and CP/M-86 at $175 (Gates, Myhrvold, and Rinearson 1995, pp. 49). This market strategy succeeded beyond Gates and his associates' wildest dreams.

Paul Allen, the co-founder of Microsoft® Corporation, also became a multi-billionaire. Allen, who was three years older than Gates, had become his friend and mentor while they attended the prestigious Lakeside School in the Seattle, Washington suburbs. In 1983, Allen was diagnosed with Hodgkin's[40] disease at the age of 30. Believing he was terminally ill, Allen resigned from Microsoft® Corporation but kept his sizable equity interest (Lesly 1996). Allen did not return to Microsoft® Corporation after the remission of his condition. During the 1990s, Allen became enthralled by the entertainment industry and invested $1.7 billion in media and technology enterprises including (Lesly 1996):

- CNET, an Internet content provider.
- USSB, a digital satellite broadcaster.
- WebTV, a supplier of Internet via television. Microsoft® Corporation acquired this enterprise in 1997.
- Dreamworks SKG, startup movie studio productions company.
- Trail Blazers, a pro-basketball team.
- Starware, a Internet content provider.
- Ticketmaster Group Inc., the world's largest entertainment ticketing company.

---

[39] USCD Pascal P-System was an operating system and development environment that was developed by Kenneth Bowles at the University of California at San Diego. The system for the early IBM PC was based on the Pascal computer language.

[40] Hodgkin's disease is a malignant, progressive, sometimes fatal disease, characterized by enlargement of the lymph nodes, spleen, and liver.

Paul Allen also invested in numerous enterprises that failed or never returned the original investment. Great wealth from technology enterprises does not necessarily imply investment or business acumen no matter what the amount. The wealth of both Gates and Allen, while astounding, has its basis in early technological entrepreneurism coupled with stochastic resonance and Arthur's (Arthur 1989) concept of *technology lockin*[41].

### 2.3.2 Michael Dell – Dell Computer Inc.

Like Gates and Allen, Michael Dell became a billionaire through the growth of the personal computer industry. Dell, who was born in 1965 and was nine years younger than Gates, also, similar to Gates, left University prior to completing his degree. Dell was also raised in an upper-middle class family. Dell's father, an orthodontist, and his mother, a stock broker, moved to Houston, Texas and wanted Michael to become a physician (Serwer 1997). Dell, while in junior high school, became obsessed with the Apple II computer and how it was built. In 1983, to please his parents, Dell enrolled at the University of Texas. While at the university, Dell bought remaindered and outmoded IBM PCs from a local retailer. Dell then proceeded to upgrade these computers in his dormitory room and sell them to university students and to local businesses (Serwer 1997). Dell's early success caused him to leave university at the end of the spring semester of his freshman year. Dell told his parents that he would return to the university if his summer sales proved disappointing. However, Dell sold over $180,000 worth of PCs in the first month of operations. During the early start-up of Dell Computer Inc., which he founded in 1984, Dell made the decision that the company would assemble computers from components and sell them at a 15 percent discount off established brand prices (Serwer 1997). By 1985, Dell Computer's revenue in one year exceeded $34 million. Annual revenue was over $800 million by 1991 and $2 billion in 1992, through direct sales to the public and industry, thereby increasing the company's margins.

Due to the phenomenally rapid growth in revenue, Dell was able to finance the company's initial expansion internally without the need for venture capital. This ability to finance the enterprise internally, similar to that of Microsoft® Corporation, resulted in Dell, Allen and Gates each retaining a significant portion of equity and control of their enterprises and thus reaping

---

[41] *Technological lockin* is when one particular technology achieves an overwhelming market dominance such that another technology, even if more productive or robust, can not achieve sufficient market penetration to survive.

phenomenal wealth. Later, Dell received bank financing using his receivables as collateral. However, problems occurred in 1993 due to over-expansion, which caused severe cash flow problems. Many technological entrepreneurs falter as a successful enterprise grows by either waiting too long as Steve Jobs of Apple Computer Inc. did before employing professional managers and then hiring the wrong type of executive or refusing altogether to seek mature professional assistance. Dell, however realized the need for mature professional management, and hired Mort Topfer, a seasoned executive from Motorola Corporation to handle day-to-day operations of the enterprise (Serwer 1997). Michael Dell also brought in other well-regarded managers. This combination of professional managers, coupled with adopting a direct sales business model, helped the enterprise to achieve high rates of growth with excellent financial returns.

### 2.3.3 Theodore W. Waitt – Gateway 2000 Inc.

Theodore ("Ted") W. Waitt was born in 1963 in Sioux City, South Dakota. When Waitt was a teenager, he delivered the *Sioux City Journal* by foot, pulling a stack of newspapers in his red wagon (Elstrom and Burrows 1997). To reduce the need to collect payment personally, Waitt devised a plan to use self-addressed envelopes in his papers. Similar to Gates and Dell, Waitt also left university before obtaining a degree. Seeing the phenomenal growth of the IBM PC, Waitt and a partner formed an enterprise which became Gateway 2000 Inc after leaving the University of Iowa in 1985 (Warner 1997). They ran the enterprise originally from a barn on Waitt's family's Iowa cattle farm having obtained a $10,000 loan from Waitt's grandmother. Waitt used a direct sales approach similar to Dell Computer Inc. Gateway 2000 Inc. had over $100,000 in sales in the first year of operation and, by 1987, the annual revenue exceeded $1.5 million. Also similar to Dell Computer Inc., Gateway 2000 Inc. built its own computers that were feature rich and hired professional managers when the enterprise grew beyond the founder's management capabilities. In 1991, Waitt hired Richard D. Snyder, an executive from Coopers and Lybrand, to bring both strategic planning and professional management to Gateway 2000 Inc. and in 1993, he hired William G. Shea a former IBM executive (Elstrom and Burrows 1997).

### 2.3.4 Scott McNealy – Sun Microsystems Inc.

McNealy was the product of a dynamic upper-middle class family. His father, R. William McNealy, was the Vice-Chairman of American Motors

Corporation ("AMC"). As a teenager, Scott McNealy spent evenings with his father, reviewing AMC memorandums and meeting with industrial leaders such as Lee A. Iacocca, the former Chairman of the Chrysler Corporation (Hof, Rebello, and Burrows 1996). Scott McNealy saw how AMC was marginalized because it never had sufficient market share and this formed the basis of his objective never to allow such marginalization to befall an enterprise he would start.

Unlike Gates, Allen, Dell and Waitt, McNealy completed his university education receiving a degree in Economics from Harvard College and a Masters of Business Administration ("MBA") from Stanford University (Hof, Rebello, and Burrows 1996). While at Stanford University, McNealy was interested in starting a small machine shop. After receiving his MBA, McNealy first joined Food Machinery Corporation ("FMC") and then directed manufacturing at Onyx Systems Inc. for ten months.

Scott McNealy and a small group of graduate engineering and business administrations students from the University of California at Berkeley and Stanford University established Sun Microsystems Inc. in 1982 (Kukalis and Kanazawa 1994). Sun Microsystems Inc. began when a former Stanford University classmate, Vinod Khosla asked McNealy to join him as a computer designer (Hof, Rebello, and Burrows 1996). Khosla and his associates understood that there was a growing demand for powerful workstation computer networks providing high-resolution graphics and extensive sharing of information. In the first year of operation, the enterprise had revenues of $9 million. By 1990, Sun Microsystems Inc. had achieved a 38 percent share of the workstation market (Kukalis and Kanazawa 1994). Scott McNealy's training in manufacturing enabled Sun Microsystems Inc. to keep up with increasing sales, which went from $9 million in 1983 to $89 million in 1984. In 1984, McNealy helped to secure financing of $20 million from Eastman Kodak Corporation to meet the expanding needs of the enterprise. One of the conditions that Eastman Kodak Corporation imposed was that Scott McNealy become the President of Sun Microsystems and Chief Operating Officer ("COO"). Due to a dispute with the board of directors, Vinod Khosla left the company and McNealy was appointed the interim CEO. Sun Microsystems Inc. growth resulted in the board of directors making McNealy the permanent CEO. Later, McNealy hired the Eastman Kodak Corporation executive who had been responsible for the initial investment as a senior executive of Sun Microsystems Inc.

## 3.0    ENTREPRENEURS OF OTHER NATIONS

While a great deal of technological innovation during the last half of the twentieth century has emanated from the USA, other nations such as Israel, Asia and the European Union ("EU") have also been contributors.

### 3.1    Cambridge University Entrepreneurs

Within the EU, England, in particular has emerged as a center of technological entrepreneurism (Flynn 1997). The University of Cambridge has served as the nucleation point for this growth, similar to that of Stanford University and MIT in the United States. In 1991, Nigel Playford and his associates formed Ionica PLC, a telephone company that competed with British Telecom. Ionica PLC completed an IPO in July 1997 and within minutes had a market capitalization of $1 billion (Flynn 1997). Initial financial success of this magnitude serves as a further stimulus for other technological entrepreneurs and by 1997 Cambridge, England had 1,200 technology enterprises with an average of 12 employees and combined revenues of $2.5 billion (Flynn 1997). This growth in the number of technology enterprises has been credited with creating 35,000 positions and reducing unemployment levels in Cambridge to 3.5 percent in 1997 below England's national average of 5.7 percent. This region covers technologies ranging from multimedia computer software to wireless communications.

University of Cambridge faculties and staff have served as early technological entrepreneurs. In 1997, Stewart Lang, a university researcher in computer graphics had established his second technological enterprise, Autostereo Systems. Autostereo Systems was established to commercialize Lang's research in three-dimensional imaging (Flynn 1997).

The success of these *children of Cambridge* fostered major technological enterprises, such as Xerox, Nokia, Olivetti, Oracle, Hitachi, Stanford Research and Microsoft® Corporation, to establish a presence in this technological center. In 1997, Microsoft® Corporation not only established an $80 million research laboratory in Cambridge, England, but also invested $16 million in a new venture fund operated by a highly successful University of Cambridge graduate, Hermann Hauser. Hauser founded Acorn Computer Group and 25 other highly successful technological enterprises including Advanced RISC Machines (Flynn 1997).

Technological entrepreneurial success operates as a positive response mechanism that develops further technological entrepreneurs. As previously mentioned, the proper culture combined with a research oriented academic institutional nucleation point are the structural elements for the feedback to form a reinforcement mechanism.

## 3.2   Israeli Entrepreneurs

Israel, with its combination of European and U.S. cultures coupled with significant national defense objectives, has served as a focus for the formation of technological enterprises in the Mediterranean region. In 1992, Yoav Nissan-Cohen and Rafael M. Levin, two employees of the National Semiconductor Corporation microchip fabrication ("FAB") facility in Migdal Ha'emek, Israel, established Tower Semiconductor Ltd. By 1995, this enterprise had become the largest microchip *foundry*[42] outside of East Asia (Sandler 1996). Nissan-Cohen and Levin, Co-CEOs of the enterprise, were able to establish their enterprise and acquire the National Semiconductor Corporation FAB facility at Migdal Ha'emek due to a $4 million investment from a successful U.S. technological entrepreneur George Morgenstein, the CEO of Data Systems and Software Inc. of Mahwah, N.J., USA.

Many of the technological enterprises in Israel have been based on developing and providing military technology. This also occurred in the United States in the 1950 – 1990 period, however, the innovations and success of many of these enterprises led to eventual technology transfer to the commercial arena. Technology transfer in Israel was at an early stage in the 1990s, when over half of the 2,000 technology enterprises were still engaged in military support.

## 3.3   Asian Entrepreneurs

Asia has been a leader in early technological innovations with the invention of papermaking, moveable type, the compass, gunpowder and other technologies that were developed and commercialized by western societies. Many technological developments in Asia were curtailed for over 800 years because of fear of cultural change until after the Second World War, when Japan and then Korea (followed by many other nations in Southeast Asia) became centers of technological growth. It is not possible to chronicle all these post-war advances adequately in this chapter, but the following technological entrepreneurial cases reflect some of the growth which has taken place in the 1990s.

---

[42] Microchip foundry is a fabrication facility that produces microchips under contract for other companies with the designs of those companies.

Japan produced many early technological entrepreneurs after the Second World War, including Masaru Lbuka[43], Konosuke Matsushita[44] and others, who led the economic revival of Japan after the end of the war in 1945. However, the culture of Japan (See Chapter 1 – Nature of Technological Entrepreneurism) did not foster many technological entrepreneurs in the last decades of the twentieth century.

An exception to this is Masayoshi Son, founder and CEO of Softbank Holdings, the largest computer enterprise in Japan in 1997. Son is the grandson of Korean immigrants. He was born on the island of Kyushu and given the Japanese surname Yosumoto because of a Japanese law, which forced assimilation into the Japanese society (Brenner and Cortese 1996). Due to Japanese discrimination against Japanese-Koreans at the time, Son's family sent him at the age of 16 to study in San Francisco, California. While attending the University of California at Berkeley and studying economics, Son started his first successful entrepreneurial venture, importing the computer video game *Space Invaders* from Japan. Son and an associate also developed an electronic dictionary that he later sold to the Sharp Corporation (Brenner and Cortese 1996).

After graduating in 1981, Son returned to Japan and established Softbank Holdings. This enterprise was established to distribute computer software to the electronics and computer retailers and to meet the need for readable technology magazines. Son found it difficult to obtain bank loans due to his Korean heritage, but finally obtained a $1 million loan from Dai-Ichi Kangyo Bank Ltd. Initially Softbank Holdings encountered problems, however, Osaka-based Joshin Denki Co. gave the enterprise a contract to supply a large quantity of software for a PC superstore. This exclusive contract was established by Son offering to supply every major software package available in Japan (Brenner and Cortese 1996).

By 1987, Softbank Holdings, after some initial reversals, had become the dominant computer software distributor in Japan. The stochastic resonance of the near collapse of ASCII Corporation, Microsoft® Corporation's original supplier, and the existence of Softbank Holding's extensive distribution network helped the enterprise to achieve this market dominance. Strategic

---

[43] **Lbuka, Masaru**, a Japanese electrical engineer, formed the Sony Corporation as the Tokyo Telecommunications Co. (Tokyo Tsushin Kogyo) with backing from sake brewing heir Akio Morita.

[44] **Matsushita, Konosuke**, who has been considered one of the greatest entrepreneurs of Japan, rebuilt Matsushita Electric Co. after the Second World War.

technology alliances with Novell Inc. and Pohang Iron and Steel Company further accelerated the growth of Softbank Holdings. By 1996, Softbank Holding's annual revenue had increased to $2.6 billion (Brenner and Cortese 1996). The enterprise's success caused Son to expand his operations into the United States by acquiring large publishing enterprises like Ziff-Davis Publishing Company's computer publication business in 1994 for $200 million, and the balance of Ziff-Davis Publishing Corporation in 1996 for $2.1 billion, and by investing in numerous Internet start-up enterprises such as Yahoo!, one of the leading WWW search-engine service companies.

Taiwan has also been a center of technological entrepreneurism in Asia. In 1973, K. T. Li, then minister without portfolio, began to build Taiwan's version of Stanford University (Moore 1997). Li provided government funding to establish the Industrial Technology Research Institute ("ITRI") with the mission of developing technologies that could serve as the nucleation point for new technological entrepreneurial ventures. One of the successful technological enterprises formed from ITRI was United Microelectronics Corporation, a semiconductor manufacturer with $1 billion in revenue in 1997 (Moore 1997). Stan Shih, the founder, Chairman and CEO of the Acer Group is another example of Taiwan's technological entrepreneurs.

In 1977, Shih established the Acer Group, whose growth has paralleled the growth of the PC market worldwide. The Acer Group was established by Shih to distribute computer microchips for Taiwanese arcade-game manufacturers (Strategy 1996). By 1996, the Acer Group was one of the world's five largest manufacturers of PCs, components and peripherals.

Shih built his enterprise based on a *fast food* business model. This model revolves around each of the company's local businesses, i.e., 39 assembly lines in 35 countries, doing local assembly from components manufactured in Taiwan. The Acer Group airships components from Taiwan, a cost effective method according to Shih, to the regional business units overseas for assembly into products (Strategy 1996). This production method accelerates the speed of new product introduction and it accelerates the inventory turnover rate.

Other nations in Southeast Asia have also continued to spawn technological entrepreneurs in the late 1990s. In the past decade, Malaysia setup economic incentives to encourage world-class technology enterprises, such as Intel Corporation, Sony Corporation and others to establish manufacturing facilities in the country. These incentives were established to increase employment, assist in technology transfer and encourage the development of locally based technological enterprises. To increase development of the country technologically, in 1997, Malaysia established a Multimedia Super Corridor south of the capital of Kuala Lumpur, a $40 billion undertaking. This corridor was established to serve as a nucleation point for technological entrepreneurism for computer software, Internet and telecommunications enterprises. However, in 1997, Malaysia lacked sufficiently trained technologists and a true entrepreneurial culture. These developments were cutback in 1998 when Malaysia and other Asian nations suffered financial crises.

## 4. OTHER ENTREPRENEURS

Not all technological entrepreneurs achieve success and wealth in their first entrepreneurial venture. In fact, many technology ventures fail and some fail spectacularly.

### 4.1 Serial Entrepreneurs

Many technological entrepreneurs do not retire after exiting from their first successful or unsuccessful enterprise. Table 2.4 is a partial listing of serial technological entrepreneurs.

Some technological entrepreneurs like Andrew Busey, the founder and CTO of ICHAT, by the age of 26, in 1997, had already founded three technology companies, worked for two others, written a successful book, and co-authored another book (Willis 1997). ICHAT, the enterprise that Busey founded in 1995, had more than 65 employees by 1997 and was the leader in providing interactive, real-time chat[45] communication products for the Internet and corporate Intranets.

---

[45] Chat is a real-time conversation via computer.

**Table 2.4**
Serial Technological Entrepreneurs

| Entrepreneur/Age in 1997 | Companies Founded |
|---|---|
| Gene M. Amdahl<br>(77) | 1970 Amdahl Corporation<br>1980 Trilogy Ltd.<br>1994 Commercial Data Service Inc. |
| Gordon A. Campbell<br>(53) | 1981 Seeq Technology Inc.<br>1984 Chips and Technologies Inc.<br>1994 3Dfx Interactive Inc. |
| Pehang Chen<br>(40) | 1989 Gain Technology Inc.<br>1993 Scebel Systems Inc.<br>1993 Broad-Vision Inc. |
| Kamran Elahian<br>(42) | 1981 CAE Systems Inc.<br>1984 Cirrus Logic Inc.<br>1989 Momenta Corporation<br>1993 NeoMagic Corporation<br>1996 Planet Web Inc.<br>1997 Centillium Technology Inc. |
| Steven T. Kirsch<br>(40) | 1982 Mouse Systems Corporation<br>1986 Frame Technology Corporation<br>1994 Infoseek Corporation |
| D. T. Mitchell<br>(55) | 1979 Seagate Technology Inc.<br>1986 Conner Peripherals Inc.<br>1994 JTS Corporation |
| Seymour I. Rubinstein<br>(63) | 1978 Micro Pro International Inc.<br>1987 Surpass Software Systems Inc.<br>1995 Prompt Software Inc. |
| Roger J. Sippl<br>(42) | 1980 Informix Software Inc.<br>1990 Vantive Corporation<br>1993 Visigenic Software Inc. |
| Nolan K. Bushnell | 1972 Atari<br>1977 Chuck E. Cheese's<br>+ 20 other enterprises |
| Steve Jobs | 1977 Apple Computer Company<br>1985 Next Computer Corporation<br>1995 Pixar Animation Studios |
| Judith L. Estrin and William<br>N. Carrico<br>(husband and wife team) | 1981 Bridge Communications Inc.<br>1988 Network Devices Inc.<br>1995 Precept Software Inc. |

(Based on data contained in Port 1997)

80

## 4.2 Managers But Not Technological Entrepreneurs

A problem arises when professional managers join technological enterprises at start-up and then proceed to apply management principals that may be successful in large enterprises but result in failure in start-up phases of a technological enterprise. Donald H. Jones, a legendary technological entrepreneur in Pittsburgh, Pennsylvania returned to Carnegie-Mellon University as a professor in 1990 (Baker 1996). Jones was intrigued with the potential of the Internet; Jones founded Nets Inc. with an online service called *Industry.Net*. *Industry.Net* service was developed to provide an online matchmaking service for companies and suppliers. *Industry.Net* was not able to reach a stage, similar to the former technological enterprises of Jones, where it could be sold.

To build this early Internet enterprise, in January 1996 Jones decided to bring in a high-profile marketing oriented manager. His choice was James P. Manzi, the former CEO of Lotus Development Corporation ("Lotus"). Manzi had successfully sold Lotus to IBM in July 1995. Jones had been impressed that Manzi had built Lotus in a very competitive market. Jones sold Manzi a large minority interest in Nets Inc., which was, in March 1996, one of the largest Internet enterprises (Baker 1996). At that time the enterprise served 4,500 manufacturers and suppliers, ranging from IBM to small tool and die manufacturers which paid $3,000 to $8,000 a year to maintain an electronic storefront on *Industry.Net*'s web site. In 1995, the enterprise had revenues of $28 million. This was one of the first enterprises to develop a business to business electronic commerce business model.

Manzi and his staff remained in Boston, Massachusetts while the operation of the enterprise remained in Pittsburgh, Pennsylvania. This attitude was similar to that of Sherman Fairchild which caused Fairchild Semiconductor Company to lose the lead in the semiconductor industry. By May of 1997, Nets Inc. had filed for Chapter 11 under the U.S. Federal Bankruptcy Code (Wilder 1997). The company under Manzi's remote management had over-extended itself. The techniques that had served in building a mature Lotus Development Corporation did not work in a new untried market but *"...Manzi wanted to get huge overnight"* according to Bruce Richardson, the Vice President of Advanced Manufacturing Research of Boston, Massachusetts (Wilder 1997).

# REFERENCES

AEA. 1997. Ground Breaking Study Defines High-Tech Industry and Shows Importance to U.S. Economy. Washington, D.C.: American Electronics Association.

Allen, David N., and Frederick Norling. 1991. Chapter 4 Exploring Perceived Threats in Faculty Commercialization of Research. In University Spin-Off Companies: Economic Development, Faculty Entrepreneurs, and Technology transfer, edited by A. M. Brett, D. V. Gilson and R. W. Smilor. Savage, MD: Rowman and Littlefield Publications Inc.

Armstrong, Larry. 1997. Hot Growth Companies. Business Week, 97/5/26, 90-102.

Arthur, W. Brian. 1989. Competing Technologies, Increasing Returns, and Lock-in by Historical Events. The Economic Journal 99 (March):116-131.

Baker, Stephen. 1996. This is My Last Startup. Business Week, 96/3/25, 81-82.

Brenner, Brian, and Amy Cortese. 1996. Cyber-Mogul. Business Week, 96/8/12, 56-62.

Busenitz, Lowell W., and Jay B. Barney. 1997. Differences between entrepreneurs and managers in large organizations: Biases and heuristics in strategic decision making. Journal of Business Venturing 12.

Cardullo, Mario W. 1996. Chief Technology Officer: A New Member of The Leadership Team. Paper read at UnIG'96: International Conference on Technology Management: University/Industry/Government Collaboration, 96/6/24-26, at Istanbul, Turkey.

Cardwell, Donald. 1995. The Norton History of Technology. New York, NY: W. W. Norton and Company.

Clancy, Heather. 1997. Bill McKiernan, CyberSource Corp. Reseller Magazine, 97/6, 144.

Clark, Don. 1996. Bidzos Holds Key to Guarding Internet Secrets. The Wall Street Journal, 96/4/16, B1, B7.

Collins, James. 1996. Winners. Time Magazine, 96/2/19, 43-47.

Cusumano, Michael A., and Richard W. Selby. 1995. Microsoft Secrets: Company Creates Technology, Shapes Markets, and Manages People. New York, NY: The Free Press.

Elstrom, Peter, and Peter Burrows. 1997. Can Gateway Round Up the Suits? Business Week, 97/5/26, 132-138.

Engardio, Pete, and Peter Burrows. 1997. Where Immigrants Find a Melting Pot of Gold. Business Week, 97/8/25, 123.

Flynn, Julia. 1997. The Hallowed Halls of Homegrown Tech. Business Week, 97/8/25, 144.

Gates, Bill, Nathan Myhrvold, and Peter Rinearson. 1995. The Road Ahead. New York, NY: Viking, Penguin Group.

Geppart, Linda. 1996. Entrepreneurial Women Engineers. IEEE Spectrum, 96/8, 28-37.

Grove, Andrew S. 1996. Only the Paranoid Survive: How to Exploit the Crisis Points that Challenge Every Company and Career. New York, NY: Currency Doubleday.

82

Hamilton, Joan O'C, and Linda Humelstein. 1997. A Wellspring Called Stanford. Business Week, 97/8/25, 82-84.

Hamm, Steve. 1997. Why Women Are So Invisible. Business Week, 97/8/25, 136.

Hellemans, Alexander, and Bryan Bunch. 1991. The Timetables of Science: A Chronology of the Most Important and People and Events in the History of Science. New York, NY: Touchstone/Simon and Schuster Inc.

Henry, Shannon. 1997. Internet Companies Rage Hot and Cold. Tech Capital, 97/Spring, 37-44.

Herring. 1997. The Digital Universe: Top 50 Private Companies: MicroStrategy. The Red Herring, 97/9, 80-81.

Higgins, Kelly Jackson. 1995. Super Mario. Virginia Business, 95/5.

Hilzenrath, David S. 1997. Hatching Start-up After Start-up: From Old Successes New Firms Emerge. Washington Business, 97/3/3, 13, 17.

Hisrick, Robert D., and Michael P. Peters. 1995. Entrepreneurship: Starting, Developing, and Managing a New Enterprise. Chicago, IL: Irwin.

Hof, Robert D., Kathy Rebello, and Peter Burrows. 1996. Scott McNealy's Rising Sun. Business Week, 96/1/23, 66-73.

IEEE. 1997. The 1997 Medallists. IEEE Spectrum, 97/6, 25.

Kukalis, Sal, and Brett Kanazawa. 1994. Sun Microsystems Reorganizes for Growth. IEEE Engineering Management Review 22 (Fall):76-82.

Lesly, Elizabeth. 1996. Paul Allen: New Age Media Mogul. Business Week, 96/11/18, 106-114.

Moore, Jonathan. 1997. Taiwan's New Grail: Innovation. Business Week, 97/8/25, 139.

Morino. 1997. Netpreneurs ride a wave of opportunity. Reston, VA: Morino Institute.

Napoli, Lisa. At the Genesis of a Web Design Firm 97/2/19 1997 [cited . Available from http;//www.nytimes.com/library/cyber/week/021997Kioken.html.

Ouellette, Tim, and Robert F. Scheier. 1997. Cobol pioneer pitches year 2000 fix. Computerworld, 97/8/11, 4.

Patterson, Lee. 1997. Two Failures That Seeded The Valley. Forbes ASAP, 97/6/2.

Port, Otis. 1997. Starting Up Again And Again And Again. Business Week, 97/8/25, 99-102.

Raymond, David. 1997. Famous Flops. Forbes ASAP, 97/6/2.

Reinhardt, Andy, Joan O'C. Hamilton, and Linda Himelstein. 1997. What Matters is How Smart You Are. Business Week, 97/8/25, 68-72.

Reuber, A. Rebecca, and Eileen M. Fischer. 1994. Entrepreneurs' Experience, Expertise, and the Performance of Technology-Based Firms. IEEE Transactions on Engineering Management 41 (4):365-374.

Roach, Ronald. 1997. High-tech entrepreneurs began young. Washington Business Journal, 97/1/17-23, 19.

Roberts, Edward B. 1991. Entrepreneurs in High Technology: Lessons from MIT and Beyond. New York, NY: Oxford University Press.

Sager, Ira. 1997. Cloning the Best of the Valley. Business Week, 97/8/25, 146-147.

Sandler, Neal. 1996. A Chip Upstart in Galilee. Business Week, 96/2/26, 68-69.

Saxenian, Annalee. 1996. Regional Advantage: Culture and Competition in Silicon Valley and Route 128. Cambridge, MA: Harvard University Press.

Schine, Eric, and Amy Barrett. 1996. Entrepreneurs: Right Party, Wrong Number. Business Week, 96/12/23, 86-87.

Serwer, Andrew E. 1997. Michael Dell Turns the PC World Inside Out. Fortune, 97/9/8, 76-86.

Silver, Jonathan. 1997. True entrepreneurs turn idea into opportunity. Washington Business Journal, 97/6/6-12, 39.

Starzynski, Bob. 1997a. Alex J. Mandl: Ex-AT&T president realizes dream in Alexandria. Washington Business Journal, 97/1/17-23, 15.

Starzynski, Bob. 1997b. Michael J. Saylor, 'Kid genius' vows to shift paradigms at MicroStrategy. Washington Business Journal, 97/7/20-25, 17.

Starzynski, Bob. 1997c. Raul J. Fernandez: Proxicom CEO fosters 'ambitious spirit' among staff. Washington Business Journal, 97/7/25-31, 17.

Stough, Roger R., James D. Rigyle, and Kulkarni. 1997. Report on The Technology Industry in Virginia. Fairfax, VA: The Center for Regional Analysis, The Institute of Public Policy, George Mason University.

Strategy. 1996. The 'Fast-Food' Computer Company: An Interview with Stan Shih. Strategy and Business, 96/Fourth Quarter, 52-56.

Stross, Randall E. 1996. The Microsoft Way: The Real Story of How the Company Outsmarts Its Competition. Reading, MA: Addison-Wesley Publishing Company, Inc.

Swisher, K. 1996. Anticipating the Internet: Good Timing, Good Deal-Making and Good Luck Turn Rich Adams' UUNet into a Star. Washington Business Journal, 96/5/6, 14.

Swisher, Kara. 1998. aol.com: How Steve Case Beat Bill Gates, Nailed the Netheads, and Made Millions in the War for the Web. New York, NY: Times Business\Random House.

Technology. 1996. High Tech Award Winners. Washington Technology, 96/5/15, 26.

Warner, Michael. 1997. Gateway to Wealth. Fortune, 97/9/8, 80.

Week, Business. 1997. Silicon Valley. Business Week, 97/8/25.

Wilder, Clinton. 1997. Manzi Venture: Early Net Casualty. Information Week, 97/5/19, 32.

Willis, Clint. 1997. Try, Try Again. Forbes ASAP, 97/6/2.

## DISCUSSION QUESTIONS

1. Choose a technological enterprise, and trace the history of the enterprise and the various entrepreneurial ventures which have developed from that enterprise.

2. Prepare a one to two page biography of a technological entrepreneur and relate this entrepreneur to the entrepreneurial characteristics discussed in Chapters 1 and 2.

3. Discuss the similarities of and differences between the various technological entrepreneurs presented in this chapter and categorize them according to their similarities and differences.
4. Prepare a case study of a technological entrepreneurial enterprise.
5. Prepare and discuss a graphical representation showing the growth of the Internet and the technological enterprises which have been spawned as a result.

# PART TWO

# PROCESS OF FORMULATING A NEW TECHNOLOGICAL ENTERPRISE

# CHAPTER 3

# Technological and Enterprise Strategic Planning

*"Fortune favors only the mind that is prepared"*
**Louis Pasteur**
1822-1895

## 1. INTRODUCTION

No enterprise starts without some form of planning. This planning may range from some preliminary review of the market for a particular technological product, process or service to a detailed analysis of the various factors that will influence the future of the technological enterprise. Technological strategic planning is an important element in developing a competitive strategy (Steele 1989, pp. 179). Technological strategic planning provides an array of technological options and priorities with which the new enterprise will compete in order to survive within the relevant technological space. While a mature enterprise may have a system of plans, a new technological enterprise should concentrate on a strategic technological and market planning process.

Many technological entrepreneurs come to the point in their careers where they have a deep understanding of the technology which will serve as the basis of their new enterprise but lack a deep understanding of the various factors which should be considered prior to the formation of a new enterprise. The objective of technological and enterprise strategic planning is to formulate a consistent strategy linking the technology and business models effectively.

In 1991, 1600 new products were introduced; only 10 percent reached their enterprise objectives (Balachardra and Friar 1997). Integration of the technological and enterprise objectives through planning should increase the number of new products that reach their assigned objectives. Figure 3.1

presents a model for placing the development of technological product, process or service in the three-dimensional technological enterprise space.

It has been proposed that there are three major groups of contextual variables for successful new products, processes, or services (Balachardra and Friar 1997):

- Nature of the innovation.
- Nature of the market.
- Nature of the technology.

The level of the innovation can vary as follows:

- Incremental.
- New generation.
- Radical.

An incremental innovation is where the basic technology remains essentially the same and the innovation contributes minor modifications to performance, flexibility, appearance and other characteristics. An incremental innovation is more suitable for an established technological market space. An example is the computer software market space where incremental innovations are used to move from one version to the next.

A new generation innovation takes a technology to a new level of effectiveness but follows the general technology developmental vector. A radical innovation is where the technology being introduced is considerably different from the earlier models. The introduction of the use of the jet engine in commercial aircraft in the 1950s quickly changed the market for aircraft propulsion systems from propeller driven to jet engines. In some cases, a radical technological innovation may be introduced into a market that did not exist before the innovation was introduced. In this case the market uncertainty is very high (Balachardra and Friar 1997).

The nature of the market for a new technological product, process or service can be categorized as existing or new. A new technological enterprise can find entering an existing market easier but filled with competitors, while a new market might be harder to enter and risky but may offer higher returns. This is the same as going to an orchard and finding that tree where the fruit has not yet been picked and choosing the fruit closer to the ground, leaving the fruit that is higher. It is easier to be the first, then to be a follower provided that the market space is ready. It takes a great deal of searching and innovative effort to find these opportunities. Entering an existing market space implies that market data are available. In the case of a new market, data are usually not available and a great deal of assumptions with associated uncertainties must be considered.

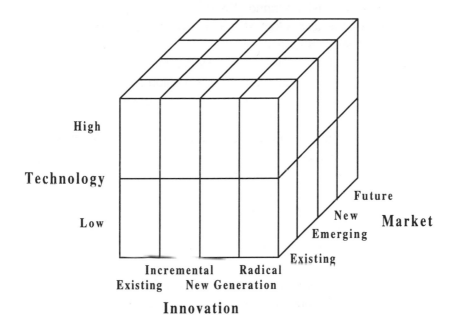

**Fig. 3.1** Technological Enterprise Space (Adapted from Balachardra and Friar 1997)

Technology space can be classified in a spectrum ranging from high to low. In the high-technology space, the technology is developing very rapidly and changes occur in terms of months. This is the region of emerging technologies, e.g., the information technology market in the 1990s, which, in some instances, appeared to be chaotic in its development. The turbulent nature of an emerging technology space will affect the perceived value of any technological advance due to the large number of advances which are occurring (Balachardra and Friar 1997). In the high-technology region, standards for the products, processes or services and their respective performances are not confirmed and a market pioneering enterprise can be seriously impacted by technological developments. Only one specification becomes the standard and this tends to result in market dominance, i.e., *technological lockin*. For example, in the late 1990s, the multiple developments for digital video disks ("DVDs") led to several different competitive standards similar to the video tape standards in the 1980s between Betamax and VHS.

In the twenty-first century, all enterprises desiring success will have to provide exceptional customer service and innovative products, processes or services (Cooper and Kleinschmidt 1993). This is amplified in the rapidly changing area of the technological market space. The reasons why new products become successful include:

- Differentiated new product based on customer driven new product design. The customer views the product as advantageous. This factor is central to the introduction of a new product.
- Early product definition before development. This includes:
  - Targeted market.
  - Product concept.
  - Product positioning.
  - Benefits to be delivered.
  - Features of specifications.
- Organized around a cross-functional team. New technological enterprises must be structured to be more than one dimensional, that is, not all team members with the same background.
- Attack from a position of strength. One of the keys to success of a new product is synergy. The core competencies that the new enterprise must assemble must form a strong position for the development and introduction of the new product, process or service.
- Focus on *quality* during the initiation of the enterprise. In the planning of a new technological enterprise, consider actions that will have to be taken to assure quality in the future.

In planning a new technological enterprise the enterprise formation team should apply the factors to ensure the success of new products. These factors can be implemented by undertaking a number of actions.

**Interface with potential customers** – The new enterprise must be market space oriented and have customer focus from its initiation onwards. While many new technological enterprises are technology focused, a common fallacy is to ignore the market space and customers during the enterprise's developmental phases. Enterprise formation teams should seek to interface with potential customers and competitors to determine if their technological and business models will meet the needs of the potential customers.

**Idea regeneration** – The most successful source of ideas will be the potential customers. The studies of von Hipple (von Hipple 1988) and Cooper and Kleinschmidt (Cooper and Kleinschmidt 1993) found that the worst source of ideas were those chosen from competitors, followed by concepts driven from technology. Customers usually know what they need. Meeting these needs will usually result in a successful technological market space entrant.

**Reliance on the voice of the potential customers** – Potential customers are a vital input into the design of a new technological product, process or service and should not be considered as just a confirmatory or after the fact check. This means, in planning in a new technological enterprise, the following questions must be answered:

- What is the value to potential customers?
- What is the benefit to potential customers?
- What are the potential customers' trade-offs between price and performance?
- What are the potential customers' needs, wants, preferences and desires?
- What must be done to delight the potential customer?

**Competitive analysis** - A thorough competitive analysis is mandatory. It is imperative that a *military* focus of *advantage* and *superiority* be maintained. The objective is to be *better* than your potential competitors. This requires understanding the industry and the enterprises that will potentially compete in the market space.

**Customer feedback during development** - When the new technological enterprise has been established and the new product, process or service is in development, it is necessary to perform a verification of the concept with the potential customers and incorporate customer responses during development and *beta-testing* (field-testing). This will include pre-testing the market to gauge customer reactions, measuring the effectiveness of the launch plans and determining expected market share and revenues.

Many technological entrepreneurs enter market space in its formative stages of development such as Bill Gates and Michael Dell. These entrepreneurs typically compete and gain market share through products, processes or services with superior performance in one or two market/customer dimensions (Wheelwright and Clark 1992, pp. 99). In some instances, an entrepreneur formulates plans to enter the market space with a technological product, process, or service that is a new generation platform, such as Netscape Communications.

Every enterprise, technological or not, is based upon a few basic concepts or assumptions (Steele 1989, pp. 9). The concept of a technological enterprise can be viewed in terms of:

- Core technological products, processes or services.
- Core competencies of the enterprise and its potential competitors.
- Competition and market space.
- Technological vector of the industry.

Technology develops through a process of creativity, invention and innovation (Cardullo 1996b, pp. 115). The development of a technological enterprise is an evolutionary process in which technology and enterprise structure evolve together.

Studies of new technological enterprises showed serious deficiencies in the technological plans of many entrepreneurs (Roberts 1991, pp. 201). Technological entrepreneurship is based upon matching evolving technological possibilities and competencies to evolving market needs and opportunities (Martin 1994, pp. 72). Identifying and exploiting technologies, which can provide the new enterprise with a competitive differentiation, is the essence of the technological enterprise planning process.

Figure 3.2 shows a technological strategic planning model. Figure 3.3 illustrates the relationship between the technology and the enterprise structure processes.

The interaction between technological and organizational knowledge will have significant implications for strategic design of the enterprise and how the technology is translated into a product, process or service which may lead the enterprise to success.

It has been proposed that Japanese enterprises are successful because of skills and *organizational knowledge creation* (Nonaka and Takeuchi 1995, pp. 3). This is defined as the capability or core competence of the entire enterprise to create new knowledge, disseminate it throughout the enterprise and *embody* it in products, processes or services. New technological enterprise planning should incorporate organizational knowledge creation. This means that even in this pre-enterprise formation stage the technological entrepreneurs should encourage a culture that will bring about innovation, continuously, incrementally and spirally. This cultural value, while difficult for Western technological entrepreneurs to implement, has served to give many Asian entrepreneurs a very agile ability to rapidly respond to the changing technological space.

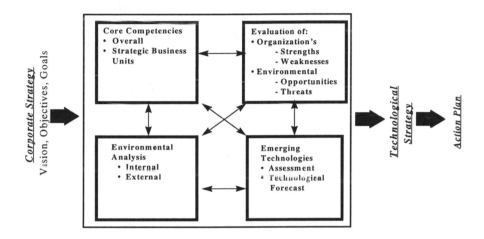

**Fig. 3.2** Technological Strategic Planning Model

Figure 3.4 shows how this process of knowledge creation leads to competitive advantage. In the rapidly changing technological space, knowledge is not another resource, but the only resource (Drucker 1993).

An enterprise can be considered as being under pressure from six forces (Grove 1996, pp. 29). These forces should be considered by a potential new enterprise in the early stages of planning. These include the power, vigor and competencies of the:

- Existing competitors.
- Complementors.
- Customers.
- Suppliers.
- Potential new competitors.

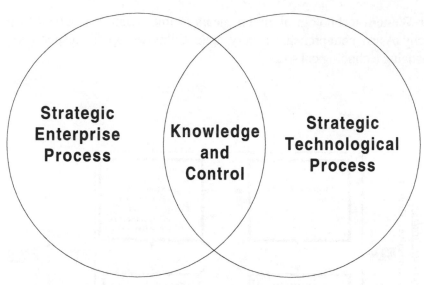

**Fig. 3.3** Relationship Between Technological and Enterprise Strategic Processes
(Adapted from Scarbrough and Corbett 1992)

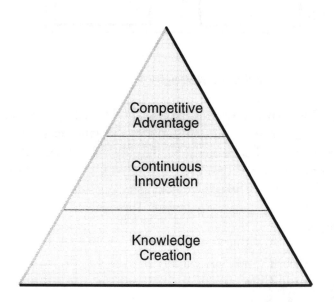

**Fig. 3.4** Knowledge Creation Pyramid (Adapted from Nonaka and Takeuchi 1995, pp. 6)

## 1.1 Technological Strategy Formation

As it has been said – *timing is everything*. It is possible to conceive, invent or innovate a new technological product, process or service and then find that the market is not prepared either to accept or even to understand the value of this new entry. The successful introduction of a new technological market entrant requires an understanding of the potential market and positive stochastic resonance, i.e., all environmental factors working to reinforce the strategy formation process. Technological enterprises can be distinguished from other enterprises by the use of research and development in producing innovative products, processes or services (Betz 1987).

Most technological enterprises use a linear development process. New technological enterprises are usually forced into this linear process mode due to limited resources. This factor alone reduces the probability of success. A linear business model strengthens the need to do intensive *front-end* technological and market planning. Table 3.1 shows the traditional strategies adopted by technological enterprises to promote growth.

**Table 3.1**
Traditional Strategies to Promote Enterprise Growth

| Strategy | Focus |
|---|---|
| Technology Push | Develop a product, process or service and then find a market |
| Technology Pull | Identify a need and develop a product, process or service to satisfy the need |
| Technology Trend | Target a new product, process or service by following an existing development path |
| Product Line Extension | Develop a related product, process or service |
| Peripheral Technology | Develop a complementary product, process or service |
| Cost Reduction Technology | Develop a product, process or service which can reduce cost of existing products, processes or services |

(Adapted from Resa 1991)

Figure 3.5 shows the relationship of these technological strategies as a function of risk and return.

96

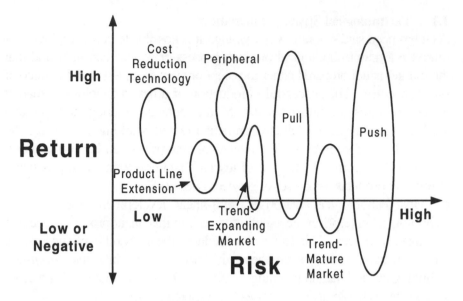

**Fig. 3.5** Technology Strategy Risk/Return Space

Technology push strategies are usually potentially high return – high-risk strategies. The introduction of a totally new technological product, process or service can start a technological trend that accelerates the enterprise's growth and captures a significant share of market space. The introduction by Apple Computer in 1974 of the first truly usable PC initiated an entire new industry. However, the introduction of the first personal digital assistant ("PDA"), i.e., the Newton by Apple Computer, with handwriting recognition software, was far from successful.

Recognizing a market need and filling that need, i.e., technology pull strategy can lead to higher returns with reduced risks. The rapid growth of small hand-held PDAs did occur in 1997, when 3Com/U.S. Robotics introduced the Palm Pilot®. This shows that a PDA which had limited capabilities but could meet market space needs would garner a larger market share than an earlier PDA, i.e., the Newton did not fully meet or deliver on the market space needs. Many new Internet entrepreneurs seek to fill perceived market space needs in their technological space.

Technological market space attractiveness is assessed by examining (Resa 1991):

- Potential demand.
- Acceptable price.
- Cost.

- Competition.

Numerous studies have indicated that an enterprise's risk of failure is greatly reduced when it operates in a familiar technological sector (Slater 1994). An enterprise can position itself to be a *technological pioneer, early technological follower,* or *late technological follower.* Figure 3.6 shows the potential returns of the three types of technological positioning. Following a technology trend in an expanding market such as telecommunications and the Internet in the 1990s has led to spectacular successes. In this strategy, technological forecasting is used to track existing development paths and then project the next likely stage in the technological evolutionary cycle. This strategy has the advantage that it relies on past successes of a technological development. Entering a mature market space calls for either large resources or a significant differentiator, and other technology-based innovations may cause the market to move in a completely different direction. Yahoo! employed this strategy, and, while it was not the first Internet search engine enterprise, by 1997 it had captured a significant market share.

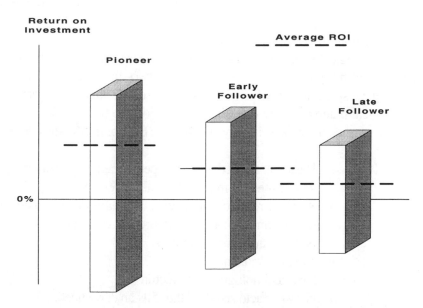

**Fig. 3.6** Potential Return of Technological Positioning (Slater 1994, 1994 IEEE Reprinted by permission)

Usually a new technological enterprise does not have the resources to employ the strategy of extending existing products, processes or services.

There are examples, such as MicroStrategy and Marimba, of enterprises which have employed this strategy by emerging from a parent entity where the initial product concepts were formulated (See Chapter 2 – Technological Entrepreneurs). Michael Saylor the CEO of MicroStrategy took a product that he and an associate had developed at DuPont Corporation and established a new enterprise. Kim Polese, the CEO of Marimba took the Java computer language concept from Sun Microsystems and moved into a new Internet market space.

The development of Windows and associated products by Microsoft® Corporation spawned a myriad of products that could be used to enhance or extend Microsoft® Corporation's products.

The objective of the cost reduction strategy is to identify and develop new technology in order to increase productivity and quality. By providing new technological products, processes or services that can reduce cost, or increase productivity or quality, it is possible to establish technological market niches with potentially high returns. A cost reduction entrant strategy by a new technological enterprise is an impact strategy (Resa 1991). This requires the new enterprise to forgo higher profits to maintain a market lead.

## 1.2    Technological Enterprise Factors

New technological enterprises can be mapped in sectors of the technological space shown in Figure 3.1. Figure 3.7 shows a two-dimensional portion of a technological space within which a new enterprise will have to operate. New technological enterprises are established to exploit the new product, process or service concept on which they are based (Bell and McNamara 1991, pp. 98):

- Basic or applied research performed at a university, in government or in an industrial laboratory.
- Applied research directed toward the development of a new technological product, process or service.
- New manufacturing process.
- New component.
- New technological architecture.
- New de facto standard that fills an early need.
- New paradigm for computing.
- New generic application made possible by a new computer system.
- New professional application.

- New user-specific product or requirement.
- New military or government requirement.
- User-developed software that serves as a demonstration, first prototype, or first release.

New technological enterprises must be agile due to a number of environmental factors. These factors include (Viscio and Pasternack 1996):

- Technological Innovation.
- Industry Structure.
- Speed Driven/Customer Driven Markets.
- Competitive Pressures.
- Regulatory Environment.
- Market Globalization.
- Information Availability.
- Evolving Capital Markets.

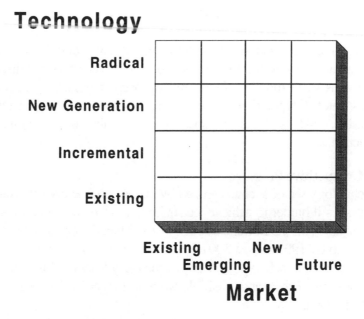

**Fig. 3.7** Two-Dimensional Technological Space

## 1.2.1 Technological Innovation

The rapidity of change forces new technological enterprises to recognize that technological innovation is a double-edge sword. While it may give a new formative enterprise a competitive advantage, it similarly serves to assist existing and potential competitors. While technological innovation creates new market opportunities, it also requires rapid adjustments, i.e., today's innovations can be quickly superceded by a competitor's innovation.

### 1.2.2 Industry Structure

While technological innovation requires enterprise agility, similarly the industry structure that the new enterprise seeks to enter may also be in a state of flux. Industries do not remain static, they evolve or disappear. A new potential enterprise must be aware of the evolutionary movement of their intended industry space. An example is the rapidly evolving telecommunications industry which, during the 1990s, moved from a monopolistic structure to an open market structure driven by regulatory changes and new technological developments such as wireless communications and the Internet.

### 1.2.3 Speed Driven/Customer Driven Markets

Business in the latter part of the twentieth century is being driven by ever rising customer expectations. In addition, life of new technological products, processes and services in some instances does not exceed 18 months, and can be as low as three months. In the microprocessor industry, manufacturers such as Intel Corporation estimate that a new microchip becomes a commodity, that is loses its specialness, within three months of its introduction.

### 1.2.4 Competitive Pressure

The technology sector is characterized by intense competitive pressure. This factor makes it harder to achieve leadership and to maintain that leadership. 149 companies on the Fortune 500 list in 1970 had disappeared from the list by 1980 and by 1990 almost 300 of the companies were no longer on the list (Viscio and Pasternack 1996). Many of the early leaders of the PC industry such as Kaypro, Hayes and, VisiCalc were no longer leaders or in existence in the late 1990s.

### 1.2.5 Regulatory Environment

The regulatory environment is having an impact on technological enterprises. Government regulations can influence not only industries, such as telecommunications, but also technology, such as computer security systems, patent law, privacy issues and others. While many new technological enterprises tend to overlook regulatory factors, it is possible to enter an industry or develop a product, process or service that can be seriously impacted by government regulation.

### 1.2.6 Market Globalization

While technological entrepreneurs usually do not consider globalization issues, such issues can have a significant impact. Questions of intellectual property and privacy can totally obviate the new product, process or service of a technological enterprise. The information revolution of the late twentieth century, led by the Internet and high speed communication, makes it possible for a new technological enterprise to enter into strategic alliances with technological enterprises in other countries. The capabilities of high-speed communication and the Internet also offer the potential for a new technological enterprise to have customers located throughout the world.

### 1.2.7 Information Availability

The availability of high-speed communications and the Internet allows new enterprises to determine market structures, competitive position, and customer information. New technological enterprises should factor this information availability not only into the formation-planning phase of the enterprise, but also into a system which will provide continual technological environmental information. In the design of a new technological enterprise, a strong informational structure, such as an Intranet for internal operation, and an Extranet linking customers and suppliers to the new enterprise, should be evaluated.

### 1.2.8 Evolving Capital Markets

The capital markets have evolved and will continue to evolve. From the beginning, a new technological enterprise must be acutely aware of the structure of the capital markets (See Chapter 6 – Initial Enterprise Financing, Chapter 8 – Next Entrepreneurial Step). Throughout the development and maturity of a technological enterprise, the entrepreneur and the leadership team must have a firm understanding of the requirements of the financial community.

### 2. SOURCES OF ENTERPRISE FORMATION
### 2.1 Technological Evolution

The source of a new technological enterprise can be traced to the fertilization of an idea within the mind of the entrepreneur. However, as in the case of the emergence of a new life from a fertilized egg, the idea is really a collective emergent property of a complex system (Kauffman 1995, pp. 19). This emergence occurs within a complex environment and, as in natural systems, the behavior of co-evolving species, in this case competitors and the market, will lead to small and large avalanches of extinction and speciation.

Technological progress occurs both in an evolutionary and a cascading manner. In evolutionary progress, technology moves by means of incremental improvements on a basic concept. In cascading progress, which many have termed radical or revolutionary, a new concept appears to have sprung *de novo* (from nothing) but in fact can be traced to prior advances which reach a critical level and cascade to form the new concept or invention.

A technological enterprise can arise from a series of factors but basically follows a natural progression from the evolution of an idea to the final innovation of a new technological product, process or service. Technological evolution is no different from the evolution of organisms (Kauffman 1995, pp. 191). Technological evolution moves from invention or discovery through innovation into a technological artifact[1]. During the evolutionary process, technological entrepreneurs cause an early explosion of diverse forms as a plethora of new possibilities are opened up by the basic scientific discovery or invention (Kauffman 1995, pp. 191). Qualitative features of technological evolution appear similar to species exponential growth during the Cambrian Period[2] (Kauffman 1995, pp. 202).

Growth is exemplified by branching to create diverse forms; it is *bushy* at the initiation point. Then the rate of branching dwindles, extinction sets in, and in a final phase, major alternative forms persist. This is similar to the growth of the PC industry, which saw many new technological enterprises emerge only to be *pruned* by the vicissitudes of the market space, leaving a few major players such as Compaq Corporation, Dell Computer while Kaypros and other similar enterprises have vanished. The early diversity of technological forms is radical in nature, and then dwindles to minor tunings or incremental improvements (Kauffman 1995, pp. 202). The *taxa*[3] fill in

---

[1] Artifact is a term used by Kauffman (Kauffman 1995) for items created by Homo Sapiens, i.e., humanity.

[2] Cambrian Period, an interval of about 70 million years, from 570 million to 500 million years before present era.

[3] Taxa is the plural of taxon which is the name applied to a taxonomic group in a formal system of nomenclature

from the top down, i.e., fundamental inventions or innovations result initially in a wide range of dramatic early experimentation with radically different forms that branch further and then settle down to a few dominant lineages.

The original PC operating systems consisted of CP/M, Pascal, DOS, Mac OS, etc., but by 1997, over 90 percent of the desktop PC operating systems were provided by Microsoft® Corporation and Apple Computer. In the case of operating systems, such as Microsoft® Corporation's Windows products, it becomes progressively harder to find further improvements. Hence, variations or new versions become progressively more moderate, even if their outward appearance may seem very different. In some instances it appears that the rate of improvement of various technologies slows with total industry expenditure, i.e., improvement in performance is rapid at first and then slows, represented by the technological "S" curve, as the physical limits of a particular technological development are reached.

The emergence of a new technological product, process or service is generally characterized by *technological push*, i.e., genuine technical novelty; or by *market pull*, i.e., use of a previously developed technology in a new market application and the other strategies shown in Table 3.1.

During the emergence period of a technological development there is a great deal of ferment. This ferment is caused by inventors, developers, and users engaging in a trial-and-error search for a technological application that meets either actual or perceived needs.

Emergence resulting from technological push is likely to be characterized by a much greater variation in the nature of the technological product, process or service, as competition is more often based on the applications characteristics than on price. These are termed technology-driven opportunities (Howard Jr. and Guile 1992, pp. 13). The challenge for entrepreneurs in this case is to find market applications and implementation strategies for the new technology.

In a technological market pull environment, the entrepreneur is dealing with a perceived market opportunity space. This perceived market opportunity space requires the use of well-understood technologies in a new market space and can be characterized as *market-driven opportunity*. In this market space, the technological entrepreneur is in search of the best technology to meet an untapped demand.

The technology industry space in which the new product, process or service is to be embedded also evolves. All technological industry spaces begin with an initial structure no matter how primitive. The entry barriers, and customer and supplier powers exist as soon as an industry space comes into existence (Porter 1980, pp. 162). This initial structure arises from a combination of the underlying economic and technical characteristics of the new industry space, the constraints of the initially small industry space and the competencies and resources of the early entrepreneurial entrants. The same process that causes technology to evolve is also in operation in the new technological industry space as a whole. The new technological industry moves toward an industry space *attractor point*[4] (Cardullo 1996b). There are a range of structures the new technology industry might achieve, depending upon the industry investment decisions taken by the various actors within the new industry space. The decisions, combined with *stochastic resonance* will tend to move the new industry toward an initial stability *attractor point*. This industry evolutionary process can be generalized by viewing each of the factors in the evolutionary industry process as a vector, i.e., having direction and magnitude. These factors include (Porter 1980, pp. 164):

- Industry growth.
- Changing customer segments.
- Customer learning.
- Reduction of uncertainty.
- Diffusion of proprietary knowledge.
- Accumulation of experience.
- Expansion or contraction of the industry.
- Changes in cost structure.
- Innovation of the technological products, processes or services within the technological industry space.
- Innovation of the marketing practices within the technological industry space
- Structural and regulatory changes in adjacent industries, such as changes in the regulatory aspects of the telecommunication industry impacting Internet enterprises.
- Regulatory policy changes within the technological industry space.
- New industry entrants and exits.

The basic characteristic of emerging technological industries such as the Internet in the 1990s is that usually they do not obey any rules of the *game*.

---

[4] Attractor point, an industry position from which it would be difficult to easily change.

The absence of rules is both a risk and an opportunity for new enterprises (Porter 1980, pp. 218).

Another characteristic of an emerging technological industry in the last decades of the twentieth century is the accelerating time-to-market of new technological products, processes or services. This means that a new technological enterprise must structure itself to meet rapidly and agilely this accelerated time-to-market paradigm. Therefore, traditional development approaches are no longer feasible in this type of environment (White and Patton 1991).

## 2.2 Technological Invention

Historians of technology have made it a cliché that one of the greatest achievements of the nineteenth century was the *invention of invention* (Drucker 1985, pp. 34). Before 1880, invention was considered a *flash of genius*. By the time of World War I, invention had become synonymous with research, a systematic and purposeful activity. A technological invention is defined as the creation of a new product, process or service. Invention is more than ensuring the end result (Cardullo 1996b, pp. 118). However, a technological invention rarely becomes an immediately successful product, process or service. Since the airplane was first flown in December 1903 at Kitty Hawk, North Carolina, it took more than thirty years before commercial aviation achieved a general market penetration. An invention is born when it is proven to work within a limited environment such as a laboratory.

## 2.3 Technological Innovation

Innovation is an economic or social term rather than a technical term and can be viewed as changing the yield of resources (Drucker 1993, pp. 33). According to economists, innovation is changing the value and satisfaction obtained from resources by the consumer. There is a critical difference between invention and innovation. An innovation is a technical solution to a particular question or problem. The innovation takes an invention or concept and adds the economic dimension so that it can enter a market space. The invention becomes an innovation when it can be replicated reliably on a large scale at an acceptable cost (Senge 1990, pp. 6). If the innovation is sufficiently important it is called a *basic* innovation and can create a new industry or transform an existing industry. The introduction of the PC by Apple Computer followed by IBM's introduction of their PC created an

106

entire new industry, while the development of the World Wide Web ("WWW") totally transformed the Internet industry from a government and academic communication medium into a rapidly growing information industry sector.

A new technological enterprise must build a seamless innovation process from its conception. Innovation is seen by the enterprise's outside environment as the facets of the enterprise, from its structure through to its actual technological output (Theis 1996). Figure 3.8 shows the innovation process as a feedback process. Successful innovation implies a double feedback process consisting of:

- Obtaining technology, marketing and customer expertise.
- Successful innovation generating the sound financial foundation for subsequent innovations.

The structure of the new technological enterprise (See Chapter 8 – Next Entrepreneural Step) is vital in developing a seamless innovation process (Theis 1996). This process means integrating horizontally, vertically and across business boundaries. All the stakeholders that are involved in the process from the initial concept to market introduction are interlinked.

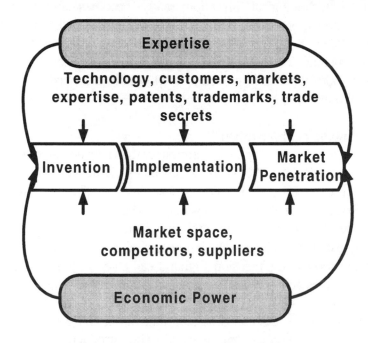

**Fig. 3.8** Innovation Feedback Process (Adapted from Theis 1996 )

### 2.3.1 Innovation Sources

The seven sources of innovation include (Drucker 1985, pp. 30-36):

**Unexpected** – This ranges from unexpected success to unexpected failure and includes unexpected environmental factors. IBM experienced unexpected success when the first PC was introduced in 1982. This started an entire new trend and product line and eventually had a serious impact on mainframe computers that were the core products of IBM. Unexpected success portents a shift or trend for an enterprise. Unexpected failure may lead to a totally new product, such as the development of *stick on notes* by the 3M Corporation after the failure of a new glue product. Unexpected environmental factors can also cause innovation. The rapid growth of the Internet caused many of the telecommunication companies to develop products and specialized services to meet the needs of this growing market.

**Incongruities** – The differences between reality and idealized states also form the basis of technological innovation. An incongruity is a discrepancy between these two potential states. An incongruity is a symptom of an opportunity to innovate Drucker (Drucker 1985, pp. 57). These incongruities can be differentiated as:

- Economic.
- Assumptions.
- Value expectations.
- Process logic.

**Process Need** – Innovations also arise to reduce process bottlenecks or inefficiencies in a process. There are three constraints in evaluating innovations based on process need:

- Clear understanding of the process need.
- Availability of knowledge to improve the process.
- Consistency of solution with the process system requirements.

**Structured Change** – As has been stated by Grove (Grove 1996), *strategic inflection points* (*10X* changes) in an industry or market can be the initiator of a major innovation. Due to *10X* changes, stable industries or markets can become very chaotic, as was the case in the telecommunication and banking industries when new de-regulation practices were introduced. These sudden and unexpected shifts necessitate innovative change.

**Demographics** – Population changes also serve as sources of innovation. As the large number of children born after World War II, who have been termed *baby boomers*, have passed through various stages in their life cycles, new opportunities for technological products, process and services have arisen.

**Perception, Mode and Meaning** – Shifts in the manner individuals, enterprises or industries view themselves create innovation opportunities. While these changes are difficult to recognize they can provide a new technological enterprise with growing market opportunities for innovative products, processes or services to meet these changes in perception, meaning or mode. The perception of enterprise outsourcing in the late 1990s provides an example of this innovative driver. Similarly, many of these drivers of innovation can be short lived and can be termed *fads*.

**New Knowledge** – Knowledge-base innovation has the longest lead-time of all innovations (Drucker 1985, pp. 107-129). However, this lead-time is changing as shown in Figure 3.9 (Cardullo 1996b, pp. 120). Knowledge-base innovation requires:

- Analysis of various factors including the knowledge itself, socio-economic and perceptual.
- Clear focus on the strategic position of the enterprise including system, market and occupancy of a strategic position.
- Learning and practice of entrepreneurial management. Entrepreneurial management is the most crucial requirement in knowledge-based innovation (Drucker 1985, pp. 119).

### 2.3.2    Innovation Types

Innovation can have various levels of economic uniqueness (Hisrick and Peters 1995, pp. 16). A technological innovation can be classified as:

- Ordinary – with little uniqueness in technology.
- Incremental – Moderate change from an existing technology with an increase in functionality or capability.
- New Generation – Technological change which differentiates new technology from old, although they share a similar basis, i.e., various developments in microprocessors moving from an 8 bit to a 64 bit architecture.
- Radical – Totally different technology to accomplish functions.

Table 3.2 compares the different types of technological innovation. The time between invention and innovation has been decreasing since the mid-1800s. Figure 3.9 shows this decreasing interval. The half-life, i.e., the time to be reduced by half, appears to be approximately 20 years.

## Ordinary Innovation

Ordinary innovations are those innovations that provide no new capabilities but may consist of cosmetic changes or repackaging. These innovations are more strategic positioning innovations. Introduction of computer software front-end graphical user interfaces ("GUIs") without adding additional capabilities is an example of an ordinary innovation. Other forms of innovation quickly supercede this type of innovation.

**Table 3.2**
Comparison of Technological Innovations

| Innovation | Discontinuity | Competency | Risk |
|---|---|---|---|
| Ordinary | None | No Change | Low |
| Incremental | Continuum | Minor Change | Minor |
| New Generation | Non-revolutionary | Enhancing | Moderate |
| Radical | Revolutionary | Destroying | High |

## Incremental Innovation

Many technological innovations are incremental in nature (Martin 1994, pp. 41). Incremental innovations are those technological products, processes or services that incrementally build on their predecessors. These are more likely to succeed than radical departures in technologies and/or markets (Cardullo 1996b, pp. 73). These incremental innovations within an existing technology are either:

- Performance improving, or
- Cost-reducing.

The Japanese technological enterprises use a continuous incremental improvement process to gain market share. The Japanese word for the process is *Kaizen*.

## Generational Innovation

Generational innovations are step-wise improvements in capabilities (Martin 1994, pp. 40). These innovations are *non-revolutionary discontinuities* since they build upon existing capabilities and are competence enhancing. The growth of capabilities manifested by Moore's Law (See Chapter 2 – Technological Entrepreneurs) illustrates generational innovation.

**Radical Innovation**

A radical innovation is a major change and is accompanied by major risks. A radical technological innovation is classified by the extent to which the enterprise incorporates embryonic and rapidly developing technology (Green, Gavis, and Ainian-Smith 1995). The radical nature of the technological innovation can also be classified by the extent to which the enterprise incorporates technology that is new to the enterprise (even thought it may be well understood outside the enterprise) and by how it departs from the existing management or business practices of the enterprise. The amount of financial risk is another measure of the radical nature of the technological innovation. The dimensions of the degree of the radical nature of the innovation are related to (Green, Gavis, and Ainian-Smith 1995):

- Technological uncertainty.
- Technological experience and knowledge.
- Business experience and knowledge.
- Fiscal risk associated with the technological innovation.

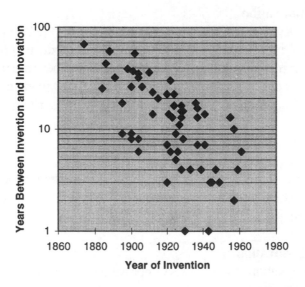

**Fig. 3.9** Relationship Between Invention and Innovation (Cardullo 1996b, pp. 120. Reprinted by Permission Research Studies Press, Ltd.)

Radical innovation can be termed *competence destroying* (Anderson and Tushnan 1991). This has been termed destruction of competency because the radical innovation destroys prior technical competencies, such as fiber optics and higher capacity over existing electrical conductors changing the nature of telecommunications.

### 2.3.3 Successful Innovation Process

Technological enterprises must look carefully on how their concepts for a new innovative product, process or service fit into the practical realities of its proposed market space, i.e., study incongruities. This requires (Mintzberg and Quinn 1991, pp. 752) a strong market orientation and a mechanism to ensure interaction between the technical and marketing segments of the proposed enterprise.

A technological entrepreneur must consider that many innovations rarely reach successful market embeddment or become profitable. Few technological innovational concepts prove profitable due to the high cost of converting a promising innovative concept into a profitable product, process or service (Pearce II and Robinson Jr. 1994, pp. 231). Between one and two percent of innovative concepts reach the marketplace (Cardullo 1996b, pp. 121).

There are a number of guidelines that can assist a technological entrepreneur in increasing the success of the innovative process (Steele 1989, pp. 284-285).

**Scale** – A new technological innovation should be scaled to meet the financial and human resources available. Tackling monumental innovative projects usually requires resources that are beyond the scope of a new entrepreneurial enterprise.

**Teamwork** – Teamwork on the part of the entrepreneurial formation team is critical. All members of the team are required to work together in bringing a new technological innovation to market. Without team cohesiveness, the likelihood of failure of the innovation and indeed the new enterprise is relatively high.

**Goals** – Realistic goals and schedules are important. However, since technological innovation must enter a rapidly changing arena, innovations requiring long developmental cycles should be discouraged.

**Belief System** – A missionary zeal should be instilled into the process. The entrepreneurial team members should fervently believe in what they are undertaking.

**Information** – A technological environmental monitoring system is key to obtaining market information early and continuously. This is vital since potential customers determine the value of the innovation. Exceedingly efficient communication among team members is vital.

**Learning Environment** – The skills of the team members must be expanded as the innovation process proceeds.

**Pioneering** – The technological innovation that is undertaken should focus on achieving a pioneering application as soon as possible. It is not necessary to develop a full-featured technological innovation, only the kernel or basic innovation. Further improvements can be achieved through a staged innovation implementation process, i.e., by adding incremental improvements.

**Financing** – It is essential that the financial requirements for the innovation be realistic. These needs must be factored into the business plan for the new technological enterprise (See Chapter 6 – Initial Enterprise Financing). Skillful financial resource management is a basic investment community indicator of successful enterprises. Financial resources should be realistically determined and parsimoniously managed.

### 2.3.4 Japanese Innovation Model

Japan has been cited in the 1980s and 1990s as having a culture where technological enterprises such as Sony, Mitsubishi and others have achieved high levels of innovation. Figure 3.10 and Table 3.3 compares the differences between the innovation cycles of Japan and the United States. The high innovation of Japanese enterprises is due to a combination of factors, which do not exist in most of the Western enterprises (Bowonder and Miyake 1993).

Coordination among individuals in Japan is through horizontal information-flow structures and semi-autonomous decision making. The operating units of the enterprise are engaged in mutually coordinating their tasks. Financial control in Japan is bank-oriented, with the main bank playing the role of manager of a loan consortium. A group of banks extends major long-term credit to the enterprise and is responsible for closely monitoring the business affairs of the enterprise. However, sometimes this has resulted in financial problems for the enterprise. Corporate management decisions of Japanese enterprises are subject to the dual control or influence of financial interests and employees' interest rather than being subject to unilateral control in the interest of the owners. Dually controlled enterprises seek innovative opportunities by developing an in-house knowledge base, rather than pursuing radical innovations. Japanese technological enterprises practice a participative mode of interaction which results in a positive cooperation strategy among enterprises.

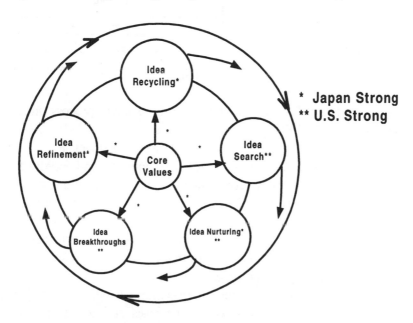

**Fig. 3.10** Japanese Innovation Cycle (Bowonder and Miyake 1993. © 1993 IEEE. Reprinted by permission)

While the Japanese innovation cycle has proven successful in developing incremental innovations in many instances, it has failed in developing radical innovations. The cultural elements expressed in this cycle would be anathema to most Western enterprises and in particular to new entrepreneurial enterprises. Table 3.3 shows the difference between the Japanese and U.S. innovation models.

While the Japanese innovation model (Figure 3.10) and system (Figure 3.11) are not totally applicable to new non-Japanese technological enterprises there are several lessons that can be extracted, including:

- Continuous scanning and assessing of the technological space via a technological monitoring system.
- Core competence building.
- Strategic partnering.
- Stress on quality and continuous improvement.

114

**Table 3.3**
Comparison of Japanese and U.S. Innovation Models

| United States (Strong) | Japan (Strong) |
|---|---|
| Idea search | Idea refinement |
| Idea nurturing | Idea recycling |
| Idea breakthrough | Idea nurturing |

(Based on data contained in Bowonder and Miyake 1993)

The lessons learned from the Japanese innovation process include (Bowonder and Miyake 1993):

- A strong institutionalized enterprise intelligence.
- A strong government role in identifying and coordinating new directions for growth and technological thrust. This lesson is in variance with the direction of governmental involvement in the United States in technological development. In the United States, the government has taken a strong role primarily in the development of military technological innovations.
- A systematic opportunity-seeking behavior looking for new ideas on a continuous basis and converting those ideas into new technological products, processes or services.
- Use of morphogenic[5] logic in which interactions continuously generate heterogeneity and new patterns of mutually beneficial relations among the heterogeneous elements.

## 3. VISION AND MISSION FORMULATION

The overall planning of a new technological enterprise should begin with the formulation of the vision and mission for the enterprise. The vision, mission and strategy can be viewed as a set of nested entities as shown in Figure 3.12. The vision is the overall guiding principle of the enterprise and the mission is the basic goals and philosophy that will shape the new enterprise strategic posture (Pearce II and Robinson Jr. 1994, pp. 31).

---

[5] Morphogensis is the formation of a structure of an organism or part; and its differentiation and growth during development.

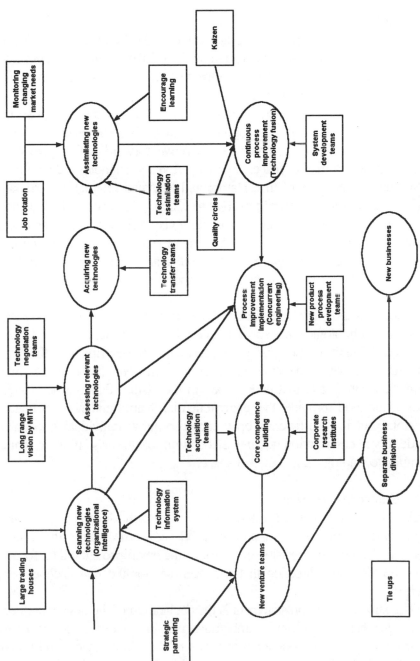

**Fig. 3.11** Japanese Innovation System (Bowonder and Miyake 1993. © 1993 IEEE Reprinted by permission)

## 3.1 Enterprise Vision

The vision of the enterprise is the aspiration of the leadership team for the future. The vision should be formulated to have a current long-ranged horizon that is relevant for future members of the enterprise; one which they can believe in and are motivated to achieve.

A vision is an ideal, i.e., imagined future state of the enterprise that differentiates between existing conditions and goals. The enterprise vision provides the focus for the enterprise to move forward with regard to its technological and market space. In a way, a vision connotes a dream or an apparition and because of this, Hamel and Prahalad (Hamel and Prahalad 1994, pp. 26) prefer the word *foresight* to *vision*. However, *vision* has been embedded in the literature. In any case, any vision must be based on a solid factual foundation. For an enterprise to remain competitive, it must be capable of enlarging its *opportunity horizon* (Hamel and Prahalad 1994, pp. 83). Thus, the vision for the new enterprise must be realistic and broad in nature.

Another important characteristic of the vision for achieving a world class successful technological enterprise is that it be shared (Schumacher 1997b). A shared vision of an enterprise means an integrated description of the future that enhances communication and motivates the entrepreneurial team to attain the desired state that is described in the vision (Schumacher 1997a). This vision will provide the entrepreneurial team guidance in making decisions, but it is sufficiently open-ended to allow individual freedom to decide upon contribution to and elaboration of the vision in a rapidly changing technological and market space.

## 3.2 Enterprise Mission

While vision is a desired future state or horizon direction for a new technological enterprise, mission is more concerned with the present direction. The current mission or vector of the enterprise should be focused upon the visionary direction that has been set for the new technological enterprise.

The strategic mission statement is the declaration of the new enterprise's *reason for being*. A clean unambiguous mission statement identifies the scope of the enterprise operation in terms of the technological and market space (David 1997, pp. 9). Studies indicate that enterprises that have a well-developed formal mission statement tend to perform better in terms of profitability. Strategic vision and mission statements are used to differentiate an enterprise from others in the technological and market space and provide identity, emphasis and direction (Thompson Jr. and Strickland III 1996, pp. 23).

**Fig. 3.12** Nested Enterprise Strategy Sets

An explicit statement of the strategic mission of the enterprise is needed to (King and Cleland 1978, pp. 124):

- Ensure unanimity of purpose.
- Provide a basis for motivating personnel and allocating resources.
- Establish an entrepreneurial climate.
- Serve as a focal point of enterprise purpose and direction.
- Facilitate the translation of objectives and goals into a work structure.
- Provide a basis for assessing and controlling cost, time and performance parameters.

The objective of any organism both at individual and community levels is to survive and grow. While many new technological enterprises are initiated each year, few manage to survive to a mature state. Growth and profitability drive survivability. Profit or its potential is the principal driving force in any enterprise. Some enterprises such as America Online Inc. have rarely achieved profitability, but growing market share indicated the potential for capturing large economic rents. Product impact studies ("PIMS") have shown that growth in market share is directly correlated with profitability (Pearce II and Robinson Jr. 1994, pp. 35).

The strategic mission statement for the new enterprise should reflect the three economic goals of the enterprise: survival, profitability and growth (Pearce II and Robinson Jr. 1994, pp. 35).

These goals should be placed in a context within the strategic mission statement that reflects various aspects of the technological and market space (David 1997, pp. 89; Pearce II and Robinson Jr. 1994, pp. 34):

- Customers.
- Markets.
- Product, process or service.
- Technology.
- Survivability.
- Growth.
- Profitability.
- Philosophy.
- Public image.
- Employees.

## 4. STRATEGIC TECHNOLOGICAL PLANNING AND ANALYSIS

Strategic technological planning and analysis is the process by which the new enterprise combines its technological planning with the overall enterprise planning process. This requires understanding the planning process, technology forecasting, the risk in any planning process, core elements of the new enterprise and the environment in which it must operate. The new enterprise must be able to meld the technological and market strategies (See Chapter 4 - Enterprise Technological Market Planning) into an overall enterprise strategy.

An iterative process focused on four technological elements results in a technological strategic plan (See Figure 3.13). These elements are (Cardullo 1997):

- Core competencies.

- Environmental analysis.
- Evaluation of the enterprise's technological strengths, weaknesses and the opportunities and threats.
- Emerging technologies.

A technological strategy to achieve competitive advantage can be driven by technological and market space (Roberts 1991, pp. 282).

**Technology Driven Strategies**

Strategies that are driven by technology rely on building a critical mass of technological skills to develop *core technology*. These strategies rely on evolving the technology by encouraging internal technology development that targets multiple and possibly unrelated technologies, i.e., multiple *core technologies* derived from the original core technology. Technology driven strategies also rely on the acquisition of new technologies through a merger and acquisition process. This avoids long-term effort of building technological skills. It is possible for a new technological enterprise to be focused on an acquisition process to assemble the critical core competencies and technologies. This process also occurs in a technological market space where a roll-up process of assembling small technological enterprises in similar technological market space is used to acquire additional market space share.

**Market Driven Strategies**

Market driven strategies employ a technological application strategy where the enterprise pursues a single product or market space with a stable selection of distribution channels. These strategies also include a leveraged technological market strategy that releases products, processes or services that address different customer groups, sharing the same functional need through the same distribution channels. Another technological strategy is characterized by products, processes or services that contain changes in customer needs, end user customer groups and distribution channels.

Technological and business strategies are interrelated (Lee and Johnson 1991) and this linkage is very important. The business strategy is driven by the market space. Thus a technological market planning process (See Chapter 4 – Enterprise Technological Market Planning) is an important element in the enterprise formation process.

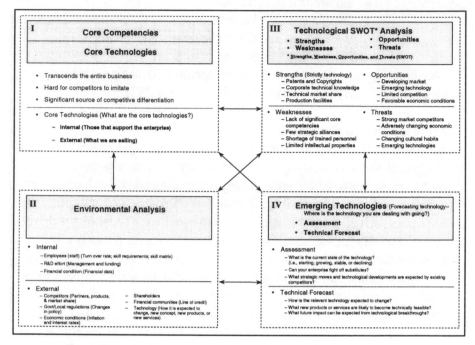

**Fig. 3.13** Technological Strategic Planning Process

Figure 3.14 shows a conceptional framework for connecting the technological and business strategy domains. The change in one plane affects the interface with the other plane. The elements of the interaction are shown in Figure 3.15 which shows the drivers and constraints for the business and technology domains.

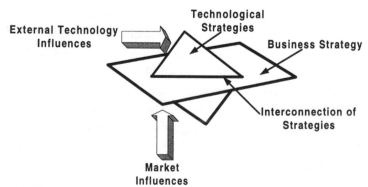

**Fig. 3.14** Intersection of Business and Technology Domains (Adapted from Lee and Johnson 1991)

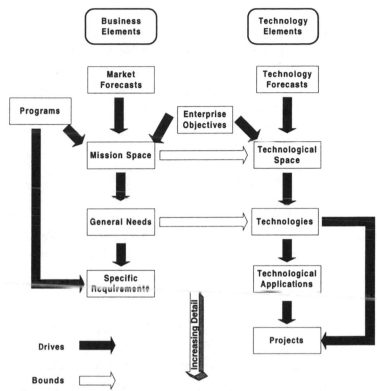

**Fig. 3.15** Key Elements of Business and Technological Strategy Domains (Lee and Johnson 1991. © 1991 IEEE. Reprinted by permission.)

## 4.1 Technological Strategic Planning Process

The technological strategic planning process equates to building a defense against the competitive forces that the enterprise will face and positioning the enterprise in the technological and market space where the competitive forces are at their weakest (Mintzberg and Quinn 1991, pp. 69). Due to the changing environment that a new technological enterprise will face, the strategy must have flexibility. An enterprise to compete more effectively in the ever-changing environment that is undergoing globalization at the end of the twentieth century, strategies must be *resource based* (Nonaka and Takeuchi 1995, pp. 46). Resource based strategies mean that competencies,

122

capabilities, skills or strategic assets[6] are the source of sustainable competitive advantage.

The technological strategic planning process provides the new venture team with a method of focusing the enterprise formation process, and is crucial in commercializing any technological concept. The technological strategic plan must clearly set forth for the technological product, process or service (Howard Jr. and Guile 1992, pp. 129):

- What it is.
- How it will be realized.
- Place in the market space.
- Introduction timing.
- Profitability.
- Future developments.

It must be realized that no enterprise will be successful unless it integrates both the technological and market strategic planning processes within the total enterprise planning process (See Chapter 6 – Initial Enterprise Financing). As stated by Howard and Guile (Howard Jr. and Guile 1992, pp. 129):

> *"Any significant innovation in technology or mission involves risks such that cost and schedule cannot be precisely known at the start."*

This uncertainty should not be the impediment to technological and market strategic planning but the reason to plan.

The development of any strategy is to compete within tomorrow's industry structure as well as within the current structure (Hamel and Prahalad 1994, pp. 42). This also implies that a technological enterprise occupies a rapidly changing market space; therefore, one must also have a continual technological environmental monitoring process in place from the enterprise's formation to gauge such changes.

Metz (Metz 1996) presents a model of *best practices* for establishing a structured technological planning process. Figure 3.16 shows the *best practices* for technological planning found among 50 enterprises which led to success. This approach is a useful framework for a new entrepreneurial enterprise to consider. Many new technological enterprises, while having a

---

[6] A strategic asset is a possession of the enterprise, such as a brand loyalty or technological expertise, that is superior to the competition; a skill is an enterprise ability that is better than its competitors (Nonaka and Takeuchi 1995, pp. 55).

vision of success (Step 1) and having defined the future basis of competition (Step 2), usually have a fixed technology and rarely evaluate other technologies which may be more robust within their technological and market space.

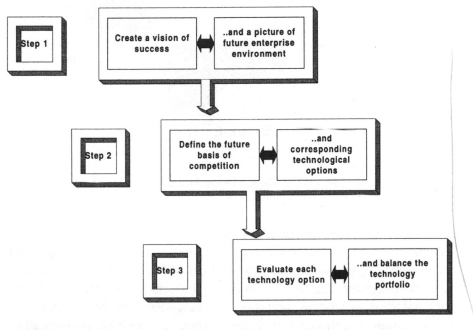

**Fig. 3.16** *Best Practices* for a structured technology planning process (Metz 1996. © 1996 IEEE. Reprinted by permission)

With very short product, process or service life cycles, sometimes measured in six to eighteen months, it is important for the technological formation team to consider the life cycle impacts on cash flow and enterprise profitability. Figure 3.17 shows a typical cash flow chart for the development of a new technological entrant.

One measure of technological success is the time to reach break-even. Break-even time is the time taken by a product, process or service to break-even on a cash flow basis (Metz 1996). Enterprises such as Hewlett-Packard use this metric to determine go/no-go decisions on project funding and as a measure of technological success.

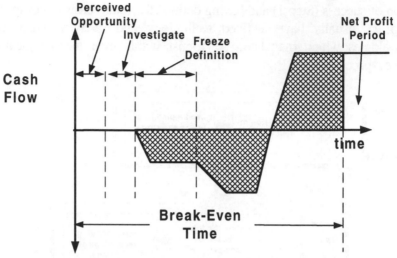

**Fig. 3.17** Break-Even Time as a Technological Success Metric (Metz 1996. © 1996 IEEE. Reprinted by permission)

## 4.2 Technological Forecasting Process

Technological strategic planning has an intimate relationship with technological forecasting. Technological forecasting is a continuous process for an enterprise, similar to technological environmental monitoring. Technological forecasting should be internally related to the monitoring of the enterprise's technological space. Thus, the technology forecasting process provides a continuous stimulus and guidance for the technological strategic planning process (Jantsch 1967, pp. 84). The technological forecasting process is used to evaluate the emerging technologies and provide an approach to reducing risk by evaluating potential new technological competitors.

Technological forecasting can be defined as the prediction of the future characteristics of useful machines, procedures or techniques. Technological forecasting is a system of logical analysis that leads to quantitative conclusions or a limited range of possibilities about technological and associated economic attributes (Bright 1968).

Technological forecasting is related to the tasks that emerge in connection with medium and long-range planning. These forecasts are basically concerned with the rates of technological progress. Jantsch, who conducted some of the initial pioneering studies, defines technological forecasting as (Jantsch 1967, pp. 23):

*"...the probabilistic assessment of future technology transfer, which ... denotes the entire range of vertical and horizontal transfer processes that constitute the advancement of technology and the effectuation of impact in technological (economic, social, military, political, etc.) terms."*

## 4.3   Technological Risk

The technological risk for a new enterprise depends on the level of technology used. Steele (Steele 1989, pp. 120) provides a framework for evaluation of risk from low through moderate to high-risk technologies. Figure 3.18 shows the risk portion of the technological space that the enterprise will face.

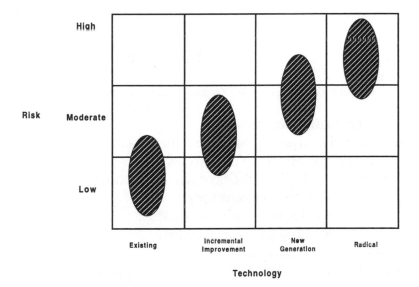

**Fig. 3.18** Technological Risk Domain

There are a number of technological strategy options for reducing risk in the R&D process (Bhrat 1991). While these options are suitable for a mature enterprise, they may not be suitable for a new technological enterprise. However, the proposed differentiation of risk is a useful way of viewing the risk domain. Figure 3.19 shows the risk domain. Each of the nine sectors of this risk domain requires a different approach to technological strategic planning.

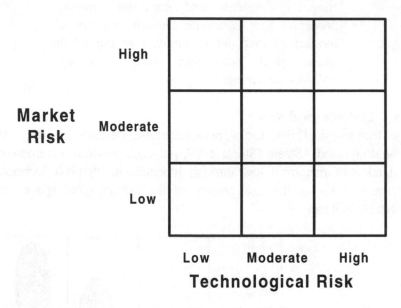

Fig. 3.19 Technological Risk Domain (Based on the construct in Bhrat 1991)

## 4.4   Technological Decisions

A technological enterprise in either the formative or operating stage is faced with three strategic decisions. This process of strategic decision making is shown in Figure 3.20. These decisions can be classified as (Tschirky 1996):

- Choice of technology.
- Acquisition of technology.
- Deployment of technology.

This trilogy poses three questions.

**First Decision** – *"Which way to go?"* – This requires an extensive analysis of current and future products, processes or services with respect to major technologies determining performance and implementation processes. This process includes technological forecasting and assessment to arrive at this decision. This decision results in the choice of the technology to be used as the basis of the new enterprise (Tschirky 1996).

**Second Decision** – *"Make or Buy?"* – This decision answers the question as to whether the chosen technology is to be obtained through acquisition, collaboration with other enterprises or through internal development.

**Third Decision** – *"Keep or Sell?"* – This decision represents whether the new technological product, process or service will be exploited through direct sales or through licenses to other enterprises. For example, Rombus Corporation (microchip designers) exploited their innovative computer memory system by licensing it to Intel Corporation. Rombus Corporation did this because of the large capital cost required to manufacture microelectronic products.

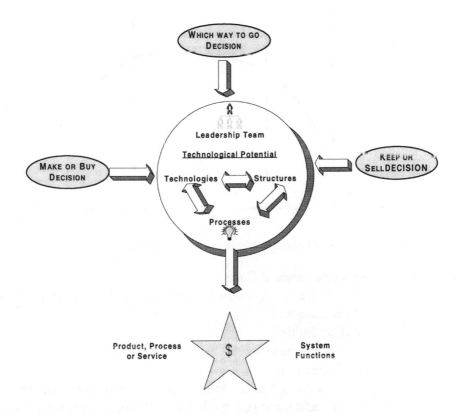

**Fig. 3.20** Trilogy of Strategic Technology Decisions (Adapted from Tschirky 1996)

Technological decisions are difficult to make due to the complexity of assessing their financial impact and the difficulty in modeling decisions. While models such as those proposed by Nair (Nair 1997) exist, they are difficult for a new formative technological enterprise to employ due to the lack of data and the complexity of each model.

128

In making technological strategic decisions, the technological formation team must be fully aware of the technological life cycle aspects of any new product, process or service introduction. Figure 3.21 shows the classical market growth curve that should be considered.

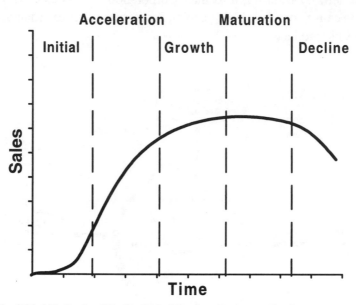

**Fig. 3.21** Life Cycle of Technological Product, Process or Service

### 4.5 Enterprise Technological Core

A technological enterprise has three basic cores that position it within its technological and market space:

- Capabilities.
- Competencies.
- Technology.

A core capability is defined as the knowledge set that distinguishes and provides a competitive advantage (Leonard-Barton 1996). A competence is defined as the bundle of skills and technologies rather than a single discrete skill or technology (Hamel and Prahalad 1994, pp. 202). A core technology is the technological basis for the new enterprise, i.e., a technology or a group of technologies, which will provide a technological competitive advantage for the enterprise.

There is a relationship between core technologies and competencies as shown in Figure 3.22. The core competencies are used to produce core technologies, which meet market needs.

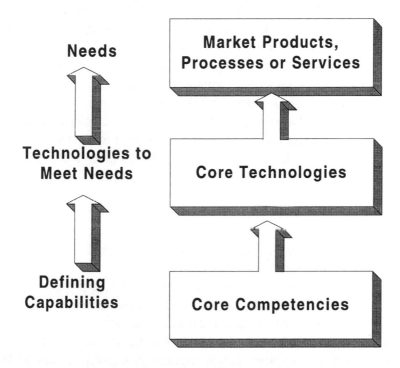

**Fig. 3.22** Relationship of Needs, Core Technologies and Competencies

### 4.5.1 Enterprise Core Capabilities

There are four dimensions to core enterprise capabilities (Leonard-Barton 1996):

- Employee knowledge and skills.
- Technical systems.
- Managerial systems.
- Values and norms.

These tacit knowledge sets can be placed into three categories (Spender 1993):

- Conscious.
- Automatic.
- Communal.

The ability of an enterprise to learn, adapt, change, and renew is important for the technological enterprise formation team to keep in focus during the planning stage of the new enterprise. These elements of the strategic orientation of the enterprise are dependent on the new enterprise's specific capabilities which are required to gain a competitive advantage within the chosen technological market space (Walsh 1996). It is important for the technological formation team to identify two sets of capabilities:

- Enterprise's specific capabilities that may result in a competitive advantage (See Chapter 4 – Enterprise Technological Market Planning).
- Identification of the requisite capabilities within the technological market and industry space that the new enterprise will enter and which have the potential for sustainable competitive advantage.

### 4.5.2 Enterprise Core Competencies

Aptitude and enterprise skill are not considered core competencies. Most enterprises have only one to three core competencies. In general a core competency must meet the following three criteria:

- Consistent throughout the entire enterprise.
- Source of competitive differentiation.
- Difficult for competitors to imitate.

If a competency can not meet the above three criteria, it is *not* a core competency of an enterprise. A new technological enterprise should develop one core competency otherwise the probability of growth, profitability and eventually survivability will be greatly diminished. According to Hamel and Prahalad (Hamel and Prahalad 1994, pp. 197):

> *"Core competencies are the gateways to future opportunities."*

Many times enterprise core competencies are confused with (Hamel and Prahalad 1994, pp. 207):

- Resources.
- Infrastructure.
- Competitive advantages.
- Critical success factors.

The core competencies of the enterprise assist the enterprise in meeting the goals arising from the vision-mission framework. A technological entrepreneurial enterprise in its formative stages may find itself with few or none technological core competencies. The investment community will not necessarily view this negatively provided a sound plan is presented to obtain at least one core competency.

The trend within all technological spaces is toward more rapid and expensive technological change and volatility if not a chaotic market space. This trend will require the new technological enterprise to focus on core competencies, which will remain relevant as the technological and market spaces evolve. Technological enterprises face an environment where the windows of opportunity for launching new products, processes or services are becoming shorter and the lead times required to develop additional core competencies are becoming longer (Dawson 1991).

### 4.5.3  Enterprise Core Technology

Any technological product, process or service is based upon an identifiable technical skill set or technology (Roberts 1991, pp. 285). A core enterprise technology in the narrowest sense can be characterized as stand-alone, i.e., it is the technological basis for the enterprise. One method of viewing core technologies is by means of its technological attractiveness (Tschirky 1996). Figure 3.23 shows a strategic technology positioning chart.

An understanding of the enterprise's core technology is critical in any technological strategic analysis. This analysis should address the basic issues of (Roberts 1991, pp. 284):

- Basic needs or user functions that the enterprise's product, process or service will satisfy.
- Groups of customers that share these needs or functional requirements and to whom the new technological product, process or service will be sold.
- Technologies that will be used to produce the new product, process or service.
- Sources of that technology.
- Distribution mechanisms that will be used to bring the successfully developed technological product, process or service to the technological market space.

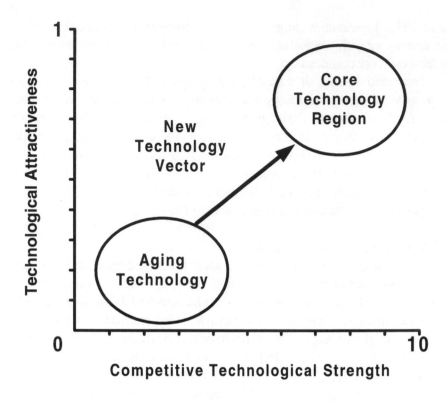

**Fig. 3.23** Strategic Technology Position (Adapted from Tschirky 1996)

In the rapidly changing technological market space, a new technological enterprise can only usually find one or possibly two specific core technologies to concentrate their developmental efforts upon (Roberts 1991, pp. 285).

### 4.5.4 Technological SWOT Analysis

A **S**trengths **W**eakness and environmental **O**pportunities and **T**hreats ("SWOT") analysis is the precursor of the formulation of a successful technological strategy. The SWOT concept derives from general enterprise strategic planning (Pearce II and Robinson Jr. 1994). A technological SWOT analysis is a systematic identification of the factors that must be considered for technological developments.

*Strengths* are the technological or other resources, skills or advantages of the enterprise. These can vary from individuals with very specialized knowledge to existing market franchises, and encompass the total set of enterprise, technologically related, strengths. Many enterprises underestimate certain human resource strengths, which provide the basis for core competencies of the enterprise.

*Weaknesses* are limitations or deficiencies in technological or other resources, skills, and capabilities that seriously impede an enterprise's effective performance. All enterprises have weaknesses when viewed in a particular context. However, in some instances these weaknesses are overlooked in optimistic atmospheres surrounding essential members of the leadership team who may be vying for internal competitive position.

*Opportunities* are favorable technological, market or other situations in an enterprise's environment. Opportunities can be found in most enterprise environments. An example is the rapid growth of direct mail sales in the computer hardware markets in the 1990s that have been successfully exploited by various enterprises.

*Threats* are major unfavorable technological, market or other situations in an enterprise's environment. Threats are important impediments to achieving strategic technological objectives. Many enterprises underestimate the threats posed by new untried technologies. The rapid rise of the Internet in the mid-1990s caught many firms unprepared, including a market leader such as Microsoft® Corporation.

Figure 3.24 shows a technological SWOT analysis. Since most formative technological enterprises have little history, a technological SWOT analysis must rely upon various assumptions. These can include alternative future scenarios and alternative technology options (Martin 1994, pp. 78).

Understanding the concept of *strategic groups* is important in developing a technological SWOT analysis. Porter in 1980 used the concept of strategic groups to discuss industry structural analysis (Porter 1980, pp. 129). A strategic group is the group of enterprises in an industry using the same strategy along the strategic dimension. The concept of strategic groups is also associated with the concept of mobility or entrance barriers (Porter 1980, pp. 132-133). Entry or mobility barriers depend on the particular strategic group that the new technological enterprise seeks to join. In technological industries such the Internet and microcomputers, the mobility barriers are very different than for other industry groups. These barriers include (Porter 1980, pp. 220):

- Proprietary technology.
- Access to distribution channels.

134

- Access to strategic resources such as high demand technical skills.
- Experiential cost advantage.
- Technological and competitive uncertainty.
- Capital barriers due to technological market space risk.

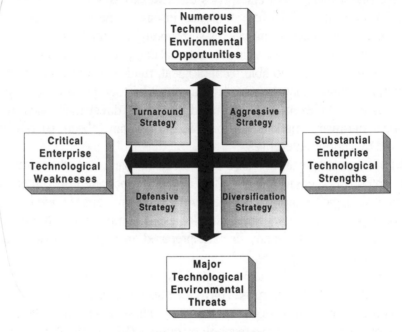

**Fig. 3.24** Technological SWOT Analysis Diagram (Adapted from Pearce II and Robinson Jr., 1994, pp. 178.)

The factors that influence an enterprise's strengths and weaknesses are (Porter 1980, pp. 149):

Factors Influencing Strengths
- Building strategic position.
- Increasing bargaining position.
- Insulating or protecting position.
- Increasing scale.
- Strong implementation.
- Availability of resources and skills.

Factors Influencing Weaknesses.
- Reducing strategic position.
- Reducing bargaining position.

- Increasing vulnerability of position.
- Increasing costs.
- Weaker implementation.
- Lack of resources.

The opportunities and threats can be characterized by the following factors (Porter 1980, pp. 150-151):

Factors Influencing Opportunities

- Create new strategic group through incremental or radical innovation.
- Shift to more favorably situated strategic group.
- Strengthen the enterprise's structural position within the existing industry group.
- Shift to a new industry group and strengthen that group's structural position.

Factors Influencing Threats or Risks

- Other enterprises entering the strategic group.
- Reducing mobility barriers of the enterprise's strategic group.
- Investment risks associated with improving enterprise position by increasing mobility barriers.
- Risks associated with attempting to increase mobility barriers into a more desirable or new strategic group.

Pearce and Robinson (Pearce II and Robinson Jr. 1994, pp. 265) present a grand strategy formulation using a SWOT analysis, which can be applied to a technological strategic planning process. Figure 3.25 presents this framework, modified for formulating an enterprise's technological strategy. Throughout the process of strategic positioning, the entrepreneurial team must try to maintain an objective view. This can be difficult under the strong emotion associated with enterprise formation.

## Quadrant I – Strong Technological Position – Growing Market or Emerging Market

The technological strategic quadrant can be characterized as the *Go-for-It* quadrant. Technological entrepreneurial enterprises that find themselves in this quadrant should concentrate on using their strengths to garner market share. This is the strategic position that Netscape had at its initiation. Netscape's technological strategy allowed for rapid initial growth that led to a successful initial public offering (See Chapter 8 – Next Entrepreneurial Step).

136

This quadrant also fosters a technological strategy of further strengthening a strong technological position by developing ancillary products, processes or services based on their core technology.

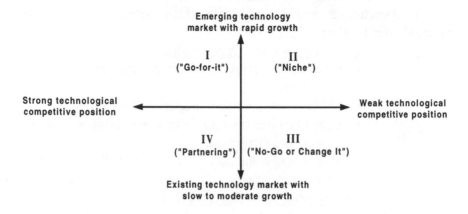

Fig. 3.25 Technological Strategic Clusters (Adapted from Pearce II and Robinson Jr. 1994, pp. 265)

## Quadrant II – Weak Technological Position – Growing or Emerging Market

Many entrepreneurial ventures can find themselves in this *Niche* quadrant. An example is the explosive growth in the 1990s of the Internet that spurred the formation of numerous small and medium sized Internet Service Providers ("ISPs"). These technological enterprises usually use existing technology and develop a niche market space position. Although the technological market space has a large upward momentum, it is possible to maintain this position. When the market reaches a point of maturity, these niche enterprises usually disappear or are *rolled-up* into other enterprises who are seeking to increase their market share. Entrepreneurial technological formation teams can use the niche market position quadrant for establishment of the new enterprise but should have a strategy either to move toward Quadrant I by developing strong technological differentiators or to secure market niches from which they execute a profitable exit strategy at the appropriate time.

**Quadrant III – Weak Technological Position – Existing or Slowing Market**
This quadrant is the *No-Go* or *Change-It* quadrant for the technological formation team. Enterprise formation teams that find themselves in this quadrant should seriously re-think the entire formation strategy. It is unlikely that a new technological enterprise in this quadrant can grow or survive. The enterprise should seek to review its core technology options and competencies before proceeding.

**Quadrant IV – Strong Technological Position – Existing or Slowing Market**
Entrepreneurial technological enterprises in this *Partner* or *Joint Venture* quadrant usually are technology spin-offs from academic or government laboratories. In this quadrant, the formation team is faced with a strong technological position usually in a mature or slowing market space. In this position, the entrepreneurial formation team strategy should seek a strategic alliance or partner to join forces with when entering the market space. The partnering enterprise must have the financial resources and/or market share which can exploit the strong technological position of the new enterprise.

**4.6    Technological Environmental Analysis**
The environment of an enterprise is the pattern of all the external and internal conditions that can and will influence its development and survivability. Technological environmental analysis allows the enterprise formation team to gain an understanding of the potential impacts of both internal and external environmental factors. The external factors are those factors outside the control of the entrepreneurial team. Although these factors are not controllable, it is important to be fully aware of their potential impact on the new technological enterprise.

A technological enterprise must be capable of maintaining and growing even if drastic changes to its environment occurs. This organic self-maintenance phenomenon is the process known as *homeostasis*. Any highly developed organism such as an enterprise should possess the ability to regulate its internal environment as the external environment changes (Laszlo 1972, pp. 41).

Technological changes are the most potentially disruptive elements within an enterprise's external environment. Figure 3.26 shows the

138

enterprise's external environment. The enterprise exists within the context of the complexities of economic, political, commercial, technological, social and cultural worlds (Del Rio Soto 1997).

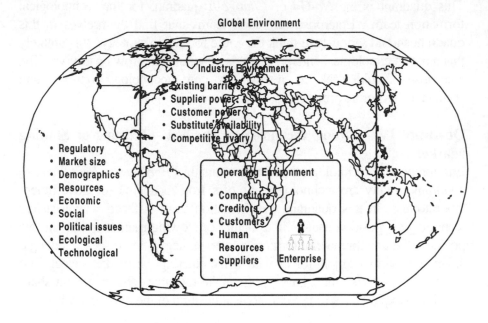

**Fig. 3.26** Enterprise External Environment (Adapted from Pearce II and Robinson Jr. 1994)

The general or global external environment of the enterprise is composed of those factors that are generally beyond the control of the enterprise and which affect all enterprises within the same technological space. This environment can be a source of opportunities and threats for the new technological enterprise. It is possible that a new technology can arise in the global environment in a manner to obviate the existing technological advantage of an enterprise. However, it is also possible that this new technology can serve as a potential opportunity that can be exploited within the enterprise's technological market space. Figure 3.27 shows the interaction of the internal and external environments of the enterprise.

It is important for the enterprise formation team to have an understanding of the various environmental factors that will affect the enterprise within the intended technological market space environment.

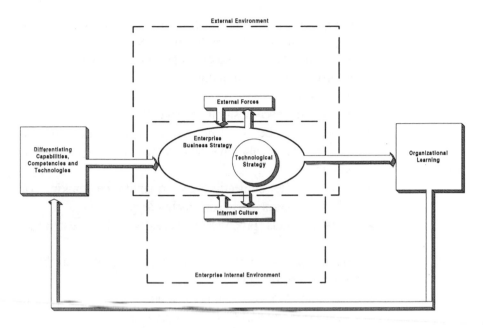

**Fig. 3.27**  Internal and External Interaction for Technological Strategic Development
(Adapted from Del Rio Soto 1997)

There are a number of questions that must be addressed in assessing the technological environment facing a new enterprise. These questions include (Petrov 1982):

- What technologies are available for the enterprise in developing its product, process or service?
- Are there critical and non-critical technologies embedded within the components that must be externally acquired?
- Which of the externally obtained technologies might become critical and why?
- Will the external technologies eventually be brought into the enterprise?
- How did the internal and external technologies evolve?
- What evolutionary changes in these technologies can be expected in the future?
- What investment must be made initially and over time in the enterprise core technologies?
- What are the historical patterns of investment in these technologies by competitors, what future investments by

competitors can be expected, and what are the implications of these trends? In terms of:

- Cash generation and earnings characteristics?
- Investment requirements?
- Growth?
- Market space position and share?

- What will be the necessary investments in the technologies by the enterprise to maintain a competitive advantage?
- What is the subjective and quantitative ranking of different enterprises in each technology?
- What products, processes or services will the enterprise offer?
- What are the critical components for the products, processes or services?
- What are the costs and value-added structures of the intended products, processes or services?
- What are the potential applications of the enterprise's technologies?
- In which applications will the enterprise participate in and why? In which applications will the enterprise not participate in and why?
- How attractive is an investment opportunity in each of these applications in terms of its market growth, it's potential for profit and/or its potential for technological leadership? Including:
  - Underlying growth characteristics.
  - Evolution of customer needs and requirements.
  - Current and emerging market segments, and segment growth rates.
  - Competitive positioning and likely strategies of key competitors.
- How critical are the enterprise's technologies to each of these applications?
- What technologies are critical to external applications?
- How do the technologies differ in each application?
- What are the competing technologies in each application?
- What are the determinants of substitution dynamics?

- What is and will be the degree of technological change in each technology?
- What should be the technological priorities?
- What technological resources will be required for the new enterprise to achieve its objectives?
- What should be the investment level and rate for the new enterprise?
- What additional technologies will be required to achieve the new enterprise's objectives?
- What are the implications of the technologies for the overall enterprise strategy?

A new entrepreneurial enterprise by definition does not have an actual internal environment. However, the process of viewing potential internal factors using a functional approach can assist the entrepreneurial formation team to put in place structures which can assist the enterprise in achieving its objectives (See Chapter 5 – Enterprise Formation). The important internal factors can be grouped into the following functional areas:

- Marketing.
- Financial.
- Production, operating and technical.
- Personnel.
- Quality management.
- Information systems.
- Organization and general management.

It is very unusual when a new technological enterprise has sufficient human and financial resources to assign different members to these functional areas. However, the enterprise formation team should divide the functions among themselves with the minimum of overlap.

## 4.7 Technological Environmental Monitoring System

It is critical that a new technological enterprise develop a technological environmental monitoring system, i.e., an *early warning system* that is integrated into the structure of the enterprise (Martino 1993, pp. 203).

A technological environmental monitoring system should have the ability to provide answers to a number of questions such as:

- What will be the probable trend in technological development in the enterprise's market space?

- What are the promising technological developments, which can influence the enterprise's core technologies positively or negatively?
- What technological vectors are competitors pursuing?
- What are the technological and business strategies of competitors and how are they changing over time?

The information needed to answer these questions comes from the technological environmental monitoring system. In the age of information, data are available from a variety of sources such as publications, journals, the Internet, personal communications, patent searches, business presses, technological presses, competitor's news releases and annual reports (if the enterprise is publicly traded), enterprise's customers and suppliers, and numerous other sources. The technological environmental monitoring system allows this diverse data to be assembled and analyzed in a manner that can provide technological guidance for the new enterprise and the leadership team.

Porter (Porter 1980, pp. 73) presents a model of a competitive intelligence system that can be modified to form the basis of an enterprise technological environmental monitoring system which can cover both the technological and market spaces of the enterprise. Figure 3.28 shows this modified environmental monitoring system.

One member of the leadership team is responsible for the environmental monitoring system. This individual is likely to be the Chief Technology Officer ("CTO") of the enterprise (See Chapter 5 – Enterprise Formation). In many new technological enterprises, the function of the CTO and the CEO may be synonymous (Cardullo 1996a). As the enterprise grows, the environmental monitoring system can be made one of the responsibilities of the CTO. The CTO will also be responsible for technological forecasting using data collected by the technological environmental monitoring system. The information that the system will collect can be used by all members of the enterprise's leadership team in the process of anticipating and reacting to changes in the technological environment from minor to *10X* changes.

As a technological enterprise moves through various stages of growth, the system can grow with the enterprise. This growth can occur from initially keeping the information in file folders or a simple database to integration into a robust Intranet system with optical storage of documents and internal intelligence agents.

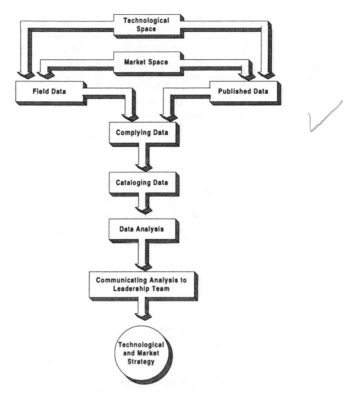

**Fig. 3.28** Enterprise Environmental Monitoring System ( Adapted fromPorter 1980)

## 4.8 Technological Value Chain

Developing a technological strategic planning process requires the new enterprise understand the concept of a *value chain*. This is a systematic approach for analyzing the series of activities an enterprise performs to provide its customers with a product, process or service. The value chain approach presents the enterprise's strategically important activities to enable understanding of the enterprise cost structure and potential sources of differentiation. A competitive advantage (See Chapter 4 – Enterprise Technological Market Planning) is achieved for the enterprise by performing these strategically important activities at a lower cost or more effectively than its competitors (Pearce II and Robinson Jr. 1994, pp. 183). Figure 3.29 presents a typical value chain model. The nine basic categories shown in Figure 3.29 are shared by most enterprises.

144

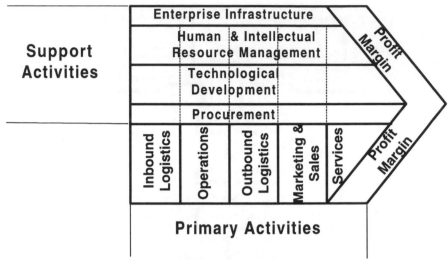

**Fig. 3.29** Typical Technological Value Chain (Adapted from Pearce II and Robinson Jr. 1994, pp. 184)

Figure 3.30 shows a process for creating value. The value chain can be evaluated by considering (Steele 1989, pp. 306):

- For each process step, determine the range of times for completing that process step.
- Human resources and skill sets required for the total value chain.
- Direct and indirect costs created in each process step.

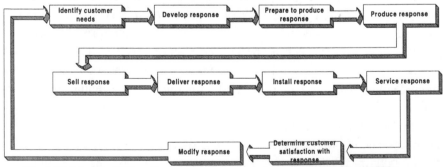

**Fig. 3.30** Modified Value Creating Chain (Adapted from Steele 1989, pp. 292)

A *system viewpoint* is essential in creating the value chain. As Figure 3.31 shows the indirect cost can increase over time for new technological entrants, obviating any direct cost saving obtained through enterprise learning.

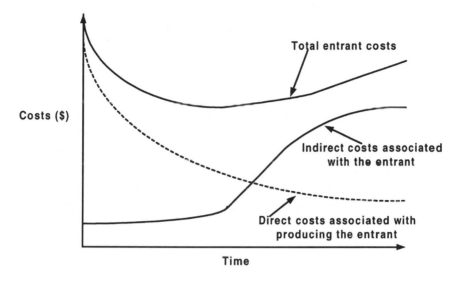

**Fig. 3.32** Typical Cost History ( Adapted from Steele 1989, pp. 300)

## 4.9 Emerging Technologies

Emerging technologies are those technologies in the embryonic stages of their development that can cause a *strategic inflection point* in the enterprise's planned or existing technological space. An understanding of emerging technologies can be developed using analytical *technological forecasting* techniques (Cardullo 1996b, pp. 79-112). Technological forecasting can be defined as the prediction of the future characteristics of useful machines, procedures or techniques (See pp. 124). These forecasts are concerned with the rates of technological progress. There are two types of forecasting techniques, normative and exploratory. It is important that the interaction of the *opportunity-oriented* (exploratory) and *needs-oriented* (normative) forecasting techniques be stated correctly.

When the forecast is needs oriented, it is termed normative. Normative technological forecasting is based upon systems analysis. Normative forecasts start with future needs and define the technological performance required to meet those needs. Normative technological forecasting approaches can be self-fulfilling prophecies. The following are normative technological forecasting techniques that can be employed:

- Decision Matrices.
  - Horizontal.
  - Vertical.
- Relevance Trees.
- Morphological Analysis.
- Network Techniques.
- Mission Flow Diagrams.
- Other Techniques.

When the forecast is opportunity oriented, it is termed exploratory. Exploratory technological forecasting uses technical data to formulate the forecast. By using measurable technical data, exploratory technological forecasting has an advantage over normative forecasting. Technical data can be grouped into three sets (Jantsch 1967, pp. 143): functional capabilities independent of any specific technology; technical parameters, and scientific and technical findings for which the relationship to functional capabilities has not yet been established. These data sets, representing past history, lend themselves to extrapolation over time by using either trend models or a Delphi[7] approach.

Most of the technological forecasting techniques can be categorized into five categories (Porter et al. 1991, pp. 64):

- Monitoring.
- Expert opinion.
- Trend extrapolation.
- Modeling.
- Scenarios.

Many forecasts of future technologies have not necessarily materialized. The majority of the errors of past forecasts have been instances of underestimating possible progress. Technological forecasting can also result in very large misjudgments of a technological development independent of the method used. A misjudgment or erroneous forecast is contributed to by (Schnaars 1989):

- Fascination with the exotic.
- Fascination with technologies which are the currently *hot*.
- Price-performance failures.
- Shifting societal trends.
- Unforeseen ultimate use.

---

[7] Delphi approach to technology forecasting is based upon using groups of experts to jointly forecast future developments.

Forecasting errors can be minimized provided that the enterprise (Porter et al. 1991, pp. 385):

- Understands the technological domain.
- Uses the right technological parameters.
- Identifies the institutions involved, socioeconomic influences, critical decision points current and future.
- Does not have a technological ideological fixation.
- Does not allow the forecasts to mirror the prevailing technological mood.
- Keeps the time horizon short.
- Does the forecast simply.

Technological change and the evolution of societal organizations are closely related. The weakness of many technological forecasting techniques is their focus with technology and assuming the societal factors to be constant, exogenous or nonexistent (Rubin 1968, pp. 243). This can be observed in how many technological enterprises originally responded to the development of the Internet in the early 1990s. Even Microsoft® Corporation originally dismissed the importance of this societal phenomenon. Technological forecasting should be the blending of two diverse approaches (Steele 1989, pp. 222):

- Technological advance results from the intrinsic characteristics of science and engineering.
- Societal needs and desires.

One useful method of considering emerging technologies is by the use of technological roadmaps. A technological roadmap is a projection of developments of the technology over time and includes (Howard Jr. and Guile 1992, pp. 79):

- Collection of data on technology life cycles.
- Learning curves.
- Competitive analysis (See Chapter 4 – Enterprise Technological Market Planning).
- Indicators of technology and market activities.

Another method for forecasting emerging technologies is by the use of multiphase life cycle analysis (Benson, Sage, and Cook 1993). The preliminary analysis for the multiphase life cycle analysis process consists of the following phases:

- Investigating and identifying requirements specifications for various technologies.

148

- Analyzing documentation concerning technological, economic and societal needs for and feasibility of the various technologies.
- Assessment and evaluation of the alternative technologies.
- Selection of appropriate technologies.

Benson et al (Benson, Sage, and Cook 1993) termed the multiphase life cycle analysis a triple-gateway methodology. This concept is based on the proposition that a technology, to obtain a stage yielding useful technological products, processes or services, must pass through three gateways:

- Technology gateway.
- Systems-management gateway.
- Market gateway.

An extremely useful technique for forecasting technology is the use of leading indicators (Martino 1991). The probabilistic approach in the use of leading indicators computes the probabilities associated with the time lag from the precursor event to the technological event to be forecasted. Historical data is used to develop a probability distribution for the lag times between a specific type precursor event and a specific type of event being forecasted.

## REFERENCES

Anderson, P., and M. L. Tushnan. 1991. Managing Through Cycles of Technological Change. Research Technology Management 34 (3):26-31.

Balachardra, R., and John H. Friar. 1997. Factors for Success in R&D Projects and New Product Innovation: A Contextual Framework. IEEE Transactions on Engineering Management 44 (3):276-287.

Bell, C. Gordon, and John E. McNamara. 1991. High-Tech Ventures: The Guide for Entrepreneurial Success. Reading, MA: Addison-Wesley Publishing Company, Inc.

Benson, Brien, Andrew P. Sage, and Gerald Cook. 1993. Emerging Technology - Evaluation Methodology: With Application to Micro-electromechanical Systems. IEEE Transactions on Engineering Management 40 (20):114-123.

Betz, Fredrick. 1987. Managing Technology: Competing Through New Ventures, Innovation and Corporate Research. Englewood Cliffs, NJ: Prentice-Hall, Inc.

Bhrat, Vasanthakumar. 1991. Generic Risk Reduction Strategies for R&D Projects. Paper read at Portland International Conference on Management of Engineering and Technology, at Portland, OR.

Bowonder, B., and T. Miyake. 1993. Japanese Technological Innovation Strategy: Recent Trends. IEEE Engineering Management Review 21 (2):38-48.

Bright, J. R. 1968. The Manager and Technological Forecasting. In Technology Forecasting for Industry and Government, edited by J. R. Bright. Englewood Cliffs: Prentice-Hall, Inc.

Cardullo, Mario W. 1996a. Chief Technology Officer: A New Member of The Leadership Team. Paper read at UnIG'96: International Conference on Technology Management: University/Industry/Government Collaboration, 96/6/24-26, at Istanbul, Turkey.

Cardullo, Mario W. 1996b. Introduction to Managing Technology. Edited by J. A. Brandon. First ed. 5 vols. Vol. 4, Engineering Management Series. Baldock, Hertfordshire, England: Research Studies Press Ltd.

Cardullo, Mario W. 1997. Development of Technological Strategic Plans: Case Study of Three Enterprises. Paper read at The Sixth International Conferernce on Management of Technology, at Goteborg, Sweden.

Cooper, Robert G., and Elko J. Kleinschmidt. 1993. Uncovering the Keys to New Product Success. IEEE Engineering Management Review 21 (4):5-18.

David, Fred R. 1997. Strategic Management. Upper Saddle River, NJ: Prentice-Hall.

Dawson, Keith. 1991. Core Competency Management in R&D Organizations. Paper read at Portland International Conference on Management of Engineering and Technology, at Portland, OR.

Del Rio Soto, Roberto. 1997. A New Approach to Corporate and Technology Strategy. Paper read at Sixth International Conference on Management of technology, at Goteborg, Sweden.

Drucker, Peter F. 1985. Innovation and Entrepreneurship: Practice and Principles, New York, NY: Harper and Row, Publishers.

Drucker, Peter F. 1993. Post-Capitalist Society. Oxford, England: Butterworth Heinemann

Green, S. G., M.B. Gavis, and L Ainian-Smith. 1995. Assessing a Multidimensional Measure of Radical Technological Innovation. IEEE Transactions on Engineering Management 42 (August):203-214.

Grove, Andrew S. 1996. Only the Paranoid Survive: How to Exploit the Crisis Points that Challenge Every Company and Career. New York, NY: Currency Doubleday.

Hamel, Gary, and C. K. Prahalad. 1994. Competing for the Future. Boston, MA: Harvard Business School Press.

Hisrick, Robert D., and Michael P. Peters. 1995. Entrepreneurship: Starting, Developing, and Managing a New Enterprise. Chicago, IL: Irwin.

Howard Jr., William G., and Bruce R. Guile. 1992. Profiting from Innovation: The Report of the Three-Year Study from the National Academy of Engineering. New York, NY: The Free Press.

Jantsch, Eric. 1967. Technological Forecasting in Perspective. Paris, France: Organization for Economic Co-Operation and Development.

Kauffman, Stuart. 1995. At Home in the Universe: The Search for Laws of Self-Organization and Complexity. New York, NY: Oxford University Press.

King, William R., and David I. Cleland. 1978. Strategic Planning and Policy. New York, NY: Van Nostrand Reinhold.

Laszlo, Ervin. 1972. The Systems View of the World: The Natural Philosophy of the New Developments in the Sciences. New York, NY: George Braziller.

Lee, David H., and Craig C. Johnson. 1991. Exploiting a Conceptual Representation To Integrate Business and Technology Strategies. Paper read at Portland International Conference on Management of Engineering and Technology, at Portland, OR.

150

Leonard-Barton, D. 1996. Core Capabilities and Core Rigidities: Paradox in Manging New product Development. Strategic Management 13:111-125.

Martin, Michael J. C. 1994. Managing Innovation and Entrepreneurship in Technology - Based Firms. Edited by D. F. Kocaoglu, Engineering and Technology Management. New York, NY: John Wiley and Sons.

Martino, Joseph P. 1991. Probabilistic Technological Forecasts Using Presursor Events. Paper read at Portland International Conference on Management of Engineering and Technology, 91/10/27-31, at Portland, OR.

Martino, Joseph P. 1993. Technological Forecasting for Decision Making. Edited by M. K. Badawy. Third ed, McGraw-Hill Engineering and Technology Management. New York, NY: McGraw-Hill, Inc.

Metz, Philip D. 1996. Integrating Technology Planning with Business Planning. IEEE Engineering Management Review 24 (4):118-120.

Mintzberg, Henry, and James Quinn. 1991. The Strategy Process: Concepts, Contexts, Cases. Second ed. Englewood Cliffs, N.J.: Prentice Hall.

Nair, Suresh K. 1997. Identifying Technology Horizons for Strategic Investment Decisions. IEEE Transactions on Engineering Management 3 (August):227-235.

Nonaka, Ikujiro, and Hirotaha Takeuchi. 1995. The Knowledge-Creating Company: How Japanese Companies Create the Dynamics of Innovation. New York, NY: Oxford University Press.

Pearce II, John A., and Richard B. Robinson Jr. 1994. Formulation, Implementation and Control of Competitive Strategy. Fifth ed. Burr Ridge, IL: Irwin.

Petrov, Boris. 1982. The Advent of the Technology Portfolio. Journal of Business Strategy (Fall).

Porter, Alan L., A. Thomas Roper, Thomas W. Mason, Frederick A. Rossini, and Jerry Banks. 1991. Forecasting and Management of Technology. Edited by D. F. Kocaoglu, Wiley Series in Engineering & Technology Management. New York, NY: John Wiley & Sons, Inc.

Porter, Michael E. 1980. Competitive Strategy: Techniques for Analyzing Industries and Competition. New York, NY: The Free Press.

Resa, Stanley C. 1991. Targeting Growth Through Technological Innovation. Paper read at Portland International Conference on Management of Engineering and Technology, at Portland, OR.

Roberts, Edward B. 1991. Entrepreneurs in High Technology: Lessons from MIT and Beyond. New York, NY: Oxford University Press.

Rubin, Theodore J. 1968. Technology, Policy and Forecasting. In Technological Forecasting for Industry and Government: Methods and Applications, edited by J. R. Bright. Englewood Cliffs, NJ: Prentice-Hall, Inc.

Scarbrough, Harry, and J. Martin Corbett. 1992. Technology and Organization: Power, meaning and design. Edited by D. C. Wilson, The Routledge Series in Analytical Management. London, England: Routledge.

Schnaars, S.P. 1989. Megamistakes. New York, NY: The Free Press.

Schumacher, Terry R. 1997a. Building Team Vision with Scenario Planning. Paper read at International Conference on Management of Engineering and Technology, 97/7/27-31, at Portland, OR.

Schumacher, Terry R. 1997b. West Coast Camelot: The Rise and Fall of an Organizational Culture. In Cultural Complexity in Organizations, edited by S. Sackman: Sage Publications.

Senge, Peter M. 1990. The Fifth Discipline: The Art and Practice of The Learning Organization. New York, NY: Currency Doubleday.

Slater, S. F. 1994. Competing in High-Velocity Markets. IEEE Engineering Management Review 22 (Summer):24 - 29.

Spender, J.C. 1993. Competitive Advantage from Tacit Knowledge? Unpacking the Concepts and Its Strategic Implications. New Brunswick, NJ: Rutgers University, Graduate School of Management.

Steele, Lowell W. 1989. Managing Technology: The Strategic View. Edited by M. K. Bradawy, McGraw-Hill Engineering and Technology Management. New York, NY: McGraw-Hill Books Company.

Theis, Dietmar. 1996. Lining Up for Innovation. Paper read at International Conference on Technology Management: University/Industry/Government Collaboration, 96/6/24-26, at Istanbul, Turkey.

Thompson Jr., Arthur A., and A. J. Strickland III. 1996. Strategic Management: Concepts and Cases. Ninth ed. Boston, MA: Irwin/McGraw-Hill.

Tschirky, Hugo. 1996. Closing the Gap Between Management Theory and Technology Reality - Approach at the Swiss Federal Institute of Technology. Paper read at International Conference on Technology Management: University/Industry/Government Collaboration, at Istanbul, Turkey.

Viscio, Albert J., and Bruce A. Pasternack. 1996. Toward a New Business Model. Strategy and Business, 96/Second Quarter, 8-14.

von Hipple, Eric. 1988. The Sources of Innovation. New York, Ny: Oxford University Press.

Walsh, Steven T. 1996. Identification Schemes for Core Technical Capabilities: Evidence from the Semiconductor Silicon Industry. Paper read at Fifth International Conference on Management of Technology, 96/2-3/27-1, at Miami, FL.

Wheelwright, Steven C., and Kim B. Clark. 1992. Revolutionizing Product Development: Quantum Leaps in Speed, Efficiency, and Quality. New York, NY: The Free Press.

White, Donald E., and John R. Patton. 1991. Accelerating Time-To-Market: Methodology and Case Study Highlights. Paper read at Portland International Conference on Management of Engineering and Technology, 91/10/27-31, at Portland, OR.

## DISCUSSION QUESTIONS

1   Choose a technology and develop a technological map tracing its evolution, growth and phase-out. Discuss the evolution in this technology and their impacts on the enterprises associated with the technology.

2   Using publicly available material such as annual reports, press releases or Security Exchange Commission ("SEC") filings, compare the vision and mission statements of five different public technology

152

companies. Discuss in detail how these statements are similar or dissimilar.

3    Choose five technological enterprises which you either familiar with or for which you can obtain data, and present their core technologies and competencies. Discuss the significance of these core factors to the current position of the enterprises.

4    Choose five technological public enterprises and develop a technological SWOT analysis for them. Discuss the differences between the strategies which they are currently appearing to employ, and those which the SWOT analysis indicates they should be using.

5    Discuss the various technological forecasting techniques and their advantages and disadvantages, as they would relate to a new technological entrepreneurial enterprise.

CHAPTER 4

# Enterprise Technological Market Planning

*"It is a bad plan that admits of no modification."*
**Publilius Syrus**
*Maxims, First Century B.C.*

## 1.    INTRODUCTION

While the technological strategic planning process is focused on the technological space (See Chapter 3 – Technological and Enterprise Strategic Planning), the technological market planning process is focused on the market space of the enterprise.  These planning processes are similar, only the *space* or *viewpoint* that is taken is different.  However, it must be realized while the viewpoint is different, the *world* being viewed is the same.  This requires harmonization of the views or spaces, i.e., each can not be considered totally separately.

### 1.1    Technological Market Plan

The result of the enterprise technological market planning process is a market strategy and plan for the new enterprise to participate in the market space. This plan should have the following characteristics (Hisrick and Peters 1995, pp. 139):

- Provide a market strategy to accomplish the enterprise's mission and goals.
- Be based on facts and verifiable assumptions.
- Allocate resources needed to enter and succeed in the chosen market space.
- Delineate an enterprise structure (See Chapter 5 – Enterprise Formation) to accomplish the market plan.
- Develop the market plan to be a *living document* that can be updated and refined for the enterprise during its lifetime.

154

- Plan should be short and to the point and not over elaborate. However, it should be sufficiently detailed to delineate the market strategy to be accomplished.
- Incorporate alternative strategies based upon possible changes in the enterprise's chosen market space.
- Contain performance criteria, which can be monitored and controlled.

Figure 4.1 shows a model for the development of the enterprise's technological market plan.

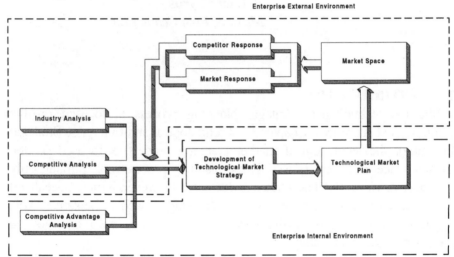

**Fig. 4.1** Enterprise Technological Market Planning Process

The technological market plan should consider the following elements in the process:

- Technological product, process or service and its position within the technological and market space. This should include capabilities and technological competitive differentiation.
- Price and pricing strategy and how it compares to the competition.
- Channels of distribution to penetrate the market space.
- Promotional activities including access to potential large customer groups.

Only 40 percent of the enterprises studied formulated a stated or implied specific marketing strategy (Roberts 1991, pp. 201). Only 30 percent had developed a sales plan, which is not a substitute for a marketing plan. It is critical that formative technological enterprises formulate robust plans. Both technological strategic and market plans will be thoroughly scrutinized by potential investors and venture capitalists.

### 1.1.1 Functionality
Within the technological market space, one important aspect is the *functionality* of the new technological product, process or service (Roberts 1991, pp. 288). Functionality is the set of potential customer needs that the new technological entrant will satisfy. The functionality is distinct from technology embedded in this new market space entrant. Competitors will deliver this functionality with their products, processes or services. Conversely, the new market entrant could use technology to deliver a new functionality to an existing or emerging market space. This was the case within the development of the early Internet World Wide Web browsers such as Mosaic that was then used by Netscape Corporation to develop a new technological enterprise.

### 1.1.2 End-user Groups
The technological market planning process should also consider *end-user customer groups*. These customer groups will each have different information, functionality and service requirements. The computer software market is an excellent example of the *end-user customer groups* in a similar market space. Products having the same embedded technology but with different functionality and information requirements can be supplied by a new technological enterprise. However, it is important that a new technological entrepreneurial enterprise should not try to serve all end-user groups initially. The new enterprise should chose the end-user group that offers the largest competitive advantage.

### 1.1.3 Distribution Channels
The channels of distribution that the enterprise will employ to penetrate its selected market space should be another consideration when developing the technological marketing plan. The distribution channels for a new technological enterprise should include (Roberts 1991, pp. 289):
- Direct sales.
- Original equipment manufacturers ("OEM") reselling.
- Value-added resellers ("VARs").
- Non value-added resellers ("NVARs").

- Mail/Internet orders.

Various highly successful technological enterprises have used each of these distribution channels. Dell Computer has been highly successful with the mail/Internet order paradigm while others such as Microsoft® Corporation, have used primarily OEM, VARs and NVARs to obtain a significant market share for its products.

## 1.2 Technological Market Planning Process

The market planning process can be classified for many of the technological enterprises as:

- Informal.
- Formal,tied to sales forecast.
- Formal, integrated with technological and business strategic planning.

In the formation of any technological market plan, market research is vital. However, the ability for technological entrepreneurs to perform market research in many instances is severely limited due either to the lack of experience or limited resources. Research strongly supports the proposition that the familiarity with existing technological attributes and uses interferes with the ability to conceive novel attributes and uses (von Hipple 1988, pp. 102).

Entrepreneurs can use certain market situations to gain a leadership position in an industry against entrenched industry enterprises (Drucker 1985, pp. 227). This is termed entrepreneurial *judo*, i.e., employing principles of balance and leverage. This entrepreneurial *judo* can be employed due to five common *bad* industry habits:

- *Not Invented Here* ("NIH") – Established enterprise industry arrogance. This also makes it difficult at times for new technological innovations to make initial penetrations.
- *Market Creaming* – Many potential customers in a technological market space are relegated to a secondary position by market leaders due to their size and profitability. This can be exploited by a new technological enterprise which meets the unfulfilled technological needs of this segment.

- *Lack of Quality* – The need to meet quality requirements at the price the customer is willing to expend is a situation that can be exploited.
- *Premium price structure of an industry* – This can allow penetration points for a new enterprise. A premium industry price structure that translates as high profits for market leaders is in effect a subsidy to the new enterprise.
- *Maximization versus optimization* – As a market grows and develops, industry leaders such as Microsoft® Corporation and Xerox try to satisfy every single user through the same product, process or service. This allows a new technological enterprise to offer more tailored functionality, which may not offered by the industry leaders.

Many entrenched market leaders in a technological market space can ignore the indications of impending replacement of their technology by a new entrant (Martino 1993, pp. 274). The current market leaders may not be aware of the interaction between growing market size and declining market share. Once the new technological entrepreneurial enterprise has reached one percent of the market, the market leader has only a relatively short time to react to the new market entrant. All technologies have an *S*-shaped life cycle, which follow the basic stages of growth, maturity and decline. A technological market positioning strategy must be sufficiently flexible to respond to this basic phenomenon. The technological market space is characterized by a rapid rate of change in the basic technology during the beginning phase of the *S*-shaped life cycle curve. During this phase the ratio of research to sales is high and there is a need for highly trained staff (Agmon and Von Glinow 1991, pp. 59). During this phase, the structure of a new technological market space is typified by strong competition with many enterprises.

The early stages of World Wide Web ("WWW") growth in the 1990s allowed for many new entrepreneurial entrants. However, as technological market space *ages* there is a movement toward consolidation of enterprises and oligopolistic competition. The Internet browser market, in a very short time, saw the market space reduced to two competitors: Microsoft® Corporation with their Internet Explorer and Netscape Corporation with their *Communicator* product.

## 1.2.1 Performance/Price Tradeoff

During the technological market planning process, the entrepreneurial formation team should consider the performance/price tradeoff in positioning their new market entrant (Betz 1993, pp. 172). This tradeoff will vary with market space.

- Military Market Space – Performance valued over price depending on need. However, during the 1990s, much military procurement has been moving toward total cost of ownership ("CTO") models for procurement.
- Industrial Market Space – Performance valued at a price justification based on return on investment ("ROI") or some other financial measure of enterprise performance.
- Business Market Space – Performance valued with an upper boundary of financial requirements such as cash flow or monthly expenses.
- Hobbyist Market Space – Performance valued within disposable recreational income constraints.

## 1.2.2 Technological Marketing Position

While technological marketing position is a very important consideration, many new technological entrepreneurs believe they can achieve an easy market dominance or a monopolistic position similar to Microsoft® Corporation or Intel Corporation by developing a *killer application*. Stochastic resonance benefited Microsoft® Corporation. These situations are not easily attainable. Many new technological entrepreneurs attempt to define an obvious, previously untapped market space which their new technological product, process or service would appear to target (Bell and McNamara 1991, pp. 233). Many new technological enterprises attack a major enterprise's customer base with a competitive replacement product, process or service. This strategy is likely to fail. This strategy can only be successful if the new technological entrant is compelling and the market entrenched enterprise cannot respond rapidly. There are certain basic flaws in the strategic plan for entering a technological market space that many new technological entrepreneurial enterprises appear to make (Bell and McNamara 1991, pp. 230-240). Many new enterprises enter new market space, resulting in them being technological pioneers and – *"Being on the edge which may result in getting cut and bleeding to death."* Some new enterprises do not understanding the S-shaped curve of emerging technological markets. Thus it will take them longer, cost more and require patience to make significant progress in an emerging technological market space.

Some new enterprises assume that they will mistakenly achieve a monopolistic market position. Without stochastic resonance, it is highly unlikely that the new enterprise will achieve such a position. Another market planning flaw is entering an always-emerging market space. The field of continuous voice and handwriting recognition, which took many years to emerge, is an example of this position.

Entering a market dominated by market leaders such as Intel is difficult and requires significant technological differentiation and considerable capital resources.

Sometimes a new enterprise will try to enter a technological market space with market entrants that are similar to existing competitor entrants and can have little chance of success unless considerable capital is expended to establish a *brand* presence. The digital subscriber line ("DSL") telecommunications market space in the late 1990s had multiple new enterprises competing with similar services in the same market space.

Attempting to obtain significant technological entrant differentiation will also cause a new enterprise to fail. The new technological product, process or service must be able to find a suitable market space niche.

Being captive to a single customer or distributor can also be a major flaw in a technological market strategy. Enterprises that enter the government contract sector, in many instances, become captive to a particular client and thus are subject to the budgetary constraints externally imposed on their client.

Attempting to enter a market space before developing the new technological entrant sufficiently is also a flawed strategy. An incomplete technological product, process or service is useless. A general technological entrant that does not target a specific customer market space segment may be considered incomplete since it is unlikely that it will fully meet all the needs in market space segments.

Right product, process or service but wrong customer is also a problem for new technological enterprises. Incorrect customer identification can divert scarce resources at a time when a new technological enterprise must be highly focused.

*Price structure* – The price structure is related to a number of factors such as the enterprise cost structure, market space pricing structure, competitive pricing and overall marketing strategy. Pricing too high or too low can be a strategic error. An example is the strategic error made by the Netscape Corporation in charging for its browser while its largest competitor, Microsoft® Corporation, gave the browser away to gain market share.

*Vaporware* – Pre-announcing a new technological entrant before its actual availability may be a serious flaw for a new technological enterprise. This pre-announcement will give existing and potential competitors information, which could cause a competitive response that the new enterprise can not fully meet.

*Right product, wrong marketing staff* – Many new technological enterprises start with very lean enterprise teams and thus may not have the right professionals to properly market their new entrant (See Chapter 5 – Enterprise Formation).

Before formulating a technological market strategy, it will be important for the enterprise formation team to estimate the potential for their new technological product, process or service. The market potential is an important concept in technological market planning (Kendall and French 1993). The value of developing a market potential is that total sales, market share, market penetration and the impact of changing marketing mix can more easily be forecasted as functions of market space potential. The concept is based upon the techniques of technological forecasting using the technological life cycle concept. This is also useful since it is bounded by market space population, which in turn is bounded by geographic population and maximum cumulative adoption (Kendall and French 1993).

The technological market space, like other non-technical market spaces has a tendency toward a gradual slide toward commoditization[1]. This commoditization occurs at the mature stage of the technological life cycle and is characterized by more service and lower prices (Rangan and Bowman 1994) (See Figure 4.2).

## 2. TECHNOLOGICAL INDUSTRY ANALYSIS

### 2.1 Technological Industry Space

In the formation of a new technological enterprise, it is critical that the enterprise leadership team has a firm understanding of the technological industry space or the industry they plan to enter. This is one of the most useful forms of strategic analysis. The analysis of the technological industry space will help the enterprise formation team determine the average level of

---

[1] Trade or commerce with little competitive differentiation.

long-term profitability of their competitors in the industry they are planning to enter. Technology industry analysis helps systematize the identification of two external components, i.e., opportunities and threats, of the technological SWOT analysis. This form of analysis will also help the new enterprise to understand the profitability differences between the various potential competitors. The differences in competitor profitability can provide (Fakey and Randall 1994, pp. 173):

- An indicator of the scope and types of strategies that result in industry leadership.
- Assistance in developing balance between required internal resources, competencies, strengths, weaknesses and the technology industry space environment.

The data on competitors can be presented in the form of the chart shown in Figure 4.3. This chart shows the return on assets versus sales over time for competitors. It is important to understand how the return has been changing for the various competitors over time and what has caused the differentiation. This analysis can give the enterprise formation team an understanding of some of the factors that are driving their potential technological industry space. The elements of an industry structure are shown in Figure 4.4. Porter's framework for an industry space is based on five forces: three of these forces are strictly competitive and two can be either cooperative or competitive. These five forces are:

- Degree of competitive rivalry.
- Entry barriers.
- Threat of substitution.
- Customer power.
- Supplier power.

An industry can be viewed according to:

- Scope.
- Resources.

The degree of scope of an industry can be divided into:

- Geographical.
- Vertical.
- Horizontal.

162

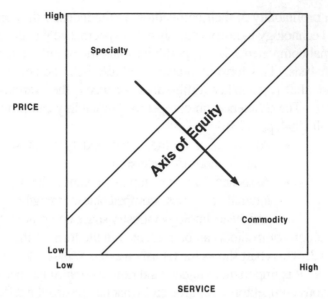

**Fig. 4.2**  Commoditization Space (Rangan and Bowman 1994. © 1994 IEEE. Reprinted by permission)

An industry can be divided into various geographical regions where physically separated markets are treated as being served by distinct industries. In the 1990s due to increasing sophistication in technology this market distinction was rapidly disappearing.  Telecommunication technology, including the Internet, allows enterprises large and small to have access to worldwide markets, through having access is not necessarily the same as being successful in widely dispersed geographical markets.  An enterprise may be able to ship to various locations, but it must also be able to provide the excellent service that the customers deserve and expect.

Technological industry spaces, as with all industry space, experiences continuous and evolutionary changes in structure.  An example is the change that occurred in the computer industry between 1980 and 1990.  Figure 4.5 shows the vertical structure of the computer industry space in 1980.  In the 1980, IBM, Digital Equipment Corporation, Sperry Univac and Wang Corporation dominated the computer industry space.  Each enterprise provided a total solution for its customers and provided all components of that solution.  However, today the computer industry structure is horizontal in nature.  Under the horizontal structure, companies provide portions of the system.  The structure of the Internet industry space in 1998 was horizontal and is shown in Figure 4.6.

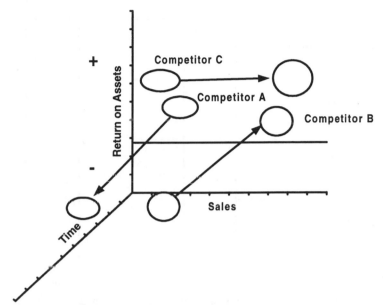

**Fig. 4.3** Competitor Analysis Based on Return on Assets

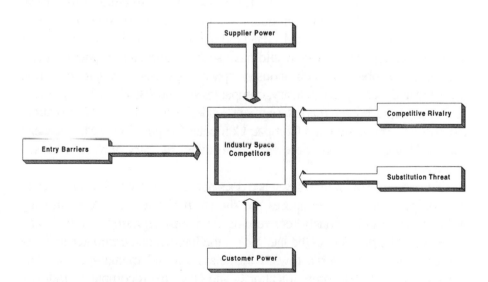

**Fig. 4.4** Factors Influencing Industry Space (Adapted from Porter 1979)

164

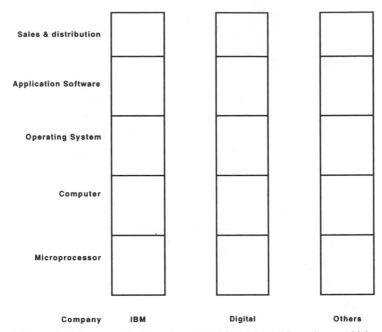

**Fig. 4.5** Vertical Computer Industry Space in 1980 (Adapted from Grove 1996, pp. 44)

The transformation of the computer industry space structure from vertical to horizontal was due to the introduction of the personal computer ("PC") by one of the vertical leaders, IBM. IBM did not realize that the introduction of a new technological product would have such a significant impact on them and other members of their industry space. As this *strategic inflection* occurred in the computer industry, companies such as IBM lost their position and were replaced by market segment leaders such as Intel Corporation, Microsoft® Corporation and Compaq Computer Corporation. Other leaders, such as Wang Computer, were reduced to minor industry players or ceased to exist.

The structure of an industry space does not remain static. The changes to the computer and Internet spaces are shown in Figure 4.6. A technology industry is simultaneously converging and disintegrating (Hamel and Prahalad 1994, pp. 37). In the late 1990s, the Internet and computer industry spaces started to converge toward the television and media spaces. The convergence of telecommunications and the microcomputer industry combined with deregulation in the United States and privatization worldwide acted to increase the convergence.

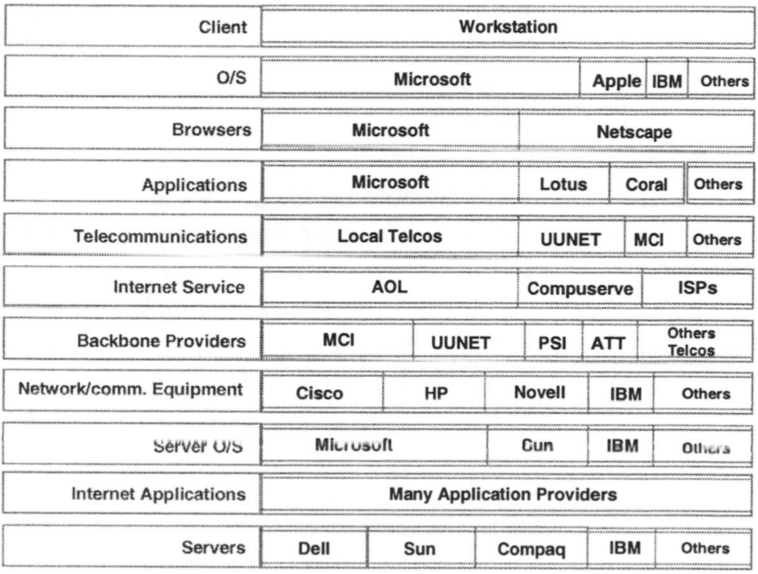

| Client | Workstation | | | |
|---|---|---|---|---|
| O/S | Microsoft | | Apple | IBM | Others |
| Browsers | Microsoft | | Netscape | |
| Applications | Microsoft | | Lotus | Coral | Others |
| Telecommunications | Local Telcos | | UUNET | MCI | Others |
| Internet Service | AOL | | Compuserve | ISPs | |
| Backbone Providers | MCI | UUNET | PSI | ATT | Others Telcos |
| Network/comm. Equipment | Cisco | HP | Novell | IBM | Others |
| Server O/S | Microsoft | | Sun | IBM | Others |
| Internet Applications | Many Application Providers | | | | |
| Servers | Dell | Sun | Compaq | IBM | Others |

**Fig. 4.6** Structure of Internet Industry Space

The structure of the technological industry space that a new enterprise will enter is critical to the strategy formation that the enterprise leadership team will need to develop. The structure of the industry space will determine the competitive environment that the new enterprise must penetrate. It is important to track the changes of each industry space component over time to understand the industry space. These factors provide strategic enterprise options within the chosen industry space (Porter 1980, pp. 127-129):

- *Specification* in terms of product, process or service focus, target customer segments or geographical markets.
- *Brand identification* such as that achieved by America Online through intense advertising or other means.
- *Push versus pull* where the enterprise positions itself directly with the end customer versus using distribution channels. This was the market strategy employed by

both Dell Computer Corporation and Gateway 2000
Computer.

- *Channel selection market strategy* positions the enterprise
  and its entrants through using particular channels for
  distributing its technology product, process or service.
- *Product quality market positioning* is based upon
  adopting a strategy that emphasises quality to achieve
  enterprise objectives.
- *Technological leadership* whereby the enterprise leads
  the technological market space in innovation. Intel
  Corporation has successfully employed this strategy in
  the microprocessor market space.
- *Vertical integration* seeks to position the enterprise by the
  extent of value added as shown in the level of forward
  and backward integration. This was the initial market
  strategy used by Apple Computer. In the horizontal
  market spaces (See Figure 4.6) existing in the 1990s in
  the computer industry this has proven more detrimental
  than advantageous.
- *Cost position market strategy* uses a low-cost position
  through investments in cost-minimizing facilities or
  processes. Over time, technological market spaces are
  driven by this strategy resulting in commoditization (See
  Figure 4.2).
- *Service market strategy* bundles ancillary services with its
  technological entrant. In this strategy the enterprise seeks
  to make their technological product, process or service
  more *total service user friendly.*
- *Price policy market strategy* positions the enterprise's
  entrant through strategically pricing. The enterprise
  might seek to price the new entrant in a manner which
  divides various segments of the offering into portions that
  encourage movement from lower to higher priced
  versions.
- *Leverage market strategy* can only be achieved by the use
  of significant financial or other resources. This form of
  market strategy is not usually available to most new
  technological enterprises.

The technological market space for a new enterprise can also be viewed in terms of a map of its structure as shown in Figure 4.7. Figure 4.7 shows a map of the computer industry market space. Each of the regions provides a technological product, process or service with varying degrees of form, substance, product, process or service.

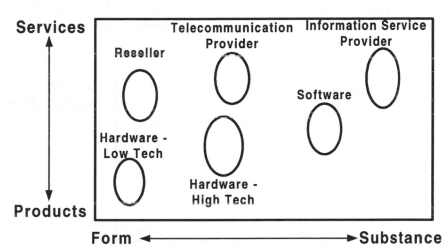

**Fig. 4.7** Computer Industry Market Space Map

## 2.2 Technological Industry Life Cycle

Industries have life cycles like all other components of this universe. It is possible that a new technological enterprise seeks to enter a market space that may be in a phase of its life cycle which will not provide a sufficient period for the enterprise to reach a stable growth position. Figure 4.8 shows this effect.

At the start of a technological industry life cycle there are a great variety of features and a large number of offerings (Steele 1989, pp. 45). As the industry matures a dominant configuration of features and attributes emerges. In the start of a technological industry, economic rent[2] is accrued to those innovations that contribute to new products and features. Each contributor seeks to become the dominant survivor. As the industry matures the innovations that stabilize the industry, as in the case of Microsoft® Corporation's Window products, contribute to the strength and market penetration of the dominant survivor. During the stabilization process improvements become important (Steele 1989, pp. 46). As maturity of the

---

[2] Profits that more than cover the opportunity cost of capital are known as *economic rents*.

industry is reached it becomes harder to introduce new technological products, processes or services with significant differentiation. As the industry ages, the market leaders may tend to feel secure in their position as IBM did in the 1960 to 1980 period. At this point, the industry may become destabilized by a totally new innovation which leads to a new industry which meets the customer needs with more functionality and at a better cost. Figure 4.9 shows this effect for the maturation of the transportation industry in the United States.

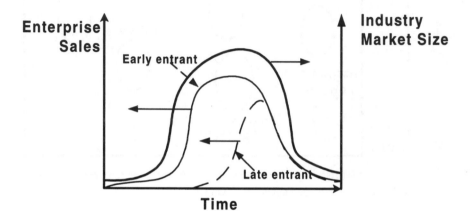

**Fig. 4.8** Interaction of Industry and Enterprise Entrant Life Cycles

## 2.3    Technological Industry Analysis

An industry can be analyzed by a number of different approaches. One method is the External Factor Evaluation ("EFE") matrix (David 1997, pp. 129). The steps in developing an EFE matrix include:

- List 10 to 20 essential external factors, including opportunities and threats, that can affect the new enterprise.
- Assign a weight to each factor from 0.0 (not important) to 1.0 (very important). The total of all factors must sum to unity (1.0). Each weight represents the relative importance of that factor in determining the success of a new enterprise in the chosen technological market space.
- Rate each factor from 1 to 4 representing how effectively the enterprise market strategy can respond to the factor:

    4 = superior

3 = above average
2 = average
1 = poor

These ratings are enterprise specific.

- Multiply each factor weight by its rating to determine the enterprise's weighted industry score. This can be done with alternative market strategies and the strategy chosen will be the one with the highest score.

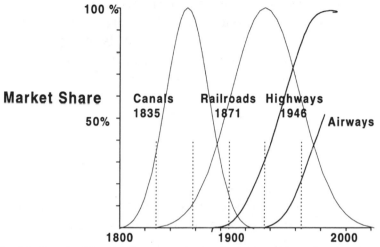

**Fig. 4.9** Growth of the U.S. Transportation Market (Adapted from Grubler 1997)

## 3. TECHNOLOGICAL COMPETITIVE ANALYSIS

### 3.1 Objectives of Competitive Analysis

An enterprise formation team should perform a detailed competitive analysis. This analysis seeks to (Pearce II and Robinson Jr. 1994, pp. 88):

- Identify existing and potential competitors in the technological market space.
- Identify existing and potential market strategies of these competitors.
- Identify effective competitive strategies for the new enterprise.

While existing competition in a technological market space may be easy to identify this might not be the case in an emerging industry or with regard to potential competitors. In developing a competitive analysis the formation team should consider a number of issues (Pearce II and Robinson Jr. 1994, pp. 88). The enterprise formation team should consider how enterprises in the chosen technological market space define the scope of their market. Similarly what are the customer derived benefits from the products, processes or services being offered. Consideration should also be given to the market commitment of existing or potential competitors since enterprises participate in markets for different reasons. A potential competitor may participate to assist its primary market and thus may not be a strong competitor in the particular market chosen by the new enterprise.

Once the competitors have been recognized, their characteristics should be defined. A competitive analysis consideration should be given to:

- Core competencies of the competitors and how they differ with those available to the enterprise formation team. It is difficult to compete in the same technological space with a core competency deficit.
- Core technologies of the competitor with advantages and disadvantages of each, compared to those that will be offered by the new entrant.
- Market strategies of the competitors, giving their strengths and weaknesses. A technological SWOT analysis of the existing and potential competitors should be performed. This analysis will allow the enterprise formation team to anticipate strategic moves of the competitors.
- A systematic identification and listing of the competitors offering features through competitive benchmarking should be performed (Betz 1993, pp. 76).

### 3.2 Components of Competitive Analysis

Figure 4.10 presents components of a competitive analysis. Figure 4.11 shows a method for evaluating the competitive technological strength and knowledge of a competitor and compared to the new enterprise.

To develop a useful technological market strategy from a competitive analysis it is important to understand the competitor's inherent factors of competitiveness that allows it to develop a strategic advantage (Wang and Guild 1997). Competitors can be analyzed by the use of a Competitive Profile Matrix ("CPM") (David 1997, pp. 130). The CPM identifies the existing and potential competitors' particular strengths and weaknesses within the technological market space. Table 4.1 shows a sample CPM analysis. This is one approach to assessing the competitive advantage of existing and potential competitors.  Various approaches are used to gain a view of the competitive space at the time when the analysis is made. However, this dynamic space requires continual update during the life of the enterprise.

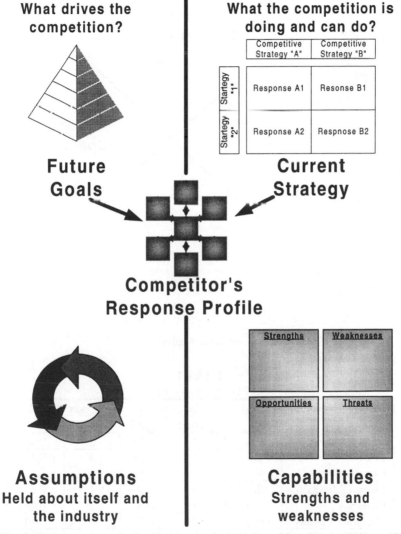

**Fig. 4.10** Components of a Competitive Analysis (Adapted from Porter 1980, pp. 49)

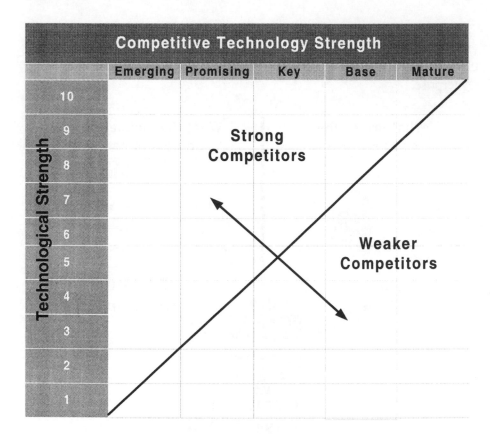

**Fig. 4.11** Technological Competitive Analysis

**Table 4.1**
CPM Competitor Analysis

| Critical Success Factors | Weight | Competitor 1 | | Competitor 2 | |
|---|---|---|---|---|---|
| | | Rating | Score | Rating | Score |
| Market Share | 0.20 | 3 | 0.60 | 2 | 0.40 |
| Price Competitiveness | 0.10 | 1 | 0.10 | 4 | 0.40 |
| Financial Position | 0.30 | 3 | 0.90 | 1 | 0.30 |
| Quality | 0.20 | 3 | 0.60 | 2 | 0.40 |
| Customer Loyalty | 0.10 | 2 | 0.20 | 4 | 0.40 |
| Technological Position | 0.10 | 4 | 0.40 | 1 | 0.10 |
| Total | 1.00 | | 2.80 | | 2.30 |

## 4. COMPETITIVE TECHNOLOGICAL ADVANTAGE

According to Kauffman (Kauffman 1995, pp. 246) all enterprises evolve and coevolve on a complex rugged, deforming, fitness landscape and face conflicting constraints. Under these general conditions, enterprises must find regions of competitive advantage to survive and grow.

### 4.1 Boston Consulting Group Matrix

A competitive advantage requires the enterprise formation team to develop total enterprise strategies, which differentiate the new technological enterprise from its competitors within the market space. The Boston Consulting Group ("BCG") uses a two-dimensional matrix approach to competitive advantage. The growth/market share matrix (See Figure 4.12) developed by BCG is used in developing an enterprise's competitive advantage position. The new enterprise position will be located in one of the four cells and each cell has a different strategic implication. The four sectors of the matrix shown in Figure 4.12 have been labeled:

- *Star* – High Growth/High Competitive Position: This position is the end point of any new technological enterprise since it represents the best long-term opportunities to achieve growth and profitability.
- *Cash Cow* – Low Growth/High Competitive Position: This sector presents enterprises with high market share in low growth market space.
- *Dog* – Low Growth/Low Competitive Position: This is the sector that should be avoided by a new technological enterprise. In this sector, the enterprise will find itself in a mature market space with a high level of competition and low profit margins. This market space is characterized by commoditization of a technology, i.e., PC hardware market in the late 1990s.
- *Question Mark* – High Growth/Low Competitive Position: In this market space, the new enterprise will be attracted to the high growth rate. However, due to low market share, the enterprise will have uncertain market potential. In most instances, many new technological entrepreneurs will find their enterprise in this quadrant. This quadrant is one that most *Netpreneurs* will face. Each enterprise hopes to move from the *Question Mark*

174

quadrant to the *Star* quadrant. To achieve this movement, the enterprise formation team will have to seek significant competitive advantage using innovative market strategies.

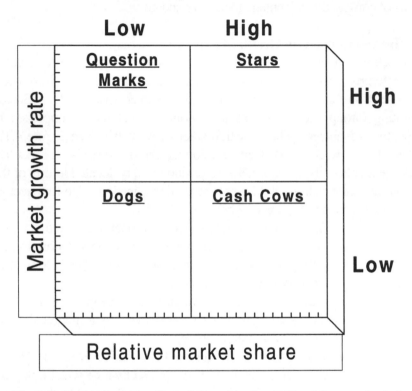

**Fig. 4.12** Boston Consulting Group Approach to Competitive Advantage Analysis

## 4.2 Competitive Advantage Impact Analysis

While the initial BCG approach is useful, it is simplistic since it assumes that high market share leads to high volume which in turn leads to lower unit cost and higher profitability. The BCG later developed a more realistic approach using two variables, the size of the enterprise's competitive advantage and the number of ways that it can be achieved. There is an underlying relationship between return-on-investment ("ROI") and market share as represented in the revised BCG matrix (Pearce II and Robinson Jr. 1994, pp. 273). Figure 4.13 shows the revised BCG matrix based upon competitive advantage.

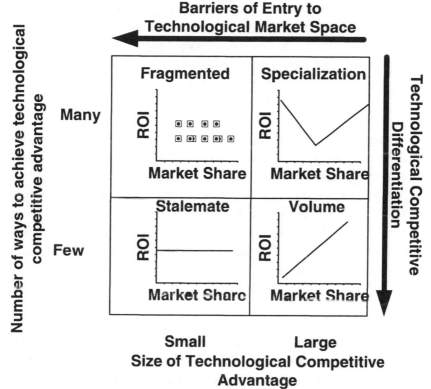

**Fig. 4.13** Impact of Competitive Advantage (Adapted from Pearce II and Robinson Jr., pp. 273)

The sectors shown in Figure 4.13 represent:

- *Fragmented* – Depending on how a new enterprise exploits the very many ways in which it can have a competitive advantage. This condition exists since the market space is fragmented.
- *Specialization* – This is the most attractive quadrant of this matrix. In this quadrant, the new technological enterprise can differentiate itself by being very focused. This sector allows new entrepreneurial enterprises to achieve profitability with small market share.
- *Stalemate* – This market space is low and has no relationship to the market share. New enterprises would find this a poor choice to enter since the investment community would not find this an attractive investment region.

- *Volume* – This market space represents market-share leadership and cost reduction strategies. This is also a difficult market space for a new technological entrepreneurial enterprise to enter since significant investment would be required to achieve large market shares and a significant competitive advantage.

## 4.3    Competitive Advantage Factors

To achieve a competitive advantage, a new enterprise can focus on a number of factors, including:

- *Application* – Meeting an unmet need by use of a proprietary technology.
- *Ease of Use* – User friendly application or device which fulfils a function that before the introduction of the new entrant had been difficult to fulfil. This was the case when the graphical user interface ("GUI") was introduced into the PC market and provided the early growth and success of Apple Computer.
- *High and Consistent Quality* – Achieving competitive advantage by delivering a new technological product, process or service at significantly higher quality standards than competitors and still maintaining a competitive price position.
- *Flexibility* – Delivering the new product, processes or services to meet individual customer needs. This has been one of the main competitive advantages of Dell Computer Corporation.
- *Service* – Providing a rapid and consistently high level of service.
- *Integration* – Providing a new technological product, process or service, which can be backward compatible with existing systems and yet provide increased levels of productivity.
- *Price* – Providing a new market space entrant which delivers increased productivity at lower prices than the products available from competitors.

A new technological enterprise may exploit many of these competitive advantages to place it in or near to the specialization quadrant of the matrix.

## 4.4   First Mover Competitive Advantage

An enterprise which first produces a new product, uses a new process, enters a new market, or provides a new service, may accrue a long-term competitive advantage (Kerin, Varadararajan, and Peterson 1993). These *first movers* have higher market shares than early followers, who in turn have higher market shares than later entrants. However, just getting there first is not the entire answer, since it is not sufficient to achieve cost and product advantages over rivals that result in maximizing market share and accruing large economic rents. To maximize the advantage of *first movers* or *market pioneering*, enterprises must possess certain competencies and capabilities, which include technological foresight, perceptive market research, skillful product and process development capabilities, and marketing acumen.

Some firms are successful leaders or *first movers* while others do better as followers. This *market pioneering* only provides opportunities: it is not the only factor in achieving market dominance. Unless an enterprise has expertise, resources, and creativity to exploit these opportunities, it will be unable to achieve dominance and produce sustainable competitive advantage. In some instances, organizations have the creativity, but lack the expertise or resources to achieve the competitive advantage. Other firms might have the internal resources, but lack the expertise needed to become the *market pioneer*. These latter enterprises might decide to acquire a successful early entrant, which does not have sustainable resources to capitalize on its *first mover* advantage. Figure 4.14 presents a model of the first mover advantage.

While achieving a competitive advantage will be an all-consuming occupation of the enterprise formation team, sustainability will be one of the principal focuses of the new enterprise's leadership team. A model of how the Japanese technological enterprises sustain competitive advantage is shown in Figure 4.15. While this model may not be totally suitable for a new technological enterprise, it offers some insights into the process. The shaded sections are those that can facilitate competitive advantages for a new technological enterprise.

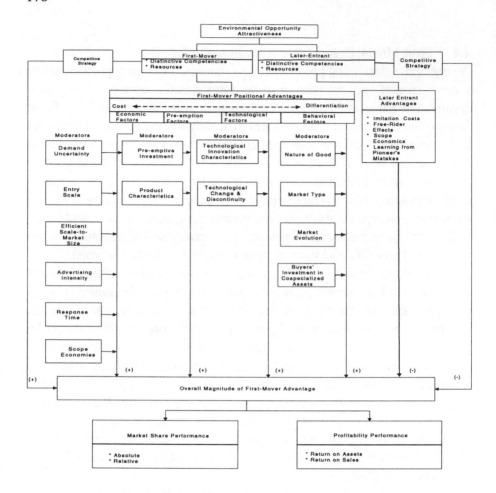

**Fig. 4.14** First Mover Advantage Model (Kerin, Varadararajan, and Peterson 1993. 1993, © 1993 IEEE. Reprinted by permission)

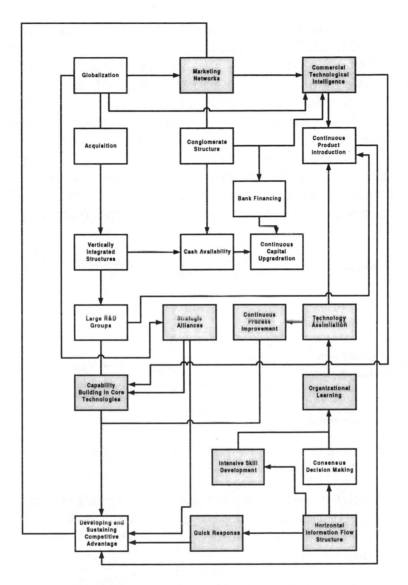

**Fig. 4.15** Model of Japanese Competitive Advantage Sustainability – Shaded Sectors for
New Technological Enterprise (Bowonder and Miyake 1993. 1993, © 1993
IEEE. Reprinted by permission)

## 5. TECHNOLOGICAL MARKET STRATEGY

Once the market space has been fully defined and the potential position of
the new enterprise determined, the final step in the process of technological
planning is the designing of the technological market strategy. There are a

180

number of methods that have been developed for creating market strategies (David 1997; Hood 1991). While each model was developed in developing an overall grand business strategy, they are applicable at the technological market strategy level. The market strategy links with the technological strategy to form the basis for the overall business strategy for the new enterprise before its formation. As the enterprise is established and starts to grow and mature, more strategic elements are added to the overall business strategy. While models for formulating the market strategy are numerous, each offers a slightly different perspective for viewing the reality of the technological market space that the new enterprise will enter. The formulation of the market strategy is a process as shown in Figure 4.16.

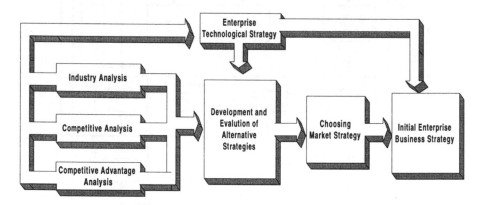

**Fig. 4.16** Interaction of Technological and Market Strategy to Form Initial Enterprise Business Strategy

The interactive model shown in Figure 4.16 represents the melding of both the technological and market strategies to form the initial business strategy, which will be used to establish the new technological entrepreneurial enterprise.

## 5.1 Technological Market Strategy Models

The function of the development and evaluation of alternative market strategies is a process of matching various aspects of the technological market space attributes. This matching process can use any or all of the developed strategy models to arrive at a market enterprise strategy which when combined with the technological strategy results in the formative strategy for the enterprise. Some of the strategy models or tools include (David 1997; Hood 1991):

- *SWOT Domain* – (See Chapter 3 –Technological and Enterprise Strategic Planning).
- *TOWS Matrix* – Extension of the SWOT model (David 1997, pp. 180) which defines the threats ("T"), opportunities ("O"), weaknesses ("W") and strengths ("S") to form a strategic matrix. This matrix is used to develop four types of strategy, each corresponding to the four quadrants of the model. These strategies can be characterized as:
  - *ST* – Using enterprise strengths to avoid or reduce external threats.
  - *WT* – Defensive strategy used to reduce internal weaknesses and avoid external threats.
  - *SO* – Use strengths to take advantage of opportunities.
  - *WO* – Overcome weaknesses by taking advantage of opportunities.

## 5.2   TOWS and QSPM Models

Figure 4.17 presents the *TOWS* matrix that should be developed for formation of a technological market strategy.

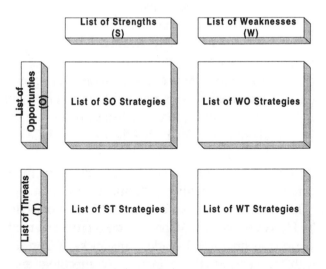

**Fig. 4.17** TOWS Matrix for Technological Market Strategies (Adapted from David 1997, pp. 182)

The TOWS matrix shown in Figure 4.17 is used to generate feasible alternative strategies. The generation of feasible technological market strategies can be accomplished using a number of analytical tools. There are many analytical tools for determining which are feasible market strategies (David 1997; Hood 1991). One of these techniques is the quantitative strategic planning matrix ("QSPM") (David 1997, pp. 193-196) . This technique uses weighting factors for each of the essential external and internal factors that influence the strategies. The process presented by David (David 1997, pp. 194) consists of:

- Listing essential external opportunities/threats and internal strengths/weaknesses for the new enterprise.
- Assigning weights to each external and internal critical success factors.
- Identifying alternative technological market strategies that the new enterprise should consider.
- Determining the *Attractiveness Score* for each alternative strategy. This is achieved by examining each alternative against each of the external and internal critical factors, determining if it affects the choice of the strategies. If the factor influences the choice then it is assigned a value of:
    - 1 = not attractive
    - 2 = somewhat attractive
    - 3 = reasonably attractive
    - 4 = highly attractive
- The total attractiveness score for each strategy is computed. This score is determined by multiplying each attractiveness score and then summing the scores for each alternative. The higher the total score the more attractive the strategy.

While the QSPM provides a quantitative measure of the strategy, this measure is derived from intuitive judgements and assumptions of the evaluators. This analysis can provide, if not performed objectively, a highly biased result. However, the QSPM process does provide a methodology for examining various technological market strategies. When this method is combined with the analysis of the industry, competitors and competitive analysis of the new enterprise, it can give a good indication of a technological market strategy that can prove successful.

It must be remembered that a technological market strategy is like a military battle plan, i.e., the first strike may be desirable but it cannot be successful without careful preparation for the attack, counterattack, penetration and consolidation to achieve lasting success.

## REFERENCES

Agmon, Tamir, and Mary Ann Von Glinow. 1991. *Technology Transfer in International Business*. New York, NY: Oxford University Press.

Bell, C. Gordon, and John E. McNamara. 1991. *High-Tech Ventures: The Guide for Entrepreneurial Success*. Reading, MA: Addison-Wesley Publishing Company, Inc.

Betz, Frederick. 1993. *Strategic Technology Management*. Edited by M. K. Badawy, *McGraw-Hill Engineering and Technology Management*. New York, NY: McGraw-Hill, Inc.

Bowonder, B., and T. Miyake. 1993. Japanese Technological Innovation Strategy: Recent Trends. *IEEE Engineering Management Review* 21 (2):38-48.

David, Fred R. 1997. *Strategic Management*. Upper Saddle River, NJ: Prentice-Hall.

Drucker, Peter F. 1985. *Innovation and Entrepreneurship: Practice and Principles*. New York, NY: Harper and Row, Publishers.

Fakey, Liam, and Robert M. Randall. 1994. *The Portable MDA in Strategy*. New York, NY: John Wiley & Sons, Inc.

Grove, Andrew S. 1996. *Only the Paranoid Survive: How to Exploit the Crisis Points that Challenge Every Company and Career*. New York, NY: Currency Doubleday.

Grubler, Arnulf. 1997. Time for a Change on the Patterns of Diffusion of Innovation. *IEEE Engineering Review* 25 (2):96-105.

Hamel, Gary, and C. K. Prahalad. 1994. *Competing for the Future*. Boston, MA: Harvard Business School Press.

Hisrick, Robert D., and Michael P. Peters. 1995. *Entrepreneurship: Starting, Developing, and Managing a New Enterprise*. Chicago, IL: Irwin.

Hood, David D. 1991. The Link Between Business Strategy and Technological Development. Paper read at Portland International Conference on Management of Engineering and Technology, at Portland, OR.

Kauffman, Stuart. 1995. *At Home in the Universe: The Search for Laws of Self-Organization and Complexity*. New York, NY: Oxford University Press.

Kendall, David L., and Michael T. French. 1993. Forecasting the Potential for New Industrial Products. *IEEE Engineering Management Review* 21 (4):40-44.

Kerin, R. A., P.R. Varadararajan, and R. A. Peterson. 1993. First-Mover Advantage - A Synthesis, Conceptual Framework and Research Proposition. *IEEE Engineering Management Review* 21 (Winter):19-33.

Martino, Joseph P. 1993. *Technological Forecasting for Decision Making*. Edited by M. K. Badawy. Third ed, *McGraw-Hill Engineering and Technology Management*. New York, NY: McGraw-Hill, Inc.

Pearce II, John A., and Richard B. Robinson Jr. 1994. *Formulation, Implementation and Control of Competitive Strategy*. Fifth ed. Burr Ridge, IL: Irwin.

Porter, Michael E. 1979. How Competitive Forces Shape Strategy. *Harvard Business Review*, 79/3-4, 137-145.

184

Porter, Michael E. 1980. *Competitive Strategy: Techniques for Analyzing Industries and Competition.* New York, NY: The Free Press.

Rangan, V. Kasturi, and George T. Bowman. 1994. Beating the Commodity Magnet. *IEEE Engineering Management Review* 22 (1):32-38.

Roberts, Edward B. 1991. *Entrepreneurs in High Technology: Lessons from MIT and Beyond.* New York, NY: Oxford University Press.

Steele, Lowell W. 1989. *Managing Technology: The Strategic View.* Edited by M. K. Bradawy, *McGraw-Hill Engineering and Technology Management.* New York, NY: McGraw-Hill Books Company.

von Hipple, Eric. 1988. *The Sources of Innovation.* New York, Ny: Oxford University Press.

Wang, Clement K., and Paul Guild. 1997. Competitive Analysis Further Upstream: Shifting the Forces of Analysis of a Japanese Multinational. Paper read at Sixth International Conference on Management of Technology, 97/6/25-28, at Goteborg, Sweden.

## DISCUSSION QUESTIONS

1. Perform and discuss an industry analysis using the concepts presented in this chapter for the following technological industries:
   - Microprocessor industry in the early 1980s and the 1990s.
   - Telecommunication industry in the 1980s and 1990s.
   - Internet service provider ("ISP") industry.
2. Prepare and discuss a competitive analysis of the Internet market space for:
   - Internet browsers in 1993 and in 1999.
   - Development tools.
3. Assume a new technological entrepreneurial enterprise is to be formed to enter the local telecommunication market space in the late 1990s. Prepare industry and competitive analyses assuming the market nitch being entered is voice and data services for small and medium sized enterprises. Decide if the wireless or high-speed access provided by digital subscriber lines ("DSL") is the technology which could be employed to gain significant market share.
4. Assume a new Netpreneur enterprise is being planned. Discuss the competitive advantages it must have to succeed. Justify your analysis based on data about the industry and potential competitors.
5. Compare and discuss the market strategies used by:
   - Microsoft®Corporation and Netscape Corporation.
   - Dell Computer, Compaq Corporation and Apple Computer.
   - Yahoo! and Infoseek.

185

6. Internet vertical portals are moving into an e-commerce primarily business-to-business ("B2B") model. Perform a competitive analysis of several of these portals.
7. Develop a competitive analysis for a technology of your choice. Use the various techniques presented in this chapter to perform the competitive analysis. Discuss in detail how each of the competitive analysis techniques in the analysis differs in term of the analysis results.
8. The globalization of technological enterprises requires market planning to be done on a broader scale than before. Discuss in detail how you would perform a strategic market planning project for an enterprise planning to enter the global market space.

CHAPTER 5

# Enterprise Formation

*"We shape our buildings: thereafter they shape us."*
**Sir Winston Churchill**
(1874–1965)

## 1.   INTRODUCTION

Enterprise structure is the formal configuration, procedures, governance and control mechanisms, and the requisite authority and decision-making process.  The enterprise structure provides direction for what is done by the enterprise and the mechanism to implement business strategies.  The enterprise formation team should have a firm concept of how it will structure the new technological enterprise and what resources it will require.   The enterprise structure chosen is a function of the strategy which the leadership team has chosen (See Chapter 3 - Technological and Enterprise Strategic Planning and Chapter 4 - Enterprise Technological Market Planning) (Pearce II and Robinson Jr. 1994, pp. 348).   All enterprises require structure to implement their strategies (Hitt, Ireland, and Hoskisson 1997, pp. 347).  The common strategy-structure sequence consists of:

- Development of enterprise strategy.
- Development of enterprise structure to meet strategic needs.
- Effective execution of strategy to achieve enterprise goals.

The success of the technological and market strategy depends upon the enterprise structure that serves as the vehicle for its implementation (Pearce II and Robinson Jr. 1991, pp.327).   Many enterprises are structured around functional units, having well-defined management hierarchies. An enterprise structured by functional units does have the advantages of clear responsibilities, activities associated with a function, and management communication channels (Juran and Gryna 1993, pp. 141).  However, while this structural concept worked well in the past, technological entrepreneurial enterprises face challenges from the rapidly evolving technological market space that may require a different construct. Functional structures can create serious communication barriers that can result in reduced enterprise flexibility. The technological enterprise environment is dynamic and unpredictable, requiring enterprises that are readily adaptable to rapidly evolving conditions, possessing a high degree of flexibility and responsiveness. Developing a flexible enterprise structure is critical for an entrepreneurial technological enterprise. Flexibility is multidimensional and requires agility and versatility, innovation and novelty; it must be robust and resilient (Bahrami 1993). This leads to stability, sustainable competitive advantage and capabilities that can evolve over time. This will require enterprises, if they are to succeed, to consist of temporary structures that are problem specific with multifunctional teams (Thamhain 1992, pp. 28).

Figure 5.1, known as the McKinsey[1] Framework (Peters and Waterman Jr. 1992, pp. 11), provides a method for identifying enterprises with superior performance. The starting point for enterprise structural development is the development of enterprise strategy. The strategy serves as the initiation point. The enterprise formation team should focus on the following enterprise elements:

- Structure.
- Systems.
- Shared values - culture.
- Skills - resources.
- Style - leadership.
- Staff - management and resources.

Like technology, enterprise structure can be seen as the outcome of interactions between the processes of invention, production and market insertion (Scarbrough and Corbett 1992, pp. 12). Figure 5.2 illustrates the relationship between enterprise structure and technology.

---

[1] McKinsey and Company is a multinational consultancy.

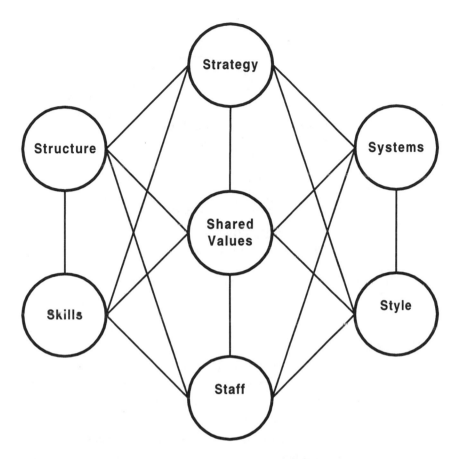

**Fig. 5.1** McKinsey Enterprise Framework (Adapted from Peters and Waterman Jr. 1992, pp. 11)

When a technological involvement is pervasive, the interaction between technological and enterprise knowledge will have significant implications for the strategic design of the enterprise and the technology (Scarbrough and Corbett 1992, pp. 13).

Technological enterprises by definition are knowledge-based enterprises. There are three requirements for knowledge-based innovation enterprises (Drucker 1985, pp. 115-119):

- Knowledge-based innovation enterprises require analysis of all the necessary factors.
- Clean focus on the strategic position including market space.
- Entrepreneurial management structure.

190

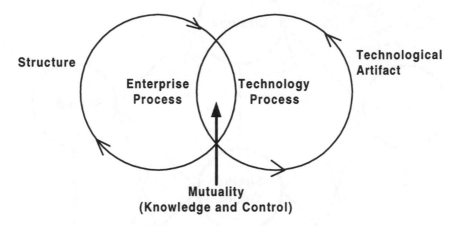

**Fig. 5.2** Technology and Enterprise Relationship (Adapted from Scarbrough and Corbett 1992, pp. 13)

The entrepreneurial structure chosen should be able to pass the following *gates* (Batz 1990, pp. 27):

- Provides early entry into technological market space.
- Provides low-risk entry into technological market space.
- Builds on entrepreneurial formation team strengths.
- Provides a growth path.
- Makes maximum use of other resources in the environment.
- Provides built-in hedges against failure, i.e., flexibility.
- Results in an enterprise that the entrepreneurial formation team envisioned.
- Provides access to capital that otherwise might not be available.
- Consistent with individual goals of the entrepreneurial formation team.

## 1.1   Historical Perspective

Enterprises have been formed throughout history. Romans before the beginning of the Common Era formed enterprises to exploit labor and resources. However, the modern form of enterprises can be traced to the Mediterranean revival in the ninth and tenth centuries (Braudel 1979, pp. 434). One of the first types of modern entrepreneurial enterprises was the *societas maris* or maritime enterprise. This was also called *societas vera* or *true* firm. The enterprise consisted of one partner that stayed on shore and one who traveled with a trading ship. Later, new forms of enterprises were developed due to the problem of liability and whether this liability should be total or limited (Braudel 1979, pp.438). These early enterprises took the form of limited partnerships or joint stock companies.

One of the first solutions to emerge to deal with liability issues was the *commandite* or limited partnership agreement. This agreement differentiated between the liability of the enterprise's directors from that of the investors who solely risked their capital (Braudel 1979, pp. 438). These limited partnerships were a combination of both individuals and capital.

The concept of joint stock companies emerged in sixteenth century France. Joint stock companies issued shares that were not only transferable but also were negotiable on the open market. The first recorded English joint stock company was the Muscovy Company established between 1553 and 1555. In 1607, the Muscovy Company, under the direction of Sir Dudley Diggs who was also a member of the Virginia Company of London, sent one of their three ships with Captain John Smith to establish at Jamestown the first English colony in the Colony of Virginia, a truly entrepreneurial venture. From these early beginnings can be traced many of the entrepreneurial enterprises that now inhabit the market landscape.

## 1.2 Evolutionary Perspective

Enterprises and the market spaces that they inhabit evolve. Kauffman (Kauffman 1995, pp. 188) views enterprises as *evolving organisms* which explore *landscapes*, i.e., market space. Growth and evolution in enterprise structure is no different from the growth and development all organisms experience if they survive beyond *infancy*. Individual organisms, be they microorganisms, human beings or enterprises evolve in structure from conception through to death. We should view technological enterprises in a similar light. A flexible enterprise that is basically self-organizing is a prerequisite for evolvability, resulting in an enterprise that is more likely to survive and grow in a highly competitive market landscape. Enterprise structures that evolve, are robust and have redundancy, i.e., can meet multiple challenges. According to Kauffman (Kauffman 1995, pp. 246):

> *"Organisms, artifacts and organizations are all evolved structures."*

Enterprise structures must change when they do not enable the enterprise to implement its strategies successfully.

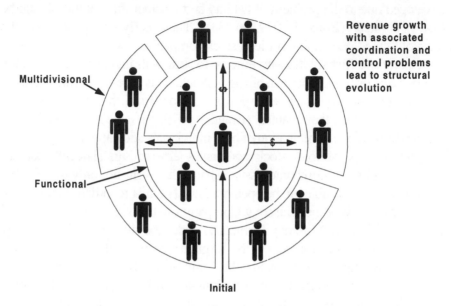

**Fig. 5.3** Pattern of Enterprise Growth (Adapted from Hitt, Ireland, and Hoskisson 1997, pp. 348)

Figure 5.3 shows a simple pattern of how enterprise structure evolves as it grows (Hitt, Ireland, and Hoskisson 1997, pp. 348). In this model, the initial or core structure of the enterprise is driven by revenue growth that usually entails coordination and control problems that the simple core structure cannot fully address. In many instances, the enterprise evolves its initial structure into a functional structure that can address the problems arising from revenue growth. As the enterprise continues to grow, the limited ability of the enterprise leadership team to process increasing information flow and increasing diversification may result in the enterprise moving from a functional framework to a multidivisional structure. However, this general model does not give a roadmap for all new technological enterprises as they grow (See Chapter 7 - Strategic Enterprise Growth) (Hitt, Ireland, and Hoskisson 1997, pp. 348).

Roberts (Roberts 1991, pp. 165) has presented a model of the early evolution of technological enterprises. This evolution is based on three concepts:

- Technological enterprises are initially based on either the sale of products, processes, repetitive services or technical consulting and contract services. Most technological enterprises evolve toward a purely product, process or repetitive service focus.
- Technological entrepreneurs are initially focused on engineering and technology, not sales and marketing. This focus must evolve toward marketing if the enterprise is to survive.
- Enterprises established by entrepreneurial teams generally evolve more rapidly than those established by an entrepreneurial individual and are focused equally on technological artifacts and sales and marketing.

## 2. LEGAL STRUCTURE

There are various legal forms that an entrepreneurial technological enterprise can take to enter the technological market space. These forms include:

- Sole proprietorship.
- Partnerships - General and Limited.
- Regular corporation ("C-Corp").
- Subchapter *S*-corporation ("S-Corp").
- Limited liability company ("LLC").

Each of these legal forms has positive and negative factors associated with ownership, taxation and liability. Before choosing which legal form the new technological enterprise should take, the enterprise formation team should consider (Cooper 1994, pp. 5):

- Tax rate.
- Liability protection.
- Allocation of tax items.
- Contribution and distribution of property.
- Existence of losses.
- Tax year.
- Limitations on ownership.
- Financial needs.
- Potential for mergers and acquisition.
- Likelihood of joint ventures.
- Compensation of entrepreneurs and employees.
- Employment taxes.

- Estate planning needs.
- State tax treatment.

These issues require consideration from both legal and financial aspects. Table 5.1 shows differences between the various legal forms of enterprise.

## 2.1 Sole Proprietorship

The earliest form of enterprise is sole proprietorship wherein ownership and operation are controlled by a single entrepreneur. The individual entrepreneur is personally liable for the obligations of the enterprise and usually any debt incurred. In this form of enterprise the entrepreneur does not create a new legal entity and usually is only required to obtain local licenses and business identification numbers. There are few legal or tax formalities when the entrepreneur creates this form of enterprise, a definite advantage.

The advantages of a sole proprietorship include that it has simplicity, it is not necessary to create a separate legal entity, legal and accounting costs are minimized and the entrepreneur has total control over the enterprise. The disadvantages of a sole proprietorship include risking the entrepreneur's personal assets due to the individual's total financial and legal liability. This can be partially offset by acquiring general liability insurance (Cooper 1994, pp. 18). The entrepreneur also has higher income tax liability as the enterprise grows, since other enterprise forms may offer certain tax advantages.

## 2.2 Partnership

Partnerships are the next step in the evolutionary process from a sole proprietorship and are a legal form of enterprise formation that results when two or more individuals form an enterprise. A partnership is not taxed as a legal entity. The tax liability flow to the individual partners depends on the type of partnership. There are two basic forms of partnership:

- General.
- Limited.

**Table 5.1**
Characteristics of Enterprise Legal Forms

| Factors | Proprietorship | Partnership | | Corporation | | Limited Liability Company |
|---|---|---|---|---|---|---|
| | | General | Limited | C-Corp | S-Corp | |
| **Ownership** | Individual | No limitation on number of partners | | No limitation on number of stockholders | Limited to 35 non foreign individual shareholders | No limitation on number of members |
| **Cost of establishing enterprise** | Filing fee for trade name | Legal partnering agreement, filing for trade name. Legal costs: function of complexity of agreement | | Created only by statute - articles of incorporation, filing fees and taxes | | Filing articles of organization |
| **Continuity of enterprise** | Death of owner | Death or withdrawal of one partners unless otherwise specified | Death or withdrawal of general partner | Only limited by financial viability | | 30 years, members die, bankruptcy or agreement to dissolve |
| **Transferability of interest** | Complete freedom to sell or transfer | General partner requires approval of all other general partners | General partner requires approval of all other general partners, limited partners can sell interest - no approval required | Most flexible, shareholders can sell or buy stock at will provided stock is not specifically restricted | Stock can only be sold to an individual | Flexible within IRS and State tax code restrictions |
| **Capital requirements** | Capital raised through personal assets or loans | Loans or new partner contributions require change in partnership agreement | | New capital raised by sale of stock, bonds or debt | | Flexible, property or cash |
| **Management control** | Owner is the chief decision maker | All parties share control equally | Only general partners have control | Majority shareholders have control, day to day control in management hands | | Members share control or appoint manager |
| **Distribution of profits** | Owner receives profits and bears losses | Depends on partnership agreement and investment | | Shareholders through dividends | | Ability to make special allocations of income, gains, losses, deductions and credit |
| **Attractiveness for raising capital** | Depends on capability of owner and business factors | Depends on general partners | | Attractiveness of investment opportunity | | Member's contribution of property is tax-free and no gain recognized because liabilities assumed |
| **Liability** | Unlimited personal liability | Joint and severally unlimited personal liability | General partners joint and severally unlimited personal liability; limited partners only to extent of investment | Amount of capital contributed | | Amount of capital contributed |
| **Taxation** | Not a separate taxable entity | Not a separate taxable entity | Not a separate taxable entity | Separate taxable entity | Shareholders taxed on the basis of ownership | Not a separate taxable entity if properly structured |

(Cooper 1994, pp. 64-65; Hisrick and Peters 1995, pp. 182-183; Mandel 1997)

The following conditions may be beneficial for the formation of a partnership (Cooper 1994, pp. 20):

- Personal liability not a significant factor.
- Simplicity and flexibility important.
- Offset partners other income by any enterprise losses.
- All profits distributed to partners.
- Special allocation of profits, losses and other tax items is desirable.

A partnership is, since it is a proprietorship, composed of two or more entrepreneurs and investors.

The advantages of partnerships include (Cooper 1994, pp. 26):

- No double taxation on distributions.
- Unlimited number and type of partners.
- Special allocation of income and losses.
- Operating and capital losses are passed through to the partners.
- Enterprise-level debt maximizes the use of losses.
- No accumulated earnings taxation.
- Unlimited investment income with no personal holding company tax.
- Tax-exempt income retains its character when passed through the partners.

The disadvantages for partnerships are similar to those of a sole proprietorship for the general partners.

## 2.2.1 General Partnership

A general partnership is usually established by a formalized partnership agreement. While there is no legal requirement for a formalized agreement, in general, a legal agreement will delineate the responsibilities and other factors relating to each partner. In general the partnership must register with the state and obtain appropriate operating licenses. The U.S. Internal Revenue Service ("IRS") tax liability treats liability as flowing to the individual partners who are also personally liable for all partnership liabilities. Therefore, each general partner has not only personal capital contributions at risk, but also personal assets that are subject to the partnership's liabilities.

## 2.2.2 Limited Partnership

A limited partnership differs from a general partnership in that it must have at least one general partner with the remaining being limited partners. Limited partners are liable only to the extent of their investment and most recent distributions of assets. The general partners are held totally liable as in the case of a general partnership. The limited partners are merely the investors while the general partners are the entrepreneurs.

A limited partnership is formed by the filing of a limited partnership agreement in the state in which the enterprise is organized. This usually requires the limited partnership to pay state filing fees to obtain articles of limited partnership. In addition, state and local licensing requirements must be met by the limited partnership.

## 2.3  Corporation

Most new technological entrepreneurial enterprises are formed as corporations. There are two basic forms of corporations:
* Regular or *C*-Corporations ("C-Corp").
* Subchapter S or *S*-Corporations ("S-Corp").

The corporation form of an enterprise is a separate legal entity that is established under the laws of each state and has a legal existence separate from the entrepreneurs and investors. To establish a corporation the entrepreneurs usually serve as the incorporators, file an application, and pay a fee to the state in which the enterprise will be incorporated.

One of the primary benefits of a corporate structure is limited personal liability for debts or actions of the corporation or its employees. The investors or shareholders are only liable to the extent of their investments. An enterprise established as a corporation is recognized by the IRS as a separate tax entity; therefore it can take advantage of many tax deductions and expenses that are not readily available to either sole proprietorships or partnerships. However, the profits of the enterprise are taxed as income to the corporation and dividends are issued as income to the stockholders for regular corporations. The problem of double taxation can sometimes be avoided by distributing the corporation's income to the entrepreneurs in the form of salaries and other benefits that then appear as enterprise expenses. This can be accomplished if there are no outside investors or if all stockholders are employees. In actual practice, most new technological enterprises do not distribute income to entrepreneurs beyond approved bonuses and normal remuneration, but re-invest that income to grow the enterprise.

### 2.3.1  *C* - Corporation
The usual corporate form of a new technological enterprise is a regular corporation of C-Corp.  The most significant aspects of a C-Corp are:
- Limited liability.
- Double taxation on earnings if distributed to shareholders.

Corporations must observe a number of legal formalities that include:
- Board of Directors.
- Annual shareholder meetings.
- Maintenance of corporate records and minutes of meetings of the Board of Directors.
- Shareholder approval of major corporate decisions.

Regular corporations have a great deal of flexibility.  This flexibility includes (Cooper 1994, pp. 44):
- Raise capital through the issuance of additional stock.
- Make a public offering (See Chapter 8 - Next Entrepreneurial Step).
- Dispose corporate assets.
- Form subsidiary corporate entities.
- Merge with other entities.
- Sell the enterprise.
- Issue incentive stock options to motivate employees.

The principal advantages of a regular corporation include:
- Limited liability.
- Ease of transferability of ownership.
- Tax treatment of fringe benefits.
- Employee stock ownership participation.
- Flexible tax year options.
- Unlimited number and type of shareholders.
- Special tax treatment based on industry, ownership and existing tax code.

The principal disadvantages of a regular corporation include:
- Double taxation on distributed income.
- Tax issues related to accumulated earnings and types of income depending on the existing tax code.

## 2.3.2  S - Corporation

The form of enterprise known as a Subchapter $S$ or $S$ -Corporation combines the advantages of partnership and a regular corporation. An $S$ - Corporation is a small business enterprise that under law elects special tax status. The income of the enterprise is passed through to the shareholders on a pro-rata basis. The U.S. Federal Tax Code provides the basic benefits for this type of enterprise. Not all states recognize the pass-through nature of $S$ - Corporations. An $S$ - Corporation is required to follow the same legal formalities as a regular corporation, including articles of incorporation, directors and shareholder meetings, corporate minutes and shareholder voting on major corporate decisions.

There are certain conditions that an enterprise must meet to qualify for status as an $S$ - Corporation (Hisrick and Peters 1995, pp. 191):

- Must be a domestic U.S. corporation, i.e., cannot have any shareholders who are not U.S. citizens.
- Cannot be a subsidiary of another corporation.
- Can only have one class of stock.
- Can not have more than 35 shareholders.
- Shareholders must be individuals, estates or certain types of trusts.
- All shareholders must elect to have the corporation formed as an $S$ - Corporation.

Both new and existing corporations may elect a subchapter $S$ status provided they meet the noted criteria.

An $S$-Corporation form of enterprise has certain advantages and disadvantages over other forms of enterprise formation. The advantages include:

- Limited liability protection of a regular or $C$ - Corporation.
- Not subject to certain taxes, depending on existing tax code, such as a minimum tax that a $C$ - Corporation might have to incur.
- Capital gain or losses are treated as personal income or losses on a pro-rata basis.
- Shares of the enterprise can have either voting or non-voting status.

- Corporate long-term capital gain or losses are directly deductible by the individual shareholders on a pro-rata basis.
- Ease of transfer of ownership similar to regular corporations.
- Continuity of the life of the enterprise similar to regular corporations.
- No accumulated earnings tax.
- Tax-exempt income retains its character when passed through to shareholders.
- Possibly, lower state taxes if provided for by statute.
- Tax-free mergers similar to a regular corporation.

The disadvantages for an $S$ - Corporation include:

- Stringent requirements to qualify as an $S$ - Corporation.
- Most fringe benefits are not tax deductible.
- Must use the calendar year for accounting purposes.
- Only one class of stock permitted.
- Net loss is limited to shareholder's stock plus loans to the business.

## 2.4 Limited Liability Company

One of the newest forms of enterprise structures available to technological entrepreneurs is the limited liability company ("LLC"). LLC is a hybrid legal entity that combines the various aspects of partnerships and corporations. An LLC offers advantages similar to those of the $S$ - Corporation but with more liberal tax rules under the Subchapter K of the U.S. Tax Code (Hisrick and Peters 1995, pp. 193). LLCs are generally treated as partnerships if they lack at least two of the four standard characteristics of a corporation (Cooper 1994, pp. 27). An LLC has members versus shareholders for a corporation and partners for a partnership. In an LLC no shares of stock are issued, and each member owns an interest in the enterprise as designated by the articles of organization. It takes unanimous written consent of the members for any member to transfer their interest. The life of an LLC is usually 30 years, however, the enterprise can be dissolved when one of the members dies, the enterprise files for bankruptcy or all the members choose to dissolve the enterprise.

Under most state laws, LLCs are usually treated as separate legal entities and require filing articles of organization. Members in an LLC have limited liability for enterprise debts and obligations, and generally are limited with respect to tort[2] liability. Depending on state laws, members may be liable for personal negligence or misconduct. The liability, if properly organized, does not extend beyond the capital contribution of the members. However, if an LLC is improperly organized, the individual members risk being jointly and severally liable for LLC obligations (Cooper 1994, pp. 28).

Members of the LLC and its management are usually taxed similarly to an *S*-Corporation without the need to conform to *S*-Corporation restrictions. The LLC structure for a new technological enterprise may be attractive for those entrepreneurs conducting high-risk research or marketing new technological products, processes or services. LLCs permit pass-through of initial losses and research expenses and the use of preferred equity interests, compensation of employees with special ownership interests and strategic joint ventures.

The advantages of an LLC include:
- No double taxation on distributed income.
- Limited liability.
- Unlimited number and type of members.
- Special allocations of income and losses.
- Operating and capital losses pass-through.
- Enterprise-level debt maximizes use of losses.
- No accumulated earnings tax.
- Investment income retains its character when passed through.
- Tax-exempt income retains its character when passed through.

The disadvantages of an LLC include:
- Non-uniformity of recognition by states.
- U.S. partnership tax code is applicable to LLCs, making tax planning more difficult.
- Not a time-tested enterprise structure as in the case of corporations or partnerships.

---

[2] Tort is damage, injury, or a wrongful act done willfully, negligently, or in circumstances involving strict liability, but not involving breach of contract, for which a civil suit can be brought.

202

- Requires attorneys and accountants familiar with LLC legal and tax requirements.

## 2.5    Summary of Enterprise Structure

Table 5.2 shows a comparison of the advantages of the various structures. The decision on the type of enterprise structure chosen can greatly influence future financing and growth prospects. The decision that may appear beneficial to initial investors may not be beneficial to the vision and exit strategies of the technological entrepreneur.

## 2.6    Enterprise Ownership

The ownership of the enterprise is a question that must be settled before obtaining the initial financing. If the new technological enterprise is formed by a single entrepreneur this is a straight forward process, i.e., the entrepreneur owns all interests in the enterprise until additional resources, capital or human, may be required (See Chapter 6 - Initial Enterprise Financing). However, many new technological enterprises are formed by several individuals, not all of whom may have conceived or fostered the concept that serves as the basis of the new venture.

There are different approaches to distribution of enterprise ownership:
- **Atavistic** - One individual keeps all the ownership interest.
- **Altruistic** - Equal sharing with all of the formation team members.
- **Contribution based** - Ownership based on the present and future contributions of formation team members.
- **Earn-in** - Each member of formation team agrees in advance a schedule of values to be placed upon each major initial task in the early stages of the enterprise formation and growth (White 1977).

Each of these approaches has benefits and disadvantages. The earn-in approach has the following advantages (Batz 1990, pp. 43):
- Eliminates arbitrariness and potential unfairness.
- Each member of the enterprise formation team is incentivized.
- Performers receive interest based on outcomes and non-performers can be eliminated from the enterprise.

**Table 5.2**
Advantages of Enterprise Structure

| Advantage | Sole Proprietorship | Partnership | Corporation | | LLC |
|---|---|---|---|---|---|
| | | | *C*-Corp | *S*-Corp | |
| Enterprise-level debt maximizes use of losses | | X | | | X |
| Certain special tax treatment depending on existing tax code | | | X | X | X |
| Continuity of enterprise life | | | X | X | |
| Employee stock ownership participation | | | X | | |
| Flexible tax year option | | | X | | |
| Investment income retains character when passed through | | X | | X | X |
| Liberal tax treatment of fringe benefits | | | X | | |
| Limited liability | | (Partners only) | X | X | X |
| No accumulated earnings tax | | X | | X | X |
| No double taxation | X | X | | X | X |
| Operating and capital loss pass-through | | X | | X | X |
| Opportunity for ordinary loss on sale of small business stock | | | X | X | |
| Possibly lower state tax if permitted by state statute | | X | | X | X |
| Simplicity | X | | | | |
| Special allocation of income and losses | | X | | | X |
| Tax-exempt income retains character when passed through | | X | | X | X |
| Tax-free mergers | | | X | X | |
| Transferability of ownership | X | | | X | |
| Unlimited investment income with no personal holding company tax | | X | | X | X |
| Unlimited number and type or partners, shareholders or members | | X | X | | X |

(Based on data contained in Cooper 1994)

The disadvantages of the earn-in ownership system include:

- Hard to gauge the relative difficulty and worth of accomplishing specific goals.
- Completion of a task can vary from acceptable to outstanding with various consequences on the enterprise.
- Future abilities and contributions of the formation team members may be unequal and of varying value to the new enterprise.

There are different methods of legally structuring the actual instrumentality of ownership. In a regular corporation preferred or common stocks are used. Preferred stock is a form of ownership which adds to the net worth of the enterprise and has preference over common stock in liquidation of the enterprise. Common stock is the most commonly used ownership instrument in an enterprise. Common stock is the junior of all securities and has no preference in liquidation.

## 2.7 Enterprise Name

The new technological enterprise name is the ultimate repository of the enterprise's goodwill. It is important to choose a name that is different from that used by another enterprise and which cannot be confused with another enterprise. The formation team must search through not only trademarks but also Internet domain[3] names to assure that the enterprise will have a clear title to its name. Unless this search is quite substantial, the enterprise can find itself faced with litigation for infringement of the rights of another entity. Some states will deny the use of an entity name that they believe is misleading.

A new technological enterprise can obtain a form of protection of their chosen name by filing with the state trademark registry (Mandel 1997, pp. 304). The most effective means of obtaining protection for the new enterprise's name is filing for U.S. Patent and Trademark Office registration. This protection is rather draconian since it provides the ultimate in protection within the United States. The enterprise is also encouraged to register the name as an Internet domain. There have been numerous incidents where major corporations were required to buy their domain names from entities that had registered their name as an Internet domain.

---

[3] Domain is an address of a network connection in the format that identifies the owner of that address in a hierarchical format.

## 2.8 Enterprise Governance

The type of formation structure chosen specifies the governance of the new enterprise.

- Sole Proprietorship - Individual entrepreneur.
- Partnership - General partners.
- Corporation - Board of Directors.
- Limited Liability Company - Members.

### 2.8.1 Board of Directors

In a corporate form of enterprise, a Board of Directors ("BOD") elected by the stockholders of the enterprise has the ultimate fiduciary responsibility. The Chief Executive Officer ("CEO") reports to the BOD. However, the only time a BOD should be involved with the daily operations of the enterprise is when the position of CEO is vacant (Bell and McNamara 1991, pp. 27). The responsibilities of the BOD include:

- Insuring the future survival and growth of the enterprise.
- Review and approval of the strategic and operational plans.
- Monitoring financial results, operational planning and resource decisions.
- Evaluation of the leadership team's performance.
- Establishing leadership succession plans.
- Providing an outlet for entrepreneurial isolation and resources in times of crisis.

The entrepreneurial formation team should not under any circumstances formulate a purely internal BOD or one populated with friends, relations or professional advisors. The BOD should consist of experienced executives and mentors who are familiar with the technological and market space the enterprise seeks to enter. In all respects, all members of the BOD should have ownership interest in the enterprise either through direct investment or through stock options. The ownership interest insures that all have a stake in the enterprise outcome.

Choosing members of the BOD is a very important process since choosing the wrong members can and will have serious consequences for the future of the enterprise. As the enterprise grows, so the size of the BOD is likely to increase (Bell and McNamara 1991, pp. 28-29).

The members of the BOD, if chosen correctly, can also serve in an additional advisory and assistance capacity:

- Assisting in developing the enterprise's business strategy.
- Acting as a sounding board for the CEO and other senior leadership team members.
- Recruiting and/or replacing the CEO and other leadership team members when warranted.
- Assisting in securing debt financing.
- Assisting in securing additional equity investment.
- Serving as an interface with investor groups.
- Monitoring but not interfering in enterprise operations.
- Establishing customer contacts.
- Serving as an interface with vendors.
- Assisting in times of crisis.

The BOD can also be augmented by a Board of Advisors ("BOA") which should be composed of individuals who have distinct professional competencies, which can assist the new enterprise. The BOA differs from the BOD in that they do not have any legal standing and thus do not have any potential liability, unlike members of the BOD. The members of the BOA are remunerated for their services and serve at the discretion of the CEO.

## 3. ORGANIZATIONAL STRUCTURE

### 3.1 Organizational Theory

Organizational theory combines structure and processes within human constraints. All enterprises, no matter what their basis, are formal structures in the sense that they represent rationally ordered instruments for achievement of stated goals (Selznick 1948). A formal organizational structure is a system of coordinated activities of two or more individuals (Barnard 1938, pp. 73). Barnard attempted to bring together the scientific management theories of Fredrick W. Taylor[4] and the human relation theories of George Elton Mayo. Taylor (Taylor 1911) prescribed *scientific* methods and procedures to organize and operate an enterprise based on the use of such tools as time and motion studies to optimize functions. Mayo's research work with the Western Electric Company in the famous *Hawthorn experiments* (Roethlisberger and Dickerson 1939) showed the importance of

---

[4] **Taylor, Frederick Winslow**, 1856-1915, was an American inventor, engineer, and efficiency expert noted for his innovations in industrial engineering and management.

various social factors such as a sense of belonging and understanding that human needs increased enterprise productivity. The various theories from Taylor, Mayo and Barnard lead to the concepts of Peter Drucker, the knowledge society and learning organizations (Nonaka and Takeuchi 1995, pp. 35-55).

Technology is developed and applied within an enterprise structure (Cardullo 1996, pp. 183). The effectiveness of not only the enterprise, but also the individual technological developments are directly related to the type, style and form of the enterprise. The enterprise structure combined with the processes used within the structure form the basis for the entire technological innovation life cycle from conception to introduction into the market space environment.

The organizational structure defines each enterprise member's position and the communication and relationships between those positions. One of the principal organizational paradigms for technological enterprises is the flexibility to deal with the rapidly evolving and changing nature of both the technological and market spaces (Bahrami 1993; Kano and Phillips 1997). Flexibility is a polymorphous concept varying with the situational context (Bahrami 1993). This includes structuring the enterprise to be agile, i.e., possessing an ability to move rapidly and take advantage of opportunities or avoid threats. Flexibility also implies that the organizational structure is versatile, i.e., able to do different things and apply different capabilities depending on the requirements of the particular situation. The concept of flexibility in the design of enterprise structure must provide a structure that is agile and versatile, associated with a rapidly changing market and technological spaces. The structure must also be robust and resilient providing stability and sustainable advantage and being capable of evolving (Bahrami 1993). Berrely (Berrely 1996) states:

> *"The fate of all complex adapting systems in the
> biosphere from single cells to economies is to
> evolve to natural state between order and chaos,
> a grand compromise between structure and
> surprise."*

A tenet of organizational structure design that is particularly important for technological organizations is to provide a structure that does not build walls between those who possess knowledge power and those who possess organization power (Grove 1996, pp. 120). Likewise, technological organization design should reflect another basic tenet of successful organizational structures, which is that they maintain very close relationships between external opportunity, strategy and internal structure (Tushman, Newman, and Romanelli 1991).

## 3.2 Structural Models

The choice of an appropriate organizational structure is a significant factor in assuring the successful implementation of both the technological and market strategies of the new enterprise (Pearce II and Robinson Jr. 1994, pp. 340). Usually a new technological enterprise is based on one single product, process or service that it intends to embed in the market space. In addition, the new enterprise will have relatively few human resources to implement a robust functional enterprise organizational structure. However, the formation team should be aware of the alternative enterprise structures available (See Chapter 7 - Strategic Enterprise Growth). A new enterprise has numerous models for structuring its organization. It must be realized that an enterprise is likely to evolve through numerous structures throughout its life cycle. Enterprise structure, like that of any organism, must adapt to changing internal and external environments. A model depicting how the enterprise processes, position and structure systems and values interact is shown in Figure 5.4 (Hammer and Champy 1993, pp. 80). This interaction results in evolution of the organizational structure to meet the challenges imposed by both the technological and market spaces.

The evolution of enterprise organizational structure is likely to follow the processes found by Chandler in the study of various enterprises over an extended period (Chandler 1962). This sequence of enterprise structure evolution consisted of:

- Development and choice of a new enterprise strategy.
- Adjustment of existing organization structure to new strategy with commensurate administrative problems and productivity impact.
- Full implementation of organizational structure to meet the enterprise strategic requirements.
- Improved profitability and strategic implementation.

A new technological enterprise usually begins its life with a basic *clean slate*. However, each member of the enterprise formation team comes to the new technological enterprise with pre-determined organizational structural beliefs based upon passed experiences. The resolution of these structural beliefs is likely to follow Chandler's model.

**Fig. 5.4** Enterprise Interaction (Adapted from Hammer and Champy 1993)

The basic enterprise structures that can be implemented by the technological enterprise over its life cycle include (Cardullo 1996, pp. 184):

- Functional.
- Geographic.
- Divisional.
- Multidimensional.
- Strategic.
- Matrix.
- Project.

Research has concluded that (Galbraith and Kazanjian 1986):

- An enterprise with a single product, process or service should employ a functional structure.
- An enterprise with several strategic business lines that are somehow related through either technological or market space should employ a multidimensional organizational structure.
- An enterprise in several unrelated strategic business lines should be organized into strategic business units ("SBUs").
- Early achievement of strategic enterprise organizational structure can be a competitive advantage (See Chapter 4 - Enterprise Technological Market Planning).

## 3.3 Strategic Leadership Team

The enterprise entrepreneurial formation team has to be able to transform itself into a strategic leadership team as the formal enterprise structure is established and evolves. The strategic leadership team of the new enterprise is composed of the entrepreneurs and associates who will be responsible for formulating and completing the new enterprise's vision. The strategic leadership team includes the officers of the new enterprise including those with the title of vice president and above.

The strategic leadership team must have the ability to anticipate, envision, maintain flexibility and empower others to create strategic change as required (Hitt, Ireland, and Hoskisson 1997, pp. 383). The most critical ability that members of the strategic leadership team must have is the ability to manage human capital. The members of the strategic leadership team should have some or all the qualities that differentiate great leaders. These qualities include (Fritz 1996, pp.209):

- Know the desired result.
- Know current position.
- Deeply care about the result.
- Able to encourage others to join them in making the vision a reality.
- Able to help others focus on reality in relation to the desired result.

- Able to translate structural tension into action that is designed to move from the existing reality to the desired reality.

The structure of the strategic leadership team could have the following senior management positions:

- Chief Executive Officer ("CEO").
- Chief Operating Officer ("COO").
- Chief Financial Officer ("CFO").
- Chief Technology Officer ("CTO").
- Chief Marketing Officer ("CMO").
- Chief Information Officer ("CIO").
- Chief Technical Operations Officer ("CTOO").

Figure 5.5 shows an organizational chart for the new technological entrepreneurial enterprise.

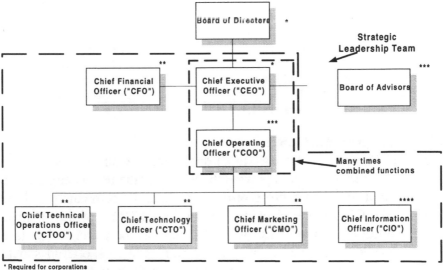

* Required for corporations
** Key strategic leadership team members
*** Desirable enterprise member
**** Structured when enterprise size and growth warrant

**Fig. 5.5** Enterprise Strategic Leadership Team

Each of these positions carries a different authority and responsibility. In many new technological enterprises, many of these responsibilities are divided between a small group of entrepreneurial founders. Table 5.3 presents the roles of essential individuals in the enterprise formation teams of major enterprises in their technological and market spaces.

**Table 5.3**
Major Technological Early Strategic Leadership Teams

| Enterprise | Individual | Founder | Role |
|---|---|---|---|
| Apple Computer, Inc. | Jobs | X | Visionary |
| | Wozniak | X | Technologist |
| | Markulo | X | Business Finance |
| | McKenna | | Board Member & PR |
| | Rick | | Board Member & Financing |
| | Scott | | First President |
| Microsoft ® Corporation | Gates | X | Visionary & Technologist |
| | Allen | X | Technologist |
| | Balmer | | Technical Operations |
| | Shirley | | Business, Marketing & Operations |
| Intel | Grove | X | Operations |
| | Moore | X | Visionary |
| | Noyce | X | Visionary & External Spokesperson |
| Sun Microsystems | Khoslo | X | First President |
| | Bechtolschein | | Hardware Designer |
| | Joy | | Software Designer |
| | McNealy | | Manufacturing |
| | Lacroute | | Operations |

(Adapted from Bell and McNamara 1991, pp. 22)

### 3.3.1  Chief Executive Officer

The Chief Executive Officer ("CEO") directs the overall operation of the enterprise. The CEO should provide the vision for the new enterprise and present it to its customers, board of directors, financial community and the public. The CEO is the chief decision-maker ("CDM") of the strategic leadership team. It is the CEO who will serve as the principal interface between the enterprise and the investment community. The CEO should follow the principles of leadership that have been put forward by Nemoto (Nemoto 1987).

**Improvement after improvement** - The CEO should provide the leadership to assure that the enterprise's environment is conducive to improvement.

**Improved coordination** - Throughout the life cycle of the enterprise the CEO should assure that there is free and open communication between members of the enterprise.

**Openness of communication** - The CEO also provides a management environment that will allow all members of the enterprise to express themselves without fear of reprisal.

**Refrain from assigning blame** - The CEO provides an environment where mistakes can be freely reported. Michael Bloomberg (Bloomberg and Winkler 1997) has stated that he does not penalize failure but actually provides a means to assure that others are not disincentivized for proposing projects that may fail.

**Teacher -** An emphasis on teaching and presentation skills is key to effective collaboration. The CEO must be able to make ideas and information come alive to persuade and teach. The communication skills of the CEO are principal elements of the enterprise in making its vision known to the financial community and the enterprise stakeholders.

**Realistic planner** - The CEO provides realistic deadlines for accomplishment of enterprise goals and objectives. Unrealistic deadlines will lead to lower enterprise moral. A realistic deadline provides an achievable outcome horizon that will incentivize the performers.

**Presenter and Coach** - Before making any presentation, the CEO should rehearse the reports and presentations. Also, the CEO should require other members of the strategic leadership team to rehearse their reports and presentations before actual presentation.

**Action oriented** - The CEO should prescribe specific remedies whenever a problem is reported. Inaction, i.e., letting a problem solve itself, is ineffective, as is delegating the responsibility to the presenter of the problem.

**Available** - The CEO should be available to enterprise members, i.e., according to Nemoto *"creating an opportunity to be heard at the top."* If the CEO and other members of the strategic leadership team are willing to assist with problems, then members of the enterprise will be more optimistic about solving problems and will take the enterprise goals more seriously.

### 3.3.2 Chief Operating Officer
The Chief Operating Officer ("COO") is responsible for the daily activities of the enterprise in accordance with the policies and objectives established by the Board of Directors and the CEO. The COO's functions usually include assisting in the development of policies of the enterprise related to operations. In many new technological entrepreneurial enterprises the functions of CEO and COO are combined. The COO also assist the CEO in formulating

214

strategic plans and acts as the Chief Planning Officer ("CPO") of the enterprise. The operations of the enterprise are the responsibility of the COO and as such the operating elements of the enterprise are usually under his/her direction.

### 3.3.3 Chief Financial Officer

The Chief Financial Officer ("CFO") is responsible for the enterprise's financial plans and policies, accounting practices, and relationships with lending institutions and the financial community. The responsibilities of the CFO include the development of accounting and statistical procedures for internal control. Many new entrepreneurial enterprises tend to delegate these responsibilities to an outside accounting professional. While this practice may be expedient due to financial resources, it is also the *Achilles' heel*[5] of the enterprise's future. The CFO is an essential element in the strategic leadership team and should be the first member added if not part of the original enterprise formation team. The investment community will in many instances judge a new entrepreneurial enterprise by the skills of its financial management and those of the CFO.

### 3.3.4 Chief Technology Officer

The Chief Technology Officer ("CTO") is the technological visionary of the enterprise. In most new technological entrepreneurial enterprises, the CTO is either the originating entrepreneur or one of the essential members of the enterprise formation team. The functions of the CEO/COO and CTO are combined in the entrepreneurial founder in many new technological enterprises. As the enterprise grows and matures, these functions will fractionate to meet the needs of the enterprise (Cardullo 1996, pp. 264-268). Colmen (Colmen 1994) argued that the CTO should set priorities and decide strategic imperatives, customer and supplier interface procedures, environmental and safety requirements, new technological products, and processes and services for the entire enterprise. A modified set of Colmen's functions for a CTO consists of:

- Developing the technological strategic plan.
- Developing and operating the technology environmental monitoring system.

---

[5] Achilles' heel is a seemingly small but mortal weakness. This is derived from the Greek hero Achilles who was vulnerable only in the heel of his foot.

- Serving as the Chief Technology Decision Maker ("CTDM").
- Acting as the technical conscience of the enterprise.
- Providing technology oversight for the enterprise.
- Serving as the enterprise's Chief Technology Transfer Officer ("CTTO").

### 3.3.5 Chief Marketing Officer

The Chief Marketing Officer ("CMO") is responsible for strategic market planning (See Chapter 4 - Enterprise Technological Market Planning) and for managing the activities of the marketing staff to achieve the enterprise's objectives regarding sales, profitability and market share. In the initial enterprise structure, the CMO may also be responsible for managing the sales efforts of the new enterprise. As the enterprise grows the enterprise structure may add a Chief Sales Officer ("CSO") who would then take on the sales responsibilities.

The position of CMO is essential to the success of the enterprise. Many new technological enterprises have failed due to concentrating their efforts and resources in the technological space and neglecting the market space.

### 3.3.6 Chief Information Officer

The Chief Information Officer ("CIO") is responsible for information flow within the enterprise, information technology system acquisition and its operation. This function may be combined with that of the CTO when the enterprise is focused in the information technology ("IT") space. However, this position should be separated from that of the CTO. This separation should exist even for IT enterprises once they reach a phase in their life cycle where internal and external information requirements dictate.

### 3.3.7 Chief Technical Operations Officer

The Chief Technological Operations Officer ("CTOO") is the individual who is responsible for translating the enterprise's technological visions into products, processes or systems which can be embedded into the market space. In the early stages of the enterprise the functions of the CTO and the CTOO are combined. The CTOO in some older enterprises is termed Chief Engineer or Vice President of Operations or some other similar title.

**3.4    Enterprise Reward System**

To attract, motivate and retain human resources requires the enterprise formation team to focus on development of a reward system within the enterprise. The system chosen will influence the current and future members of the enterprise but also it is a strategic input into developing the financial plans required to obtain enterprise financing (See Chapter 6 - Initial Enterprise Financing). Hence, the enterprise leadership team should highly value the reward and motivational systems of the enterprise. These systems are powerful tools for motivating the enterprise to meet its strategic objectives. The reward system should have a flexible philosophy that is open to change as the internal and external environments warrant. The enterprise's reward system must align the actions and objectives of both the enterprise members and those of the enterprise (Pearce II and Robinson Jr. 1994, pp. 364). The reward system chosen should also focus both on the near and far horizons of the enterprise.

There are different types of reward systems; there is no perfect system. Each new technological enterprise must tailor its reward system to meet the circumstances. There are many variations available depending upon the existing tax codes and inventiveness of professional compensation consultants. Reward systems can be classified as direct and indirect. Pearce and Robinson (Pearce II and Robinson Jr. 1994, pp. 367-372) provide guidelines for structuring an effective reward system that the enterprise formation team should consider. The guidelines include linking the reward system with the enterprise's strategic plans (See Chapter 3 - Technological and Enterprise Strategic Planning and Chapter 4 - Enterprise Technological Market Planning). A uniform incentive program throughout the enterprise is important and should vary from 25 to 60 percent of an individual's compensation depending upon the degree of successful execution of the individual's responsibilities. The rewards and incentives must be linked to an individual's position and performance. The reward system should link performance to success, instead of the hierarchical enterprise position. In some instances the technology specialist may be rewarded, in financial terms, more than a founder with major equity interest in the enterprise. All members of the enterprise should be rewarded without major discrepancies between enterprise levels. The reward system should be scrupulously fair, accurate and informative. Even if individuals are not fully successful they should be rewarded; the reward can be generous when fully meeting or exceeding expectations but the system should also reward failure, to a much lesser degree, in order to incentivize future performance.

### 3.4.1 Direct Compensation

Direct compensation includes:

- Salary.
- Vacation, sick leave, and holidays.
- Insurance, i.e., health and life.
- Training.

These elements are considered in all compensation systems. While there may be a tendency to provide compensation below the market rate, the enterprise formation team should consider other factors, recognizing that technological personnel in the late 1990s and into the twenty-first century are scarce resources. Salary packages close to market rates with additional rewards based on outcomes and in terms of stock options may serve as an excellent incentivization system.

Vacation, sick leave, holidays policies are a function of the region where the enterprise is based and in some instances are dictated by National and International conventions requirements such as maternity and family leave. Medical insurance is an important consideration in any employee's benefit package. Hence, even though medical coverage tends to be expensive for a new entrepreneurial enterprise, it is important that the formation team consider at least a modest health plan with high deductibles and minimal benefits rather than inducing financial stress in employees that will both be unfair to the employee and impact the individual's productivity.

### 3.4.2 Incentive Compensation

Incentivized reward systems include:

- Stock plans.
- Profit sharing plans.
- Bonuses and commissions.
- Educational payments.

Incentive compensation systems can be categorized into those related to the profits earned by the enterprise, i.e., goals achieved, and those that are related to the total value of the enterprise and are tied to the equity of the enterprise. The profit sharing portion of the reward is directly linked to the total enterprise profitability and the contribution of the employee to that profitability. Although profits for most new technological enterprises will be in the future and thus cannot be used to incentivize, *401-K* plans can be put in place that permit tax deferred savings by employees, with optimal matching by the enterprise. The enterprise can increase their contribution when financial circumstances permit.

Stock plans provide one method for incentivizing productivity by offering the employees a stake in the enterprise's future. Since many new technological entrepreneurial enterprises have made founding employees exceedingly wealthy as in the case of the over 1,000 millionaires and half a dozen billionaires in Microsoft® Corporation. Publications, both general and industrial, were replete throughout the 1990s with success stories of technological entrepreneurial enterprises and the wealth that accrued to many of their employees.

Stock plans are of two varieties: direct stock purchase and option plans. As in previous areas, the key to any stock plan is the flexibility to meet every changing need of the enterprise. It is important to tie the stock plans to performance, such that equity interest becomes available over a reasonable time and in some instances must be sold back to the enterprise if the employee leaves before a particular time. Any stock plan should be firmly in place before hiring staff outside of the enterprise formation team. The entrepreneurial formation team should have formal agreements as to their compensation and ownership. It must be realized that initial venture financing could radically change the reward and ownership structure (See Chapter 6 - Initial Enterprise Financing).

Depending on the existing tax code, it is possible to structure variations to the stock and options systems. Variations in the U.S. Tax Code in the 1990s changed the landscape and caused economic reversals for various incentive systems. It is important to consult tax professionals before placing any stock plan or incentive system in place. However, barring the unforeseen tax consequences, stock plans in all their *flavors* can highly motivate both the enterprise formation team members and future employees.

In 1994, Jeffrey Bezos founded Amazon.com with an initial investment of $10,000. Amazon.com was founded to sell books over the Internet. By mid-1997, Amazon.com had sold $32 million worth of books (Norris 1997). The initial public offering ("IPO") (See Chapter 8 - Next Entrepreneurial Step) had increased by mid-1997 Bezos' $10,000 investment to over $200 million.

Figure 5.6 shows a 1997 study of 900 fast growth enterprises and the percentage of employee stock ownership versus the percentage of enterprises.

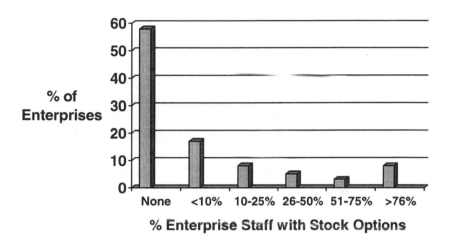

**Fig. 5.6** Employee Stock Ownership (Adapted from Sexten and Seale 1997)

One of the leading practices to maintain enterprise control is to grant employee stock ownership selectively (Sexten and Seale 1997, pp. 19). In a 1997 study of fast growth enterprises, it was found that 42 percent of these enterprises shared some ownership with their employees. It was also determined that the stock ownership sharing does not typically result in the employees having control of voting shares. Thus, entrepreneurs of fast growth enterprises can usually obtain higher levels of productivity through employee stock ownership plans while retaining controlling stock ownership.

When profit sharing plans are not suitable for new technological enterprises, bonuses and commissions are good managerial motivational tools (Batz 1990, pp. 145). Bonuses and commissions have been the standard reward system. However, the strategic leadership team can apply innovative techniques to these methods. These innovations can include non-cash bonuses, such as airline mileage tied to sales, or membership to clubs or other items that, depending on the tax code, may be non-taxable items for the employee.

## 4. ENTERPRISE RESOURCES

The formation of a new technological enterprise is an exercise in bringing to bear a set of resources to implement strategic decisions. Without or with limited pre-requisite resources, the future of the new enterprise may not be promising. The technological entrepreneurial formation team must consider four types of resources when planning the enterprise. These resources include:

- Human.
- Physical.
- Intellectual.
- Financial (See Chapter 6 - Initial Enterprise Financing).

Another way to view the required enterprise resources is the resource-based view (Miller 1993, pp. 119-123). The resource-based view of the enterprise consists of the collection of tangible and intangible assets combined with enterprise capabilities for the use of the assets to develop competencies and achieve a competitive advantage. This concept is well adapted to knowledge based technological enterprises (Miller 1993, pp. 119). An example of the tangible assets include:

- Intellectual property such as patents, copyrights and trade secrets.
- Physical facilities.
- Inventory.
- Distribution networks.

Intangible assets include:

- Skill sets of employees.
- Enterprise culture.
- Strategic leadership team.
- Enterprise structure.
- Visionary entrepreneur with strong motivation and communication skills.

### 4.1 Human Resources

While the enterprise formation team will serve as the initial human resources complement for the enterprise, it must aggressively seek others in order to bring the vision of the enterprise to fruition. However, it is important first to determine what skill sets, talents or capabilities the enterprise will require initially and as it grows. Associated with defining requirements is the cost of satisfying them. This requires the entrepreneurial formation team to develop a human resource plan that contains:

- Forecast and estimate of the human resources in terms of skill sets.
- Salary and compensation structure.
- Strategy for acquiring these human resources, i.e., advertising, Internet, networking, etc.

The acquisition of resources should be tied to enterprise growth. In many instances, new technological entrepreneurial enterprises acquire human resources in anticipation of revenue. This is exceedingly dangerous since revenue projections are rarely accurate when an enterprise has little historical perspective. Figure 5.7 shows the growth of Microsoft ® Corporation from 1975 through to 1995. According to Microsoft® Corporation, the company *"has a conscious policy to hire about half the number of people we think we need"* (Cusumano and Selby 1995, pp. 94).

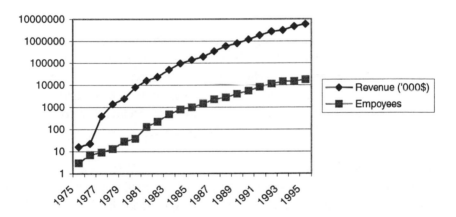

**Fig. 5.7** Growth of Microsoft ® Corporation (Based on data contained in Cusumano and Selby 1995)

## 4.2 Physical Resources

All enterprises must have some form of physical resources, even if it is a room with one computer. While the concept of virtual enterprises, i.e., enterprises with no fixed resources base, has grown with the growth of the Internet, it is still not the standard means of enterprise formation. The enterprise formation team will have to consider where to locate and what will be required to establish the venture. These requirements will include equipment and facilities to implement the entrepreneurial vision and will have an impact on the initial capital required for the enterprise (See Chapter 6 - Initial Enterprise Financing)

## 4.3    Intellectual Assets

Intellectual assets consist of intellectual capital and property. These assets, while not easily quantifiable, are the *heart* of a technological enterprise. In new technological enterprises, these assets are usually embedded within the enterprise formation team.

### 4.3.1  Intellectual Capital

The intellectual capital of the enterprise consists of both knowledge and innovations. Intellectual capital has been defined as the combination of intangible assets that add value to the enterprise when implementing the entrepreneurial vision (Masoulas 1997).

### 4.3.2  Intellectual Property

Intellectual property is an intangible right that can be bought and sold, leased or rented, or otherwise transferred between parties in much the same way that rights to real property or other personal property can be transferred. Intellectual property can consist of patents, trade secrets and expertise, copyrights, designs, expertise, and trademarks. Intellectual property rights are most often transferred through contracts or licenses.

### Inventions and Patents

Invention is the act or process of discovering something new, physical or conceptual. A United States patent is an agreement between the United States government and the inventor. This agreement grants the inventor the right to exclude others from making, using, or selling the invention for a defined period of time within the United States. The patent law of the United States specifies that any person who

> *"invents or discovers any new and useful*
> *process, machine, manufacture, or composition*
> *of matter, or any new and useful improvements*
> *thereof, may obtain a patent."*

A patent does not give the inventor the right to practice his or her invention, only the right to exclude others from doing so (von Hipple 1988, pp. 47). The inventor is given exclusive use of the invention and the right to assign that use. However, a grant of a patent has been found not to be useful for excluding imitators and/or capturing royalty income in most industries. A grant of a patent is often likely to offer little benefit to its holder. Patents gives the patentee the right to exclude others from its use, but this does not give the patentee the right to use the patent if such use infringes on the patents of others. The United States patent system places the burden on the patentee to detect any infringers to sue for redress. A patent covers a particular means of achieving a given end, but not the end itself, even if the end and, perhaps the market it identifies, are novel.

## Trade Secrets and Know-how

Trade secrets and expertise are other forms of intellectual property that can be used for technology transfer. A trade secret is any commercial formula, device, pattern, process, or information that affords an enterprise an advantage over others who do not know it. The information is not generally known and has value. Trade secrets must be maintained by avoiding public disclosure.

In contrast, expertise is a broader term that describes factual knowledge not usually amenable to a precise description. Expertise is usually accumulated knowledge as a result of trial and error. Expertise typically gives an enterprise the ability to produce something that could not be produced as accurately or successfully without it. Expertise may include trade secrets and cannot be protected or licensed unless it is first recorded in a tangible medium.

Unlike patents, in the U.S., trade secrets are protected by state, rather than federal, laws. These laws allow the trade secret owner to prosecute someone for unauthorized use or theft of such information. However, state laws generally require that its owner must protect a trade secret if it is to retain trade secret status. If the owner allows the information to become public information through publication, public use, observation, or lack of adequate security measures, the information moves into the public domain and loses protection under trade secret law. Trade secrets are an effective means to protect product innovations (von Hipple 1988, pp. 54). Trade secrets incorporate various technological barriers to analysis, and process innovations that can be hidden from exposure.

## Copyrights

A copyright is an exclusive right granted by the United States government to authors, composers, artists, or their assignees for the life of the individual plus fifty years, to copy, exhibit, distribute, or perform their work. As with patent rights, these rights go to the individual creating the work, unless provisions are made to the contrary.

A copyright exists when a work is created. The law no longer requires the work to be marked with a copyright notice, but it is good practice to do so. Registration of copyrights with the federal government is optional and can be done at any time during the life of the copyright. Registration also permits using the federal court system to prosecute infringers and provides certain mandatory federal damages against those convicted of infringement. Registration may be recommended if software is the subject of a license agreement.

## Trademarks

A trademark is a word, name, symbol, device, letter, numeral, or picture, or any combination thereof, in any form or arrangement that is used to identify the origin of goods or services. A trademark must be individually identifiable and distinguishable from those of others for similar goods or services. Trademarks assure the buyer of the authenticity of a product or service and imply that the seller has some standards of quality associated with the trademark. An enterprise or person may establish a trademark simply by using it in interstate commerce. Like copyrights, trademarks may also be registered.

## Licensing

Licensing is the transfer of less than ownership rights in intellectual property to a third party, to permit the third party to use intellectual property. Licensing can be exclusive, non-exclusive, for a specific field of use, and for a specific geographical area. If ownership is transferred, it is called an assignment.

The transfer of technology through licensing is a useful method for capturing economic rents for technological innovations. Small technology enterprises can benefit from technological licensing. A new technological enterprise usually benefits more by licensing its technology than trying to commercialize it. The commercialization of new technologies requires a high expenditure of resources, generally beyond the means of many small entrepreneurial enterprises. However, in order to benefit from technological licensing, small enterprises must overcome their initial naiveté by concentrating on the economic and strategic aspects of the process (Chung 1995). These small enterprises must broaden operational perspective, scope, and build credibility and expertise. To further benefit from technological licensing, new technological enterprises should improve exchange and interaction capabilities, and enhance experience and responsibility.

## REFERENCES

Bahrami, Hema. 1993. The Emerging Flexible Organization: Perspective from Silicon Valley. *IEEE Engineering Management Review* 21 (4):94-102.

Barnard, Chester L. 1938. *The Functions of the Executive*. Cambridge, MA: Harvard University Press.

Batz, Gordon B. 1990. *Entrepreneurship for the Nineties*. Englewood Cliffs, NJ: Prentice Hall.

Bell, C. Gordon, and John E. McNamara. 1991. *High-Tech Ventures: The Guide for Entrepreneurial Success*. Reading, MA: Addison-Wesley Publishing Company, Inc.

Berrely, David. 1996. Between Chaos and Order: What Complexity Theory Can Teach Business. *Strategy and Business* Second Quarter (3):76-84.

Bloomberg, Michael, and Matthew Winkler. 1997. *Bloomberg by Bloomberg*. New York: J. Wiley.

Braudel, Fernand. 1979. *The Wheels of Commerce: Civilization and Capitalism 15th - 18th Century - Volume 2*. Translated by Reynolds, S. 2 vols. Vol. 2. New York, NY: Harper and Row, Publishers.

Cardullo, Mario W. 1996. *Introduction to Managing Technology*. Edited by J. A. Brandon. First ed. 5 vols. Vol. 4, *Engineering Management Series*. Baldock, Hertfordshire, England: Research Studies Press Ltd.

Chandler, Alfred D. 1962. *Strategy and Structure*. Cambridge, MA: MIT Press.

Chung, Kam B. 1995. Technology Licensing for the Small Firm. Paper read at 1995 IEEE Annual International Engineering Management Conference, 95/6/28-30, at Singapore.

Colmen, Kenneth S. 1994. Benchmarking the Delivery of Technical Support. *IEEE Engineering Management Review* 22 (Winter 1994):47 - 51.

Cooper. 1994. *Choosing a Business Entity in the 1990s*. Washington, D.C.: Cooper and Lybrand L.L.P.

Cusumano, Michael A., and Richard W. Selby. 1995. *Microsoft Secrets: Company Creates Technology, Shapes Markets, and Manages People*. New York, NY: The Free Press.

Drucker, Peter F. 1985. *Innovation and Entrepreneurship: Practice and Principles*. New York, NY: Harper and Row, Publishers.

Fritz, Robert. 1996. *Corporate Tides: The Inescapable Laws of Organizational Structure*. San Francisco, CA: Berrett-Koehler Publishers.

Galbraith, V. R., and R. K. Kazanjian. 1986. *Strategy Implementation: Structure, Systems, and Processes*. St. Paul, MN: West Publishing.

226

Grove, Andrew S. 1996. *Only the Paranoid Survive: How to Exploit the Crisis Points that Challenge Every Company and Career.* New York, NY: Currency Doubleday.

Hammer, Michael, and James Champy. 1993. *Reengineering The Corporation: A Manifesto for Business Revolution.* New York, NY: Harper Business.

Hisrick, Robert D., and Michael P. Peters. 1995. *Entrepreneurship: Starting, Developing, and Managing a New Enterprise.* Chicago, IL: Irwin.

Hitt, Michael A., R. Duane Ireland, and Robert E. Hoskisson. 1997. *Strategic Management: Competitiveness and Globalization - Concepts.* Second ed. Minneapolis/St. Paul, MN: West Publishing Company.

Juran, J.M., and Frank M. Gryna. 1993. *Quality Planning and Analysis: From Product Development through Use.* Third ed. New York, NY: McGraw-Hill, Inc.

Kano, Jun, and Fred Phillips. 1997. The Evolutionary Organization as a Complex Adaptive System. Paper read at Portland International Conference on Management of Engineering and Technology - 1997, 97/7/27-31, at Portland, OR.

Kauffman, Stuart. 1995. *At Home in the Universe: The Search for Laws of Self-Organization and Complexity.* New York, NY: Oxford University Press.

Mandel, Richard P. 1997. Chapter 10 Legal and Tax Issues. In *The Portable MBA in Entrepreneurship*, edited by W. D. Bygrave. New York, NY: John Wiley and Sons, Inc.

Masoulas, Vasilis. 1997. Participative Development of Systems to Manage Organizational Intellectual Capital (Knowledge and Innovation) based on Individual and Organizational Requirements. Paper read at Sixth International Conference on Management of Technology, at Goteborg, Sweden.

Miller, Alex. 1993. *Strategic Management.* Third ed. Boston, MA: Irwin/McGraw-Hill.

Nemoto, Masao. 1987. *Total Quality Control for Management: Strategies and Tactics from Toyota and Toyoda Gasei.* Translated by Lu, David. Englewood Cliffs, NJ: Prentice Hall.

Nonaka, Ikujiro, and Hirotaha Takeuchi. 1995. *The Knowledge-Creating Company: How Japanese Companies Create the Dynamics of Innovation.* New York, NY: Oxford University Press.

Norris, Floyd. 1997. *The Money Is in the Stock, Not the Books* [web site]. The New York Times, 1997 [cited 97/5/18 1997]. Available from www.nytimes.com/yr/mo/day/news/financial/market-watch-ado18.htm.

Pearce II, John A., and Richard B. Robinson Jr. 1991. *Strategic Management: Formulation, Implementation and Control.* Fourth ed. Homewood, IL: Irwin.

Pearce II, John A., and Richard B. Robinson Jr. 1994. *Formulation, Implementation and Control of Competitive Strategy.* Fifth ed. Burr Ridge, IL: Irwin.

Peters, Thomas J, and Robert H. Waterman Jr. 1992. *In Search of Excellence.* New York, NY: Harper and Row.

Roberts, Edward B. 1991. *Entrepreneurs in High Technology: Lessons from MIT and Beyond.* New York, NY: Oxford University Press.

Roethlisberger, F. J., and E. J. Dickerson. 1939. *Management and the Worker.* Cambridge, MA: Harvard University Press.

227

Scarbrough, Harry, and J. Martin Corbett. 1992. *Technology and Organization: Power, meaning and design.* Edited by D. C. Wilson, *The Routledge Series in Analytical Management.* London, England: Routledge.

Selznick, Philip. 1948. Foundation of the Theory of Organization. *American Sociological Review* 13 (February):25-35.

Sexten, Donald L., and Forrest I. Seale. 1997. Leading Practices of Fast Growth Entrepreneurs: Pathways for High Performance: National Center for Entrepreneurship Research.

Taylor, Frederick W. 1911. *The Principles of Scientific Management.* New York, NY: Harper and Brothers.

Thamhain, Hans J. 1992. *Engineering Management: Managing Effectively in Technology-Based Organizations.* Edited by D. F. Kocaoglu, *Wiley Series in Engineering and Technology Management.* New York, NY: John Wiley and Sons, Inc.

Tushman, Michael L., William H. Newman, and Elaine Romanelli. 1991. Convergence and Upheaval: Managing the Unsteady Pace of Organizational Evolution. In *The Strategy Process: Concepts, Context, Cases,* edited by H. Mintzberg and J. B. Quinn. Englewood Cliffs, NJ: Prentice Hall.

von Hipple, Eric. 1988. *The Sources of Innovation.* New York, NY: Oxford University Press.

White, Richard M. 1977. *Entrepreneur's Manual: Business Startups, Spinoffs, and Innovation Management.* Radnor, PA: Chilton Book Co.

## DISCUSSION QUESTIONS

1. Development of a new technological enterprise requires time. Develop a time line for formation of a new technological enterprise, starting with initial conception through to legal formation. Discuss your assumptions and the potential obstacles, both human and legal, that may be encountered.

2. Choose three technological public enterprises and prepare a historical timetable of their development based on your research. Discuss the problems encountered by the entrepreneurs as they moved from initial concept stage to enterprise formation.

3. A new entrepreneurial venture that develops over time into a large enterprise must change in its technological and market spaces. Discuss these changes to the enterprise structure.

4. Choose five public technological enterprises in a particular technological space and obtain their upper management salary structure by researching the Securities and Exchange Commission ("SEC") filings. Compare the compensation packages as a function of the revenue, profits, stock price and price earnings ratios over a three-year period. Discuss in detail the potential reasons for any differences.

5. Enterprise resources, both tangible and intangible, serve as the basis of enterprise competitive advantage. Choose two technological

enterprises and compare them based on their tangible and intangible resources and discuss how the resources contribute to the enterprise's competitive advantages.

6. The U.S. Tax Code has changed over the last fifty years. Prepare a table of those changes that have affected enterprise structure and in particular those changes directly applicable to technological resources.

7. Intellectual property is the mainstay of technological enterprises. Choose two well-known technological products and discuss in detail the patents, trademarks and any trade secrets associated with them.

# CHAPTER 6

# Enterprise Initial Financing

*"No better friend - No worse enemy."*
**Epitaph on tomb of Lucius Cornelius Sulla, Dictator of Rome and Uncle of Gaius Julius Caesar, 138 - 78 B.C.**

## 1.   INTRODUCTION

The word *capital* derives from the Late Latin word *capitale* based on the Latin *caput* meaning head.   The term capital emerged in the twelfth to thirteenth centuries as relating to funds, stock of merchandise, sum of money or money carrying interest (Braudel 1979, pp.232). The word capitalist dates from the mid-seventeenth century.  In a sense, the early merchant bankers of Europe, such as the Buonsignnori of Siena[1], that funded trade expeditions were the first venture capitalists (Braudel 1979, pp. 376). All technological entrepreneurs participating in the evolution of an enterprise will need to seek financing at some point in the evolutionary process.  In many instances, this starts with the initiation of the enterprise.  It is critical that the technological entrepreneur understands and prepares strategically to enter the financial space.   The entrepreneur must keep focused on two important elements (Zimmer and Scarborough 1996, pp. 377):

- Capital is available and it is important to know where to seek it.
- Creative seeking is critical to find non-conventional sources of capital, such as large strategic partners, suppliers, and the Internet.

The penultimate step in establishing a new technological enterprise is the acquisition of prerequisite capital to bring the strategic plan into existence.

---

[1] **Buonsignnori of Siena**, operated the *Magna Tavola*, a large firm exclusively devoted to banking and have been characterized as the Rothschilds of the thirteenth century.

230

Many technological entrepreneurs start with this step. However, as it has been shown in prior chapters, this could prove to be a fatal error. Without the prerequisite technological and market strategic planning (See Chapter 3 - Technological and Enterprise Strategic Planning and Chapter 4 - Enterprise Technological Market Planning) many embryonic technological enterprises either fail to obtain the required capital resources or seek insufficient funding.

The initial venture financing requires the technological entrepreneur and the enterprise formation team to:

- Develop a robust business plan that summarizes the vision, concepts, objectives and the method for their achievement and for the presentation of the prerequisite capital resources.
- Develop a financial plan, which is summarized within the initial business plan, that is realistically tempered with optimism.
- Seek the prerequisite capital resources. This requires both a plan and a strategy for seeking the capital.
- Finalize the capital acquisition with the sources of capital. With the proper investors, this may provide a source of professional and financial assistance as the enterprise grows.

There appears to be a positive relationship between the investment and financing strategies for new technology and enterprise performance levels (Carrière and Gasse 1996). While many new technological enterprises seek financing from conventional sources, such as friends, angels[2], venture capitalists and banks; others seek capital from potential strategic partners (Carayannis and Kossicieh 1997). Beyond the capital available from potential large strategic partners, such as Intel Corporation, Dell Computer and others, are the technical and management skills these strategic partners can bring to bear. However, establishment of such strategic alliances has been found to take a surprisingly long time, and these alliance may not be a suitable source of seed or start-up capital (Carayannis and Kossicieh 1997). The seed capital available through strategic alliances is in many instances complemented with traditional capital sources.

---

[2] Angels are financially able individuals or informal investors who do not have any relationship with the enterprise initially.

The technological entrepreneur has to understand not only the conventional sources of capital but also the life cycle of enterprise financing. Like all systems, financing has a life cycle. Each phase of that life cycle has different needs and participants. These requirements and participants are different in both form and substance. The sources of financing vary from personal sources, which may be easily available to the technological entrepreneur (such as personal assets and credit cards) through to sophisticated venture capitalists with individual financial objectives and exit strategies. During the initiation of a new technological enterprise, the entrepreneur and the enterprise formation team will also be faced with numerous choices as to the amount of ownership interest that will need to be given to secure the initial financing. Some decisions that may have euphoric elements can easily determine the future of the enterprise.

The acquisition of capital for the new enterprise is also determined by the risk which potential investors view as associated with the enterprise. Figure 6.1 shows a relationship between risk and the potential return investors may require to secure their investment. This return when coupled with the future value of the enterprise at the time of investor *exit*[3] will determine the amount of equity that the investors will require.

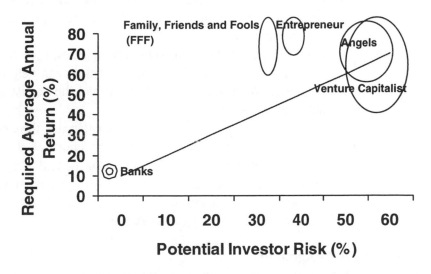

**Fig. 6.1** Perceived Risk - Return Investment Space

---

[3] Exit is the point where equity in the enterprise can be easily converted to monetary value.

Figure 6.1 forms part of the financial space that a new technological enterprise must consider as it seeks initial financing. It is critical that the enterprise formulation team prepares robust business and financial plans capable of convincing the prospective investors that the enterprise vision and objectives are not only well founded but will provide return commensurate with the risk they are taking.

Seeking initial enterprise financing can be an arduous process (Jacobus and Gottlieb 1997). In many instances new technological enterprises fail to obtain their initial capital due to a number of reasons, some of which may not be associated with the technology, strategies, or their experience but with the way the material is presented to the prospective investors. It is important that the entrepreneur (DeFife 1997):

- Develop a robust business plan that clearly defines the enterprise and the plan for its financing.
- Focus on the enterprise formation team since it is the team that will implement the business and financial plan.
- Target investors by having a funding strategy and plan.
- Find a mentor that *"has been there, done that"* who can act as an advisor in reviewing the business plan and funding strategy.
- Publicize the enterprise through news releases, speeches, etc. This publicity while seeming frivolous can help to establish a *buzz* about the enterprise and thus assist in attracting investors.
- Build momentum for interest in the enterprise through building strategic alliances. Press coverage of these strategic alliances can further attract and build momentum behind the financing strategy and move potential investors to closure.
- Participate in networking organizations.

## 1.1 Historical Background

Entrepreneurs and the search for capital have historic roots that are deep. The word funding is based on Latin noun *fonds* that represented goods of early merchants (Braudel 1979, pp. 233). Funds and capital became analogous in the early eighteenth century. By 1759, Jean-Jacques Rousseau wrote to a friend *"I am not a great lord nor a capitalist; I am poor and happy"* (Braudel 1979, pp. 235).

While creative entrepreneurs have always sought capital to implement their vision, the sources of capital did not markedly changed until the mid-twentieth century. After the Second World War, with the rise of technological enterprises, the formal venture capital community started to appear in the financing space. Before that time the financing space for new enterprises was the province of individual investors and the banking community. The formal venture capital industry became a major funding source following the success of such technological enterprises as the Polaroid Corporation and the spectacular financial growth of American Research and Development ("ARD"). ARD invested several million dollars to fund Digital Equipment Corporation. ARD had been started by George Doriot, an eminent professor at Harvard University. By 1997, the venture capital community was investing in ventures at the rate of $12.8 billion per year (PW 1998). In 1997, nearly 2,700 enterprises had received venture funding with new technological ventures receiving the largest share of venture financing, i.e., 45 percent.

## 1.2 Financing Life Cycle

Like all processes, financing has a life cycle that matches that of the enterprise. Figure 6.2 shows the general financial cycle. The financing of a new enterprise changes as the enterprise and its financial requirements grow. A different investor group with separate investing objectives dominates each phase of financing. The early and seed capital financing stage is dominated usually by the entrepreneur, and family, friends and *fools*[4] ("FFF"). This initial investment covers the cost of establishing the technological enterprise and the expected difference between revenue and the expenses required to bring the technology to market and to achieve a presence in the market space. Recently this phase has also become the region in which *angels* have begun to invest. Increasingly *angels* have joined together in networks, such as the Private Investor Network ("PIN") in the Washington, D.C. metropolitan region. These networks provide a means to screen potential investment targets. These informal venture capital networks exist throughout the United States and Europe.

---

[4] These non-related investors are termed *fools* since many simply invest based on the exuberance of the entrepreneur and rarely due any depth of analysis of the investment.

234

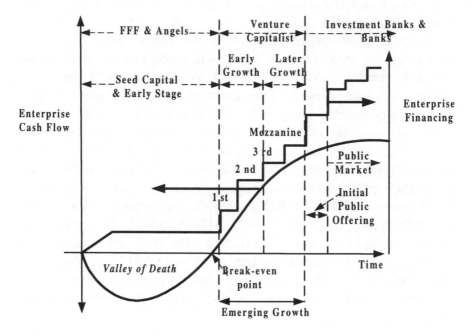

**Fig. 6.2** Financing Life Cycle (Adapted from Fitzpatrick 1991)

The venture capitalists tend to invest in early and later growth stage financing of the enterprise development. However, as the 1997 data shows, venture capitalists are increasingly investing in early stage enterprise financing (PW 1998).

### 1.3 Initial Stage Financing Strategies

Development of a business plan is a necessary but not a sufficient condition for obtaining seed capital. Strategies for increasing the probability of obtaining financing are necessary, and are one of the principal objectives of the initial business plan (DeFife 1997).

**Robust Business Plan** - The business plan is the primary introduction of the enterprise to the prospective investors. The prospective investors will look initially at the executive summary, leadership team and financials. If these sections are not sufficiently robust and well presented it is unlikely that the reader will go further. It is also important that the business plan shows how the enterprise will use the proceeds of the initial financing and what will be the *exit* or *harvest strategy* (See Chapter 8 - Next Entrepreneurial Step). The *exit strategy* is the means by which the potential investors will not only recover their initial investment but the high returns warranted for investing in a high-risk venture.

**Robust and Knowledgeable Leadership Team** - While coupling the financial vision to the entrepreneurial vision is essential, it is the leadership team that must bring the enterprise to fruition. It is therefore important to demonstrate to the prospective investors that the leadership team has the experience and expertise to accomplish the robust enterprise vision, i.e., the enterprise formation team having *"been there, done that."* While this may be difficult in a new technological and market space, robust backgrounds and achievements will provide some assurance that the enterprise leadership team can meet potential problems. The leadership team's strengths and weaknesses are the guides the potential investors will, in the end, base their investment decision upon, all other factors being equal.

**Investor Focus** - The investment space is large and variegated, with different investment regions and objectives. Hence, it is important to target the correct investor space region. This can be accomplished by:

- Networking among as many potential investor groups as possible.
- Determine if the investors do initial, i.e., seed, financing.
- Determine the investor definition of early stage financing.
- Determine if the prospective investors have available capital for early stage financing and their timeline for making investments.
- If the new enterprise is not within a prospective investor space, then determine if the prospective investors would be willing to introduce you to other investor groups, which may be suitable for early stage financing.

Before selecting prospective investors, it is important to understand that investors can add value to the new enterprise by adding experience, expertise, ideas, partnerships and contacts beyond the initial financing. Therefore, it is critical to take similar care when choosing the investors as when choosing the members of the enterprise leadership team.

**Robust Advisors** - While many technological entrepreneurs have initial self-assurance, it is important to have outside advisors. The advisors should have exceptional business experience and be willing to serve as the enterprise's mentors. These advisors should have experience, if possible, in the same or contiguous technological and market spaces.

**Robust Public Relations** - It is important to create a *buzz* about the new technological enterprise. This can be achieved by a strategy of issuing a structured group of press releases, making industry presentations, writing articles and other items that will help to create a presence if not a *branding* of the new enterprise.

**Build Relationships** - Building momentum behind the business plan can be achieved through building relationships with prospective customers, suppliers and other potential strategic partners. This can be achieved even without initial enterprise financing, by building strategic relations and signing contingent contracts. These relationships can illustrate to potential investors the robustness of the entrepreneurial vision.

## 2. INITIAL BUSINESS PLAN
### 2.1 Initial Business Plan Focus

A business plan is a written statement of what the enterprise intends to do in the future, how it plans to implement its vision and how the leadership team will achieve the results (Zimmer and Scarborough 1996, pp. 326).

The initial business plan is where the vision and objectives of the technological entrepreneur are presented with the supporting financial statements in a manner that enables not only potential investors, but also the enterprise to accept and participate in the entrepreneurial vision.

The business plan incorporates the results of the technological and market strategic planning processes (See Chapter 3 - Technological and Enterprise Strategic Planning and Chapter 4 - Enterprise Technological Market Planning). An initial business plan serves as both as a roadmap to manage the enterprise and as a means to raise the initial capital resources needed to mechanize the roadmap. The technological entrepreneur and the enterprise formation team need to keep these two objectives of the business plan in focus as it is crafted.

The initial enterprise business plan should highlight the critical framework elements for any enterprise (Sahlman 1998). These elements include the people, opportunity, context, and risks and rewards of the proposed new technological enterprise.

**The People** - The entrepreneur and the enterprise leadership team and any outside groups providing important services or resources, including lawyers, accountants, and suppliers, are the first important element of the business plan.

**The Opportunity** – The business model is the part of the framework that covers what the enterprise is selling and its potential market space. This enumerates the economics and potential barriers to be faced by the new technological enterprise.

**The Context** - The context of the business plan includes the uncontrollable environmental variables such as regulatory environment, interest rates, demographic trends, inflation and similar factors not under the control of the entrepreneur and the leadership team.

**Risks and Rewards** - All ventures are formed to exploit either a real or a potential competitive advantage. As such, it is critical that the initial business plan delineates both the potential risks and rewards. In any circumstance, there is always a response strategy for dealing with potential problems. The initial business plan is a scenario of future events and as such must deal with potential risks. The business plan presents a plausible and coherent story of the future enterprise's position in both the technological and market spaces. Therefore, the initial business plan must unflinchingly confront the risks that the enterprise might face.

The initial business plan provides potential investors with an opportunity to determine if the entrepreneur and the enterprise formation team have identified a competitive advantage and have the entrepreneurial and management skills to exploit the business opportunity and the competitive advantage. The plan should present the strategies in a manner that will persuade the potential investors that there is a reasonable probability of achieving high returns.

The initial business plan has a number of benefits associated with its development. These benefits include providing documentation of the strategic technological and market planning, the competitive advantages of the business model, the associated risks in achieving the enterprise vision, and proposed strategies for dealing with these risks. This documentation provides assurance that a realistic business model exists. The initial business plan presents the enterprise structure and documents the advantages of the enterprise formation team. The plan establishes the financial and other objectives that can be used to manage the new technological enterprise. The plan can also present the technological enterprise in a light that can attract the necessary capital resources to bring the entrepreneurial vision to reality. The plan should also define and anticipate potential risks, problems, and trade-offs.

In many instances, the business plan is the first enterprise product that prospective investors see. Thus, it is critical that the plan be both complete and concise. The business plan is not an offering memorandum. However, the initial business plan must not only present the enterprise vision and the means of achieving that vision, but also the capital requirements. The plan should not contain the outline of the *deal* the entrepreneur is seeking since that could likely place it in the light of an investment memorandum with the associated legal constraints.

Technological entrepreneurs visualize how their enterprise should be presented and how to achieve the initial vision objectives (Rockey 1986, pp. 344). Any business plan, not only the initial but also future plans, should provide validity, realism, truthfulness and full disclosure (Vesper 1993, pp. 332).

The high returns drive the investment rationale not the technology. A business plan is a *selling document* that conveys the excitement and promise of the enterprise to the potential investors and thus provides a basis for ensuring the potential high returns sought (Gumpert 1997). Prospective investors have short spans of attention when considering business plans. The entrepreneur is faced with various *gates* that must be passed before obtaining venture financing. These gates include full reading of the business plan, full investigation, and finally negotiation for the investment. In turn, the investors are faced with high risks for their investments. Estimates of the probability of passing the various venture capital *gates* and risk domains are shown in Table 6.1.

Therefore, potential investors are faced with the knowledge that one to two plans in a thousand submitted are likely to produce sufficiently high returns to justify the risk domain. Thus, it is critical for the technological entrepreneur and the enterprise formation team to build the initial business plan that can penetrate these formidable investment barriers.

The initial business plan must be a carefully thought out and crafted document. The business plan should include a robust market analysis with a full explanation of how and why the plan will make the entrepreneurial vision a reality (Teague 1980).

**Table 6.1**
Entrepreneurial Financing Gates

| Investor Actions | Business Plan Acceptance Rates |
|---|---|
| Full Reading | 10 - 13 % |
| Full Investigation (Due Diligence) | 2 - 5 % |
| Negotiation | 1 - 3 % |
| Initial Financing | 0.5 - 1 % |

Venture Capital Risk Domain

| Investment Results | Investments |
|---|---|
| Total Failure | 25 - 30 % |
| Marginal (*Walking Dead*) | 50 - 60 % |
| Highly Profitable | 10 - 15 % |

Investors do not like to see an excessively lengthy business plan that could easily be made more concise (Vesper 1993, pp. 333). The plan should be between twenty-five and thirty pages with only relevant appendixes. Irrelevant information that does not lend itself to establishing the basic logic of the business plan should not be included. The framers of the plan should not include self-congratulatory words and phrases. However, the plan should be clear on the background of the leadership team of the new enterprise. Also critical data on the enterprise, which are associated with its core competencies, technologies and potential competitive advantages, are important to include.

Poor writing including spelling and grammatical errors can easily discourage investors. This can be overcome by having the plan reviewed by outside advisors. These reviews may not only improve the writing of the plan but can be used to ferret-out logical inconsistencies. However, professionally prepared plans that are not the direct product of the technological entrepreneur and the enterprise formation team will reduce the confidence of the prospective investors in the enterprise. Using a financial consultant to review the plan and provide suggestions may be helpful in placing the financial plan in a format and consistency that venture capitalists usually seek.

A business plan presented to prospective investors in particular venture capitals without a personal introduction or personal presentation lacks the *human element* that is critical in obtaining any initial financing. This personal contact is in many instances more important than the business plan

240

since it is the characteristics of the entrepreneur and the enterprise formation team that will turn the technological entrepreneurial vision into a reality.

## 2.2 Initial Business Plan Format

The initial business plan can be of varying length depending on the nature of the new enterprise. However, the initial business plan must be complete in that it fully delineates the entrepreneurial vision, the strategy for implementing the vision, the technological and market space, the enterprise leadership team and the financial resources needed to bring the vision to fruition. Table 6.2 presents a general outline for a technological enterprise initial business plan that should contain the following major sections:

- Cover Page.
- Table of Contents.
- Executive Summary.
- Technological and Market Space.
- Strategic Technological and Market Plan.
- Enterprise Structure and Leadership Team.
- Risk Management Plan.
- Financial Plan.
- Appendixes.

**Table 6.2**
General Initial Business Plan Format

Cover Page
Table of Contents
1.  Executive Summary (2 to 4 pages)
    1.1.    Entrepreneurial vision
    1.2.    Summary of technological space and strategy
    1.3.    Summary of market space and strategy
    1.4.    Summary of strengths of enterprise leadership team
    1.5.    Summary of potential risks and enterprise responses
    1.6.    Summary statement of financial requirements
2.  Technological and Market Space
    2.1.    Technological Space and Strategy
        2.1.1.    Short description of the technological basis for the enterprise, i.e., enterprise core technology
        2.1.2.    Technological space the enterprise is entering and potential positive and negative developments, i.e., technological environmental analysis

## 2.2.1 Cover Page and Table of Contents

The cover page has a number of purposes. It should include the enterprise name, logo (if it exists), address and principal contact including telephone numbers and e-mail addresses. The cover page should also contain a warning as to the proprietary nature of the material contained within the business plan. The front page should also include a copy number for tracking purposes.

The table of contents follows the cover page. This section should be as detailed as possible so potential investors can easily find material. Many investors read business plans not necessarily in the order presented and may read marketing or financial sections before reading the executive summary.

### 2.2.2 Executive Summary
The objective of the executive summary is to summarize in two to four pages the enterprise and the strategy for transforming the entrepreneurial vision into value for the stakeholders. Prospective investors use the executive summary to make an initial determination as to the value of proceeding further with the business plan. It is important that this section of the business plan be concise, convincing and should include the nature of the enterprise, capital requirements, summary of technological and market space potentials, risks and alternative strategies.

### 2.2.3 Technological and Market Space
It is in this section of the business plan where the entrepreneur and the leadership team present the enterprise strategy for entering an existing or new market space with their technological entrant. It is important that this section be succinct and easily grasped. Many prospective investors may not have the in-depth technological background to follow detailed technical descriptions. In fact, a verbose presentation of the technology may in fact serve as a deterrent to an investment.

This section also presents the analysis of the technological industry including existing and potential competitors. The section should clearly delineate the anticipated technological and competitive advantages and their sustainability. Included is a general description of the marketing strategy. While it has been argued that the business plan should contain a detailed marketing plan, it must be understood that eventually the plan will be read by the enterprise's competitors, and, as has been stated by Andy Grove, Former Chairman of Intel Corporation, *"Only the paranoid survive"* (Grove 1996). Hence, only a general market plan and strategy should be presented. A separate, detailed strategic market plan (See Chapter 4 - Enterprise

Technological Market Planning) should also be prepared, but it is only prudent that this not be widely circulated except to investors during their due diligence process.

### 2.2.4 Risk Management Plan
All enterprises will face some risks especially those trying to embed new or radical technologies into an existing market space or establish a totally new market space. Based upon the SWOT analysis (See Chapter 3 - Technological and Enterprise Strategic Planning) of the new enterprise, risks associated with the technologies employed and the market should be identified and addressed as to their elimination or mitigation. This should include contingency plans. This approach will indicate to potential investors that the enterprise is prepared to deal with the vicissitudes of a rapidly changing technological and market space.

### 2.2.5 Financial Plan
This section of the initial business plan presents the capital required to implement the technological entrepreneurial vision. A detailed discussion of the initial financial plan is presented in Section 3 of this chapter. It is the financial plan that presents the investment required and the economic feasibility of the enterprise. The financial plan contains the sales forecasts and how these translate into cash flow and an increase in value of the potential investment. Also contained in this section is the financial and other assumptions used to generate the analysis. The financial plan is a critical requirement for obtaining the initial financing of the enterprise.

### 2.2.6 Appendixes
The background material that substantiates the business plan is placed in the appendixes. This can contain detail managerial profiles, product or service literature if available, market research data, and any other material directly related to the enterprise.

### 2.3 Business Plan Failure
Initial business plans face a number of hurdles even if well conceived. Initial business plans are rejected by venture capitalists due to a number of reasons (Roberts 1983). Table 6.3 shows the data reported by Roberts for deficiencies of business plans.

**Table 6.3**
Deficiencies of Initial Business Plans

| Deficiencies Due To | Percentage of Business Plans Containing Problems |
|---|:---:|
| Detailed identification of competition lacking | 75 |
| Discussion of intellectual property protection inadequate | 55 |
| Leadership team lacked marketing experience, and marketing strategy was not fully detailed | 40 |
| Financial plans lacked sufficient details | 10 - 15 |

The greater the initial plan deficiencies the more likely the potential investors will decline investing in the new venture. Many new business plan failures are due to one or more classic factors (Hisrick and Peters 1995, pp. 129):

- Unreasonable goals.
- Non-measurable goals.
- Lack of total entrepreneurial commitment.
- Lack of entrepreneurial experience in proposed market space.
- Failure to recognize and adequately address potential threats facing the new enterprise.
- Lack of satisfying customer needs.

Evidence exists that the entrepreneur's expertise is more strongly correlated with enterprise performance than was the entrepreneur's experience. They also found those different types of expertise were associated with different types of experience (Reuber and Fischer 1994). These empirical studies showed that experience is an inadequate surrogate for expertise. It is suggested that prospective investors focus explicitly on learning, in order to understand better how and what entrepreneurs learn from their experience. Synergies may arise from having small amounts of different types of experience rather than from having large amounts of one type of experience (Reuber and Fischer 1994). Thus having industry, large firm, and start-up experience, could provide a more comprehensive body of experience than having the same amount of one type of experience.

## 2.4 Initial Business Plan Evaluation

The technological entrepreneur and the enterprise formation team should evaluate their initial business plan before submitting it to prospective investors. This evaluation should be undertaken using the guidelines similar to that employed by many venture capitalists. The entrepreneur and the leadership team should try to develop an analytic approach to evaluate their initial business plan similar to that shown in Table 6.4.

**Table 6.4**
Initial Business Plan Evaluation

| Criteria | Valuation (Scale 1 to 10 where 1 is poor and 10 is outstanding) |
|---|---|
| **1. Leadership Team** (10 max each) | |
|    1.1.    Entrepreneurial Experience and Expertise | |
|       1.1.1.    Varied experience ( 5 max) | |
|       1.1.2.    Experience in market space ( 5 max) | |
|    1.2.    Technical Members | |
|    1.3.    Marketing Members | |
|    1.4.    Financial Members | |
| **Total Leadership Team** | (40 max) |
| **2. Technological Space** (10 max each) | |
|    2.1.    Technological Competitive Advantage (10 max) | |
|       2.1.1.    Existing Technology | |
|       2.1.2.    Incremental Technology | |
|       2.1.3.    New Generation Technology | |
|       2.1.4.    Radical Technology | |
|    2.2.    Potential Technological Risk ( 1 = high, 10 = low) | |
| **Total Technological Space** | (20 max) |
| **3. Market Space** (10 max each) | |
|    3.1.    Market Competitive Advantage | |
|    3.2.    Market Growth Potential (1 = low, 10 = high) | |
| **Total Market Space** | (20 max) |
| **4. Financial Space** (10 max each) | |
|    4.1.    Capital Requirements (1 = insufficient or excessive, 10 = sufficient with some margin for uncertainty) | |
|    4.2.    Return - Short Term (1 to 3 years) | |
|    4.3.    Return - Long Term (5 years) (1 = less than 10 percent, 10 = greater than 60 percent annually) | |

4.4.     Economic Value Added ("EVA")[5] with 50 percent use of
         capital after 5 years (1 = negative, 10 = positive, the higher
         the better)

                                    **Total Financial Space**     (40 max)

5.   **Initial Business Plan Internals** (10 max each)
     5.1.     Describes enterprise vision in an easily understood manner
     5.2.     Market detail description
     5.3.     Realistic evaluation of competitors
     5.4.     Technological strategy (1 = no mention, 10 = robust
              strategy)
     5.5.     Market strategy (1 = no mention, 10 = robust strategy)
     5.6.     Financial plan (1 = missing one or more standard elements,
              10 = robust and contains all prerequisite elements and is not
              overly complex)

                          **Total Business Plan Internals**     (60 max)
                              **Total Initial Business Plan**     **(180 max)**

A twelve-factor method, based on a scale of one to ten, for evaluating
business plans includes (Scarbrough and Corbett 1992, pp. 352 - 355):

- Marketability of enterprise concept, with one being
  assigned if the plan describes hypothetical customers to
  ten for firm purchase orders or contracts.
- Short-term profit potential for the enterprise, with one for
  annual return of ten percent or less with ten assigned to
  return exceeding fifty percent or more.
- Market size or growth potential, with one for small
  specialty market with little or no growth potential and ten
  for a potentially large market with high growth potential.
- Competitive advantage of enterprise, with one for
  products, processes or services that can be supplied by
  existing competitors, i.e., little or no competitive
  advantage, and ten for a high competitive advantage.
- Enterprise ability to control distribution channels and
  quality, with one if core competencies must be

---

[5] EVA = Net operating profit after taxes ("NOPAT") less capital invested times expected
return on capital, for a new high risk venture this return should be approximately 50 percent
or higher.

outsourced and a factor of ten for total enterprise control of both distribution channels and quality.

- Enterprise skills and experience sets, with one for inexperience and expertise and ten for a higher level of relevant experience and expertise.
- Complexity of the new enterprise business model, with one assigned for an enterprise with a high degree of complexity and one or a few products, processes or services provided to customer who understand the benefits of items being provided by the enterprise. Ten is assigned for a simple new enterprise business model, with one or more products, processes or services.
- Degree of personal investment by the entrepreneur and other key members of the new enterprise leadership with one for only for *sweat equity* to ten for total financial commitment.
- The degree to which the technological entrant being offered by the new enterprise offers the potential customers long term benefits, with one for little or no long term benefits to ten for excellent long-term customer benefits.
- Degree of robustness of the technological and market strategies presented, with one assigned if no or little strategy is presented to ten for a well designed, clearly formulated robust strategy.
- Degree to which the financial plan presented realistically presents financial projections, including, most likely, pessimistic and optimistic scenarios, with one assigned to little or no financial projections to ten for a complete robust financial model that can be adjusted to show *what-if* scenarios.
- Degree to which the initial business plan communicates the entrepreneurial vision, with one assigned to a business plan that is not clear and concise and ten for a professionally written initial business plan which is clear and concise.

It was found that initial business plans that scored between 108 and 120 points had a good chance of obtaining initial financing, while a score between 96 and 107 indicated an initial business plan that was likely to attract some financing, but could improve their scores by some additional work (Zimmer and Scarborough 1996, pp. 355). A score between 72 and 95 indicated there was the possibility that the initial business plan would result in financing, but it would take time and be difficult to secure. With a score of less than 71, it was unlikely that the initial business plan would obtain financing and, the enterprise business model should be totally reworked.

## 2.5 Initial Business Plan Presentation

After preparing the initial business plan, at some point the technological entrepreneur will have to make a presentation to potential investors. This presentation can range from a one-on-one meeting to a presentation before a group of angel investors. There are three impediments to a successful presentation (Jacobus and Gottlieb 1997).

**Reading versus speaking** - A prevalent mistake is to read the business presentation rather than speak it. An excellent oral presentation will allow the entrepreneur to energize and motivate prospective investors. While not all speakers are charismatic, entrepreneurial excitement coupled with a realistic approach will achieve results.

**Focusing on the process not the objective of the presentation** - The objective of the presentation is to solicit sufficient interest so follow-up meetings with potential investors will occur. The technological entrepreneur must realize that the process of obtaining financing will take time and a number of meetings. The material to be presented should be convincing and to the point. Visual aides such as overhead transparencies, slides, and presentations such as available in Microsoft's® PowerPoint, can help keep the presentation focused. The entrepreneur should also keep the presentation within the time allotted. In most instances, technological entrepreneurs have between eight and twenty minutes to present the essence of their initial business plan to potential investors at venture fairs. A typical investor presentation follows a topical structure covering the technological product, process or service being offered by the new enterprise, the targeted market space, sales and marketing plan, leadership team, financial arrangements and exit strategy. Other useful formats are to use either chronological or a question and answer presentation approach.

**Lack of attention to the needs and desires of the potential investors** - It is important not to explain the enterprise technology in detail. The potential investors are more concerned with the entrepreneur and the leadership team, market strategy, financial projections, the validation of the assumptions used to derive the financial and market space and potential exit strategies.

The business plan presentation can benefit from professional advice to create a credible and professional presentation that will garner confidence and enthusiasm from prospective investors. It is important that the entrepreneur have a number of rehearsals of the presentation before a critical, but non-investor, audience. The combination of using a presentation coach and dress rehearsals will increase the probability of obtaining the interest that may secure the initial financing.

## 3. INITIAL FINANCIAL PLAN

The development of a logical and robust initial financial plan is one of the keys to obtaining the prerequisite financing to implement the entrepreneurial vision. Hence, the initial financial plan for the enterprise should be approached with the same diligence that the entrepreneur and leadership team employ when developing the technological and market strategy. It is important to visualize the financial plan in terms of a financial model. Figure 6.3 shows a form of a financial model that will allow the entrepreneur and leadership team to test various *what-if-scenarios* before finalizing the initial financial plan. These *what-if-scenarios* will allow the entrepreneur to present to prospective investors the range of investment parameters.

The initial financial plan should contain a number of elements including (Snyder 1997):

- Historical financials, if available. However, most new technological enterprises do not have any history. If historical financials are available then professionally prepared audited statements should be included.
- Forecasts for the first year of operation on a quarterly basis and a five-year forecast on a yearly basis. These forecasts should include:
  - Pro forma income statement.
  - Pro forma balance sheet.
  - Pro forma cash flow statement.
- Financial assumptions.
- Sales forecasts and essential variables that are linked to the basic financial statements.

250

- Sensitivity analysis of the essential variables indicating the impact on the net profit after taxes.
- Summary of enterprise business ratios.

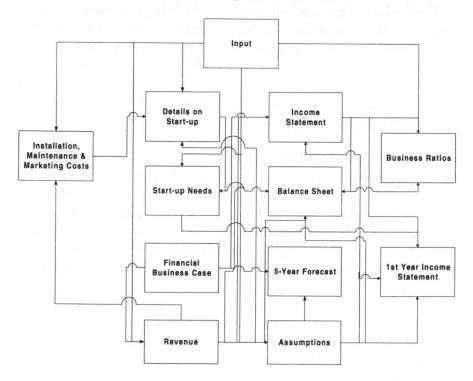

**Fig. 6.3** Financial Plan Model

## 3.1 Initial Capital Requirements

The accurate assessment of the initial capital requirements of the new enterprise is critical. Prospective investors will make an independent assessment of these capital requirements. If their results differ significantly from the requirements presented in the financial plan the confidence in the entrepreneur and the leadership team to manage the enterprise will be put in doubt.

The initial requirements for the new venture can be determined from financial projections, outside observation and funding timing (Batz 1990, pp. 97-98).

**Financial Projections** - Development of a profit and loss ("P&L") statement based on realistic sales forecasts is the principal method used to compute the capital requirements. This will yield a cash flow projection that will show the amount of cash required during each period of the forecast. The cash flow is very sensitive to small variations in growth rate, development cost, and enterprise overheads and accounts receivable.

**Outside Observation** - Observing what capital has been obtained for comparable new enterprises in the chosen technological and market space. The equity interest that has been demanded can also be ascertained from outside observation.

**Funding Timing** - All funding that the new enterprise will obtain will be scheduled to meet the enterprise development stage. A prudent investor will schedule the investment to meet the cash flow requirements of the enterprise. The cash flow analysis will give an indication of this funding schedule. The funding is likely to be tied to meeting enterprise milestones, such as prototype availability, sales goals, etc.

It is important to anticipate potential problems that can cause cash flow crises for the new enterprise. Delays and other operational problems that will negatively influence the projections can cause such crises. Prospective investors will also be interested if the investment can be phased. Investment transfers based on enterprise milestones provide prospective investors with a means of reducing investment risks.

## 3.2    Financial Projections

The objective of preparing financial projections is to determine the enterprise revenue, gross net profits, net worth, cash flow and economic valued added. These projections should be made for the first year of the new enterprise operations on a monthly basis and, if that is not possible due to uncertainty, on a quarterly basis. Additional projections should also be performed for three to five years on a yearly basis if not a quarterly basis. It is unusual for a new technological enterprise to have sufficient information about the technological and market space to prepare an accurate three to five year forecast on a quarterly basis beyond the first year of operation. This implies that a series of scenarios need to be prepared and the important variables parsed within potential ranges to determine impact on capital requirements and critical cash flow periods.

These projections are elements within the pro forma income statement, balance sheet, and operating ratios. As shown in Figure 6.3, all these elements are related in a dynamic manner. Appendix A at the end of this chapter presents financial projections associated with the model, shown for a proposed new communications enterprise, RoyalTel Communications, Ltd. The financial projections for this enterprise illustrate the interactive nature of the inputs and assumptions.

Integrated financial projections that are consistent require:

- Development of a block diagram model showing how the various model components are related to the desired outputs.
- Development of a sales forecast based upon the diagrammatic model.
- Development of a pro forma income statement.
- Development of the expenses required to meet the revenue projections. An example is the number of salespersons and maintenance personnel required. These staffing requirements are in turn related to the number of sales calls per day and the customer capture rate.
- Development of the pro forma balance sheet.
- Development of a pro forma cash flow statement by approximating the net cash flow by taking the net operating profit after taxes ("NOPAT") and adding back depreciation and other accounting items that net real cash outflow. The beginning and ending balance sheets can also be used to determine the cash flow. The entrepreneur and the leadership team should consider potential cash outflow events that can be easily masked in the beginning and end periods being considered.

The development of an internally consistent financial model provides a means for:

- Explicitly linking assumptions to financial projections.
- Linking all statements, i.e., revenue forecasts, projected expenses, income statement, balance sheet and ratios.
- Providing linkages to enterprise financial ratios, breakeven analysis, and enterprise valuation.
- Developing *what-if* projections easily.

Figure 6.4 shows simplified financial model linkages.

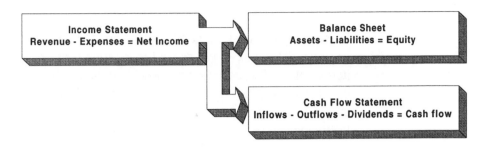

**Fig. 6.4** Example of Financial Projection Linkages

## 3.3 Pro Forma[6] Statements

The initial financial plan contains as a minimum the following pro forma statements:

- Income Statement
- Balance Sheet
- Cash Flow
- Breakeven Analysis
- Financial Ratios

### 3.3.1 Pro Forma Income Statement

The pro forma income statement is known as a profit and loss ("P&L") statement. This statement presents the differences between the revenue and the expenses to produce these revenues. The pro forma income statement is prepared by:

- Determining sales revenue for the period of the forecast, i.e., monthly, quarterly or yearly. These revenues should include potential income that can accrue to the enterprise from sales and services. Revenues include potential additional income sources such as investment interest, rents, royalties, etc. The sum of these revenues is known as *gross revenues.*
- Subtracting potential returns refunds from the *gross revenues.* The remaining revenue is known as the *net sales revenue.*

---

[6] Pro Forma is from New Latin *pro formâ: pro*, for the sake of, + *formâ*, ablative of *forma*, form. Its principal definition is: done as a formality; perfunctory.

- Subtracting the cost of goods sold from the *net sales revenue*. The *cost of goods sold* is the total cost of the items sold. These costs are those cost items that are directly passed through to the customer. Total cost includes shipping of the items sold. Typically, technological service enterprises do not have cost of goods sold. The result of subtracting the *cost of goods sold* from the *net sales revenue* is the *gross margin on sales*.
- Dividing the expenses that will be incurred by the new technological enterprise between:
  - Operating Expenses - Costs that contribute directly to products, processes or services provided. These could include sales, manufacturing and distribution expenses.
  - General Expenses - Indirect costs incurred in operating the enterprise, such as benefits, clerical staff, and interest on notes, mortgages, and debentures[7].
  - Other Expenses - All other expenses that cannot be classified as operating or general expenses.
- Subtracting the sum of all expenses from the *gross margin on sales*. This yields the *net operating profit* or *loss* before taxes.
- Depreciation is a deductible expense on the income statement although it is not part of the cash flow of the enterprise. Deducting the depreciation from the *net operating profit* or *loss* provides the amount that is subject to taxation. If this amount is negative it provides a tax loss carry forward that can be used in the future forecast periods to offset positive net income that can be subject to taxation.

### 3.3.2 Pro Forma Balance Sheet

The pro forma balance sheet provides a forecast of the new enterprise's net worth on a given date. The balance sheet is also known as the statement of financial position of the new enterprise. The pro forma balance sheet is

---

[7] Debentures are unsecured bonds backed only by the general credit of the issuing enterprise.

based on the accounting equation: *Assets* = *Liabilities plus stockholders'*
*equity or net worth.* This requires that any change in one side of the equation
be equal to the change in the other side of the equation.

The assets of the enterprise consist of everything owned by or owed to
the enterprise. The assets are divided between:

- Current Assets - Includes cash, accounts receivable (less
  allowances for doubtful accounts), inventory, and prepaid
  expenses.
- Fixed Assets - Including land, buildings (less
  accumulated depreciation), equipment (less accumulated
  depreciation), and furniture and fixtures (less
  accumulated depreciation).
- Intangible Assets - This can include items such as
  goodwill, copyrights and patents, that are valuable, but do
  not have a tangible value.

The liabilities of the enterprise consist of creditors' claims against the
enterprise. These include:

- Current Liabilities - Debts that must be paid within one
  year or enterprise financial cycle such as accounts
  payable, notes payable, accrued wages payable, accrued
  interest payable, and accrued taxes payable.
- Long-term Liabilities - These are debts due after one year
  and include such items as mortgages debentures and
  notes payable.

The equity of the enterprise consists of the value of the owner's
investment in the business. The equity represents the excess of all assets over
all liabilities, i.e., it represents the *net worth* of the enterprise. All revenue can
increase assets and net worth of the enterprise. The profit from the
operations of the enterprise will increase the *net worth* as *retained earnings.*
All expenses decrease *net worth* and either increase liabilities or decrease
assets. The equity of the enterprise is thus the sum of:

- Capital Stock - In a corporation this is represented by the
  preferred and common stocks of the enterprise. These
  shares are represented by the stock certificates issued by
  the corporation to its stockholders. The enterprise can
  issue several different classes of shares, each having
  different attributes such as voting rights and dividends.

- Capital Surplus - This part of the equity of the enterprise is the amount paid in by the owners over the par or legal value of each share in an enterprise.
- Accumulated Retained Earnings - This is also known as earned surplus. When the enterprise is initiated, it has no accumulated retained earnings. However, each operating period will produce either a profit or loss that is accounted for in the earned surplus.

### 3.3.3 Pro Forma Cash Flow Statement

The projected cash flow of the enterprise is the difference between the projected cash receipts and cash payments and presents the changes in the enterprise's working capital. This is not the same as profits or losses, which is the revenue less the expenses. This is because revenues and expenses may lag or lead the actual receipts or payments.

The principal financial problem that may face new technological enterprises is cash flow. Therefore, profits may not be a true metric of long-term enterprise success if there is a significant negative cash flow.

The cash flow statement contains all the receipts of revenue in the projected period less the total disbursements expected. The principal problem in preparing a cash flow statement is determining the staging of receipts and disbursements. In preparing an initial financial plan the entrepreneur and the leadership team should use conservative estimates, i.e., it will usually take longer to receive payments from customers while suppliers and other creditors will seek faster payments. Thus, a forecast should assume a lag in receipts, which exceeds the lag in the need to pay expenses associated with the sales.

It is also recommended that these initial projections for the business plan contain several scenarios: optimistic, most likely and pessimistic. Such scenario presentation will allow prospective investors to gauge the range of investments that are required by the enterprise. The management of the enterprise's cash flow is an exercise in strategic management of resources. A professional Chief Financial Offer ("CFO") will provide the experience and expertise to manage this strategic exercise.

It is important that the entrepreneur and the CFO revise cash flow projections as operating experience for the new enterprise is acquired.

### 3.3.4 Breakeven Analysis

The prospective investors will be interested in four types of breakeven for the new enterprise:

- Point in time when profit and losses are equal.
- Point in time when initial capital has been recovered through profit.
- Point in time when net operating profit after taxes less risk based interest on the enterprise capital becomes positive. (This is known as *Economic Valued Added* ("EVA") breakeven.)
- Number of sales or service units required to breakeven.

The revenue unit breakeven formula is given by (Hisrick and Peters 1995, pp. 163)

$$B/E(Q) \equiv \frac{TFC}{SP - VC / unit \text{ (marginal contribution)}}$$

Where:

$B/E(Q)$ = breakeven revenue units
$TFC$ = total fixed costs[8]
$SP$ = selling price per revenue unit
$VC$ = variable cost[9] per revenue unit

Figure 6.5 shows the various types of breakeven. Various investors will base their investment decisions on different types of breakeven. It is important that the technological entrepreneur understand the type of breakeven that prospective investors will base their investment decisions upon. The business plan, however, should only contain one breakeven chart: usually a cash flow breakeven chart.

---

[8] Fixed costs are costs that, without change in present production capacity, are not impacted by changes in output volume.
[9] Variable costs are costs that are impacted by changes in output volume.

258

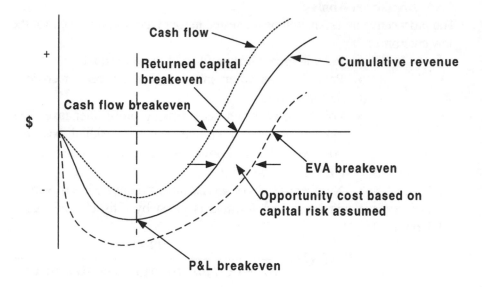

**Fig. 6.5** Breakeven Regions

### 3.3.5 Financial Ratios

Ratio analysis is used as a means for financial analysis by prospective investors. The ratios show relationships between financial accounts. While for a new technological enterprise, there is usually insufficient data to use financial ratios, they can be used with the pro forma statements to project potential financial conditions. The ratios are used to compare the enterprise with industry averages. As the enterprise matures, actual operational data can be used to analyze the financial conditions. These ratios can be divided into:

- Liquidity Ratios.
- Asset Management Ratios.
- Debt Management Ratios.
- Profitability Ratios.
- Market Value Ratios.

**Liquidity Ratios** - These ratios provide a means for determining if the enterprise will have trouble satisfying its financial obligations. The two commonly used liquidity ratios are the *Current Ratio* and the *Quick or Acid Test Ratio*. The *Current Ratio* is based on dividing current assets by current liabilities. The current assets usually include cash, marketable securities, accounts receivable, and inventories. An enterprise in difficulty usually pays its account payables more slowly thereby building up liabilities. A falling *Current Ratio* is a good metric of potential short-term enterprise solvency.

*Quick or Acid Test Ratio* is based on deducting inventories from current assets and dividing the remainder by current liabilities. This shows the enterprises ability to meet short-term obligations without relying on sale of inventories, the least liquid of the current assets.

**Asset Management Ratios** -These ratios measure the effectiveness of the management of the enterprise's assets. These ratios provide a means to determine if each type of asset being reported by the enterprise is too high or low in reference to the current and projected operations of the enterprise. The usual ratios employed are *Inventory Turnover, Average Collection Period, Fixed Assets Turnover*, and *Total Asset Turnover.*

*Inventory Turnover* or *inventory utilization ratio* is computed by dividing sales by inventories. The first problem associated with this ratio occurs due to the fact that sales are based on market prices while the inventories are based on cost, thus overstating the true turnover ratio. The second problem is that sales occur over a period, usually over an entire year, while inventories are point in time value. Therefore, a truer measure is the average inventory over the period of sales.

*Average Collection Period* is used to measure the accounts receivable and is determined by dividing the average daily sales into the accounts receivable to find the number of days' sales tied up in receivables and comparing this to the enterprise's terms on which the sales are made.

*Fixed Assets Turnover* or *fixed assets utilization ratio* is the metric of how effectively the enterprise uses its equipment and other fixed assets such as its facilities. This measure is determined by dividing sales by the fixed assets. However, a potential problem exists during periods of inflation that can understate the true value of fixed assets. *Total Assets Turnover* measures the utilization of the entire enterprise's assets. This metric is determined by dividing sales by total assets.

**Debt Management Ratios** - These ratios measure the enterprise's financial leverage. The amount of financial leverage increases the expected return to potential investors since interest is deductible, debt financing lowers the amount of taxes while making available more of the enterprise's operating income and, if the rate of return on assets exceeds the interest rate on the debt, then the debt can be used to finance assets, pay the interest on the debt and increase assets. Debt management ratios include *Debt Ratio, Times*

*Interest Earned Ratio, Fixed Charge Coverage Ratio* and *Cash Flow Coverage Ratio.*

*Debt Ratio,* also known as *total debt to total assets ratio,* is a measure of the total funds that will be provided by creditors. The *total debt* is defined as the current liabilities and long-term debt. Creditors would like to see a low debt ratio for an enterprise in order to minimize their potential losses if the enterprise enters liquidation. The entrepreneur and investors would seek a high leverage to magnify earning.

*Times Interest Earned Ratio* is obtained by dividing earning, before interest and taxes ("EBIT"), by interest charges. This ratio measures the extent that operating income can decline before the enterprise can no longer meet its annual interest charges.

*Fixed Charge Coverage Ratio* recognizes that enterprise lease assets can incur long-term obligations from lease contracts. This ratio is computed by adding lease payments to the EBIT and then dividing the total by the sum of the interest charges plus the lease payment. Enterprises such as America Online, Inc. and others have used leases to finance their expansions in the 1990s. Such enterprises can also manipulate income statements so as to appear to have sizable EBITs to cover the fact they are highly leveraged through leasing the majority of their assets.

*Cash Flow Coverage Ratio* is composed of the fixed charge coverage ratio and other factors including depreciation, preferred dividends, principal repayments placed on a before tax basis. These adjust show the margin by which the operating cash flows cover financial requirements. The following equation presents the method for computing this ratio.

$$\text{Cash Flow Coverage Ratio} = \frac{\text{EBIT} + \text{Lease Payments} + \text{Depreciation}}{\text{Interest} + \text{Lease Payments} + \dfrac{\text{Dividends on Preferred Stock}}{(1 - \text{Tax Rate})} + \dfrac{\text{Debt Repayment}}{(1 - \text{Tax Rate})}}$$

**Profitability Ratios** - These ratios provide information on the profitability of the enterprise's operations including the combined impact of liquidity, asset and debt management. These ratios include *Profit Margin on Sales Ratio, Basic Earning Power Ratio, Return on Assets,* and *Return on Common Equity.*

*Profit Margin on Sales Ratio* is obtained by dividing the net operating income after taxes ("NOPAT") by sales.

*Basic Earning Power Ratio* is obtained by dividing the EBIT by the total assets. This ratio shows the ability of the enterprise's assets, before impact of taxes and interest, to generate income.

*Return on Total Assets Ratio* is the ratio of the net income to total assets after taxes and interest.

*Return on Common Equity Ratio* is the ratio of NOPAT to common equity and is a measure of the rate of return on the investment of the stockholders.

**Market Value Ratios** give an indication of the way investors value the enterprise. While new enterprises do not necessarily have a market for their stock, an indication can be obtained from seeing how public enterprises in the same or similar technological and market space are valued (See Chapter 8 - Next Entrepreneurial Step.) These ratios give an indication of the way investors in a similar technological and market space value an enterprise's past and future performances. These ratios include *Price to Earnings Ratio* and *Market to Book Ratio.*

*Price to Earnings ("P/E") Ratio* is an indication of how much investors are willing to pay per reported profits. This ratio varies with industry averages such as the Standard and Poors ("S&P") Index. In the late 1990s, some technological spaces, such as Internet enterprises, reached exuberant ratios even for enterprises with little or no profits or substantial losses.

*Market to Book Ratio* gives an indication of how investors regard similar enterprises. Enterprises with high rates of return on equity usually have their stock selling at higher multiples of book value than those enterprises with low returns. The book value per share is computed by dividing the amount of common equity by the number of shares outstanding. To obtain the *Market to Book Ratio* the market price per share is divided by the book value per share.

## 4. INITIAL FINANCING

In some instances, initial financing is relatively painless, as in the case of Doug Borchard, President of iMarket Inc, a database marketing software manufacturer in Waltham, Massachusetts. Borchard obtained the initial financing from a private investor who was a relative of one of the other founders (Edge 1998). In other instances, it can take many months to find the correct financing and investors.

While financing of the initial enterprise is primary, the type of investors and their ability to assist the enterprise is also very important. The initial financing of a new technological enterprise requires the search for the type of investors that can add more than simply money. In fact, *"not all money is equal."* Some prospective investors who may be interested in investing in the new enterprise may in fact be the *wrong* types of investor for this stage of investment. It is important to perform due diligence on the prospective investors as they in turn investigate the enterprise.

## 4.1 Financial Strategies

Creating a financial strategy and funding plan is the essential element in initiating the new enterprise. Figure 6.6 shows a financial strategy framework (Timmons 1994, pp. 451). This framework is based on the premise that:

> *"...opportunity leads and drives the business*
> *strategy, which in turn drives the financial*
> *requirements, the sources and deal structures,*
> *and the financial strategy."* (Timmons 1994, pp.
> 450)

When developing an initial financing strategy the entrepreneur and the leadership team should consider:

- Quid Pro Quo, i.e., acceptable cost of capital: What will the enterprise be willing to give to obtain the initial capital?
- Risk - Return: What realistic return should the potential investor expect from the technological and market space the enterprise will be entering? This can be determined by reviewing returns from similar technological entrepreneurial enterprises in similar technological and market spaces. Prospective investors in a high-risk space would normally expect to obtain 50 to 100 percent annual returns on capital invested.
- Debt: Is the enterprise willing and capable of taking on short- and long-term debts and what would be the instrumentalities such as convertible debentures?

The factors that can influence the initial financing strategy include:

- Perceived risk.
- Technological and market space.
- Exit strategy.

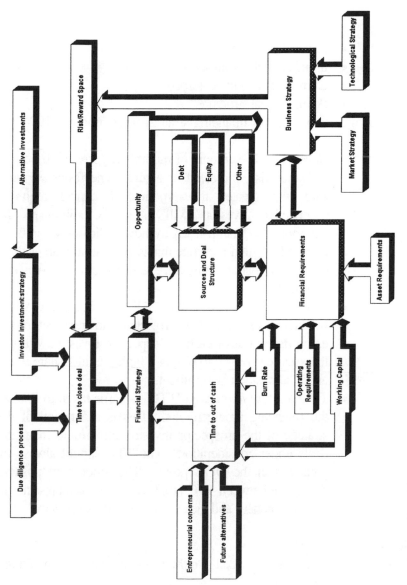

**Fig. 6.6** Financial Strategy Framework (Adapted from Timmons 1994, pp 452)

- Return - risk domain.
- Initial capital requirements.
- Current state of the enterprise.
- Potential deal structure.

The critical determinants for financing strategy are (Timmons 1994, pp. 451):

- *Burn rate* - The amount of monthly negative cash flow of the enterprise, projected or actual. The faster *the burn rate*, the greater the amount of capital required. Prospective investors will judge the ability of the enterprise leadership team by how judiciously capital is invested. A high burn rate that is generating market share can lead to market dominance as was the case of America Online, Inc.
- *Out of cash* ("OOC") - The OOC represents how many months, at the current or projected burn rate, before the enterprise is out of cash. Prospective investors will use this metric possibly to obtain a higher equity share when an OOC position is imminent.
- *Time to close financing* ("TTC") - Time taken to finalize the financing arrangements. This is a function of the strategy of the prospector investor and similar financing deals under consideration. The TTC should always be greater than the OOC point. The amount of positive difference between TTC and OOC will place pressure on the entrepreneur and the enterprise leadership team.

### 4.2 Financing Life Cycle

The financing life cycle can be divided into the following phases (See Figure 6.2):

- Seed and Startup.
- Early Stage.
- Later Stage.
- Initial and Post Public Offering (See Chapter 8 - Next Entrepreneurial Step).

As shown in Figure 6.2, a technological enterprise will need to seek capital throughout its life cycle. This financing life cycle starts before the formal establishment of the enterprise, as soon as the technological entrepreneur starts to expend resources. Figure 6.7 shows the early stage of this cycle as the enterprise is established and begins the climb to profitability.

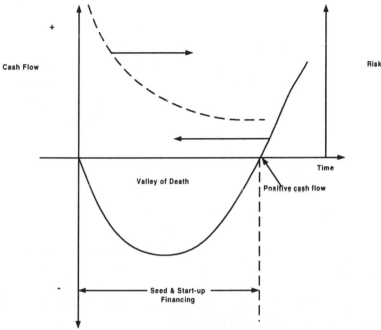

**Fig 6.7** Domain of Family, Friends, Fools , Angels and Some Venture Capitalists

The risk is greatest immediately at enterprise initiation and tends to decrease as positive cash flow and profitability are reached. During this early phase, financing usually is derived from:

- Entrepreneur - The entrepreneur usually provides initial resources to establish the enterprise.
- Family, Friends and Fools ("FFF") - Early stage investors who know or are related to the entrepreneur and who are willing to accept very high risk for potentially high returns. The fools are those individuals who are willing to invest without a true understanding of the risks, technology and market spaces and do not know the entrepreneur, but invest because of an unfounded exuberance.

- Angels - Individual knowledgeable investors who may not have any direct relationship with the new technological enterprise. Angels are usually substantial investors who believe the potential return from an investment in the new enterprise is worth the potential risks. This group is also known as *informal investors.*
- Strategic Alliances - Enterprises united together and seeking access to new technologies or markets.
- Government Agencies - Governmental guaranteed loans.
- Venture Capitalists - Few venture funds invest in the early stages of technological enterprises. Venture capital funding is usually available during the emerging growth stage of the enterprise.

The beginning portion of the financing life cycle is referred to as the *Valley of Death.* This reference is due to the fact that many new technological entrepreneurial enterprises never reach a positive cash flow or revenue position, and thus the enterprise *dies*, i.e., goes out of business. However, many technological enterprises take years to reach a positive revenue position and manage to garner worldwide branding, e.g., American Online ("AOL"). AOL, for much of its history from 1980s through the 1990s, did not have a positive revenue position. In fact, if the *Valley of Death* is redefined as the cumulative revenue, AOL as of 1998, had not recaptured all its losses or had a positive EVA.

### 4.2.1 Seed and Startup Capital Financing

Seed and startup capital financing consists of the capital required by the entrepreneur to implement the technological entrepreneurial vision. During this phase, the prospective investors realize the large risks involved that have been classified as extreme (Wetzel Jr. 1979). These investments should be sufficient to cover the projected negative cash flow as the enterprise starts to make a penetration in its chosen technological market space. The levels of investments from the various sources of seed and startup funding usually range from:

- FFF: Under $250,000.
- Angels (Small): $50,000 to $100,000.
- Angels (Large): $100,000 to $1 million.
- Strategic alliances: $250,000 and greater.

In certain instances, formal investors and venture capital groups may participate usually with investments of $500,000 and beyond. These circumstances are usually associated with well known entrepreneurs who have proven records of accomplishment in establishing and growing new technological enterprises.

On average, one out of two new enterprises make it out of the *Valley of Death* (Zimmer and Scarborough 1996, pp. 461). However, for those enterprises that move out of the *Valley of Death*, the risk to prospective investors may decrease from the higher levels associated with enterprises that are not profitable. Under some conditions, the risk can actually increase as large competitors notice the market penetration and take defensive market steps. The Seed and Start-up phase investors have return expectations between 50 and 100 percent per year on their investments (Zimmer and Scarborough 1996, pp. 461) due to the extreme risks associated with this phase of the financing life cycle.

Figure 6.8 shows an approximation of the return on investment ("ROI") expected by prospective investors during various rounds of financing in the emerging growth financing phase.

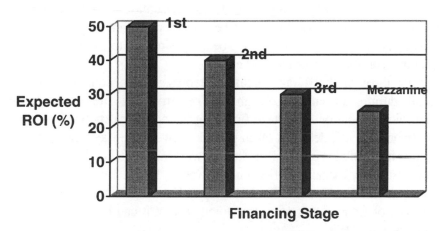

**Fig. 6.8** Approximate ROI during Emerging Growth Stage (Adopted from data in Wetzel Jr. 1997)

A source of seed and startup capital for some new technological enterprises is from strategic alliances (See Chapter 7 - Strategic Enterprise Growth). These strategic partners may supply capital to obtain rights to radical technologies. In many instances, it is easier for the strategic partner to finance a new enterprise than to develop a competing technology internally. In other instances, strategic allies may supply capital to a former employee who wants to implement a complementary technology or enter a new market space.

### 4.2.2 Emerging Growth Enterprise Financing

It is the emerging growth enterprise financing that the venture capitalists usually invest. The sources used to finance the enterprise in the seed and startup capital stage may not be sufficient to provide the capital during the enterprise growth stage. In this growth stage, the new technological enterprise will likely need a number of rounds of capital additions or financing. These financing rounds consist of:

- First.
- Second.
- Third and beyond.
- Mezzanine.

These financing rounds are usually provided by formal venture capitalist groups or through large strategic alliance partners. As the enterprise revenue increases, the associated investor risk tends to decrease. However, there are exceptions to this relationship as can be attested by technological enterprises who falter even as revenue appears to be increasing due to a radical change in either the technological or the market space.

First through third stage financing represents the continual need for capital during an enterprise's growth or emerging life cycle phases. Mezzanine capital or final stage financing is capital that is between senior debt financing, i.e., debt that takes precedent over other debt, and common stock. This capital is used for marketing, working capital and other uses. In some instances, mezzanine financing serves as bridge financing before an initial public offering ("IPO") (See Chapter 8 - Next Entrepreneural Step). This type of financing is often structured so that it can be repaid from the proceeds of the IPO.

### 4.3 Types of Enterprise Capital

There are two types of capital: equity and debt. Equity is an ownership interest in the new technological enterprise, while debt is loaned capital that requires repayment. The amount of equity to sacrifice in order to obtain capital for establishing a new enterprise is a question that all technological entrepreneurs will struggle to answer.

There are many variations or *flavors* to both equity and debt; the new enterprise can obtain financing from the following:

- Sale of common stock, with voting and non-voting interest.
- Sale of preferred stock.
- Sale of warrants, options or rights.
- Sale of bonds or notes that can be subordinated or not.
- Sale of debentures, which are notes that can be exchanged for stock at a future date.

Each of these forms of financing have advantages and disadvantages for the entrepreneur and future financing of the enterprise in its growth and, possibly, initial public offering. Table 6.5 provides a comparison of the various types of equity and debt. Figure 6.9 shows the general relationship between equity, debt, cost and risk.

**Fig. 6.9** Financing Space (Adapted from E&Y 1994)

Figure 6.9 illustrates the financing space facing a new technological enterprise. The long term cost to the enterprise is higher for equity due to the higher risk the prospective investors will have to endure. This is because the total after-tax cost makes it more expensive than debt. Debt results in higher overall financial risk for the enterprise since interest payments must be made and eventually the debt principal repaid.

Debt capital is usually very difficult for most new technological enterprises to obtain. Rarely do technological entrepreneurs seek debt capital unless there are substantial personal or intellectual assets that can be hypothecated[10], serving as security for the debt. However, as the enterprise starts to have revenue, then it may be able to secure debt from commercial sources such as banks (See Chapter 7 - Strategic Enterprise Growth). The debt can be:

- Short Term.
  - Line of credit.
  - Loan against accounts receivables.
  - Loan against inventory.
- Long Term.
  - Equipment leases[11].
  - Commercial mortgages for facilities.
  - Termed loan guaranteed by sources such as the Small Business Administration ("SBA") or others.

In most instances, the financial institutions providing the debt capital will require guarantees. The guarantees are promises from either the entrepreneur or others that they will be responsible for the repayment of the debt if the new enterprise fails to meet its obligations. It is possible for the entrepreneur to find a potential individual or enterprise willing to serve as a co-signer or guarantor of the debt in return for an interest in the enterprise. This can provide the capital required, but at the price that the new enterprise is saddled with both debt and having to part with an ownership interest.

Bonds are a source of debt financing not usually considered by new enterprises (Zimmer and Scarborough 1996, pp. 433). However, during the emerging growth phase of the new enterprise this form of financing may become a viable alternative (See Chapter 7 - Strategic Enterprise Growth).

---

[10] Hypothecate:to pledge property as security or collateral for a debt without transfer of title or possession.

[11] This type of loan was used to provide the majority of capital for the expansion of America Online.

**Table 6.5**
Types of New Enterprise Capital

| | Debt | | | Equity | | | |
| --- | --- | --- | --- | --- | --- | --- | --- |
| | | | | Common Stock | | Preferred Stock | Options, Warrants, & Rights |
| | Short Term | Long Term | Debenture | Voting | Non-Voting | | |
| Ease of Obtaining | Depends on security provided - usually difficult for new enterprises | | Not common | Yes | Maybe | Maybe | Not usual |
| Payback | Yes | Yes | Yes if not converted; to equity | No | No | No | No |
| Interest payments | Yes | Yes | Yes until converted sometimes rolled into note | No | No | No | No |
| Voting control | No | No | Only when converted | Yes | No | Yes | No |
| Restrictive covenants | Maybe | Maybe | Maybe | No | No | No | No |
| ROI Expected | Bank rates | Bank rates | Bank rates + | 50-100% | 50-100% | 50-100% | Depends |
| Risk to Investor | Usually secured | Usually secured | Can be secured but not generally, the investor is only at risk for the principal | Investor risk | Investor risk | Investor risk | Investor risk |
| Payback period | 1 year or less | 3 to 5 years | 1 to 5 years | 3 to 5 years | 3 to 5 years | 3 to 5 years | 3 to 5 years |

272

## 4.4    Sources of New Enterprise Capital

There are many sources of capital, however, not all of these are readily available to new technological enterprises.  In the 1990s, new enterprises obtained capital from (Zimmer and Scarborough 1996, pp. 377):

- Private Investors (FFF and Angels) - 35 percent.
- Corporations (Strategic Alliances) - 35 percent.
- Federal Research Grants (SBIR[12]) - 10 percent.
- Venture Capitalists - 10 percent.
- State, Local and other Governmental Agencies - 10 percent.

The most likely sources of capital for new enterprises are compared in Table 6.6.  Figure 6.10 shows a perceived risk-return space for various investor groups (See also Figure 6.1.)

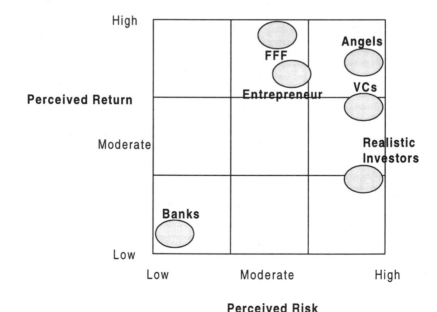

**Fig. 6.10** Investor Perceived Risk-Return Space

### 4.4.1  Private or Informal Sources of Capital

Private investors constitute the prevalent groups that provide financing for new technological enterprises and are classified as part of the informal

---

[12] SBIR = Small Business Innovation Research.

venture capital market (Harrison and Mason 1996). While Harrison and Masson do not classify entrepreneurs and FFF in this category, these groups are still informal and not professional investors. The private investor group consists of:

- Entrepreneur and members of enterprise formation team.
- Family, friend and fools.
- Angels, both small and large.

Entrepreneur and Enterprise Formation Team: Usually it is the entrepreneur and sometimes other members of the enterprise formation team that supply the initial capital to begin the new technological enterprise. This financing can come from personal savings, use of credit cards, loans or whatever personal resources that may be available. The entrepreneur and members of the enterprise formation team fervently believe in the entrepreneurial vision. This belief is also strengthened by the potential ephemeral and monetary rewards of succeeding in this new venture. While the monetary rewards may seem like the principal driver, the degree of the reward, i.e., how financially successful the enterprise will be, is not the primary psychological motivation. Usually the entrepreneur and the enterprise formation team underestimate the risks and overestimate the potential return from the new venture.

Family, Friends, and Fools: Family and friends are the next realistic source of initial financing for the new enterprise. This group tends to become the next fervent believers in the entrepreneurial vision after the entrepreneur and the enterprise formation team. These individuals perceive that there is risk, usually underestimated, but the belief in the entrepreneur and the entrepreneurial vision encourages limited investment. This group also tends to assume that the return will be relatively high. This group usually does little or no due diligence to determine the true viability of the entrepreneurial vision and thus invests solely because of relationships. To this category must be added *fools*, i.e., individuals who are not directly related to the entrepreneur or the enterprise formation team members and invest solely on the basis of the entrepreneurial vision without performing a validity check on the vision and lacking an understanding of the technological or market space the enterprise is planning to enter.

274

**Table 6.6**
Sources of Capital for New Technological Enterprises

| Source | Enterprise Life Cycle | | | Control | | | Cost | | | |
|---|---|---|---|---|---|---|---|---|---|---|
| | Seed | Operational | Growth | Covenants | Voting Rights | Guarantees of Debt | Zero | Interest | Equity | % Profits |
| **Equity** | | | | | | | | | | |
| Entrepreneur | X | X | ? | | X | | X | | X | |
| FFF | X | X | ? | | X | X | | | X | |
| Angels | X | X | | X | X | X | | | X | |
| Strategic Alliances | X | ? | ? | ? | ? | X | | | X | ? |
| Venture Capitalist | X | X | X | X | X | X | | ? | X | |
| Investment Funds | | | X | X | X | | | ? | X | ? |
| Public Offering | | | X | | X | | | | X | |
| **Debt** | | | | | | | | | | |
| Commercial Banks | | X | X | X | | X | | X | | |
| Asset leased lenders/lessors | | ? | X | X | | | | X | | |
| **Government Agencies** | | | | | | | | | | |
| SBA | X | X | X | X | | X | | | | X |
| SBIC/MESBIC | ? | X | | X | | X | | | | X |
| **Other Sources** | | | | | | | | | | |
| SBIR | X | X | ? | X | | | X | | | |
| Tax shelters | X | X | X | X | ? | | | ? | ? | ? |

(Based on data contained in Stevenson et al. 1994, pp. 240; Zimmer and Scarborough 1996, pp. 381)

Angels:   Another segment of the informal venture capital group are business angels.  The term *angel* is a term that is traditionally associated with investors in theatrical productions.   These individuals provide risk capital directly to new and growing enterprises in which they have no prior connection.  This category can be divided between small and large angels. The differentiation is based upon the amount of capital and the instrumentalities of the deal.   Small angels tend to invest $10,000 to $100,000 and rarely have term sheets[13] for the investments.  Large angels tend to invest in the manner of true venture capitalists and invest up to several million dollars.  These large angels usually handle the investment transaction with professional assistance.

Angels represent one of the largest sources of risk capital for technological entrepreneurs in the United States (Wetzel Jr. 1986, pp. 121) and are a growing investment source in both the United States and the European Union ("EU") (Harrison and Mason 1996, pp. 8 - 9).   The Advisory Committee on Science and Technology ("ACOST") of the United Kingdom has concluded that an informal venture capital market, i.e., angels and angel networks, are major pre-requisites for a vigorous entrepreneurial economy (ACOST 1990, pp. 41).

Angels usually provide Seed and Early-Stage investment capital and only one round of financing.  Venture capitalists usually invest larger amounts than angels and participate in more than one round of financing.  Angels usually look beyond the pure enterprise proposition and want to know and understand the entrepreneur (Gaydos 1997).  Angels want to embrace the entrepreneurial vision while venture capitalists tend not to be as emotionally involved in the enterprises in which they invest.  Angels also tend to want to assist the entrepreneur build a successful enterprise.   This usually is associated with the fact that many angels are or have been successful technological entrepreneurs and desire to recapture their past experiences (Gaydos 1997).

The characteristics of angels are (Hisrick and Peters 1995, pp. 265):
- Well educated, many having advanced degrees.
- Primarily financing new enterprises within a one-day travel radius from their primary residence.

---

[13] A term sheet is a document presented to the entrepreneur which outlines the proposed investment deal.

- Often wanting to have an active role in the new enterprise.
- Usually operating within an angel network that provides deal flow and preliminary screening.
- Making investments in the range of $10,000 to $100,000 for small angels and larger sums for large angels.
- Making one to two investments per year.

Figure 6.11 presents the risk-return space for angels based on enterprise operational experience. As the enterprise gains operational experience, the risk should decrease. However, the degree of risk is not solely limited to the experience level of an enterprise since the technology or market space can change even for enterprises which have substantial experience. The technological landscape is littered with enterprises such as Wang Computer, Digital Equipment and others that could not survive when *10X* changes occurred.

The primary sources of investment opportunities, i.e., *deal flow*, for angels are through referral sources such as angel networks. These referral sources include (Wetzel Jr. 1984, pp. 114):

- Business associates.
- Angel networks and venture fairs.
- Friends.
- Active personal search.
- Investment bankers.
- Business bankers.
- Commercial bankers.
- Attorneys.
- Accountants.

The number and diversity of these sources make it critical that the technological entrepreneur and the enterprise formation team seek to have their entrepreneurial vision and initial business plan presented to as many individuals as possible. If the vision and business plan have merit, one or more informal investors will eventually see it.

Many angel networks are sponsored by Universities such as the Private Investor Network ("PIN") Baltimore-Washington Venture Group which is sponsored by the Dingman Center for Entrepreneurship of the University of Maryland, the Grubstake Breakfast sponsored by the Century Club of George Mason University in Northern Virginia, or the Venture Capital

Network sponsored by the Massachusetts Institute of Technology ("MIT"). Some are sponsored by industry such as the Greater Washington Venture Conference and some by networks of investors such as the Mid-Atlantic Venture Fair. These informal angel networks exist in the United States, Canada, United Kingdom, Sweden, and in several European Community countries such as France and Germany.

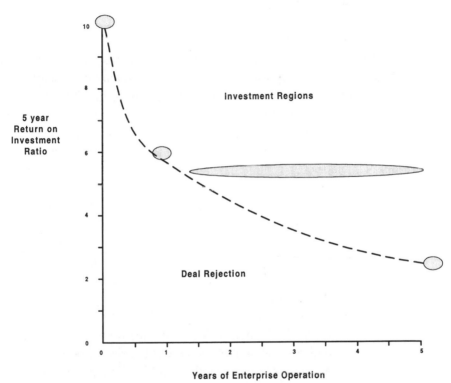

**Fig. 6.11** Angel Risk - Return Space (Based upon data contained in Hisrick and Peters 1995, pp. 265)

Many angel networks and others sponsor venture fairs. The venture fairs allow the technological entrepreneur to present the entrepreneurial vision to a large audience. However, the entrepreneur usually only has eight to ten minutes to present the enterprise. A survey of five years of venture fairs produced by the Mid-Atlantic Venture Association ("MAVA") showed that approximately 53 percent of the enterprises received funding (Anderson 1998). The investments ranged between $500,000 and $32 million with average investments of $5.3 million.

### 4.4.2 Traditional or Formal Sources of Capital

Traditional or formal sources of financing for a new technological enterprise are:

- Venture Capitalists.
- Investment Banks.
- Commercial Banks.
- Private Placement.
- Governmental Sources.

All formal sources of financing for new ventures will require the entrepreneur and the enterprise formation team to overcome many more barriers than with informal sources. However, many of the formal sources also provide professional management assistance beyond those available from individual investors. These sources will also provide financing beyond the Seed and Early-Stage and Start-up Phases of the financing life cycle.

Venture Capitalists: A venture capitalist is an individual associated with an investment enterprise who can provide capital. Venture capitalists consider three key factors in making their investment decisions. These factors still persist at the end of the twentieth century (Fischer 1971, pp. 76 - 77):

- Sound Management - The entrepreneur and the enterprise formation leadership team have a realistic approach to dealing with enterprise problems.
- Sense of Responsibility - The entrepreneur and the enterprise formation leadership team have a real stake in and commitment to the new enterprise. They must have a sense of responsibility and willingness to put their commitment on the line with that of the venture capitalists.
- Business Acumen - Venture capitalists usually only invest in the entrepreneur and leadership team who have demonstrated enterprise ability.

Venture capitalists usually require membership on the enterprise's board of directors, monthly financial statements with annual audits, and substantial life insurance policies on the entrepreneur and key members of the leadership team (Vesper 1993, pp. 188). Some studies indicate that professional venture capitalists do not add value beyond capital to the new enterprise since their investments do not usually obtain better returns than the overall average for all types of sources. According to the highly successful entrepreneur, Michael Bloomberg (Bloomberg and Winkler 1997, pp. 43), *"...banks and venture capitalists (are) your vast enemies."* Figure 6.12 presents the risk-return space for venture capitalists based on enterprise operational experience.

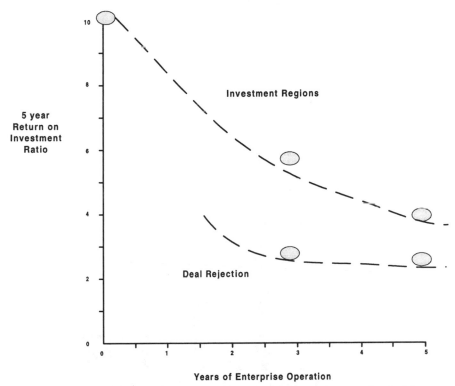

**Fig. 6.12** Venture Capitalist Risk - Return Space (Based upon data contained in Vesper 1993, pp. 191)

The venture capitalist has a portfolio of enterprises in which he/she has invested. The actual return in many instances does not match the expected returns on an overall average. Venture capitalists' actual annual portfolio return has ranged from 13 to 35 percent to a loss of 40 percent in the 1970 to 1990s period (Vesper 1993, pp. 191). However, with the high economic rates of growth and in particular in the technological sector in the late 1990s, many of the venture capitalists were obtaining substantial returns on their investments as were other investors in this sector. These returns were heightened substantially by Internet exuberance in the late 1990s with

280

companies such as Amazon.com, Inc., eBay and others that had market values beyond historical norms for new ventures. Venture capitalists require high returns because of the investment-risk domain associated with new technological enterprises. Figure 6.13 shows percentage of venture capitalist investments in various result categories.

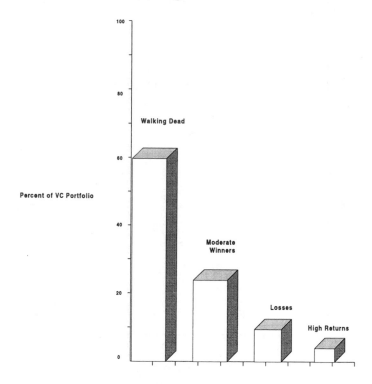

**Fig. 6.13** Venture Capitalist Portfolios (Based on data contained in Vesper 1993, pp. 191)

*Walking dead* are those venture capital investments where the capital remains tied up in the enterprise, i.e., the venture capitalists cannot recover their investments.

Investment Banks: Investment banks are usually associated with enterprises that are ready for an initial public offering ("IPO") (See Chapter 8 - Next Entrepreneurial Step). However, if an investment bank believes that a new technological enterprise has a high potential, they may syndicate a private placement of stock to a small group of sophisticated investors (Batz 1990, pp. 75). Investment banks usually only work with relatively large placements, $20 to $25 million or greater. They receive a substantial fee and they do not underwrite the offer and perform these services on a *best-efforts* [14]basis.

Commercial Banks: Commercial banks are the principal source of debt financing for new entrepreneurial ventures. In the 1990s, commercial banks represented 63 percent of these sources (Zimmer and Scarborough 1996, pp. 421). Commercial banks provide this capital for an interest payment varying between 3 and 10 percent beyond their cost of capital depending upon the guarantees supplied. Most new entrepreneurs and enterprises are usually not capable of providing guarantees beyond their personal property.

The types of debt consist of short-term loans that are extended for less than one year or long-term loans for three or more years. The majority of entrepreneurs operate their enterprises with short-term loans. These short-term loans are divided into three types:

- Commercial traditional loans.
- Lines of credit: a short-term loan that provides for cash flow during operations. These loans must be re-capitalized each year.
- *Floor planning* loans that are related to major capital items such as equipment and facilities in which the bank holds the title as collateral.

Banks also provide long-term loans. These loans are used to assist enterprise growth. Long-term loans are usually not available to serve as seed or early stage capital for the new enterprise.

Private Placement Memorandum: A private placement memorandum is a legal document that offers the stock of a new enterprise to knowledgeable investors. These offerings are very different from an IPO. An IPO is used for obtaining substantial amounts of capital from the public and requires registration with the Securities and Exchange Commission ("SEC"). The offering itself is a complex legal document and is expensive to prepare. Beyond the SEC requirements, each of the States in the United States has certain requirements. Once the private placement memorandum is prepared, the entrepreneur can offer the securities to a limited number of investors who meet the following criteria:

- Sufficient business acumen to evaluate the enterprise.

---

[14] A best-efforts deal requires the enterprise to pay the associated fees independent of whether or not financing is obtained.

- Access to enterprise data so they can perform evaluations of the risks associated with a potential investment.

In the United States, the Securities Act of 1933 ("1933 Act") and rules issued by SEC govern these transactions. The complexity of the legal issues involved requires the entrepreneur to seek professional legal assistance if this source of financing is chosen. The availability of a private placement memorandum does not guarantee that the enterprise will obtain the required funding.

Governmental Sources of Capital: Many national governments have various means of providing capital to new technological enterprises. In the United States, this is accomplished through grants and guarantees associated with debt. The Small Business Administration ("SBA") of the U.S. Government is one of the methods for new technological enterprises to obtain debt financing. The SBA provides a guarantee and does not make the loan directly to the new enterprise in most cases, but delegates the application process, the lending decision, and other details to the lending institution. The SBA guarantees up to 75 percent of the loan with a minimum guarantee of $100,000 and a maximum of $500,000. The SBA also makes direct loans with no lending institution participating and these loans do not exceed $150,000.

The U.S. Government, like many other governments, provides research grants to new and existing technological enterprises. In the United States, these are usually provided through Small Business Innovative Research ("SBIR") contracts. These contracts can be used to assist in developing new technology concepts. However, some small technological enterprises use SBIR funding to sustain their enterprises for many years. This type of funding should be used judicially otherwise a new technological enterprise can quickly become a *life-style* company relying on this and other types of government funding for substance.

The Small Business Investment Companies ("SBICs") were established to provide private long-term capital and federal guaranteed debt to small enterprises. The SBA in 1969 created the Minority Enterprise Small Business Investment Companies ("MESBICs") to provide private credit and capital to small minority-owned enterprises. The SBICs and MESBICs are regulated by the SBA.

### 4.4.3 Innovative Sources of Capital

The proliferation of the Internet has opened a vast landscape for new technological enterprises seeking capital. The Internet has been used in enterprise-investor matching services such as EDIE Online to the sale of equities through a registered public offering. The Internet has the potential to provide the new technological enterprise with extensive investment information.

The global Internet system allows small new enterprises to establish a worldwide presence easily. Obtaining capital from any source is a process that will take time and requires thought and patience.

## 5 VENTURE CAPITAL

### 5.1 Venture Capital Funds

Traditional venture capital has the following characteristics (Wetzel Jr. 1997, pp. 180):

- Early-stage equity or equity linked financing.
- High risk.
- Lack of liquidity or marketability.
- Returns are primarily from capital gains.
- Typically provided by patient investors able to offer valued-added advice.

In the period since the end of the Second World War, venture capitalists have become a major economic driver of technology. Venture capital enterprises have been an important element in technological entrepreneurial growth in the late 1990s. This growth has included a large growth in the information technology ("IT") space that in the 1993 to 1998 period has accounted for 25 percent of the real economic growth of the United States (Houston 1998). While venture capital funds remain an important source, in the late 1990s they have become somewhat restricted to financing enterprises who have passed the *bottom* of the *Valley of Death*, i.e., enterprises that have achieved some market presence and have a positive cash flow.

Venture capital enterprises also participate in networks, both formal and informal, to find potential investments. Venture capital enterprises form relationships or networks between the companies in their investment portfolios. These relationships have been termed *keiretsu* (Gove 1998). *Keiretsu* is a Japanese term for a set of interlocking relationships among suppliers and manufacturers. *Keiretsu* is based on the principle that the best way to build a new enterprise is to work with partners. This interlocking network of companies is an added advantage of venture capital financing.

Venture capital enterprises are established, like most private sector enterprises, to provide capital growth to their stakeholders. The investment policies of these entities cover a wide range of preferences in:

- Investment size.
- Stage of enterprise development.
- Technology space.
- Market space.

The types and preferences of the myriad of venture capital funds can be determined by searching a number of directories of venture capital enterprises such as *Pratt's Guide to Venture Capital Sources* (Morris, S., and Knowles 1997). The venture capital community has various evaluation criteria for making their investment decisions. In general the criteria are:

- Strong management team.
- Sustainable unique competitive advantage.
- Risk-Return space (See Figure 6.12).

Each criterion is evaluated by venture capital enterprises differently. However, the strength of the management team is usually the primary focus. If the new enterprise has a very *strong* sustainable competitive advantage, such as unique defendable intellectual capital, venture capitalists may invest with the condition that they bring in a strong management team to exploit this advantage.

The venture capitalist will consider a number of questions before starting and completing the investment process. These questions include (VC 1997):

- How compelling is the enterprise's competitive advantage?
- What level of investment is required to sustain this competitive advantage?
- How unique is the enterprise's technological market position and differentiation?
- Who is the competition and what is their competitive advantage?
- Does the enterprise have adequate distribution channels?
- Does the business model of the enterprise generate sufficient operating leverage?

- How does the capital intensity of the enterprise compare to enterprises in the similar technological and market space?
- What is the investment and valuation of the enterprise relative to comparable enterprises?
- If the enterprise has existing customers, are they satisfied and committed to the enterprise's technological products, processes or services offered?
- What is the existing or potential sales momentum?

The venture capital community usually includes long-term investors searching for capital gains within their risk-return space. All venture capitalists look at long-term as three to five years.

The *exit strategy* or *harvest strategy* (See Chapter 8 - Next Entrepreneurial Step) is a principal concern of most investors. This is especially true for the venture capital community. The *exit strategy* is the means by which all investors may achieve the rewards for their investments. In some instances, these rewards are achieved through registration and sale of some or all of the investor's interest during or after an initial public offering ("IPO") (See Chapter 8 - Next Entrepreneurial Step.) In other cases, this can occur through the sale, merger or acquisition of the enterprise by another enterprise. This can entail cash buyout, debt, or exchange of stock or a combination of instrumentalities.

## 5.2 Venture Capital Markets

In 1970, the venture capital community in the United States invested $83 million in enterprises. By 1995 this had increased to $7.5 billion (PW 1998). In 1997, venture capitalists invested $12.8 billion in 2,700 enterprises, a 34 percent increase from the $9.5 billion invested in 1996. Table 6.7 shows the distribution of venture capital invested in 1997 in the United States.

**Table 6.7**
Venture Capital Investments in the United States in 1997

| Region | No. | Investment | % of Total |
|---|---|---|---|
| Silicon Valley | 698 | $3.66 billion | 28.6 |
| New England | 361 | $1.54 billion | 12.0 |
| Southeast | 265 | $1.24 billion | 9.7 |
| New York Metro | 161 | $1.03 billion | 8.0 |
| Midwest | 204 | $959 million | 7.5 |

| | | | |
|---|---|---|---|
| Texas | 137 | $936 million | 7.3 |
| Los Angeles/Orange County | 125 | $722 million | 5.6 |
| Northwest | 111 | $478 million | 3.7 |
| DC/Metroplex | 97 | $400 million | 3.1 |
| **Sector** | | | |
| Software & Information | 856 | $3.18 billion | 24.8 |
| Telecommunications | 411 | $2.86 billion | 22.4 |
| Healthcare | 238 | $1.25 billion | 9.8 |
| Business Services | 141 | $713 million | 5.6 |
| Distribution/Retail | 124 | $700 million | 5.5 |
| Consumer Products | 137 | $693 million | 5.4 |
| Biotechnology | 134 | $670 million | 5.2 |
| **Financing Stage** | | | |
| Seed & Early | 226 | $574 million | 4.5 |
| First | 480 | $1.97 billion | 15.4 |
| Second | 508 | $2.54 billion | 19.9 |
| Third | 264 | $1.70 billion | 13.3 |
| Fourth & Beyond[15] | 107 | $838 million | 6.8 |
| Follow-on[13] | 409 | $1.595 billion | 12.5 |
| Bridge/Mezzanine | 276 | $811 million | 6.3 |

(Based on data contained in PW 1998)

As Table 6.7 shows, venture capital funds tend to concentrate their resources in regions, i.e., Silicon Valley (28.6 percent), sectors, e.g., software, information and telecommunications (47.2 percent), and the emerging growth portion of the financing space (61.7 percent).

While venture capital appears strongest in the United States, there is growing venture capital market in the European Community, primarily in the United Kingdom and in Israel.

# 6  INITIAL FINANCING DEAL

When all is said and done, the entrepreneur and the enterprise formation team, if successful in obtaining investors, must focus on the *deal*. The *deal* formalizes the relationship between the new enterprise and the investors and results in the flow of capital to the enterprise. The deal can be divided into:

---

[15] Fourth and other stages before an IPO are not shown in Figure 6.2 but can be considered as a portion of third round or later stage financing.

- Investor Risk.
- Valuation of the Enterprise.
- Structure of the Deal.
- Negotiations and Closing.

## 6.1 Investor Risk

Potential risk is associated with the:

- Technological space.
- Market space.
- Stage of the enterprise.
- Leadership team.
- Financial considerations.
- Exit strategy.

The level of development of the technology can be used to classify the technological space risk. A technology that is a radical development may be more risk prone than a technological product, process or service that is an incremental improvement. Figure 6.14 shows a technological risk-return space. High risk requires high return and, similarly, investing in existing technology is likely to result in a low risk/low return profile. Each venture capitalist assigns different values to risk associated with the technological risk-return space, based on his/her individual experience.

The technological market risk space factor is a function of the development stage of the market and the competitors and their position within the space. Figure 6.15 shows the technological market risk space. The position within this space will determine the potential risk to the prospective investors.

Each stage of development of the technological enterprise also has associated risk. Capital associated with a start-up or early stage financing has the highest risk and should yield the highest return. Figure 6.16 shows the risk-return space based on the stages of enterprise development compared with other potential investments.

The entrepreneur and enterprise formation team can similarly be placed in a management risk-return space, based on such factors as experience and expertise within the technological market space. Figure 6.17 shows the management risk-return space.

While Figures 6.15, 6.16 and 6.17 present expected risk - return spaces, anomalies occur where individuals such as Bill Gates and Michael Dell enter new market and technological spaces with little or no management

288

experience and expertise and become Schumpeter's creative destructor by totally changing the technological and market paradigm. However, experience indicates that in most cases the heuristic rules given by these expected spaces will govern.

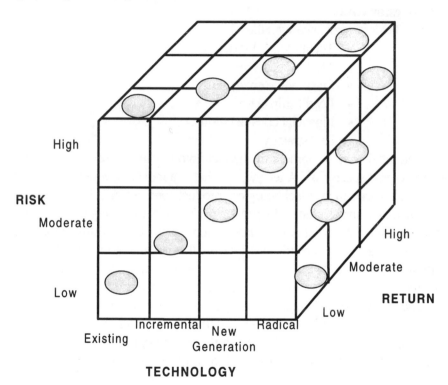

**Fig. 6.14** Technological Risk-Return Space

The financial considerations of a new venture have an associated risk. The venture capitalist has to determine the amount of capital and its phasing that will bring the new technological enterprise to a stage where the return justifies the risk. Many excellent technological concepts inadequately funded have failed while moderate technologies, i.e., incremental improvements, with sufficient funding have been highly successful financially. Similarly, some large investments have yielded low returns or losses.

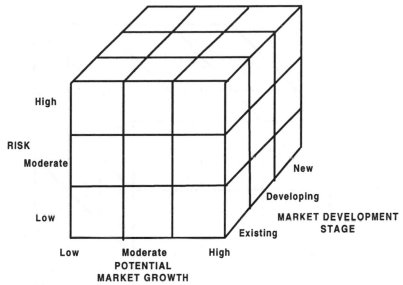

**Fig. 6.15** Technological Market Risk Space

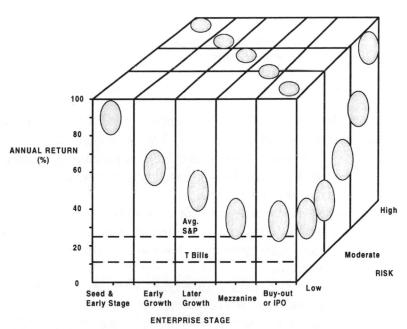

**Fig. 6.16** Enterprise Risk-Return Space

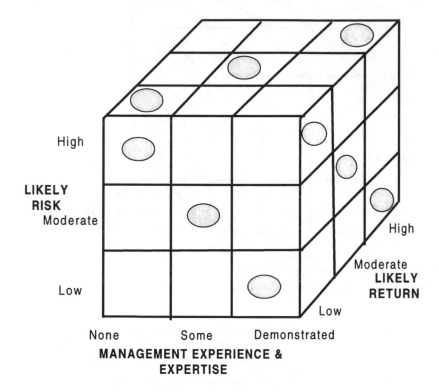

**Fig. 6.17** Management Risk-Return Space

Davenport (Davenport 1992, pp. 16) combines various factors to place the potential investment in a risk-return space. The risk is classified as:

- Most risky - New enterprise that is a startup with a radical market entrant for which the investors have to provide the majority of the capital.
- Risky - Enterprise with a prototype of a commercial product, i.e., a working model, that is an innovative entrant; the entrepreneur has some investment in the new enterprise.
- Moderate risk - Enterprise with an innovative or evolutionary market entrant at the commercialization stage with less than two years to breakeven.
- Low risk - Profitable enterprise at the expansion stage with an innovative entrant.

Figure 6.18 shows the risk-return space as defined by Davenport.

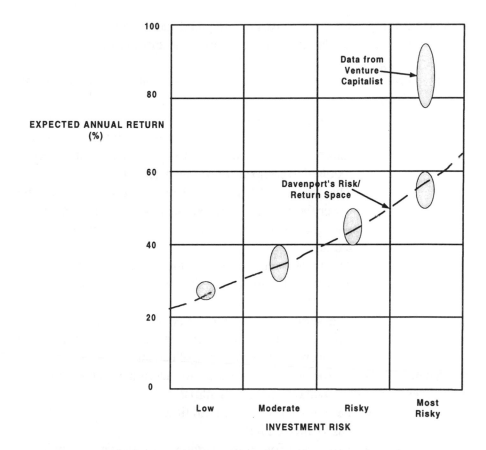

**Fig. 6.18** Davenport's Investment Risk - Return Space (Based on data contained in Cardullo 1998; Davenport 1992, pp. 12)

## 6.2 New Enterprise Valuation

In order to gauge the potential of an investment into a new enterprise, investors must make an assessment of the valuation of the new enterprise. This valuation should be based on a concurrent evaluation of comparable enterprises in the same technological and market spaces and a forecasted return analysis on the basis of either forecasted internal rate of return ("IRR") and/or economic value added ("EVA").

The analysis methods, criteria and other factors used in standard enterprise financing have *severe limitations* when valuating a new technological entrepreneurial enterprise (Timmons 1994, pp. 509). The valuation is impacted by the investor's required rate of return for different enterprise stages, the duration of the investment and the potential *exit* or *harvest strategies*.

Four principles which can be used for enterprise valuation are (Wetzel Jr. 1997, pp. 199):

- Division of ownership between the entrepreneur and prospective investors is determined by the expected future value of the enterprise and the equity interest required to compensate for the potential risks.
- The longer the track record of the new enterprise, the lower the risk and therefore the lower cost of capital and thus the lower proportion of equity the investors will require.
- The greater the expected value of the new enterprise in the future, the lower the share of equity required for the same capital.
- The shorter the time required for prospective investor exit, i.e., cash-out, the lower the share of equity required to obtain any given amount of capital.

There are various methods that are used to determine valuation of the new enterprise. These methods include (Sahlman 1988):

- Present value of future cash flow.
- Discounted cash flow.
- Earnings - Forecasted earnings and applying an industry price earnings ratio ("P/E").
- Future required value based on equity interest.
- First Chicago Method - Use of a discount applied to the average of three possible cash flow scenarios with each scenario weighted according to its perceived probability.

Each method will provide a different equity distribution between the prospective investors and the entrepreneur. A new technological enterprise should return between 50 to 70 percent annually for prospective investors. Figure 6.19 shows the prospective expected returns for price earnings ratio between 20 and 40 in the late 1990s. The prospective investors are likely to require equity ownership based on certain assumptions as to earnings and the likely value of the enterprise in the future. One approach is given by the equation:

$$\text{Required Equity Ownership} \equiv \frac{\text{Investment} * \left(1 + \text{IRR}\right)^n}{\left(\frac{P}{E}\right) * \text{NOPAT}_n}$$

or

$$\text{Required Equity Ownership} \equiv \left(\frac{\text{Investment}}{\text{NOPAT}_n}\right) * \left[\frac{\left(1 + \text{IRR}\right)^n}{P/E}\right]$$

where

P/E = price earnings ratio for enterprises in the same technological and market space.

$\text{NOPAT}_n$ = net operating profit after taxes in year $n$.

$n$ = number of years after the initial investment.

IRR = expected investor internal rate of return for investments with similar assumed risk.

The required equity is basically driven by two components:
- Ratio of investment to net profits at the point of exercise of the exit strategy.
- Expected return to industry ratio at the same stage of development.

Thus, an enterprise that has the potential to produce outstanding earnings will result in less equity that must be given to the prospective investors.

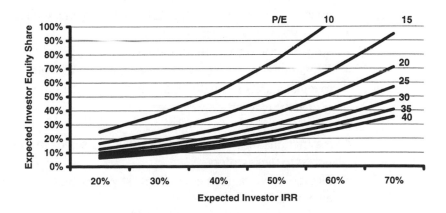

**Fig. 6.19** Expected Investor Interest (Based on a $1 million investment and $1 million NOPAT after 5 years)

294

## 6.3 Investment Structure

The valuation of the new enterprise will lead to the legal structuring of the investment, i.e., *the deal*. This requires the entrepreneur and the enterprise formation team to understand (Stevenson, Roberts, and Grousbeck 1994, pp. 243):

- Economics associated with the new enterprise, and the technological and market space.
- Prospective risk-return space.
- Entrepreneur's and enterprise's needs.

The terms and conditions of *the deal* are negotiable. The equity for a new enterprise ranges from common stock (individual investors) to convertible preferred stock (venture capitalists) and subordinated convertible debentures (SBICs and MESBICs).

The practice of most large angels and venture capitalists is to delineate the terms and conditions of *the deal* in a *term sheet*. The *term sheet* will state the number of shares, price, liquidation preference, options for redemption, conversion price, automatic conversion events, anti-dilution protection, voting rights, closing conditions, registration rights expenses, waivers, and other items that the prospective investors deem important (Halloran, Benton, and Lovejoy 1990, pp. 259). The *term sheet* is not a legal document, but is used to prepare the actual legal document covering the terms. It is important that the entrepreneur and the enterprise formation team have competent legal advice from lawyers who have venture capital experience.

A typical deal structure from a venture capitalist will have items such as:

- Convertibility of preferred stock.
- Anti-dilution protection for the investor.
- Registration rights, i.e., the investors will have the ability to register and eventually sell their equity at the time of an IPO at the enterprise's expense.
- Mandatory redemption rights.
- Restrictions on issuing securities that are senior to those issued to the investors.
- Non-compete agreements from key members of the enterprise.
- Approval on major enterprise actions such acquisitions, divestitures, new ventures, etc.
- Position on the Board of Directors.

- Rights of first refusal on additional equity investments.

## 6.4 Negotiation and Closing of the Initial Financing

Negotiation and closing of the initial financing is the process by which the entrepreneur and the enterprise formation team obtain the required capital resources to implement the entrepreneurial vision and initial business plan. While many claim negotiations can be managed by entrepreneurs without professional assistance, it is important for entrepreneurs to have such professional assistance when available. Most technological entrepreneurs are trained to approach a problem logically and use a scientific method, either consciously or unconsciously. Negotiations also require an understanding of psychology and strategy. It is in this phase of the initial financing process that the technological entrepreneur places in motion a set of forces that can determine the future of the enterprise and the reaping of rewards.

The process of negotiation is one in which both parties desire something. This is essentially a two party *zero sum game* where each side wants to maximize its position while minimizing what it must give in return. However, there are bounds that each participant has which can not be easily exceeded. Thus, as Figure 6.20 illustrates, there is a window of opportunity in the negotiation space within which the two parties reach an amicable solution that is a *win-win* for the participants. The negotiation space will cover such issues as:

- Equity interest including type.
- Capital additions, including amount, timing and conversion from debt to equity.
- Participation on Board of Directors.
- Payment of fees.
- Covenants and restrictions.
- Timing of initial public offering.

In some instances, the negotiation space can be relatively narrow; in others, it can provide significant negotiation latitude. For the purpose of negotiation, the technological entrepreneur and the enterprise formation team should consider (Batz 1990, pp. 108 -109; Zimmer and Scarborough 1996, pp. 385 - 386):

- Obtaining legal assistance with good negotiation skills.
- Investigating prospective investors, their prior investments, and deals.
- Preparing a *term sheet* with ranges for the enterprise.

- Summarizing the prospective investors *term sheet.*
- Comparing the prospective investor's *term sheet* with that prepared for the enterprise.
- Listing all the issues that surface during the actual negotiation.
- Maintaining an atmosphere of openness and geniality.
- Trying to keep the deal simple.
- Avoiding confrontation that can *kill* the deal or prevent a *win-win* outcome.
- Developing alternative initial financing paths and what-if scenarios

Once the terms of the initial financing have been agreed upon, then legal documentation is prepared.

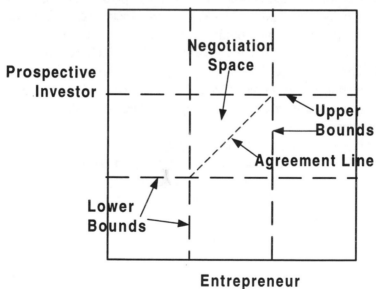

**Fig. 6.20** Negotiation Space

## REFERENCES


ACOST. 1990. The Enterprise Challenge: Overcoming barriers to growth in small firms. London, UK: Advisory Council on Science and Technology, HMSO.

Anderson, Tania. 1998. Desperately Seeking Schmoozing: Playing the Venture Fair. *Tech Capital*, 98/7-8, 29-30.

Batz, Gordon B. 1990. *Entrepreneurship for the Nineties*. Englewood Cliffs, NJ: Prentice Hall.

Bloomberg, Michael, and Matthew Winkler. 1997. *Bloomberg by Bloomberg*. New York: J. Wiley.

Braudel, Fernand. 1979. *The Wheels of Commerce: Civilization and Capitalism 15th - 18th Century - Volume 2*. Translated by Reynolds, S. 2 vols. Vol. 2. New York, NY: Harper and Row, Publishers.

Carayannis, Elias G., and Suleiman K. Kossicieh. 1997. Financing Technological Entrepreneurship: The Role of Strategic Alliances in Procuring Early-Stage Seed Capital. Paper read at Portland International Conference on Management of Engineering and Technology, 97/7/27-31, at Portland, OR.

Cardullo, Mario W. 1998. Discussion with various venture capitalists.

Carrière, Jean-Bernard, and Yvon Gasse. 1996. Investing and Financing New Technologies in Entrepreneurial Firms: A Strategic Study. Paper read at Fifth International Conference on Management of Technology, 96/2/27, at Miami, FL.

Davenport, Robert W. 1992. *Venture Capital and Economic Development*. New York, NY: National Development Council.

DeFife, Susan Williams. 1997. *Seven Strategies for Getting Early Stage Financing* [Internet]. Netpreneur Exchange - Capital Growth Interactive, 1997 [cited 97/11/22 1997]. Available from netpreneur.org/funding/earlystage/defife.html.

E&Y. 1994. *Mergers and Acquisitions: Back-to-Basics Techniques for the '90s*. New York, NY: John Wiley & Sons, Inc.

Edge, Entrepreneurial. 1998. Entrepreneurs Roundtable. *Entrepreneurial Edge*, 1998, 80-81.

Fischer, Philip A. 1971. What the Venture Capitalist Seeks. In *How to Raise and Invest Venture Capital*, edited by S. M. Rubel and E. G. Novotny. New York, NY: Presidents Publishing House, Inc.

Fitzpatrick, Peter. 1991. Chart of Timing of Venture Capital Financing. Potomac, MD: Peter Fitzpatrick.

Gaydos, Valerie S. 1997. Capital Adventures: Dollars From Heaven. *Tech Capital*, 15-16.

Gove, Alex. 1998. American Keiretsu. *The Red Herring*, 98/2, 52-55.

Grove, Andrew S. 1996. *Only the Paranoid Survive: How to Exploit the Crisis Points that Challenge Every Company and Career*. New York, NY: Currency Doubleday.

Gumpert, David. 1997. Creating a Successful Business Plan. In *The Portable MBA in Entrepreneurship*, edited by W. D. Bygrave. New York, NY: John Wiley & Sons, Inc.

Halloran, Michael J., Lee F Benton, and Jesse Robert Lovejoy. 1990. *Venture Capital and Public Offering Negotiation*. New York, NY: Harcourt.

Harrison, Richard T., and Colin M. Mason. 1996. Informal Venture Capital: Evaluating the impact of business introduction services. In *Informal Venture Capital*, edited by R. T. Harrison and C. M. Mason. London, UK: Prentice Hall/Woodhead-Faulkner.

Hisrick, Robert D., and Michael P. Peters. 1995. *Entrepreneurship: Starting, Developing, and Managing a New Enterprise*. Chicago, IL: Irwin.

298

Houston, Patrick. 1998. *New $350 M venture capital fund invetsed* Zdnet, 1998 [cited 98/4/20 1998]. Available from www.zdnet.com/zdnn/content/zdnn/20420/308750.html.

Jacobus, Lynne L., and Alvin D. Gottlieb. 1997. *Presenting Your Company to Investors* [Internet]. Edge Magazine Online, 1997 [cited 97/10/24 1997]. Available from www.edgeonline.com/main/edgemag/archives/investor.shtm.

Morris, J., Isenstein S., and A. Knowles. 1997. *Pratt's Guide to Venture Capital Sources.* New York, NY: SDC Publishing, Inc.

PW. 1998. National Venture Capital Survey: Topline Results - Full Year 1997. New York, NY: Price Waterhouse.

Reuber, A. Rebecca, and Eileen M. Fischer. 1994. Entrepreneurs' Experience, Expertise, and the Performance of Technology-Based Firms. *IEEE Transactions on Engineering Management* 41 (4):365-374.

Roberts, Edward B. 1983. Business Planning in the Start-up High-Technology Enterprise. In *Frontiers of Entrepreneurship Research 1983*, edited by J. Hornady. Wellesly, MA: Babson Center for Entrepreneurial Studies.

Rockey, Edward H. 1986. Envisioning New Business: How Entrepreneurs Perceive the Benefits of Visualization. In *Frontiers of Entrepreneurship Research 1986*, edited by R. Ronstadt, R. P. Hornaday and K. H. Vesper. Wellesley, MA: Babson Center for Entrepreneurial Studies.

Sahlman, William A. 1988. A Method for Valuing High-Risk, Long-Term Investments. Cambridge, MA: Harvard Business School.

Sahlman, William A. 1998. How to Write a Great Business Plan. *IEEE Engineering Management Review* 26 (Spring):87-95.

Scarbrough, Harry, and J. Martin Corbett. 1992. *Technology and Organization: Power, meaning and design.* Edited by D. C. Wilson, *The Routledge Series in Analytical Management.* London, England: Routledge.

Snyder, Edward. 1997. *Business Plan Financials That Work* [Internet]. Netpreneur Exchange - Capital Growth Interactive, 1997 [cited 97/11/22 1997]. Available from netpreneur.org/funding/cg/snyder.html.

Stevenson, Howard H., Michael J. Roberts, and H. Irving Grousbeck. 1994. *New Business Ventures and the Entrepreneur.* Fourth ed. Boston. MA: Irwin/McGraw-Hill.

Teague, Burton W. 1980. Venture Capital, Who Gets It and Why. *Inc*, 80/6, 70.

Timmons, Jeffry A. 1994. *New Venture Creation: Entrepreneurship for the 21st Century.* Fourth ed. Boston, MA: Irwin/McGraw-Hill.

VC. 1997. *A Venture Capital Analysis: Frequently Asked Question* morebusiness.com, 1997 [cited 97/11/22 1997]. Available from morebusiness.com/financing/vent-cap.html.

Vesper, Karl H. 1993. *New Venture Mechanisms.* Englewood Cliffs, Nj: Prentice Hall.

Wetzel Jr., W. E. 1984. Venture Capital Network, Inc.: An Experiment in Capital Formation. Paper read at 1984 Conference on Entrepreneurship, 84/4.

Wetzel Jr., W.E. 1986. Entrepreneurs, angles and economic renaissance. In *Entrepreneurship, Intrapreneurship and Venture Capital*, edited by R. D. Hisrick. Lexington, MA: Lexington Books.

Wetzel Jr., William E. 1997. Venture Capital. In *The Portable MBA in Entrepreneurship*, edited by W. D. Bygrave. New York, NY: John Wiley & Sons, Inc.

Wetzel Jr., W. H. 1979. The Cost of Availability of Credit and Risk Capital in New England. In *A Region's Struggling Savior: Small Business in New England*, edited by J. A. Timmons and D. E. Gumpert. Waltham, MA: Small Business Foundation of America.

Zimmer, Thomas W., and Norman M Scarborough. 1996. *Entrepreneurship and New Venture Formation.* Upper Saddle River, NJ: Prentice Hall.

## DISCUSSION QUESTIONS

1. Using the Internet and other reference material prepare a list of sources which can be used to develop business plans. Compare these sources as to the degree of relevancy to technological entrepreneurs.

2. Risk management is an important element in a business plan. Discuss the types of risks that should be presented in the business plan for the following types of technological and market spaces that the enterprise would be entering:

    • Radical technology in an existing market space.
    • Radical technology in a new market space.
    • Incremental technology in an existing market space.
    • Existing technology in a new market space.

3. Prepare an analytical method for analyzing initial plans that can provide the entrepreneur with a basis for determining the potential financiability of the plan.

4. Discuss the differences between pro forma income statement, pro forma cash flow and pro forma balance sheet. Discuss how the pro forma balance sheet reflects enterprise transactions.

5. Prepare a lexicon of terms a technological entrepreneur will need to understand in order to prepare the initial business and financial plans for a new enterprise.

6. The financing life cycle for a new technological enterprise offers many options. Discuss the various financing options available and the rationale a technological entrepreneur would use to choose the appropriate method.

7. Using the Internet, determine what electronic means an entrepreneur would have in making potential investors aware of the new enterprise and the potential investment opportunity without violating security laws and governmental regulations.

8. Discuss in detail the various innovative sources available to technological entrepreneurs for obtaining initial financing.

9. Research the availability of angel networks and venture capital in:

- European Community.
- Eastern Europe.
- Africa.
- Middle East.

10. Compare venture capital availability in the following regions of the United States:
    - Eastern.
    - Western.
    - West Coast.

Discuss the differences and why such differences exist.

11. Valuation of a technological enterprise is both an analytical and a qualitative process. Prepare an analysis of the valuation of an enterprise based on the financial model given in Appendix A.

12. Risk analysis is required in structuring the initial financing *deal*. Discuss the different approaches to analyzing risk from an investor's viewpoint - show examples where possible.

# APPENDIX - FINANCIAL MODEL - ROYALTEL COMMUNICATIONS, LTD.

RoyalTel Communications, Ltd. is a proposed new competitive local exchange carrier ("CLEC"). The company proposes to provide full telecommunication services to small and medium businesses using advanced communication technology such as digital subscriber lines ("DSL"). Income and balance statements for this proposed enterprise can be developed using the financial model shown below.

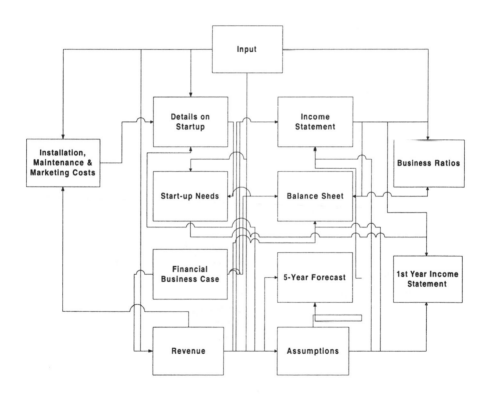

## Financial Model

The following are the data for each module of the financial model.

## Input Module

This module contains the various variables used to develop the financial model.

| | | |
|---|---|---|
| Starting Year | 1999 | |
| **Financial Assumptions (Starting Year)** | | |
| Short-term interest rate | 10.00% | |
| Long-term interest rate | 6.50% | |
| Tax rate | 42.00% | |
| Personnel burden | 30.00% | |
| | | |
| **Head End Cost** | $500 | per subscriber |
| **Installation Cost** | | |
| Installer Cost ($/hr) | $100 | |
| Rolls Per Day | 4 | |
| **Maintenance Costs** | | |
| Customers Requiring Rolls | 50.00% | |

| Cost (Subscriber) | ADSL Modem | Splitter | Hrs per Installation |
|---|---|---|---|
| Small Business | $300 | $100 | 2 |
| Association | $700 | $100 | 4 |
| Telecommuting | $100 | $50 | 1 |

| | | |
|---|---|---|
| **Telephone Support Cost** | | |
| Service Calls per Year | 10 | |
| Customers Calling | 50.00% | |
| **Billing Costs** | | |
| Software | $300,000 | amortized over 3 years |
| Staff | 50.00% | of Call Center Staffing |
| **Marketing, Sales & Promotion Costs** | | |
| Sales Calls per day per salesperson | 4 | |

| | Capture Rate |
|---|---|
| Small Businesses | 5.00% |
| Associations | 7.00% |

## Cost of Sales

| | | |
|---|---|---|
| Long Distance Service - Small/Medium Business | 90.00% | of revenue |
| Other Telecommunication Related Services | 90.00% | of revenue |
| Franchise Fees & Sales | 30.00% | of revenue |

**Interconnection Fees ($ per subscriber per yr)** — $250

| | | |
|---|---|---|
| Minimum Return | 60.00% | |
| Minimum Opening Cash Balance | $3.00 | million |

| Legal Cost | Time (hr) | Rate ($/hr) |
|---|---|---|
| Filing for CLEC | 40 | $300 |
| Negotiations with Bell Atlantic | 1000 | $300 |
| General Legal | 500 | $300 |

| Initial Staffing | Staff Size | Base Salary |
|---|---|---|
| CEO | 1 | $80,000 |
| COO | 1 | $120,000 |
| CFO | 1 | $100,000 |
| V.P. Marketing | 1 | $120,000 |
| Accounting | 2 | $40,000 |
| Clerical | 2 | $25,000 |
| Engineering | 3 | $60,000 |
| Costing | 3 | $50,000 |
| **Administrative Burden** | 50.00% | |
| **Salary (+ Commission)** | | $60,000 |
| **Commission** | 10.00% | |
| **Ad & Promotion Budget** | 40.00% of sales once sales begin | |
| Start-up Budget | $500,000 | |

| Initial Market | Total | 1999 Market Share | Annual Increase Market Share |
|---|---|---|---|
| Small Businesses | 75,000 | 0.50% | 2.00% |
| Associations | 2,500 | 0.50% | 2.00% |
| Telecommuting | 75,000 | 0.00% | 0.50% |
| Long Distance Service - Small/Medium Business | | 0.00% | 0.50% |
| Other Telecommunication Related Services | | 0.00% | 0.50% |
| Growth Rate per year | | 2.00% | |

| Average Subscriber Fees | Initial | Annual Growth Rate |
|---|---|---|
| Small Businesses | $300 | 3.00% |
| Associations | $600 | 3.00% |
| Telecommuting | $60 | 3.00% |
| Initial Installation Fees | | |
| Small Businesses | $500 | 3.00% |
| Associations | $700 | 3.00% |
| Telecommuting | $150 | 3.00% |

## Assumption Model

## RoyalTel Communications, Ltd. Financial Assumptions

Starting Year     1999

| | 1999 | 2000 | 2001 | 2002 | 2003 |
|---|---|---|---|---|---|
| Short-term interest rate | 10.00% | 10.00% | 10.00% | 10.00% | 10.00% |
| Long-term interest rate | 6.50% | 6.50% | 6.50% | 6.50% | 6.50% |
| Tax rate | 42.00% | 42.00% | 42.00% | 42.00% | 42.00% |
| Personnel burden | 30.00% | 30.00% | 30.00% | 30.00% | 30.00% |

# Installation, Maintenance and Marketing Cost Module

| | Time per Installation | | Installer Cost | Cost Per Install or Service Call | ADSL Modem | Splitter | Total Subscriber Investment | Total Investment per circuit |
|---|---|---|---|---|---|---|---|---|
| Installation | (hrs per Install) | | ($ per hr) | ($ per Install) | ($) | ($) | ($) | ($) |
| Small Business | 2 | | $100 | $200 | $300 | $100 | $400 | $900 |
| Association | 4 | | $100 | $400 | $700 | $100 | $800 | $1,300 |
| Telecommuter | 1 | | $100 | $100 | $100 | $50 | $150 | $650 |

| | | |
|---|---|---|
| Install Staff | Calls Per Day | Installer Cost |
| Installer | 4 | $100 |

| Telephone Support Cost Cost per Year per Customer per Call | Service Calls per Year | % Customers Calling | % Customers Req. Rolls |
|---|---|---|---|
| $35.87 | 10 | 50.00% | 50.00% |

| Installation & Maintenance Cost | 1999 | 2000 | 2001 | 2002 | 2003 |
|---|---|---|---|---|---|
| No. Calls per year | 1,938 | 11,794 | 22,043 | 32,698 | 43,771 |
| Avg. Calls per day | 11 | 32 | 61 | 90 | 120 |
| No. Rolls per year | 194 | 1,179 | 2,204 | 3,270 | 4,377 |
| No. Rolls per Day | 3 | 3 | 6 | 9 | 12 |
| Call Center Staff Required | 3 | 7 | 11 | 14 | 18 |
| Installers Required | 2 | 5 | 10 | 15 | 20 |
| Installation Cost | $80,000 | $366,250 | $460,868 | $762,174 | $872,298 |
| Telephone Support Cost | $180,000 | $423,003 | $790,627 | $1,172,787 | $1,569,917 |
| Maintenance Cost | $40,000 | $223,125 | $413,559 | $611,521 | $817,236 |
| Total Installation & Maintenance Cost | $300,000 | $1,012,378 | $1,665,054 | $2,546,482 | $3,259,451 |
| Total Billing Cost | $61,667 | $228,168 | $333,763 | $426,866 | $540,936 |
| Installation & Maintenance & Billing Cost per Subscriber | $933 | $526 | $453 | $455 | $434 |

| Billing Cost | | | | | |
|---|---|---|---|---|---|
| Software Procurement (Capitalized) | $50,000 | | | $50,000 | |
| Staff | 2 | 4 | 5 | 7 | 9 |
| Full Staff Cost | $45,000 | $211,502 | $317,096 | $426,866 | $540,936 |
| Total Billing Cost | $61,667 | $228,168 | $333,763 | $426,866 | $540,936 |

| Marketing, Sales & Promotion Costs | |
|---|---|
| Sales Assumptions | |
| Sales Calls per day per salesperson | 4 |
| Capture Rate | |
| Small Businesses | 5.0% |
| Associations | 7.0% |

# Details on Start-up Module

|  | (hr) | ($/hr) | ($) |
|---|---|---|---|
| Filing for CLEC | 40 | $300 | $12,000 |
| Negotiations with Bell Atlantic | 1,000 | $300 | $300,000 |
| General Legal | 500 | $300 | $150,000 |
| Total | 1,540 | | $462,000 |

| Staffing (G&A) | Number | Base Salary | Start-up | 1999 | 2000 | 2001 | 2002 | 2003 |
|---|---|---|---|---|---|---|---|---|
| CEO | 1 | $80,000 | $20,000 | $40,000 | $84,000 | $88,200 | $92,610 | $97,241 |
| COO | 1 | $120,000 | $30,000 | $60,000 | $84,000 | $88,200 | $92,610 | $97,241 |
| CFO | 1 | $100,000 | $25,000 | $50,000 | $105,000 | $110,250 | $115,763 | $121,551 |
| V.P. Marketing | 1 | $120,000 | $30,000 | $60,000 | $126,000 | $132,300 | $138,915 | $145,861 |
| Accounting | 2 | $40,000 | $20,000 | $40,000 | $84,000 | $88,200 | $138,915 | $145,861 |
| Clerical | 2 | $25,000 | $12,500 | $25,000 | $52,500 | $55,125 | $86,822 | $91,163 |
| Engineering | 3 | $60,000 | $45,000 | $60,000 | $189,000 | $198,450 | $277,830 | $291,722 |
| Costing | 3 | $50,000 | $37,500 | $75,000 | $105,000 | $110,250 | $115,763 | $121,551 |
| Total | 14 | | $220,000 | $410,000 | $829,500 | $870,975 | $1,059,227 | $1,112,188 |
| Personnel Burden | | | $66,000 | $123,000 | $248,850 | $261,293 | $317,768 | $333,656 |
| Administrative Burden | 50.0% | | $110,000 | $205,000 | $414,750 | $435,488 | $529,613 | $556,094 |
| Total G&A | | | $396,000 | $738,000 | $1,493,100 | $1,567,755 | $1,906,608 | $2,001,939 |
| G&A per Subscriber | | | | $1,905 | $633 | $356 | $292 | $229 |
| Sales Costs | | | | | | | | |
| Salary (x Commission) | | $60,000 | $30,000 | $442,995 | $1,816,277 | $1,888,751 | $1,963,398 | $2,040,274 |
| Commission | 10% | | | $135,000 | $574,155 | $631,914 | $694,048 | $760,852 |
| Total Salary + Commission | | | $30,000 | $577,995 | $2,390,432 | $2,520,665 | $2,657,446 | $2,801,126 |
| G&A | | | $24,000 | $462,396 | $1,912,346 | $2,016,532 | $2,125,956 | $2,240,901 |
| Total Cost of Sales | | | $54,000 | $1,040,390 | $4,302,778 | $4,537,197 | $4,783,402 | $5,042,027 |
| Sales Cost per New Subscriber | | | | $2,685 | $2,183 | $2,213 | $2,245 | $2,277 |
| Ad & Promotion Budget | 40% of sales | | $500,000 | $654,500 | $3,905,642 | $7,204,475 | $10,867,775 | $14,961,270 |
| Ad & Promotion Budget per New Subscriber | | | | $3,079 | $1,981 | $3,514 | $5,100 | $6,756 |
| Acquisition Cost per New Subscriber | | | | $5,764 | $4,164 | $5,728 | $7,345 | $9,033 |
| Sales & Promotion per all Subscribers | | | | $4,374 | $3,480 | $2,663 | $2,393 | $2,285 |

| Start-up Capital Equipment | |
|---|---|
| Trucks | $100,000 |
| Computers | $85,000 |
| Head-End Equipment | $193,750 |
| ADSL Modems | $121,250 |
| Splitters | $41,250 |
| Software | $50,000 |
| Furniture | $100,000 |
| Total Equipment | $591,250 |

| Staffing | Start-up | 1999 | 2000 | 2001 | 2002 | 2003 |
|---|---|---|---|---|---|---|
| CEO | 1 | 1 | 1 | 1 | 1 | 1 |
| COO | 1 | 1 | 1 | 1 | 1 | 1 |
| CFO | 1 | 1 | 1 | 1 | 1 | 1 |
| V.P. Marketing | 1 | 1 | 1 | 1 | 1 | 1 |
| Salespersons | 2 | 15 | 30 | 31 | 33 | 34 |
| Accounting | 2 | 2 | 2 | 2 | 3 | 3 |
| Clerical | 2 | 2 | 2 | 2 | 3 | 3 |
| Engineering | 3 | 3 | 3 | 3 | 4 | 4 |
| Installation & Maintenance | | 2 | 5 | 10 | 15 | 20 |
| Call Center | | 3 | 7 | 11 | 14 | 18 |
| Costing | 3 | 2 | 2 | 2 | 2 | 2 |
| Total | 16 | 32 | 56 | 65 | 78 | 88 |

# Year 1 Forecast Module

## RoyalTel Communications, Ltd. 1999 Sales Forecast

| | Q1-99 | Q2-99 | Q3-99 | Q4-99 | 1999 |
|---|---|---|---|---|---|
| **Sales** | | | | | |
| Small Businesses | $0 | $307,500 | $461,250 | $768,750 | $1,537,500 |
| Associations | $0 | $9,875 | $19,750 | $69,125 | $98,750 |
| Telecommuting | $0 | $0 | $0 | $0 | $0 |
| Long Distance Service - Small/Medium Business | $0 | $0 | $0 | $0 | $0 |
| Other Telecommunication Related Services | $0 | $0 | $0 | $0 | $0 |
| Franchise Fees & Sales | $0 | $0 | $0 | $0 | $0 |
| **Total** | $0 | $317,375 | $481,000 | $837,875 | $1,636,250 |
| **Cost of sales** | | | | | |
| Small Businesses | $0 | $10,417 | $15,625 | $31,250 | $46,875 |
| Associations | $0 | $347 | $521 | $1,042 | $1,563 |
| Telecommuting | $0 | $0 | $0 | $0 | $0 |
| Long Distance Service - Small/Medium Business | $0 | $0 | $0 | $0 | $0 |
| Other Telecommunication Related Services | $0 | $0 | $0 | $0 | $0 |
| Other | $0 | $0 | $0 | $0 | $0 |
| **Total** | $0 | $10,764 | $16,146 | $32,292 | $48,438 |

## 1999 Pro Forma RoyalTel Communications, Ltd. Income Statement

| | Q1-99 | Q2-99 | Q3-99 | Q4-99 | 1999 |
|---|---|---|---|---|---|
| **Sales** | 0 | 317,375 | 481,000 | 837,875 | 1,636,250 |
| **Cost of sales** | | | | | |
| Cost of sales | 0 | 10,764 | 16,146 | 32,292 | 59,201 |
| **Total** | $0 | $306,611 | $464,854 | $805,583 | $1,577,049 |
| **Gross margin** | | | | | |
| Percent | 0.00% | 96.61% | 96.64% | 96.15% | 97.04% |
| **Operating expenses** | | | | | |
| Depreciation | $0 | $6,787 | $13,574 | $47,508 | $67,868 |
| Total Operating Cost | $0 | $36,167 | $72,333 | $253,167 | $361,667 |
| Sales & Promotion | | $169,489 | $338,978 | $1,186,423 | $1,694,890 |
| G&A | $0 | $73,800 | $147,600 | $516,600 | $738,000 |
| **Total** | $0 | $286,243 | $572,485 | $2,003,698 | $2,862,425 |
| **Percent of sales** | 0.00% | 90.19% | 119.02% | 239.14% | 174.94% |
| **Pre-tax profit** | $0 | $20,369 | -$107,631 | -$1,198,114 | -$1,285,376 |
| Short-term interest | 0 | 0 | 0 | 0 | 0 |
| Long-term interest | 0 | 0 | 0 | 0 | 0 |
| Taxes incurred | 0 | 8,555 | -45,205 | 0 | -36,650 |
| One-Time Startup Costs | | 1,962,000 | | | 1,962,000 |
| **Net profit** | $0 | ($1,950,186) | ($62,426) | ($1,198,114) | ($3,210,726) |
| **Net profit/sales** | 0.00% | -614.47% | -12.98% | -142.99% | -196.22% |

# 5-Year Forecast Module

## 5-Year Total Market Forecast

### SMALL/MEDIUM TELECOMMUNICATIONS MARKET (Millions $)

|  | 1999 | 2000 | 2001 | 2002 | 2003 |
|---|---|---|---|---|---|
| Small Businesses | 270 | 284 | 298 | 313 | 329 |
| Associations | 18 | 19 | 20 | 21 | 22 |
| Telecommuting | 54 | 57 | 60 | 63 | 66 |
| Long Distance Service - Small/Medium Business | 171 | 180 | 189 | 198 | 208 |
| Other Telecommunication Related Services | 5 | 6 | 7 | 9 | 10 |
| **Total market** | $518 | $545 | $573 | $604 | $635 |

## RoyalTel Communications, Ltd. Market Share Objectives

### PER MARKET SEGMENT

|  | 1999 | 2000 | 2001 | 2002 | 2003 |
|---|---|---|---|---|---|
| Small Businesses | 0.50% | 2.50% | 4.50% | 6.50% | 8.50% |
| Associations | 0.50% | 2.50% | 4.50% | 6.50% | 8.50% |
| Telecommuting | 0.00% | 0.50% | 1.00% | 1.50% | 2.00% |
| Long Distance Service - Small/Medium Business | 0.00% | 0.50% | 1.00% | 1.50% | 2.00% |
| Other Telecommunication Related Services | 0.00% | 0.50% | 1.00% | 1.50% | 2.00% |

## 5-Year Sales Forecast

### TOTAL SALES ($ Millions)

|  | 1999 | 2000 | 2001 | 2002 | 2003 |
|---|---|---|---|---|---|
| Small Businesses | $1.54 | $7.88 | $14.26 | $21.26 | $28.93 |
| Associations | $0.10 | $0.51 | $0.93 | $1.40 | $1.91 |
| Telecommuting | $0.00 | $0.34 | $0.66 | $1.01 | $1.39 |
| Long Distance Service - Small/Medium Business | $0.00 | $0.90 | $1.89 | $2.97 | $4.17 |
| Other Telecommunication Related Services | $0.00 | $0.03 | $0.07 | $0.13 | $0.21 |
| Franchise Fees & Sales | $0.00 | $0.10 | $0.20 | $0.40 | $0.80 |
| **Total** | $1.64 | $9.76 | $18.01 | $27.17 | $37.40 |

### TOTAL COST OF SALES ($ Millions)

|  | 1999 | 2000 | 2001 | 2002 | 2003 |
|---|---|---|---|---|---|
| Small Businesses | $0.05 | $0.48 | $0.88 | $1.29 | $1.73 |
| Associations | $0.00 | $0.02 | $0.03 | $0.04 | $0.06 |
| Telecommuting | $0.00 | $0.10 | $0.20 | $0.30 | $0.41 |
| Long Distance Service - Small/Medium Business | $0.00 | $0.81 | $1.70 | $2.68 | $3.75 |
| Other Telecommunication Related Services | $0.00 | $0.03 | $0.06 | $0.12 | $0.19 |
| Franchise Fees & Sales | $0.00 | $0.03 | $0.06 | $0.12 | $0.24 |
| **Total** | $0.05 | $1.46 | $2.93 | $4.55 | $6.37 |

# Start-Up Needs Module

## RoyalTel Communications, Ltd. Start-Up Costs and Capitalization

| | | List | Subtotals | Totals |
|---|---|---|---|---|
| **START-UP EXPENSES ($ Millions)** | | | | |
| | **General and administrative** | | | |
| | Legal and accounting | $0.46 | | |
| | Salaries | $0.45 | | |
| | Other | $0.00 | $0.91 | |
| | **Sales and marketing** | | | |
| | Advertising | $0.50 | | |
| | Promotion | $0.50 | | |
| | Deposits & Insurance | $0.05 | $1.05 | |
| | **Other expenses** | | | |
| | Other | $0.00 | | |
| | Other | $0.00 | | |
| | Other | $0.00 | $0.00 | $1.96 |
| | **Total start-up expenses** | $1.96 | $1.96 | |

## Start-Up Costs and Capitalization

| | | List | Subtotals | Totals |
|---|---|---|---|---|
| **START-UP ASSETS ($ Millions)** | | | | |
| | **Opening cash (min. balance)** | $3.00 | $3.00 | |
| | **Capital equipment** | | | |
| | Furniture | $0.10 | | |
| | Equipment | $0.59 | | |
| | Other | $0.00 | $0.69 | |
| | **Other assets** | | | |
| | Other | $0.00 | $0.00 | $3.69 |
| | **Total start-up assets** | $3.69 | $3.69 | |
| | **Start-up requirements** | $5.65 | $5.65 | $5.65 |

## Start-Up Costs and Capitalization

| | | List | Subtotals | Totals |
|---|---|---|---|---|
| **START-UP CAPITALIZATION ($ Millions)** | | | | |
| | **Owners' investment** | | | |
| | Venture Capital | $10.00 | | |
| | Other | $0.00 | $10.00 | |
| | **Bank loans** | | | |
| | Bank 1 | $0.00 | | |
| | Bank 2 | $0.00 | | |
| | Other | $0.00 | | |
| | Other | $0.00 | $0.00 | |
| | **Other loans** | | | |
| | Other | $0.00 | | |
| | Other | $0.00 | | |
| | Other | $0.00 | $0.00 | $10.00 |
| | **Total capitalization** | $10.00 | $10.00 | |
| | **Capitalization deficit** | $4.35 | $4.35 | $4.35 |

310

# Revenue Module

| REVENUE ASSUMPTIONS & ANALYSIS | | | | | |
|---|---|---|---|---|---|
| Revenue Source | 1999 | 2000 | 2001 | 2002 | 2003 |
| Small Businesses | 75,000 | 76,500 | 78,030 | 79,591 | 81,182 |
| Associations | 2,500 | 2,550 | 2,601 | 2,653 | 2,706 |
| Telecommuting | 75,000 | 76,500 | 78,030 | 79,591 | 81,182 |
| Market Share | | | | | |
| Small Business | 0.50% | 2.50% | 4.50% | 6.50% | 8.50% |
| Association | 0.50% | 2.50% | 4.50% | 6.50% | 8.50% |
| Telecommuting | 0.00% | 0.50% | 1.00% | 1.50% | 2.00% |
| Long Distance Service - Small/Medium Business | 0.00% | 0.50% | 1.00% | 1.50% | 2.00% |
| Other Telecommunication Related Services | 0.00% | 0.50% | 1.00% | 1.50% | 2.00% |
| Customers | | | | | |
| Small Business | 375 | 1,913 | 3,511 | 5,173 | 6,901 |
| Association | 13 | 64 | 117 | 172 | 230 |
| Telecommuting | 0 | 383 | 780 | 1,194 | 1,624 |
| Circuit Revenue per Month/Subscriber | | | | | |
| Small Business | $300 | $309 | $318 | $328 | $338 |
| Association | $600 | $618 | $637 | $656 | $675 |
| Telecommuting | $60 | $62 | $64 | $66 | $68 |
| DSL Circuit Revenue | | | | | |
| Small Business | $1,350,000 | $7,091,550 | $13,410,688 | $20,351,167 | $27,959,685 |
| Association | $90,000 | $472,770 | $894,046 | $1,356,744 | $1,863,979 |
| Telecommuting | $0 | $283,662 | $596,031 | $939,285 | $1,315,750 |
| TOTAL SUBSCRIBER REVENUE | $1,440,000 | $7,847,982 | $14,900,765 | $22,647,196 | $31,139,414 |
| Revenue for Installation | | | | | |
| Small Business | $500 | $515 | $530 | $546 | $563 |
| Association | $700 | $721 | $743 | $765 | $788 |
| Telecommuting | $150 | $155 | $159 | $164 | $169 |
| Cost of Sales | | | | | |
| Long Distance Service - Small/Medium Business | 90% | 90% | 90% | 90% | 90% |
| Other Telecommunication Related Services | 90% | 90% | 90% | 90% | 90% |
| Franchise Fees & Sales | 30% | 30% | 30% | 30% | 30% |
| Network Interconnection Fees to Bell Atlantic ($ per subscriber per yr) | $250 | $250 | $250 | $250 | $250 |

# Financial Business Case - Per Subscriber Module

|  | Startup ($) | 1999 ($) | 2000 ($) | 2001 ($) | 2002 ($) | 2003 ($) |
|---|---|---|---|---|---|---|
| *Revenue per circuit per year* |  | $1,858 | $3,327 | $3,380 | $3,463 | $3,557 |
| *Revenue for Installation* |  | $506 | $462 | $470 | $482 | $496 |
| *Total Revenue* |  | $2,365 | $3,789 | $3,850 | $3,945 | $4,053 |
| *Depreciation* |  | $183 | $174 | $173 | $173 | $173 |
| *Total Operating Cost* |  | $933 | $526 | $453 | $455 | $434 |
| *Sales & Promotion* |  | $4,374 | $3,480 | $2,663 | $2,393 | $2,285 |
| *G&A* |  | $1,905 | $633 | $356 | $292 | $229 |
| *Income Before Tax* |  | -$656 | $2,456 | $2,868 | $3,026 | $3,217 |
| *Taxes* |  | $0 | $1,032 | $1,205 | $1,271 | $1,351 |
| *Net Income* |  | -$656 | $1,425 | $1,663 | $1,755 | $1,866 |
| *Cash Flow* | -$876 | -$473 | $1,599 | $1,837 | $1,928 | $2,039 |
| *Total Investment* | $876 | $913 | $870 | $866 | $865 | $864 |
| *Net Present Value (@10%)* | $4,854 |  |  |  |  |  |
| *Internal Rate of Return* | 78% |  |  |  |  |  |
| *Revenue per Circuit per month* | $291 | 310 | 277 | 282 | 289 | 296 |

Based on average values for all subscribers

## Income Statement Module

### 5-Year Total Market Forecast

**SMALL/MEDIUM TELECOMMUNICATIONS MARKET (Millions $)**

| | 1999 | 2000 | 2001 | 2002 | 2003 |
|---|---|---|---|---|---|
| Small Businesses | 270 | 284 | 298 | 313 | 329 |
| Associations | 18 | 19 | 20 | 21 | 22 |
| Telecommuting | 54 | 57 | 60 | 63 | 66 |
| Long Distance Service - Small/Medium Business | 171 | 180 | 189 | 198 | 208 |
| Other Telecommunication Related Services | 5 | 6 | 7 | 9 | 10 |
| **Total market** | **$518** | **$545** | **$573** | **$604** | **$635** |

### RoyalTel Communications, Ltd. Market Share Objectives

**PER MARKET SEGMENT**

| | 1999 | 2000 | 2001 | 2002 | 2003 |
|---|---|---|---|---|---|
| Small Businesses | 0.50% | 2.50% | 4.50% | 6.50% | 8.50% |
| Associations | 0.50% | 2.50% | 4.50% | 6.50% | 8.50% |
| Telecommuting | 0.00% | 0.50% | 1.00% | 1.50% | 2.00% |
| Long Distance Service - Small/Medium Business | 0.00% | 0.50% | 1.00% | 1.50% | 2.00% |
| Other Telecommunication Related Services | 0.00% | 0.50% | 1.00% | 1.50% | 2.00% |

### 5-Year Sales Forecast

**TOTAL SALES ($ Millions)**

| | 1999 | 2000 | 2001 | 2002 | 2003 |
|---|---|---|---|---|---|
| Small Businesses | $1.54 | $7.88 | $14.26 | $21.26 | $28.93 |
| Associations | $0.10 | $0.51 | $0.93 | $1.40 | $1.91 |
| Telecommuting | $0.00 | $0.34 | $0.66 | $1.01 | $1.39 |
| Long Distance Service - Small/Medium Business | $0.00 | $0.90 | $1.89 | $2.97 | $4.17 |
| Other Telecommunication Related Services | $0.00 | $0.03 | $0.07 | $0.13 | $0.21 |
| Franchise Fees & Sales | $0.00 | $0.10 | $0.20 | $0.40 | $0.80 |
| **Total** | **$1.64** | **$9.76** | **$18.01** | **$27.17** | **$37.40** |

**TOTAL COST OF SALES ($ Millions)**

| | 1999 | 2000 | 2001 | 2002 | 2003 |
|---|---|---|---|---|---|
| Small Businesses | $0.05 | $0.48 | $0.88 | $1.29 | $1.73 |
| Associations | $0.00 | $0.02 | $0.03 | $0.04 | $0.06 |
| Telecommuting | $0.00 | $0.10 | $0.20 | $0.30 | $0.41 |
| Long Distance Service - Small/Medium Business | $0.00 | $0.81 | $1.70 | $2.68 | $3.75 |
| Other Telecommunication Related Services | $0.00 | $0.03 | $0.06 | $0.12 | $0.19 |
| Franchise Fees & Sales | $0.00 | $0.03 | $0.06 | $0.12 | $0.24 |
| **Total** | **$0.05** | **$1.46** | **$2.93** | **$4.55** | **$6.37** |

### Profitability Details

| | 1999 | 2000 | 2001 | 2002 | 2003 |
|---|---|---|---|---|---|
| Cost of sales | $0.05 | $1.46 | $2.93 | $4.55 | $6.37 |
| Operating expenses | $2.86 | $11.36 | $16.08 | $21.68 | $27.34 |
| Interest | $0.00 | $0.00 | $0.00 | $0.00 | $0.00 |
| Tax | -$0.54 | -$1.28 | -$0.42 | $0.40 | $1.55 |
| Profits | -$2.70 | -$1.77 | -$0.58 | $0.55 | $2.15 |
| Sales | $1.64 | $9.76 | $18.01 | $27.17 | $37.40 |

## Balance Sheet Module

### 5-Year RoyalTel Communications, Ltd. Pro Forma Balance Sheet

| | 1999 | 2000 | 2001 | 2002 | 2003 |
|---|---|---|---|---|---|
| **ASSETS** | | | | | |
| **Short-term assets** | | | | | |
| Cash | $3.34 | $3.95 | $2.35 | $2.17 | $3.91 |
| Accounts receivable | $0.00 | $0.00 | $0.00 | $0.00 | $0.00 |
| Inventory | $0.00 | $0.00 | $0.00 | $0.00 | $0.00 |
| Other short-term assets | $0.00 | $0.00 | $0.00 | $0.00 | $0.00 |
| Total | $3.34 | $3.95 | $2.35 | $2.17 | $3.91 |
| **Long-term assets** | | | | | |
| Capital assets | $4.03 | $2.07 | $3.86 | $5.73 | $7.67 |
| Accumulated depreciation | $0.07 | $0.48 | $1.25 | $2.40 | $3.93 |
| Total | $3.96 | $1.58 | $2.61 | $3.33 | $3.73 |
| Total assets | $7.30 | $5.53 | $4.95 | $5.50 | $7.65 |
| **DEBT AND EQUITY** | | | | | |
| **Short-term liabilities** | | | | | |
| Accounts payable | $0.00 | $0.00 | $0.00 | $0.00 | $0.00 |
| Short-term notes | $0.00 | $0.00 | $0.00 | $0.00 | $0.00 |
| Other short-term liabilities | $0.00 | $0.00 | $0.00 | $0.00 | $0.00 |
| Total | $0.00 | $0.00 | $0.00 | $0.00 | $0.00 |
| **Long-term liabilities** | $0.00 | $0.00 | $0.00 | $0.00 | $0.00 |
| Total liabilities | $0.00 | $0.00 | $0.00 | $0.00 | $0.00 |
| **Equity** | | | | | |
| Paid-in capital | $10.00 | $10.00 | $10.00 | $10.00 | $10.00 |
| Retained earnings | $0.00 | -$2.70 | -$4.47 | -$5.05 | -$4.50 |
| Earnings | -$2.70 | -$1.77 | -$0.58 | $0.55 | $2.15 |
| Total | $7.30 | $5.53 | $4.95 | $5.50 | $7.65 |
| Total debt and equity | $7.30 | $5.53 | $4.95 | $5.50 | $7.65 |
| Check line | $0.00 | $0.00 | $0.00 | $0.00 | $0.00 |
| Net worth | $7.30 | $5.53 | $4.95 | $5.50 | $7.65 |

## RoyalTel Communications, Ltd. Business Ratios

| | 1999 | 2000 | 2001 | 2002 | 2003 |
|---|---|---|---|---|---|
| Gross margin | 97% | 85% | 84% | 83% | 83% |
| Net margin | -165% | -18% | -3% | 2% | 6% |
| Return on equity | -37% | -32% | -12% | 10% | 28% |
| Return on investment | -27% | -18% | -6% | 5% | 21% |
| Return on assets | -37% | -32% | -12% | 10% | 28% |
| Net worth (million $) | $7.3 | $5.5 | $5.0 | $5.5 | $7.6 |
| Economic Value Added* (million $) | -$7.08 | -$5.09 | -$3.55 | -$2.75 | -$2.44 |

Note: Economic Value Added = EVA = NOPAT less Capital Charges, where Capital Charges = Assets x Minimum Return
Minimum Return = 60%

314

| Business Ratios (Percentage of Total Revenue) | 1999 (%) | 2000 (%) | 2001 (%) | 2002 (%) | 2003 (%) |
|---|---|---|---|---|---|
| Revenue per circuit per year | 78.6% | 87.8% | 87.8% | 87.8% | 87.8% |
| Revenue for Installation | 21.4% | 12.2% | 12.2% | 12.2% | 12.2% |
| Total Revenue | 100.0% | 100.0% | 100.0% | 100.0% | 100.0% |
| Depreciation | 7.7% | 4.6% | 4.5% | 4.4% | 4.3% |
| Total Operating Cost | 39.5% | 13.9% | 11.8% | 11.5% | 10.7% |
| Sales & Promotion | 185.0% | 91.8% | 69.2% | 60.7% | 56.4% |
| G&A | 80.5% | 16.7% | 9.2% | 7.4% | 5.6% |
| Income Before Tax | -27.7% | 64.8% | 74.5% | 76.7% | 79.4% |
| Taxes | 0.0% | 27.2% | 31.3% | 32.2% | 33.3% |
| Net Income | -27.7% | 37.6% | 43.2% | 44.5% | 46.0% |
| Cash Flow | -20.0% | 42.2% | 47.7% | 48.9% | 50.3% |

# PART THREE

# PROCESS OF GROWTH
# AND
# HARVEST

CHAPTER 7

# Strategic Enterprise Growth

*"There's no resting place for an enterprise in a competitive economy."*
**Alfred P. Sloan**
*1875-1966, industrialist, philanthropist; Chairman, General Motors*

## 1. INTRODUCTION

The initial financing of an enterprise is only the beginning of the process of growing. A new technological enterprise not only must grow but also must *get to the future first* (Hamel and Prahalad 1994, pp. 177). The rewards for *getting to the future first* are substantial but such a strategy does involve risks. Microsoft® Corporation has garnered substantial rewards and some say monopolistic rents but has never gotten to the future first. Intel Corporation has used a *getting to the future first* philosophy to achieve and maintain microprocessor dominance. There is a significant body of data that indicates that a *quick follower* is better positioned than a pioneer (Senge 1990, pp. 128; Tellis and Golder 1996, pp. 65). The empirical data seem to indicate that the pioneer role is inherently risky and that the pioneering enterprise will, inevitably stumble, offering an opportunity for *quick* and *later* followers to garner market share (Hamel and Prahalad 1994, pp. 178). Thus, while Hamel and Prahalad (Hamel and Prahalad 1994, pp. 177) emphasize the importance of moving rapidly the evidence and their counsel indicate the need to be a *quick follower* to reduce risk.

Figure 7.1 presents the stages of a technological enterprise (Bell and McNamara 1991, pp. 256-262). While Figure 7.1 covers the entire spectrum from conception to steady state, this chapter covers the later part of the cycle, i.e., stages three through five.

318

The early portion of the enterprise growth cycle is the transversing of the *Valley of Death* (See Chapter 6 – Initial Enterprise Financing). According to Andrew Grove, Chairman of Intel Corporation (Grove 1996, pp. 140):

> *"To make it through the valley of death*
> *successfully, your first task is to form a mental*
> *image of what the company should look like*
> *when you get to the other side."*

Thus the technological entrepreneur must have and communicate the vision of the new enterprise as a growing and dynamic enterprise.

The technological market space that a new enterprise is entering and preparing to grow in is characterized by a new enterprise paradigm. This new paradigm is based upon:

- Knowledge generation and the growth of that knowledge through learning culture.
- Responding to customers and their needs and providing those needs with high quality entrants. This also includes a focus on customization where possible.
- Collaborating through development of strategic alliances and other mechanisms. This partnering provides a synergy that would not necessarily be attainable through a single entity. This can involve creation of consortia, joint ventures, cross licensing or other strategic mechanisms (Tapscott and Caston 1993, pp. 9).
- Internationalization or globalization of the market space that the new technological enterprise is planning to enter. The pervasiveness of the Internet and lowering cost of high-speed telecommunications is accelerating this trend.
- The ability to outsource capabilities that are not associated with core competencies can help the enterprise to remain lean and focus on those capabilities that are critical to the enterprise's success. However, this outsourcing must be judicious to protect the enterprise's key areas of value-added capability.

Once the new enterprise has passed through the first and second stages (see prior chapters), the new technological enterprise enters the development stage. In this stage, the objective is to build the staff while simultaneously, designing and performing initial testing of the new technological entrant.

This stage can take from six months to several years depending upon the complexity of the new entrant. This stage also contains the initial testing phase of the new entrant, i.e., alpha[1] and beta[2] testing. The objective of these tests is to stress the entrant to maximize operability and determine what modifications will be required in light of the test results.

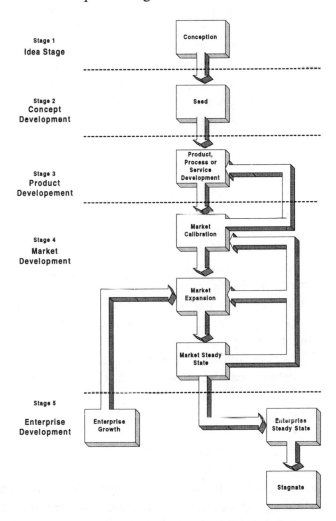

**Fig. 7.1** Stages of Enterprise Growth (Adapted from Bell and McNamara 1991, pp. 257)

---

[1] Alpha testing is the initial testing of the entrant under conditions as stringent as those of actual use.

[2] Beta testing is testing with a select group of actual users of the product in their environment.

The market development stage sometimes begins even when the new entrant is still in the development stage. In many cases, the market strategy combined with the results of the market development stage in many cases will set the environment for the success or failure of the enterprise.

The market development stage, contains three substages: calibration, expansion, and steady state (Bell and McNamara 1991, pp. 260-261). The market calibration substage begins with the initial introduction of the new technological entrant to the market space. This can be considered a market-beta-testing phase. The objective of this substage is to determine the price for the new entrant, cost of sales and potential growth rates. During this stage, the new entrant is *tuned* in reference to pricing and sales plans to achieve profitability.

During the market expansion substage, the enterprise continues to calibrate and modify its market strategy to gain market share. Once an acceptable market space position is reached, the enterprise uses this position to fund future versions and growth of the entrant or other new entrants that can continually grow the enterprise and thereby achieve profitability.

While Bell (Bell and McNamara 1991, pp. 261-262) poses a final steady state enterprise position, no enterprise can survive in this stage,

*"An enterprise that is not growing is dying."*

Growth and managing that growth is the *sina qua non* of survival. The growth of a technological enterprise is a function of its technological and market space and its management.

Figure 7.2 shows the new enterprise growth space where new technological ventures can be classified as (Hisrick and Peters 1995, pp. 401):

- Life-style.
- Marginal.
- Successful and growing.
- High-growth.

Some technological enterprises, particularly those that depend on government funding through such mechanisms as research grants and contracts, do not seek to grow but to become *life-style enterprises.* In this case, the entrepreneur is satisfied with the level of activity and rewards. This type of enterprise can only benefit the entrepreneur and usually is of little or no interest to prospective investors. Thus, the *life-style enterprise* is an *end-point* of entrepreneurial growth.

The management factors are important elements that affects enterprise growth (Hisrick and Peters 1995, pp. 400). These management factors include the ability to manage growth combined with the psychological propensity for growth. The ability to manage growth requires that the technological entrepreneur either grows managerially or brings in a professional manager who will be able to deal with the increasing enterprise complexity.

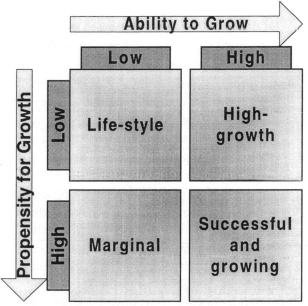

**Fig. 7.2** New Enterprise Growth Space (Adapted from Hisrick and Peters 1995, pp. 401)

Entrepreneurial and professional management styles are very different. The entrepreneurial management style usually consists of (Stevenson, Roberts, and Grousbeck 1994, pp. 527):

- Centralized decision-making where the entrepreneur makes all the decisions. This characteristic is acceptable where a new enterprise is small and all information is easily assimilated by one individual. However, as the enterprise grows and the complexity increases exponentially, the enterprise cannot be managed successfully by one individual.
- Informal control by the technological entrepreneur. While informal control can provide an entrepreneurial

culture to a small enterprise it can cause serious problems as the complexity of the enterprise increases with growth.

The management style of a professional manager differs significantly from that of an entrepreneur and includes (Stevenson, Roberts, and Grousbeck 1994, pp. 528):

- Delegation of decision-making responsibility, which is desirable as the enterprise grows. This allows for rapidity of response, making it easier to react to technological and market space threats. However, such delegation must be placed within a strategic framework.
- Formal control systems that stay within the strategic framework and that measure the performance of the enterprise and its members. The formal control system includes the setting of enterprise objectives, monitoring and rewarding performance. The formal guidelines allow the enterprise to determine its condition. The negative aspects of some formal control mechanisms are that they can stifle innovation and an entrepreneurial culture within the enterprise if not properly implemented.

Microsoft® Corporation managed the growth from its early beginnings as an entrepreneurial enterprise to the leader in its market space by use of four basic principles (Cusumano and Selby 1995, pp. 21):

- Acquire a Chief Executive Officer ("CEO") with a deep understanding of the technological and market space.
- Use a flexible organizational structure around and across markets and business functions.
- Acquire the most intelligent managers obtainable, who have a deep understanding of the technological and market space.
- Acquire the most intelligent employees obtainable, who have a deep understanding of the technological and market space.

These principles had a profound impact on Microsoft® Corporation and the software and computer industries.

The growth of a new technological enterprise should be managed on three axes (Shenhar 1991):

- Skills and expertise.

- Assets.
- Processes.

Figure 7.3 shows this complex three-dimensional model for managing a technological enterprise. This space increases in complexity as the enterprise grows requiring the management to grow with the enterprise.

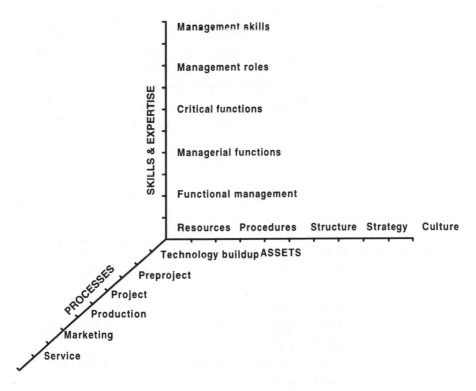

**Fig. 7.3** Three-Dimensional Technological Management Model (Adapted from Shenhar 1991)

## 1.1 Theory of Enterprise Growth

The growth of a new technological enterprise should be based upon increasing long-term stakeholder value by growing revenues and profitability (Asim and Lucier 1996). This growth in revenue is achieved by:

- Pursuing growing market spaces.
- Developing new customers.
- Retaining customers.

The increase in long-term stakeholder value is achieved either through a managed or innovative growth paradigm. In the managed growth paradigm the focus is on the market space and the cost positions that are superior to the competition's. This is achieved through better strategic planning and management of the enterprise. The innovative-growth paradigm produces higher stakeholder value growth than the managed growth paradigm (Asim and Lucier 1996). A successful enterprise using the innovative-growth paradigm creates rapid growth in revenue, profit and stakeholder value. This is accomplished through strategic innovation, or a stream of product, process or service innovations or both. Using the innovative-growth paradigm, an enterprise differentiates itself from its competition and its customers perceive innovative actions to be of significantly superior value, thus enhancing the enterprise's superiority. This superiority is composed of customer value and profitability.

Growth, while necessary, is not a sufficient condition to ensure enterprise survival. It is possible for an enterprise to grow at such a rapid rate that it is no longer possible to sustain or manage that growth rate. However, finding the optimal growth rate for the new enterprise is not an easy task. The factors that influence the optimum growth rate include (Bhide 1996):

- Economies of scale, scope or customer network.
- Ability to lock-in customer or scarce resources.
- Competitor's growth.
- Resource constraints.
- Internal financing capability.
- Tolerant customers.
- Personal temperament and goals of the technological entrepreneur.

The growth of a new technological enterprise also involves a number of issues that must be dealt with by the entrepreneur and the enterprise formation team. These issues cover:

- Strategy.
- Technology.
- Organizational.
- Financing.
- Entrepreneurship.

## 1.2    Strategic Space Issues

There are three generic strategic approaches for an enterprise to grow by outperforming other enterprises in its market space. These strategies include (Porter 1980, pp. 35):

- **Achieving overall cost leadership** - A strategy that requires efficient scale facilities, vigorous pursuit of cost reductions based on experience, tight cost and overhead control, avoidance of marginal accounts, and other cost minimization approaches.
- **Differentiating** the new technological product, process or service by creating an entrant that is perceived within the technological and market space as being unique.
- **Focus** provides the enterprise with the ability to concentrate on a particular narrow sector of the market or technological space.

Figure 7.4 illustrates how these generic strategies aid in developing an enterprise's strategic competitive advantage. While Porter postulated these three generic growth strategies in 1980, since then the empirical data indicate that value for the stakeholders must be the major outcome of these strategies.

The growth of the new enterprise is directly related to strategy for value creation (Prahalad, Fahey, and Randall 1994). This strategy for value creation is linked with:

- Strategic intent - The articulation of the enterprise's aspirations. This creates a focus for mobility barrier-breaking initiatives. These barrier-breaking initiatives include identifying radical new vectors for enterprise opportunities.
- Strategic architecture - Provides the necessary enterprise framework for leveraging resources that is consistent with strategic intent. For example the strategic architecture provides a means to identify the enterprise's core competencies and those which need to be either developed or acquired
- Core competencies (See Chapter 3 - Technological and Enterprise Strategic Planning)

326

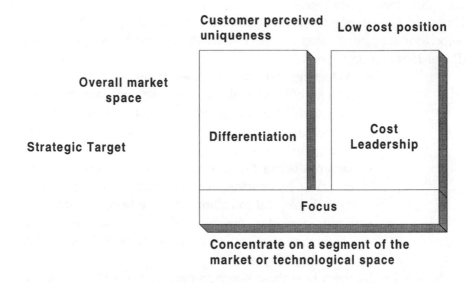

**Fig. 7.4** Porter's Three Generic Strategies (Adapted from Porter 1980, pp. 39)

For a new enterprise to achieve *super-success* is far from simple. Roberts (Roberts 1991, pp. 309-313), defines success as a function of return on equity ("ROE") and growth rate. The success space is shown in Figure 7.5. In this space *super-success* enterprises have ROE's of greater than 15 percent coupled with growth rates exceeding 30 percent annually. To achieve *super-success* in the rapidly changing technological landscape and market space requires the enterprise's strategy to have the ability to (Pearce II and Robinson Jr. 1991, pp. 178):

- Shape the market space structure based on timing of entry, reputation, success in related market and technological spaces and an acknowledged market space position.
- Rapidly improve customer value through improved quality and performance features.
- Develop strategic relationships with key suppliers and promising distribution channels.
- Establish the enterprise's technology as the dominant technology and maintain that dominance through incremental and radical changes with the technological space.

- Acquire a core group of loyal customers and expand the customer base through entrant changes, alternative pricing and promotion.
- Forecast future competitors and develop response strategies to the strategies that potential competitors are likely to employ.

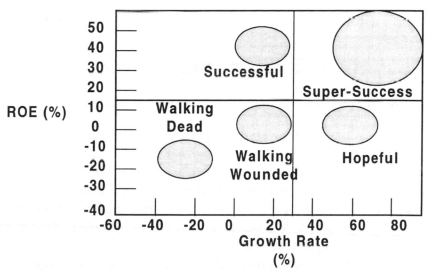

**Fig. 7.5** Enterprise Success Space (Based on data conatined in Roberts 1991, pp. 313)

## 1.3    Technological Space Issues

The principal technological space issue is the ever-shrinking technological life cycle. The life cycle of any technology is the time from inception to the period when it is no longer viable in the market space.   The average technological life cycle has been decreasing. The life cycle was about 10 years in the 1960s (Edosomwan 1989, pp. 21). By 1986, this life cycle had decreased to approximately two years.    This exponential decay in technological life cycle appears to have a half-life[3] of 12 years.  In 1998, the life cycle was reduced to approximately 12 to 16 months.

A new technological enterprise also faces issues arising from convergence in many technological spaces.   Technological convergence shifts the basis of competition from superior technologies to customization, efficiency, quality, ease-of-use and other conditions (Werther 1997).   This

---

[3] Half-life is the time required for the radioactivity of material to decay to half its initial value.

328

forces the enterprise to change its focus from technology to strategy as the life cycle of the technology and market space evolve. Figure 7.6 shows this change.

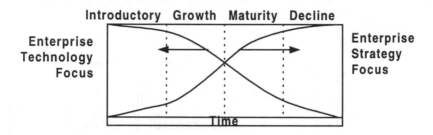

**Fig. 7.6** Strategy and Technological Focus (Adapted from Werther 1997)

New technological enterprises will also have to deal with how their technological entrants will be integrated within the enterprise from development through sales through service. This requires the entrepreneur and the enterprise leadership team to deal with a shift from a technological space to a market space focus. This will require reallocation of responsibilities along a continuum of activities (Cespedes 1996) with decreasing life cycles accelerating the need for iteration of roles and processes within the enterprise. This implies that the new enterprise must develop a structure, system and processes that encourage better concurrent marketing and the use of a multifunctional team approach during the entrant's life cycle.

### 1.4    Market Space Issues
In an era where the technological market space is being driven by communization[4], customization and a high degree of competitiveness, the new enterprise is faced with a number of marketing issues. The enterprise must decide the preferences of the current and potential customers and develop market space strategies that are very focused. This customer focus must be integrated throughout the enterprise during the growth of the enterprise. The enterprise must also develop market space strategies that are effective and contribute to profitability. The new enterprise must seek a balance that strives for profitability while providing the customers what they

---

[4] Communization is the formation of communities of users.

want with a value orientation. This in turn should lead to sustainable competitive advantage.

Another market space issue that the new enterprise must focus upon is the diversity of the customers. Customers vary in their needs and the reasons they acquire certain new technological products, processes or services. Some acquisitions by customers are driven by price, others by location, others by functions available, and others by a multiplicity of issues (Goodman and Lawless 1994, pp. 23-24). This variance among customers has led to the growth of customization of many technological products and services.

International competition or globalization is another market space issue facing the growing technological enterprises. The emerging economies in much of the world offer both a market space opportunity and a threat. A new technological enterprise can employ new technologies such as the Internet and electronic commerce to achieve a market space visibility. Companies such as Amazon.com, Yahoo!, Broadcast.com and others have used these technological instrumentalities to grow rapidly to become major players within existing and new market spaces.

Similar new technological entrants become aware of both the customer and competitor portions of the market space. This rapidity of communication contributes to the ever decreasing technological life cycle. This issue can be dealt with by seeking strategic alliances within the market space that can leverage the enterprise's technological or market space competitive advantage.

## 1.5 Enterprise Space Issues

The growing technological enterprise is faced with many issues, but those issues related to managing the enterprise in many instances are the most vexing for the leadership team. New technological enterprises are usually flat in nature with all decisions centralized by the entrepreneur (Hisrick and Peters 1995, pp. 401); financial decisions are made on a sequential basis. As the enterprise grows, the structure grows in a manner similar to that which Max Weber[5] catalogued in the late ninetieth century (Bendix 1960, pp. 418-425). This growth of bureaucratic organization is difficult to counter, as structure is necessary to deal with the growth in complexity of the new enterprise.

---

[5] **Max Weber, (1864-1920)**, was a German economist and social historian, known for his systematic approach to world history and the development of Western civilization. His classical work on bureaucracies defined the various stages of their development.

An important issue for the enterprise is keeping the entrepreneurial spirit alive as the enterprise complexity increases and the need for control increases. This need for control and the delegation of decision-making has two critical dimensions (Stevenson, Roberts, and Grousbeck 1994, pp. 529):

- Efficiency of the new enterprise in achieving the entrepreneurial vision and goals with minimum resources.
- Effectiveness of the new enterprise in adapting the entrepreneurial vision and goals in response to changing requirements of the technological and market spaces.

To achieve a tradeoff between these two dimensions, delegation and control issues must be resolved in a manner that allows the new enterprise to grow without stifling the entrepreneurial spirit.

The new enterprise is also faced with maintaining its competitive advantage through continuous knowledge creation (Nonaka and Takeuchi 1995, pp. 6). This requires the new enterprise to become a learning organization where a free exchange of information exists even as it grows in size and complexity (Senge 1990).

## 1.6 Financing Issues

As the enterprise grows, the financing issues will rarely be far from the top of the issues facing the enterprise leadership team. The management of cash flow is one of the issues that can determine the success of the new enterprise. A lack of cash has caused many new technological enterprises to fail and seek bankruptcy protection. Thus developing and maintaining a robust cash forecast is important for the new enterprise because in many instances early profits do not generate sufficient cash levels (Zimmer and Scarborough 1996, pp. 289).

The enterprise leadership team will also be faced with finding additional financing as the new enterprise grows. To obtain this additional financing will require the enterprise to seek new sources and types of funding. The search for additional capital will likely require going beyond the sources that provide primary seed and start-up funding. Thus, business plans will have to be continuously updated and produced to meet the requirements of new investor sources. As the enterprise starts to grow out of the *Valley of Death*, the entrepreneur and the enterprise leadership team will start to deal with venture capitalists and investment bankers. These new sources of capital have a totally different risk-return domain than that of the original investors (See Chapter 6 - Initial Enterprise Financing).

The issue of additional financing will also raise subsidiary issues as to the choice of types of additional investors, form of financing, what the enterprise leadership team is willing to give for this additional financing and the impact on and response of the initial investors.

## 1.7 Entrepreneurial Issues

The growth of the new enterprise is also coupled with the need to provide professional managers. In many instances, the entrepreneurial characteristics that provided for the establishment of the new enterprise are deleterious to the function of a more mature enterprise. There are few individuals such as Bill Gates of Microsoft® Corporation or Michael Dell of Dell Computer are able to meet the managerial demands of the more mature and growing enterprise. Thus, the enterprise leadership team may have either to delegate the management to more professional managers or to leave the enterprise. Therefore, for the technological enterprise to grow successfully, the entrepreneur will need to change management to encourage leadership by others (Wyrick 1997).

All entrepreneurs are eventually determining their individual harvesting or exit strategy (See Chapter 8 - Next Entrepreneurial Step.) This issue to capitalize on the enterprise's success also raises the issue of succession in the management of the enterprise. While the entrepreneur may harvest some or all of the value of the individual enterprise ownership, there will be the issue of who will be the Chief Decision-Maker ("CDM") for the enterprise.

## 2 TECHNOLOGICAL GROWTH

The technological space is an ever-changing landscape and only the robust survive. This rapidly changing technological landscape has an impact on a number of factors such as:

- Entrant life cycle.
- Speed to market
- Acquisition of technology either generated internally or acquired externally.

This requires that growing technological enterprises consider the process of technological growth and the means of generating or acquiring the technology. A new technological enterprise, while usually having its first market space entrant defined, must consider the follow on entrants. These

332

future technological products, processes or services are the instrumentalities that will provide the growth engine for the enterprise.

## 2.1 Technological Processes

Technological progress is either evolutionary or revolutionary. This progress results from:

- Increasing basic performance of technologies.
- Quest to exploit increases in performance of technologies within existing and new market spaces.

A technological enterprise can pursue either an evolutionary or a revolutionary path in developing new technological entrants. The evolutionary process moves along the path shown in Figure 7.7 which illustrates how new classes form and how older classes in a technological space are reimplemented with new technology as a function of time.

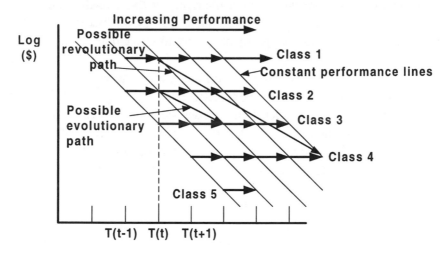

**Fig. 7.7** Price versus Time for Technological Progress (Adapted from Bell and McNamara 1991, pp. 170)

Moving from one class to another class along an increasing performance path is evolutionary. Increasing performance by moving to an advanced class is revolutionary. An example of an evolutionary movement is the growth of Microsoft ® Corporation's Windows ™ operating system, while the daring step of Boeing Corporation to develop a 707 jet engine powered airliner in the 1960s was considered daring and revolutionary in nature.

The new technological enterprise must focus on rising consumer expectations, shorter life cycles, the rapidly changing technological space and many other factors (Hall 1997). The enterprise's future technological entrants must be based upon what has been identified by appropriate research on customer needs. Figure 7.8 shows the process of developing the design requirements for future market space entrants.

The development of a new technological entrant to drive the growth of the enterprise is also a function of the enterprise's ability to innovate. A new technological enterprise can grow and be exceedingly successful, increasing value for its stakeholders by being innovative. Innovation is the creation and introduction of any kind of change that results from focused, purposeful action; however, it must create value for customers (Steele 1989, pp. 268). This innovation ability can result in the development of a *killer application* (Gates, Myhrvold, and Rinearson 1995, pp. 68). A *killer application* is a technology so attractive to consumers that it fuels the market space and makes the application indispensable. However, while many new technological enterprises seek a *killer application*, few entrants achieve this status.

The creation of value for the customer requires a sequence of activities. This value creation process begins by the identification of customer needs or to want once they perceive the need it would satisfy, such as the ability of the Internet to provide a means to acquire information easily. The enterprise must realize that technological innovation involves uncertainty because it requires market response as well as technical performance.

Due to the rapidly changing technological space, timing to market is critical. An enterprise that develops a high-quality new technological entrant must consider the timing of the introduction of the new entrant (Wheelwright and Clark 1992, pp. 16-20). The enterprise may seek to:

- Start a new technological entrant development project concurrently with similar projects developed by competitors, but introduce the entrant before the competition.
- Delay the start of the new technological entrant in order to obtain better information about the market and technological space and, as a result, bring the new entrant to market at the same time as its competitors with features better suited to the customer needs.

334

Mismanaging the introduction of the new entrant can seriously influence the cumulative profits from the sale of the new entrant in the enterprise's life cycle. Figure 7.9 shows that an enterprise can gain significant profit advantage by introducing a new entrant before its competitor. However, if the enterprise misjudges the market space readiness it can suffer a significant loss. An enterprise with a technological growth strategy of timing and quality can produce sales growth similar to that shown in Figure 7.10. The sales are built up by strategically introducing change before the prior entrant is in the decline phase of its life cycle.

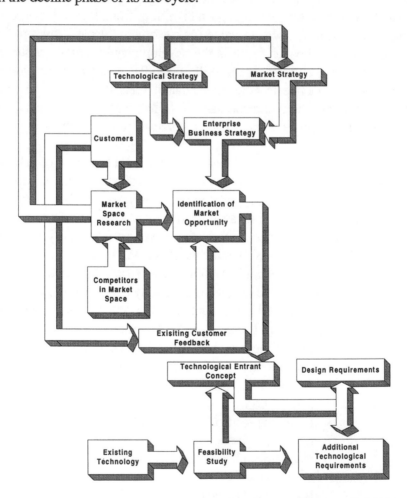

**Fig. 7.8** Technological Process for Growth (Adapted and modified from Hall 1997, pp. 64)

**Cumulative Profits over
Life of Technological
Product Relative to
Market Space Average**

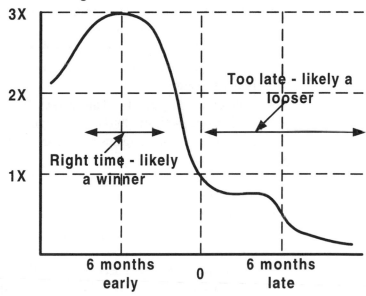

**Fig. 7.9** Time to market relative to competitor (Adapted from Wheelwright and Clark 1992)

The cumulative revenue pattern is built up of individual revenue cycles of entrants in various stages of maturity. The cumulative revenue will form an *S* shaped boundary if each entrant has an identical growth and decline pattern. However, if the new entrants have increasing sales the cumulative envelope will continue on a growth trajectory.

Accelerating the time-to-market of a new technological entrant is a critical competitive requirement for the growth of the enterprise. To achieve an acceleration of the time-to-market, the enterprise will require (White and Patton 1991):

- Commitment and support of the enterprise leadership team. When the enterprise is in its early stage of growth, this may be quite easy since the entrepreneur and/or the leadership team is the implementer. As the complexity of the enterprise increases it may not be so easily attainable.

- Simple and flexible control system, capable of operating in the chaotic technological environment. This allows the technological enterprise to adjust priorities quickly as unforeseen events arise.
- Clear and communicated priorities that focus resources on the most important enterprise requirements. This provides the enterprise with a clear direction so that it can quickly resolve resource conflicts and quickly implement needed change.
- Enterprise integration - This allows the organizational goals to be achieved through integration of the external stakeholders, including customers, suppliers and strategic allies.
- Clear, open timely and free-flowing communications at all levels and across all functions.
- Understanding of customer expectations. This is achieved by early, focused and repeated customer contact.
- An empowered team leadership with a minimum of hierarchical structure. The team leader must be given the responsibility and the authority to implement changes as appropriate.
- Sufficient resources to implement the plan for the new entrant. If resources are insufficient the team members will not only be frustrated, but alsothe enterprise is unlikely to meet the set objectives. It would be better to choose a *doable* project for market acceleration than an insufficiently supported project that is only likely to expend scarce resources without achieving the market entrant objectives.

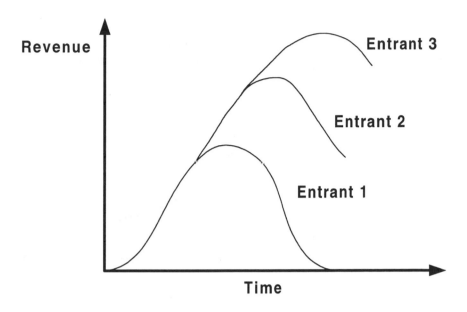

**Fig. 7.10** Cumulative Revenue from Strategically Introduced New Technological
Entrants

To produce increasing returns from technological products, processes or
services, the enterprise has to deal with the half-life of technological
knowledge. This requires the enterprise to maintain a technological
knowledge base that is the basis of any new technological entrant. This
knowledge base is influenced by (Vanini 1997):

- Continuous technological progress.
- Imitation by competitors.
- Decreasing demand devaluating existing knowledge.
- Retention of technological knowledge within the
  enterprise by retaining those enterprise members who are
  the storehouse of this knowledge.

These factors cause the original technological knowledge base of the
enterprise to decrease as shown in Figure 7.11. To compensate for this
decrease, the enterprise will have to add to this original base. If this original
knowledge base is left uncompensated it will affect and reduce the growth
potential of the new enterprise.

338

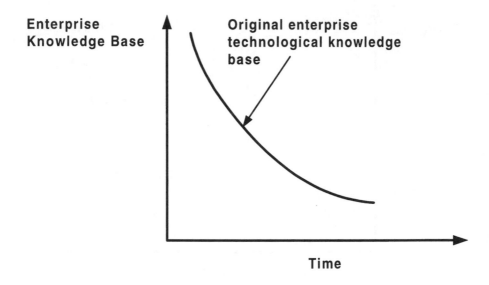

**Fig. 7.11** Enterprise Technological Knowledge Base

## 2.2    Technological Acquisition

A growing technological enterprise is faced with developing and market embedding not just one but a series of new entrants.  Embedding a new entrant is like the birth of a new child with all the accompanying pain and pleasure.  Like a new addition to the family, it can be a product of internal family conception or through the process of adoption.  Each process has its advantages and disadvantages for the growth of the enterprise.  Like any growth in a family, the enterprise must plan and manage this growth.

### 2.2.1  Management of Technological Acquisition

The acquisition of technology, either internally by development or through external acquisition, must be planned.  Figure 7.12 shows an approach to viewing a new entrant expansion space.

The enterprise must choose the new entrant expansion space strategy that best suits the technological development stage, i.e., existing technology, incremental improvement, new generation or radical entrant.  The new entrant development must be managed along four dimensions (Grant 1994):

- Technological feasibility.
- Behavior effects.
- Scheduling sequence.

- Economic costs and benefits.

The enterprise leadership team must be capable of managing usually a complex technological entrant with consideration to these four dimensions. Any error along these four dimensions can have serious consequences for the new and growing enterprise.

**Fig. 7.12** New Entrant Expansion Space

Outstanding new entrant developments have the following characteristics (Wheelwright and Clark 1992, pp. 14):

- Clear and shared objectives by all members of the enterprise who are involved directly and indirectly in bringing the new technological entrant to fruition.
- Anticipation of future customer needs and provision for those needs in a continuous manner. This means that offerings of the enterprise should be primarily incremental in nature. Radical entrants can in some instances actually lose customer support due to the disruptive nature of the entrant and its associated operational costs and risks.
- Brought to the intended market space as rapidly as possible. This must be achieved by considering all aspects of the development system.

- Test and validating in a manner that does not violate the rapid development cycle yet provides sufficient validation to minimize failure risks for the customers.
- Employment of multifunctional teams, with leadership empowered to make crucial decisions and allocate scarce resources.

A technological enterprise in its growth phase must choose which new entrant to develop and bring to market. This requires that the enterprise leadership team choose among alternative entrants to implement and allocate scarce enterprise resources. This choice requires an understanding of the opportunities lost by choosing one alternative over another. This in turn requires the enterprise leadership team to account for the various risks and uncertainties associated with various alternatives.

One method of making this determination is using an evaluation method based on net present value ("$NPV_R$") of the expected return from each new potential entrant; the probability ("P") of success of each potential entrant in the market space, and the $NPV_I$ of the corresponding investments ("I") required by the enterprise. Combining these factors enables determination of an index of value ("V") of each potential alternative (Steele 1989, pp. 103).

$$V = \frac{NPV_R * P}{NPV_I}$$

where

$$NPV_R = \sum_{t=0}^{N} \frac{R_t - C_t}{(1+i)^t}$$

$$NPV_I = \sum_{t=0}^{N} \frac{I_t}{(1+i)^t}$$

$R_t$ = revenue of potential entrant in year "t"
$C_t$ = cost of producing the potential entrant in year "t"
$I_t$ = investment required in year "t"
$i$ = discount rate
$N$ = life of the entrant in the market space

The NPV itself can be used as a measure of potential entrant viability. However, by combining the NPV with the enterprise investment required and a subjective judgement of the probability of success of the potential technological entrant, the enterprise can determine the fitness of various alternatives.

Another method for choosing which alternative entrant development to implement is the use of the technology-investment space concept shown in Figure 7.13 that provides a means for identifying technological investment priorities (Martin 1994, pp. 79-80).

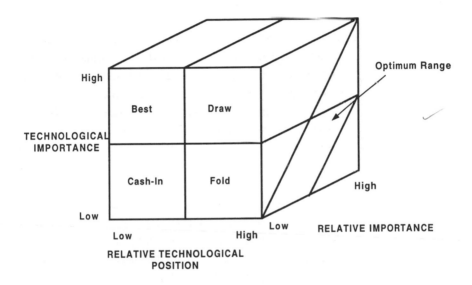

**Fig. 7.13** Technology-Investment Space (Adapted from Martin 1994, pp. 80)

Once the choice of the new technological entrant to develop has been made, the enterprise should consider the six principles used by highly successful technological enterprises such as Microsoft® Corporation to bring new entrants to the market space (Cusumano and Selby 1995, pp. 187). These principles are:

- Division of large projects into multiple milestone cycles.
- Provide a vision statement for the development and communicate that statement to all members of the development team. This also includes clearly defining the specifications for the new entrant.
- Incorporate prioritized features which customer research has shown are needed.

- Use modular and horizontal design architecture such that the entrant's structure is mirrored in the project structure.
- Control by individual commitments to small tasks and milestones.
- Do everything in parallel with frequent synchronization.

During the development process, the new technological entrant team can employ a variety of technology management tools including (Levy 1998, pp. 115-117):

- Control charts – These charts shows the variation of measures of performance over time. Limits, both lower and upper, are set that are used to manage the entrant development and maintain specifications.
- Cause and effect diagrams (also known as *fish-bone* charts). These charts show potentially major causes for an identified problem as main branches of a tree. Minor causes associated with each major cause are shown as leaves on a branch.
- Pareto[6] chart - These charts display the relative contribution of each subproblem to the total problem. This method is based on the Pareto principle which states that usually 20 percent of all possible factors cause 80 percent of all given phenomena.
- Slip charts - These charts show expected milestone completion dates as a function of the date of the estimate. These charts help to identify if the schedule will be met and offer the team a method to identify which milestones are seriously slipping behind their scheduled completion dates.

The timing and impact of management and its influence in meeting problems decreases as the project moves through the development cycle prior to market embeddment. The enterprise leadership team has its greatest influence in the early stages of development. This influence greatly diminishes as the project moves into its design and pilot production stages. Throughout the development, a balance must be maintained between the

---

[6] **Pareto, Vilfredo** (1848-1923) was an Italian sociologist and economist whose controversial theory concerning the superiority of an elite class is generally associated with the development of fascism in Italy.

technical and management processes (Shenhar and Dvir 1996). The technical process includes all the technical activities, both internal and external to the enterprise, that result in the new market entrant. The management process involves the management activities that are needed to allocate and monitor the use of project resources.

## 2.2.2 Internal Technology Acquisition

Many new technological enterprises in their early growth stages choose to introduce new market entrants based upon internally developed technologies. The actual process of transferring technology within the enterprise involves a number of decisions (Garvin 1992, pp. 326-328). One of the decisions is on timing, i.e., when the technology is ready to move from R&D to production and finally to market. Timing is driven by the need for preemption of competition. A late market introduction can have significant adverse effects on technology profitability; however, premature release can also have major adverse impacts. The timing of internal technology transfer is therefore critical.

Location within the enterprise for the responsibility of technology transfer is a critical decision factor, which includes whether the new technology should reside in an existing or a new portion of the enterprise. This location decision requires an understanding of the relationship between technology and R&D elements, i.e., should the technology be placed in an existing portion of the enterprise or in a new organizational element which is close in both physical proximity and/or culture to the R&D element? The organizational location decision must take into account the relationship of the technology to suppliers and customers, and the availability of technical and marketing skills of the responsible enterprise element. Other factors impacting location of the responsibility of the technology transfer process are the existing technology product and process requirements, and the need for organizational learning, i.e., the need to increase the technical capability of the entire enterprise.

Deciding which staff members should be involved in the internal technology transfer process is an element of the process (Garvin 1992, pp. 327). Multifunctional teams composed of the developers and receivers of the technology are the most effective in ensuring a smooth transfer. Communication between the various enterprise elements involved in the internal technology transfer process is a critical factor in the decision process. It is important to develop effective communication methods for bridging the

344

cultural, informational and geographic differences those often-separate enterprise elements in an internal technology transfer process. Multifunctional teams with responsibilities throughout the entire project greatly enhance communication. Where multifunctional teams do not exist, then direct transfer of personnel and formal documentation can assist communication.

The internal transfer or integration of technology differs within an enterprise depending on the nature of the technology being transferred from R&D or applied basic science to the product or production stage of development (Iansiti 1995). Figure 7.14 shows the informational relationship between research, technology integration, and the product development process. The model serves as a framework for understanding the development process of new technology that has both a high level of complexity and component uncertainty.

The success of the internal technology transfer determines the overall effectiveness of the total enterprise developmental process. The research indicates that those enterprises that are more successful are characterized by a system focused on the integration process of technology (Iansiti 1995). These enterprises emphasize the importance of gathering accurate information on how the technical factors would influence functionality and cost. This information should be obtained before moving the technology from R&D to product development. The problems that may occur in later stages of product development are directly linked to the decision in the critical internal technology integration or transfer stage.

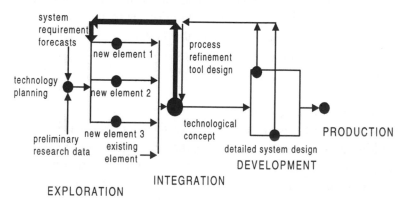

**Fig. 7.14** Information Process Framework (Iansiti 1995, © 1995 IEEE, Reprinted by permission)

There are a number of internal barriers to the transfer of technology between research and development and production (Vasconcellos 1994). Vasconcellos' study indicated ineffective communication systems between production and R&D constitutes the primary barrier to the technology transfer. The next strongest barrier was that the testing of new processes and products paralyzed the production line, especially in smaller enterprises. In addition, production is resistant to innovation and is bound by routine, causing another barrier to effective technology transfer from R&D.

Vasconcellos' study of technology enterprises also indicated that using multifunctional teams to develop the technological strategic plan could significantly reduce barriers. Decentralization of R&D, with personnel from these units being placed closer to production, will also reduce the barriers. A better understanding of the culture of both enterprise elements can be achieved by internal position rotation between production and R&D. Finally, Vasconcellos also showed that linking and participation of marketing elements in the transfer process between R&D and production is important since it offers insights into customer requirements.

Even if the technology is internally developed for the new entrant, outside suppliers of components and subsidiary technology may be involved. This can include *black box sourcing*. *Black box sourcing* is the practice of handing over the general specifications of a component to suppliers and having them design and produce the component to meet these specifications (Liker et al. 1995). This requires the enterprise to rely on the supplier to:

- Produce a high-quality design.
- Pre-test the design.
- Build the prototype within a set-time frame.
- Continually produce the final component within specifications.

The complexity of the new technological entrant will determine how the enterprise has to organize and emphasize the entrant's operational support. The entrant's development team will have to prepare a plan to test and validate the entrant. The enterprise will also have to provide for the support and training of staff before introduction of the new entrant. The amount of management attention will shift from entrant development to entrant support once it is embedded in its intended market space.

Empirical studies (Grzinich, Thompson, and Sentovich 1997) have shown that the top two drivers of schedule slips in new entrant development are poor definition of product requirements and unanticipated technical difficulties. These drivers are found to have the greatest impact on new or breakthrough entrants.

### 2.2.3 External Technology Acquisition

Outsourcing became a byword of the late 1990s in the technological space. This outsourcing included even the acquisition of technology. Empirical studies of the effectiveness of the external acquisition of technological knowledge indicate a variance among products, processes and industries. (Harabi 1996).

The decision to acquire technology external to the enterprise has a number of significant ramifications and is intimately tied to the technological strategy the new enterprise has chosen (See Chapter 3 - Technological and Enterprise Strategic Planning). Figure 7.15 shows a model of an internal versus external acquisition strategy for the enterprise. The primary drivers of the decision are:

- Degree of Competition - The greater the likelihood that a number of competitors will develop a similar technological entrant, the greater the benefit of external technology and this will result in reducing the time required to get to the market space.
- Degree of Protection - The less legally and physically protected the needed technology is expected to be, the more likely an enterprise may seek the technology externally.
- Life of Technology - The shorter the expected life of the technology, the greater the benefit of external acquisition.
- Technological Relatedness - Technologies that are not closely related to existing core enterprise technologies are more likely to be externally acquired.

A basic tension within the enterprise is caused by the decision to acquire technology externally. This tension arises due to two opposing forces (Goodman and Lawless 1994, pp. 256-261):

- Need of the enterprise to use the best available technology in developing its proposed new technological entrant.

- Need to have absolute control over the technology embedded in its new technological entrant.

Successful external technology acquisition depends on a number of factors including:

- Type.
- Complexity.
- Transfer mechanism.
- Relationships.
- Core competencies.
- Organizational culture.

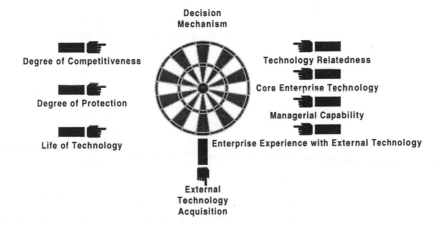

**Fig. 7.15** Internal-External Technology Acquisition Model (Adapted from Kurokawa 1997)

It has been stated that *"no enterprise is an island"* (Håkansson and Snehota 1989). Figure 7.16 shows the groups that interact with an enterprise (Gemünden, Heydebreck, and Heider 1994). These external relationships are an important strategic consideration for amplifying internal capabilities and skills. One benefit is the resulting synergy effects upon value and cost, i.e., increased value through increased quality and reduced cost through sharing resources and learning curves.

Studies of four hundred and ninety-two enterprises showed a relevance of technology-oriented relationships to an enterprise's innovation capabilities. Figure 7.17 shows R&D intensity and co-operation as determinants of technological innovation success. The methods a technological enterprise can employ to acquire external technology include (Ramanathan 1996):

- Hiring technical consultants, training technical personnel in companies and universities, encouraging and supporting technical staff in technical seminars, workshops and conferences, informal contacts and hiring technical staff from competitors.
- Joint ventures for gaining technology and training of internal staff from an allied enterprise.
- Subcontracting of technological components to an enterprise with an existing core technology.
- Licensing a technology from an enterprise or university that has developed an essential technology for the new market space entrant.
- Strategic alliances where the partners join to develop a new technology and maintain their independence and how the technology will be individually deployed.

Strategic alliances have grown significantly as a means of acquiring technology externally. In general, strategic alliances are also a competitive strategy tool. Technological strategic alliances have the following attributes (Carayannis and Alexander 1998):

- The presence of a champion in the potential ally is highly associated with the success of seed-capital financed strategic alliances.
- Capital assets from a strategic alliance are used in acquiring and developing proprietary technology and acquiring and developing skills and knowledge possessed by essential management personnel.
- Established enterprises in strategic alliances receive the primary technology-related intellectual property rights and marketing rights in exchange for investing in the new enterprise in the alliance.
- The partners in a strategic alliance could either become competitors or have a licensing agreement.

Table 7.1 shows a Pareto ranking of the effectiveness of alternative means of acquiring technological knowledge.

**Table 7.1**

Pareto Ranking of External Technological Knowledge Acquisition

| Processes | Measure of Effectiveness* |
|---|---|
| Independent R&D | 5.18 |
| Publications or Technical Meetings | 4.58 |
| Conversations with employees of innovative enterprises | 4.40 |
| Reverse engineering | 4.20 |
| Licensing technology | 3.83 |
| Hiring employees of innovative enterprises | 3.62 |
| Patent disclosures | 3.42 |

| Products | |
|---|---|
| Independent R&D | 5.30 |
| Reverse engineering | 4.60 |
| Publications or Technical Meetings | 4.42 |
| Conversations with employees of innovative enterprises | 4.24 |
| Licensing technology | 3.92 |
| Hiring employees of innovative enterprises | 3.67 |
| Patent disclosures | 3.54 |

* where 1 is not at all effective and 7 is very effective
(Based on the data contained in Harabi 1996)

Strategic alliances for acquiring technology externally have a number of organizational forms that often involve an intense technological cooperation not only in the local market space but also in spaces of the partner supplying the technology (Pucik 1994). The use of these alliances can result in competitive collaboration, where the partners are competitors but for a selected technological project may actually exchange technologies within certain limits.

350

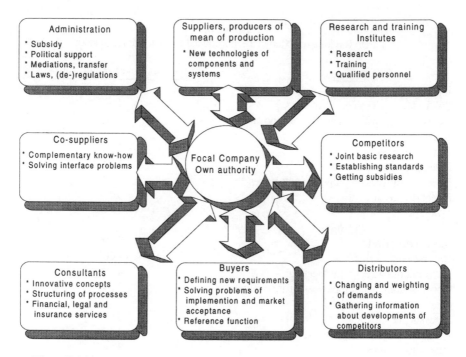

**Fig. 7.16** External Enterprise Relationships (Adapted from Gemünden, Heydebreck, and Heider 1994)

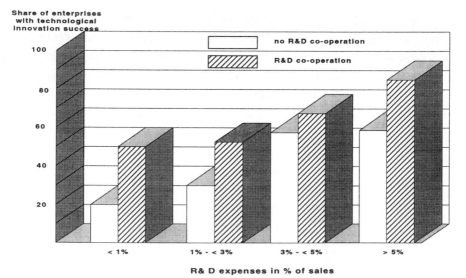

**Fig. 7.17** R&D Intensity and Co-operation Impact (Gemünden, Heydebreck, and Heider 1994,© 1994 IEEE. Reprinted by permission)

## 3. MARKET GROWTH
### 3.1 Technological Marketing

The concept of marketing has a long history (Braudel 1979, pp. 138-230). During this long history of market space developments, many of the concepts being employed by technological enterprises were honed and perfected. These included concepts such as *killer applications,* strategic alliances, branding and customization. *Killer applications* like the Gutenberg's[7] printing press, gun powder, and xerography have a long history. A *killer application* is a use of technology so attractive that it drives market forces and makes the device or concept all but indispensable (Gates, Myhrvold, and Rinearson 1995, pp. 68). Many of the uses of these technologies were never even considered by the inventor or innovator.

Inventions and innovations drive enterprises to introduce new technologies seeking a *killer application*, but not all technology-driven innovations are economic successes (Levy 1998, pp. 15). Many new technological entrants may have the potential to be *killer applications*, but the enterprise may lack the skills necessary to successfully market the entrant. Successful marketing of new technological entrants has been paraphrased as *war,* where no individual may die but where the very existence or life of the technological enterprises is at stake (Levy 1998, pp. 152).

Tracy (Tracy 1995) states that technological marketing staff must have the following qualities:

- Imagination and Creativity - The enterprise must approach its market space in a manner that will allow it to deal with the ever-changing landscape with imagination and creativity.
- Communication Ability - The technological marketing staff should be skilled in their ability to communicate clearly to its customers, suppliers and staff.
- Technical Competency - The potential customers should interface with the enterprise through enterprise representatives who exude technical knowledge.
- Reliability - The enterprise and its marketing staff should inspire confidence both internally and externally.

---

[7]**Gutenberg, Johann** or **Johannes** (1400-1468), German printer who is traditionally considered the inventor of movable type.

352

- Enthusiasm, Devotion and Perseverance - These qualities should be embedded into the total enterprise culture.

The technological marketing-goals of the enterprise must be tied to the enterprise goals. Similarly, to all technological products, processes or services the marketing must also follow a life cycle. Figure 7.18 illustrates the interaction of these cycles where marketing first generates the sales growth followed by a decline as the entrant's life cycle starts to decline. In some instances, marketing expenses may lag the sales decline as a product matures. If the enterprise has not anticipated this decline and tries to increase sales in a declining entrant life cycle, losses will increase.

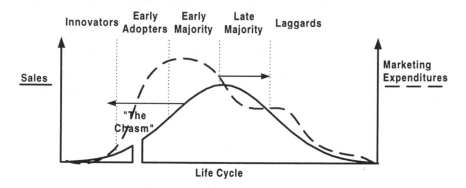

**Fig. 7.18** Sales and Marketing Life Cycles

Technological marketing should be based on the following concepts (Hills 1997):

- Customer needs and wants.
- Enterprise integrated marketing strategy.
- Realistic marketing goals.

To achieve customer orientation requires that the enterprise continually collect data on the exact needs of their existing and potential customers. The enterprise must also focus as an entity and integrate marketing into the developmental and production processes of the new entrant. Unrealistic goals can be negatively self-fulfilling and hence should be avoided.

The technological enterprise is faced with a number of different channels to make their new technological entrants available to the customers. Figure 7.19 shows the alternative marketing channels available to the enterprise. These channels include:

- Distributor - Takes products from various suppliers and provides them to either retailers, or resellers.
- Agent/Broker - Arranges sales but does not take possession of the product. Usually places orders for the enterprise with distributors, retailers or resellers.
- Reseller - Takes product and resells the product possibly with added value to end-users.
- Retailer - Sells the product to the end user.

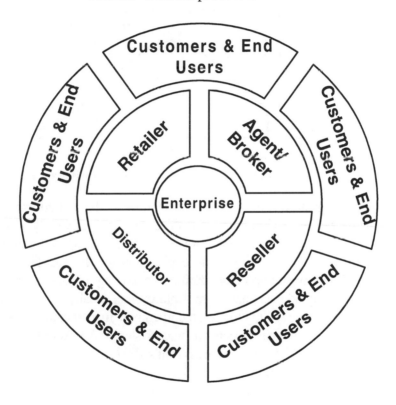

**Fig. 7.19** Technological Marketing Channels

## 3.2    Technological Marketing Segments

Many technological markets follow an adoption pattern similar to that shown in Figure 7.20. The technological market environment is usually composed of the following adopters (Hills 1997; Mather 1998):

- Innovators - Enthusiasts.
- Early adopters - Visionaries.

354

- Early majority - Pragmatics.
- Late majority - Conservatives.
- Laggards - Skeptics.

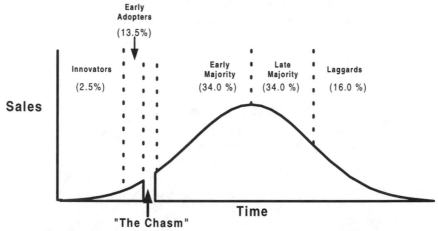

**Fig. 7.20** Technological Adopter Cycle (Based on data contained in Rogers 1995)

The technological market can be segmented by the type of adopters and follows the pattern shown in Figure 7.20. The innovators and early adopters are the first to accept a new entrant. However, there is a gap between these adopters and the early majority. The explanation for the gap lies in the execution of the decision process during the buying process, since the innovators and early adopters are more venturesome, usually well-educated, more affluent and more willing to use an untried new market entrant. All the adopters will follow the same decision process steps. Adopters follow the following steps during the buying process (Hills 1997):

- Awareness.
- Interest.
- Evaluation.
- Trial.
- Adoption.

While all adopters follow the same processes, the primary difference between them is the time taken to move from one step to another. Thus, the technological enterprise must develop marketing strategies that will assist potential adopters in reducing the cycle time in the adoption process.

## 3.3    Technological Branding

While a technological enterprise must continuously develop and embed new entrants in its chosen market space, it similarly must develop a recognized presence.  This presence is termed *brand*[8].  By establishing a *brand*, the enterprise creates perceived differences and develops customer loyalty that increases enterprise recognition and results in growth.  The development of this technological *brand* and *brand equity*[9] requires (Keller 1998):

- Memorability - The brand is easily recognized and recalled by customers.
- Meaningfulness - The brand has meaning for the customer and suggests quality and value.
- Transferability - The customer recognizes the brand when new market entrants are introduced by the enterprise.
- Adaptability - The brand can be easily updated and made contemporary.  (An example is the Microsoft® brand extending from DOS to the Windows™ products.)
- Protectability - The brand is protected through trademark registration that must then be enforced.

The results of technological branding help the enterprise to grow and secure larger margins.  Technological enterprises should (Keller 1998):

- Create a corporate brand with strongly associated enterprise credibility.
- Leverage quality through associations such as third-party endorsements.
- Link non-product-related associations in distinguishing near-party entrants.
- Craft the design and brand portfolios and hierarchies so that new entrants appear to be extensions of already branded products, e.g., Windows 3.1, Windows 95, and Windows 98 by Microsoft® Corporation.

Advertising is a marketing approach that can build brand awareness and brand equity, advertising also provides information about the new entrant to prospective customers. Advertising is an important element of technological

---

[8] American Marketing Association definition of a *brand* is a name, term, sign, symbol or design, or a combination thereof, intended to identify goods and services of one seller or group of sellers and to differentiate them from those of competitors.

[9] Keller (Keller 1998) defines *brand equity* "…as the differential effect that consumers' brand knowledge has on their response to marketing of that brand."

356

branding and marketing. Carefully crafted technological advertisements help
to persuade customers about the benefits of the products and generate leads
for inquires or orders to the enterprise (Gerstner and Naik 1998). Figure 7.21
shows the objectives and tasks for advertising technological market entrants.

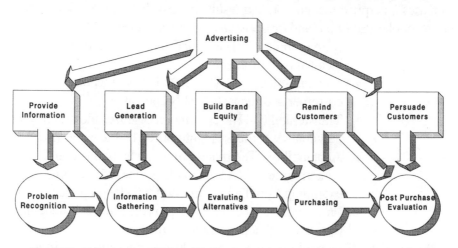

**Fig. 7.21** Objectives and Tasks of Technological Advertising (Gerstner and Naik 1998
© 1998 IEEE. Reprinted by permission)

### 3.4 Technological Customization

The customer's requirements and how well a new technological market
entrant meets those requirements will determine if the customer will seek to
acquire the new entrant. The closer those requirements match the
characteristics of the entrant the higher probability of a sale. Designing new
entrants with flexibility to be easily customized to the prospective customer
needs is called *customization*. To achieve *customization* or *individualization*
of a technological product, process or service requires user involvement
(Sioukas 1995).

In general the higher cost of an item, the higher degree of customization.
Thus, a U.S. Navy aircraft carrier such as the U.S.S. Truman, which cost
$4.5+ billion in 1998 to construct, was built exactly to the customer
requirements. A passenger aircraft such as the Boeing 777 costs over $500
million and whilst it is customized for a particular airline buyer it is less
customized than the aircraft carrier. A hamburger only costs $1.75 and has
very little customization. As technology is introduced into a system, the
degree of customization increases for the same cost. Thus, Dell Computer

Corporation can offer customization due to the reduced cost and functionality of direct marketing and the use of electronic commerce via the Internet. Figure 7.22 shows the impact of technology on the degree of customization. The Internet is an example of using technology that results in lowering cost while increasing customization.

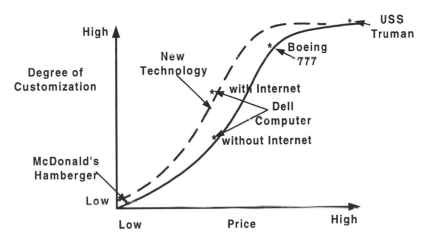

**Fig. 7.22** Impact of Technology on Customization

## 3.5 Strategic Alliances

Strategic alliances have been used throughout history to achieve market leverage. Strategic alliances are formed to combine the superior design technology of one of the partners with the efficient manufacturing of the other partner. This type of alliance results in diversifying the risks inherent in developing new products, processes or services. Long-term strategic alliances allow enterprise insight into competencies that are deeply buried within the fabric of a partner. These alliances do occur between competitors. *Complementary enemies* form a symbiotic relationship where each partner achieves objectives and yet maintains a competitive position. At times Microsoft® Corporation and IBM Corporation and Sun Microsystems have been strategic partners.

Each partner seeks to maximize their economic rents[10] (von Hipple 1988, pp. 76-92). The use of strategic alliances is one method of *borrowing* the resources of other enterprises (Hamel and Prahalad 1994, pp. 167).

---

[10] Economic rent is the revenue yielded by a property that is more than that yielded by the poorest or least favorably property under equal market conditions.

In the majority of strategic alliances, the dominant pattern of activity is the exchange of technology for technology (Simon 1994). According to Simon, strategic alliances usually emphasize a bilateral flow of technology, while joint ventures tend to emphasize a unilateral flow of technology. Strategic alliances caused the flow of technology before the technology's full market value has been exploited. Strategic alliances such as SEMATECH, PowerPC® and others usually allow faster development (Cardullo 1996, pp. 20-23). Hitt et al (Hitt, Ireland, and Hoskisson 1997, pp. 286-285) classified strategic alliances at a business or corporate level. These can be further differentiated as:

Business Level
- Complementary.
- Competitive reduction.
- Competitive response.
- Uncertainty reduction.

Corporate Level
- Diversifying.
- Synergistic.
- Franchising.

Technological strategic alliances can take many forms:
- Technical exchange and cross-licensing.
- Co-production and marketing agreements.
- Joint product development programs.
- Stand-alone joint venture enterprises with equity distribution among participants.

The formation of a strategic alliance cannot be taken lightly. Figure 7.23 shows strategic alliance formulation methodology.

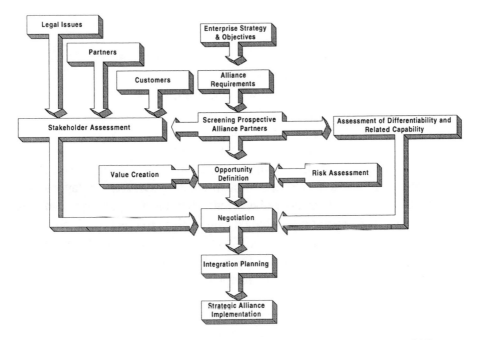

**Fig. 7.23** Strategic Alliance Formulation Methodology (Adapted from Knott 1997)

In the rapidly changing technological market space, strategic alliances offer a means to increase the speed of entrant development and/or market space entry and possibly to garner strategic competitiveness (Hitt, Ireland, and Hoskisson 1997, pp. 283-284). These strategic alliances in a fast cycle market space s are useful to (Hitt, Ireland, and Hoskisson 1997, pp. 284):

- Reduce time from development to market entry.
- Maintain market leadership.
- Establish an industry standard.
- Reduce R&D risk.
- Reduce technological and market uncertainty.

The strategic intent behind each partner in forming the alliance is very important. According to Pucik (Pucik 1994), the change from competitive rivalry to collaboration is merely a tactical adjustment aimed at specific market conditions.

A potential competitive relationship between partners distinguishes strategic alliances that involve competitive collaboration from more traditional complementary ventures (Hamel and Prahalad 1994, pp. 213). The following is a comparison between co-operative and competitive collaboration:

360

Co-operative Collaboration
- Feasibility.
- Desirability.
- Long-term win/win outcomes.

Competitive Collaboration
- Strategic market intent.
- No long-term win/win outcomes likely.

Large enterprises such as Intel Corporation may become investors in many new technological start-ups through creating symbiotic relationships, as was the case in their investment into Rambus Corporation. In this example, Intel Corporation obtained innovative microchip design and Rambus Corporation obtained capital and manufacturing knowledge, which helped it to achieve better designs. Figure 7.24 shows some of the forms of strategic alliances that can assist an enterprise's growth.

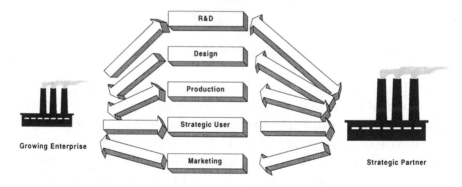

**Fig. 7.24** Models of Technological Alliances

The complementary strategic alliances can be either horizontal or vertical. The horizontal strategic alliances consist of partners at the same stage in a value chain and are used to increase strategic competitiveness of each of the alliance members. Vertical strategic alliances are where two or more competitors join and include R&D, distribution, suppliers, and outsourcing alliances.

### 3.6 International Technology Marketing

The technological space itself is fostering international marketing even for new growing enterprises. The development of electronic commerce is allowing new technological enterprises to sell their new technological products, processes and services globally. This type of marketing is accelerating with the pervasiveness of lower cost communication systems and the growth of the Internet.

There are a number of reasons why a technological enterprise would seek an international presence including (Hitt, Ireland, and Hoskisson 1997, pp. 296):

- Increased market size.
- Increased return on investment.
- Economies of scale.
- Location advantage.

The relaxing of world wide trade restrictions fostered by the General Agreement on Tariffs and Trade ("GATT") and the establishment of the World Trade Organization ("WTO") has resulted in a more open market space for technological enterprises (Levy 1998, pp. 186-208).

Enterprises considering operating in the international market space must consider differences in:

- Culture.
- Legal requirements.
- Cost of operating in various countries.
- Market space in various countries.
- Foreign government structures and their roles in the market space.
- Competitors in terms of goals, resources and competencies.

Operations in the international environment place new requirements upon an enterprise seeking to use a learning organizational archetype. These needs include an understanding of the cultural differences and how to effectively communicate and learn in this environment (Munter 1995). Figure 7.25 shows a mapping of the differences in high and low context cultures that managers of technology must understand in order to be able to operate effectively in an international environment. Cultures range from *high context*, i.e., establishing a context or relation first, to *low context*, i.e., getting right down to business.

In an international technology environment, a manager must understand that various cultures have different attitudes on what determines communication credibility. Communication credibility is enhanced by the relative importance of the rank of the communicator.

362

Relationships and personal records of accomplishment or goodwill are also of importance in the communication process. Many cultures place a higher value on expertise than on trust.

Perceptions about image, i.e., age versus youth, male versus female, and class, are an important element in some cultures. The importance of shared values cannot be underestimated in communications.

Language can also serve as a barrier to effective cross-cultural communication and learning. This barrier is caused, according to Munter, by:

- Semantics.
- Word connotations.
- Tone differences.
- Perceptions.

Managers of technology, who will be interacting with other cultures, can develop an understanding of the culture by reading about and discussing the culture before going to the country. While the manager is in the country, listening, reacting, and interpreting the culture is very important. It is important that technology managers encourage group members to learn by example, especially in relation to non-verbal communication, maintaining an open attitude of patience, tolerance, objectivity, empathy, and respect.

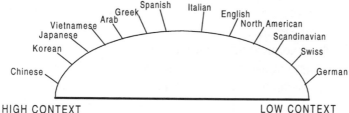

| HIGH CONTEXT | LOW CONTEXT |
|---|---|
| * Establish social trust first | * Get down to business first |
| * Value personal relations and goodwill | * Value expertise and performance |
| * Agreement by general trust | * Agreement by specific, legalistic contract |
| * Negotiations slow and ritualistic | * Negotiations as efficient as possible |

**Fig. 7.25** Differences Between High and Low Context Cultures (Munter 1995, © 1995 IEEE. Reprinted by permission)

The legal considerations in some instances can be insurmountable. For example, in some nations, enterprises must have a majority partner who is a national of the country in which the enterprise intends to operate.

All of these factors require that enterprises perform substantial country research before attempting to enter international markets. International marketing research requires the same understanding as within domestic markets, focusing on the differences between:

- Customers.
- Brand development strategies.
- Distribution channels.
- Pricing strategies.

Use of a strategic alliance is a marketing strategy that can assist a technological enterprise in entering the international market space through a strategic alliance. In this case, the strategic alliance partner either is an enterprise located in the foreign country or a domestic entity that has a strong market space presence in the selected country. In development of a strategic alliance, it is critical to understand the cultural differences between the partners and then consider developing the relationship.

## 4. ORGANIZATIONAL GROWTH

The enterprise in its growth stage will require organizational perturbations to deal with various problems. Figure 7.26 shows a Pareto chart of the problems of evolving enterprises. As Figure 7.26 shows the primary problem that technological enterprises had to manage concerned sales and personnel (Roberts 1991, pp. 184). While many authors have stressed problems caused by the lack of sufficient financing, it is the problems associated with sales, lack of or decreasing, that cause the basis of most enterprise problems, including the lack of financing. Financial success stems from sales driven by human resources. Problems in either of these factors will influence the financial success of the enterprise.

Planning these changes to cope with these problems will require an understanding of the enterprise and its various interactions with the supporting environment (Youngblood 1993, pp. 56). The organizational levers for implementing change include:

- Structure.
- Process.
- Systems.
- Human Resources.

These changes will occur in:

- Structure of the enterprise.
- Leadership characteristics.
- Culture of the enterprise.
- Management processes.

- Resources, both intellectual and human, used by the enterprise.

The way the enterprise handles these changes will have a profound impact on its growth and profitability.

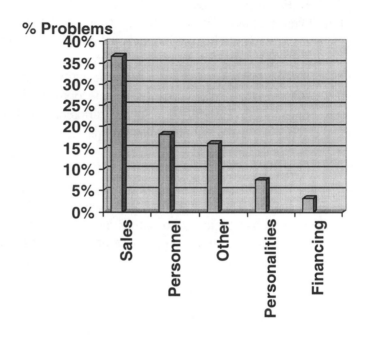

**Fig. 7.26** Major Management Problems During Growth (Based on data contained in Roberts 1991, pp. 184)

## 4.1  Enterprise Structure

The structure is the enterprise's formal role configuration, procedures, governance, control mechanism, authority, and decision-making processes. There are many ways of viewing the structure of an enterprise. A formal organization is the structural expression of rational action (Selznick 1948). The enterprise structure is an integration of skills and resources using processes and systems to accomplish the enterprise's goals, and as such, the enterprise is technically an *economy* and an *adaptive social structure*.

Enterprises as they grow appear to follow certain structural paths (See Chapter 5 - Enterprise Formation). There are two basic organizational theories to understand how an organizational structure can change as the enterprise grows. These theories are oriented (Anthony, Dearden, and Bedford 1984, pp. 40-41):

- Internally - Based on viewing the enterprise as an independent entity that functions without excessive concern for the external environment. This theory assumes a hierarchical assignment of responsibilities and decision making.
- Externally - Based on open-systems theory of enterprise-individual behavior. In this theory, the enterprise is viewed as a group of independent parts that interrelate and the entire enterprise interrelates with its environment.

An open adaptive system is what is required as the enterprise grows, so it can respond to changes in its environment. An adaptive structure can be  viewed as in the form of a grouping of responsibility centers at each level of the organizational chart (Anthony, Dearden, and Bedford 1984, pp. 232). The sum of all these *responsibility* centers forms the enterprise. The responsibility centers exists to accomplish one or more objectives (See Figure 7.27) with the financial performance of a responsibility center being measured in terms of profit, i.e., the difference between revenues and expenses. These centers are sometimes termed *profit centers*.

**Fig. 7.27** System Model of Responsibility Center (Adapted from Anthony, Dearden, and Bedford 1984)

Another way to view a responsibility center is in terms of return on investment ("ROI"). In this case, the enterprise unit is measured in terms of the return on capital used to produce the profit and can be valued through the economic value added concepts previously discussed in this text.

Enterprise structure follows inescapable structural laws (Fritz 1996, pp.3). The enterprise can be designed around various models and evolve as the environment changes (See Chapter 5 - Enterprise Formation). The enterprise as it grows must be adaptive to maximize its effectiveness and produce significant returns for its stakeholders.

Tapscott and Caston (Tapscott and Caston 1993, pp. 10-11) proposed that enterprise structure must change from a multi-layered hierarchy to flatter structures or even relatively autonomous enterprises. Table 7.2 shows how the enterprise migration should occur to achieve an open networked enterprise. The new open networked enterprise provides the flexibility to meet the challenges of the rapidly changing technology landscape.

**Table 7.2**
Migration Path to Open Networked Enterprise

| Element | Multilayered Hierarchy Structure | Open Network Structure |
|---|---|---|
| Scope | Internal/closed | External/open |
| Resource | Capital | Human, information |
| State | Static, stable | Dynamic, changing |
| Personnel | Managers | Professionals |
| Enterprise drivers | Reward & punishment | Commitment |
| Direction | Management commands | Self-management |
| Basis of action | Control | Empowerment to act |
| Individual motivation | Satisfy superiors | Achieve team goals |
| Learning | Specific skills | Broader competencies |
| Basis for compensation | Position in hierarchy | Accomplishment, competence level |
| Relationships | Competitive | Cooperation |
| Dominance requirements | Sound management | Leadership |

Source: (Adapted from Tapscott and Caston 1993, pp. 11)

An open enterprise networked structure can easily adapt to a changing landscape, while a fixed hierarchical structure lacks this flexibility. In thermodynamic terms, a fixed closed hierarchical structure leads to increased entropy[11] and eventually to *thermodynamic death*, i.e., and loss of the enterprise or acquisition.

The employment of a model that is more adaptive and open than the traditional structure is necessitated by the rapid changes occurring in the technological and market spaces. The adaptive and open enterprise structure has led Nonaka and Konno (Nonaka and Takeuchi 1995, pp. 166) to propose

---

[11] Entropy is a measure of the disorder or randomness in a closed system and in a closed system it inevitably and steadily leads to the deterioration of the system.

a *hypertext* organization. A *hypertext* organization is composed of interconnected layers or context, i.e., the business system, the project team and the knowledge base. In the business system layer, the normal, routine operations are conducted. The project team layer is composed of multiple project teams engaged in knowledge-creating activities. The teams are multifunctional in nature and are crosscutting from within the enterprise. The *knowledge-base* layer is where enterprise knowledge is created. This layer does not actually exist as an enterprise entity and is the combination of the enterprise vision, culture and technology (Nonaka and Takeuchi 1995, pp. 166-171).

As the enterprise grows it is critical to keep technological entrepreneurship alive. Burgelman (Burgelman 1984) defined a number of organizational structures for keeping the entrepreneurial culture alive within the enterprise. Figure 7.28 shows the enterprise design space for maintaining entrepreneurism within the enterprise.

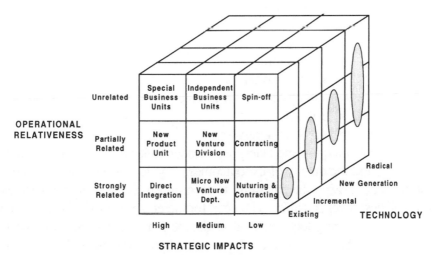

**Fig. 7.28** Enterprise Design Space (Adapted from Burgelman 1984)

The growing technological enterprise must not only keep the entrepreneurial spirit alive within the enterprise, but also must structure itself to dynamic and adaptive, i.e., a *living* enterprise (de Geus 1997). This *living organism* can become self-perpetuating as it adapts to the various challengers it will face as it grows.

368

## 4.2  Enterprise Strategic Leadership

Leadership will determine how well the enterprise adapts as it grows.  The leadership role has many facets including (Thompson Jr. and Strickland III 1996, pp. 307):

- Chief technological entrepreneur.
- Strategist.
- Chief enterprise administrator.
- Strategy implementer.
- Culture builder.
- Supervisor.
- Crisis solver.
- Taskmaster.
- Spokesperson.
- Resource allocator.
- Negotiator.
- Motivator.
- Adviser.
- Arbitrator.
- Consensus builder.
- Policy maker and enforcer.
- Mentor.
- Head *cheerleader.*

These roles require the enterprise's leader to keep cognizant of what is happening and the quality of the outcomes.  The leader must also promote a culture that *energizes* the enterprise to accomplish all the strategic objectives at the highest level possible.  The need for the enterprise to be responsive to the rapidly changing technological landscape places a responsibility on the leadership to be fully aware of potential opportunities within both the technological and market spaces.  The enterprise leadership must also build consensus within the enterprise.  The ethos[12] of the enterprise is also the function of the leadership.

The leadership of the enterprise can also be categorized by the leadership space (Figure 7.29).  The general trend of technological enterprise leadership is to move from a high human resource and high technological orientation to

---

[12] Ethos is the disposition, character, or fundamental values peculiar to a specific person, people, culture, or movement.

low people focus as the enterprise matures and moves to the public market stage.

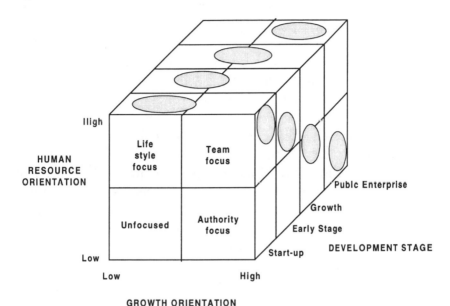

GROWTH ORIENTATION

**Fig. 7.29** Technology Leadership Space

The leadership style of the enterprise must also exhibit an adaptive nature, since technological enterprises require different kinds of leadership for each stage of growth (Herring 1997). Rarely does a technological entrepreneur stay as the Chief Executive Officer ("CEO") during the entire growth cycle of the enterprise although there are exceptions such as Bill Gates of Microsoft® Corporation. The start-up technological entrepreneur is a *visionary*. However, as the start-up moves through its various life cycle phases, a point is reached where the skills of the original technological entrepreneur are insufficient to manage the enterprise's growth. It is difficult and expensive to change the CEO of a growing enterprise. The greatest cause of failure is the lack of sufficient management and personal skills to deal with a rapidly growing enterprise. Many successful technological enterprises as UUNET and Yahoo! have been able to handle growth by turning the enterprise's leadership role to highly competent managers. The importance of leadership abilities is underestimated many times by investors.

## 4.3 Enterprise Culture

Enterprise culture is the set of in many instances unstated assumptions that the members of the enterprise share (Pearce II and Robinson Jr. 1991, pp. 344). Culture is internalized beliefs and values that all members of the enterprise share. The culture that permeates an enterprise is like the breath of life. The uniformity of that culture and its composition will greatly assist in growing the enterprise. Thus, if the culture is not uniform throughout the enterprise, disagreement and conflict can result and in turn serve as a deterrent to growth. The culture of highly successful enterprises guides the behavior and orientation of the members. The guiding philosophies and principles assist the members of the enterprise to amplify their individual efforts. Aligning the enterprise culture with strategic issues will provide synergistic benefits. In the rapidly changing technological landscape, the culture, similar to the enterprise structure, must be adaptive if the enterprise is to achieve a sustainable long-term performance.

The entrepreneur and the leadership team must engender a culture of a sustainable technological entrepreneurial spirit within the enterprise as growth occurs (Drucker 1985, pp. 143-146). This can be achieved by fostering individuality while focusing on the enterprise's strategic objectives. Multifunctional teams that are fully empowered have been shown to help foster enterprise entrepreneurism.

An important enterprise cultural element is *learning* (Senge 1990). According to Sitkin et al (Sitkin, Sutcliffe, and Weick 1998), enterprise learning is a change in an enterprise's response characteristics, i.e., it becomes highly responsive to change in its environments. An adaptive learning culture within an enterprise will assist the enterprise in achieving a sustainable competitive advantage (Franco 1997). Highly successful technological enterprises such as Microsoft® Corporation have built a learning culture for their enterprises. This has been achieved by improving the enterprise through continuous self-critiquing, feedback and sharing (Cusumano and Selby 1995, pp. 327). This learning culture includes systematically learning from past and present enterprise activities. This is accomplished through using quantitative metrics and benchmarks and providing this feedback to all members of the enterprise. In this manner, the enterprise members can continuously improve their performance.

The enterprise must act as one *organism* by promoting linkages and sharing across all enterprise elements. This results in an adaptive conscious improvement in enterprise knowledge, action and performance.

## 4.4 Enterprise Process Management

The management of the enterprise consists of a series of processes. While the enterprise structure and culture must be adaptive, the management of the enterprise must be creative to achieve superior performance results. Flexibility within limits should be the byword for enterprise management.

Figure 7.30 presents elements of the enterprise process management.

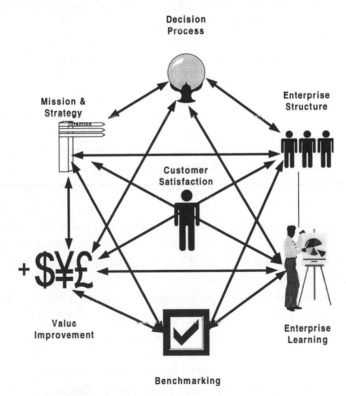

**Fig. 7.30** Enterprise Management Process

The management process must be implemented in a flexible manner to handle the operations of the enterprise in a rapidly changing environment. The process must be able to handle the variety of problems that arise during growth of the enterprise and that were shown to be the drivers of changes in process itself.

The technological management process must focus on:
- Technology selection.
- Improving enterprise competency.
- Sources of technology.
- Human and financial resources.
- Managing the enterprise adaptive process..

A management technique that allows the enterprise to respond to the changing technological landscape is the use of teams. The most effective team is one composed of various enterprise elements, i.e., multifunctional teams. A multifunctional team, also known as cross-functional team ("CFT"), is defined as (Wilemon 1995):

> *"Members of different departments and disciplines brought together under one manager to make development decisions and enlist support for them throughout the organization".*

The development of multifunctional teams evolved because traditional approaches for developing new technologically based products, processes or services were not effective. The cause of this ineffectiveness was limited internal integration, i.e., among R&D, manufacturing, marketing, and limited external integration, i.e., among customers, suppliers, partners and technologies. Other contributing factors were poorly executed or ignored developmental steps, combined with the important initial steps being rushed. These factors produced technical problems later in the developmental process. Low information sharing among enterprise sectors and limited learning across projects and organizations were others.

It is important that enterprises construct an internal environment where multifunctional teams can successfully operate. True multifunctional integration occurs at the working level where communication is very critical. The benefits of multifunctional teams include:
- Synergy, i.e., more than the sum of the parts.
- Improved customer focus and satisfaction.
- Reduced lead-time to market for new products, processes or services.
- Higher quality decisions and work.
- Fewer communication breakdowns.
- Enhanced organizational learning.

While multifunctional teams enable these important benefits, they also have limitations (Wilemon 1995). Team collaborations are often tentative, fragile, threatened by confusion, stressful, conflicting and skeptical, and team member contributions are quite variable. There is also the paradox of preserving differences among team members while attempting to integrate the differences into a whole. In addition, there is definite team tension as individuals adjust to becoming team members.

Multifunctional teams can be enhanced through a number of actions(Wilemon 1995). Figure 7.31 presents the building blocks for an effective multifunctional team. Limitation of team size to eight or fewer members will reduce interface problems. It is important to take a proactive stance toward interface problems by openly discussing them, seeking resolutions, and eliminating small problems early. Involving all parties early in the project life cycle also enhances team performance.

By making open communication the responsibility of every team member, performance of the multifunctional team is enhanced. Clarifying the decision-making authorities can assist performance. Altering the basis for allocating responsibility for goal achievements from controllers to direct participants, e.g., change managers from resource controllers to resource suppliers, is another technique. An important factor in enhancing performance is empowering teams and not individual team members. The team is like a family when the team is empowered rather than the individual team members. It is important to give professionals the ability to choose their assignments within the structure. Successful multifunctional teams balance leadership with membership, i.e., they use a *flat structure* rather than a hierarchy. All team members should be trained for teamwork. The use of multifunctional teams has resulted in: more products, processes and services; faster realization times; higher product quality; and the creation of products, processes and services which better reflect the needs of both the customers and the enterprise.

374

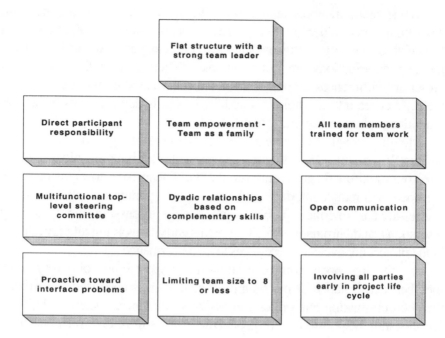

**Fig. 7.31**  Building Blocks to Successful Multifunctional Teams

Teams fail for a number of reasons.  Failure is defined as the team falling significantly short of reaching its full potential (Beyerlein, Beyerlein, and Jordan 1997).  In many instances, these failures have occurred because the enterprise failed to do sufficient planning before implementing teams or the teams were teams in name only.  In some instances, the failures occurred due to confusion in defining the team and the outcomes expected.

## 4.5   Internal Enterprise Resources
A growing technological enterprise must deal primarily with two types of internal resources: intellectual and human.  These resources form the basis for the enterprise sustainable competitive advantage.  Various ways to leverage resources to achieve sustainable competitive advantage have been identified, including (Hamel and Prahalad 1994, pp. 160):

- Concentrating resources on essential strategic enterprise goals.
- Efficiently accumulating resources.
- Synergistic effect of complementing resources of one type with those of another.

- Conserving resources wherever possible.
- Rapidly recovering resources by reducing the time between expenditure and payback for the resource.

## 4.5.1 Intellectual Resources

Intellectual resources consist of the intellectual capital of the enterprise and form one of the essential elements to a sustainable competitive advantage for a growing technological enterprise (See Chapter 5 - Enterprise Formation). In many enterprises, intellectual capital management has expanded from licensing of enterprise technology to becoming the basic element in technology strategy (Grindley and Teece 1998). The concept of licensing and cross licensing is not solely limited to large mature enterprises. Growing technological enterprises can also benefit from a licensing strategy. Technological innovations are an important strategic variable and as such can serve as generators of revenue (Chung 1995).

Determination of what patents are suited for licensing requires the application of a patent portfolio concept (Ernst 1997), e.g., the patent portfolio space concept shown in Figure 7.32. This space shows the relative position of the enterprise's patents as a function of their technological attractiveness. The relative enterprise patent position in a particular technological field is measured by the number of patents owned by the enterprise relative to the number of patents of a competitor in the same technological space. The overall technological attractiveness is measured by calculating the growth rates of patent applications in the technological space.

## 4.5.2 Human Resources

The human resources of the growing enterprise are the means by which the vision is translated into reality. As such, the acquiring of the necessary *best* human resources to assist the enterprise to grow is of vital importance (See Chapter 5 - Enterprise Formation). As the enterprise grows the degree of contact between the founding enterprise members and the employees tends to decrease (Zimmer and Scarborough 1996, pp. 483). Thus, the acquisition of human resources with characteristics that help to maintain the entrepreneurial spirit is important. A human resource strategy for the growing technological enterprise is essential. The leadership team should make the development of this human resource strategy and its implementation an important element within the overall system of strategic plans the enterprise maintains.

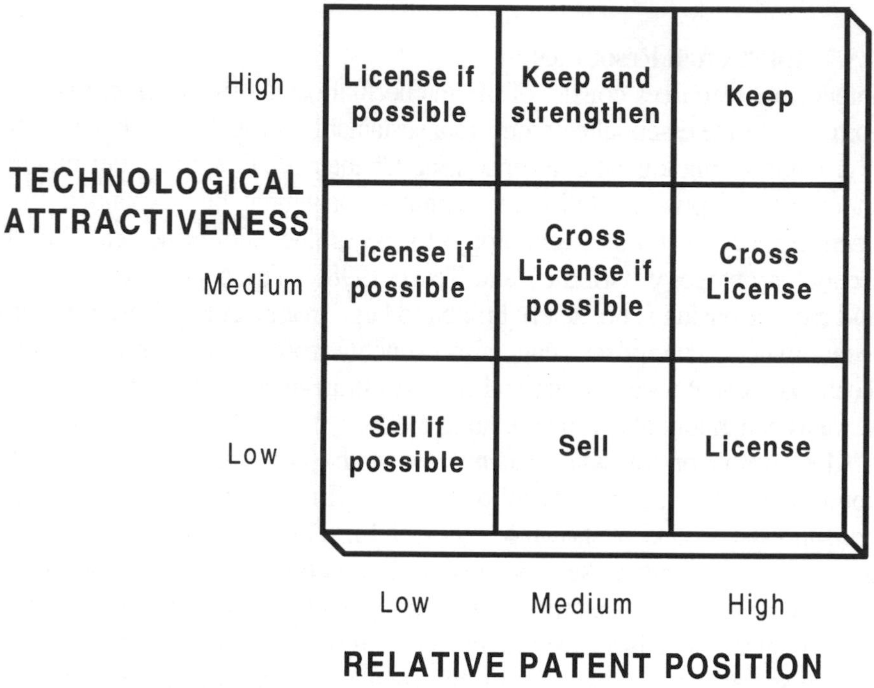

| | Low | Medium | High |
|---|---|---|---|
| **High** | License if possible | Keep and strengthen | Keep |
| **Medium** | License if possible | Cross License if possible | Cross License |
| **Low** | Sell if possible | Sell | License |

**TECHNOLOGICAL ATTRACTIVENESS**

Low   Medium   High

**RELATIVE PATENT POSITION**

**Fig. 7.32** Patent Portfolio Space (Adapted from Ernst 1997)

The growing technological enterprise should seek to acquire human resources that have both technological and market space skills. This requires that the enterprise locate, acquire, motivate, and retain these human resources. In the late 1990s recruitment techniques expanded with the introduction of the Internet. In the twenty-first century, recruitment of human resources will become increasingly challenging, requiring enterprises to explore alternative recruitment options (von Glinow and Scandura 1998).

To attract human resources requires that the enterprise develop an understanding of what sets it apart from other technological enterprises. The enterprise must clearly delineate what skill sets are required and what it is willing to trade-off to obtain them. Once acquired the enterprise must be able to retain this increasingly scarce resource. Many enterprises have chosen to emphasize their unique cultures to attract and retain employees (Henry 1998). The use of culture as an employee retention factor is illustrated by

MicroStrategy and its dynamic CEO, Michael J. Saylor (See Chapter 2 - Technological Entrepreneurs), who emphasizes the culture and his enterprise's ethics and loyalty. Michael J. Saylor looked for employees who were *".... bright, passionate, even done something decently, whether it's rocketry or badminton."* (Henry 1998).

## 5. FINANCIAL GROWTH

A growing technological enterprise will need additional financing. This need (See Chapter 6 Initial Enterprise Financing) continues throughout the life of the enterprise. Growth financing can be obtained from:

- Bank loans.
- Accounts receivable financing.
- Second, third and mezzanine private and venture capital equity additions.
- Convertible debentures.
- Licensing of intellectual property.
- Revenues.

### 5.1 Financing Growth

The second round of financing can prove very time consuming and daunting during the initial growth of the enterprise (Martin 1994, pp. 309). During this early stage of enterprise growth, the prospective investors will closely watch how the enterprise is making progress toward its goals. Once the enterprise has moved beyond the *Valley of Death*, venture capitalists operating in the enterprise's technological and market space will be more easily attracted to at least investigating the possibilities of investing in the enterprise. An important element in the later stages of financing is the financial and cost management of the enterprise. According to Roberts (Roberts 1991, pp. 188-197), 60 percent of the technological enterprises sampled obtain second round financing and about 30 percent obtain third round financing. Figures 7.33 and 7.34 show Pareto charts of the sources of the second and third round enterprise growth financing.

There is no optimal source of growth capital for technological enterprises (Roberts 1991, pp. 194). While some internal funding is available from re-investment of profits and licensing fees, the principal financial growth sources are equity and debt financing.

378

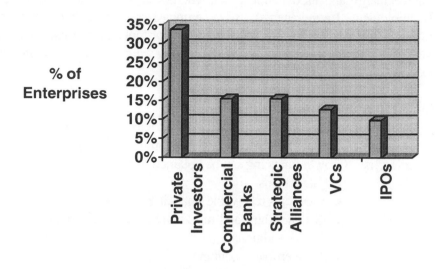

**Fig. 7.33** Principal Sources of Growth Financing - Second Round (Based on data contained in Roberts 1991, pp. 191)

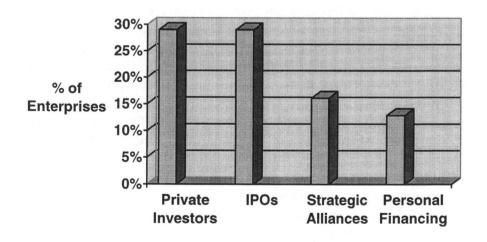

**Fig. 7.34** Principal Sources of Growth Financing - Third Round (Based on data contained in Roberts 1991, pp. 191)

### 5.1.1 Equity Financing

Equity financing is obtained by selling additional interest in the new technological enterprise. The entrepreneur, the leadership team, and the original seed and startup investors have to decide how much capital to raise from prospective investors and from whom to raise this capital. Using pro forma income and balance sheet projections (See Chapter 6 - Initial Enterprise Financing) and its capital budgeting process, the enterprise determines the amount of additional capital needed. The weighted cost of capital can be calculated from (Keeley 1998, pp. 8-22):

$$R_{Cap} = \left(\frac{D}{D+E}\right) R_D (1 - T_C) + \left(\frac{S}{D+E}\right) R_C$$

where

$R_{Cap}$ = weighted average cost of capital (%)
E    = equity ($)
D    = debt ($)
Cap  = enterprise total capital = E + D
$R_D$  = cost of debt (%)
$R_C$  = cost of equity (%)
$T_C$  = corporate income tax rate (%)

The cost of equity can be calculated from:

$$R_C = R_f + P_{Risk} * R_{Risk}$$

where

$R_f$      = cost of capital for a risk free investment.
$P_{Risk}$     = equity risk premium.

The $P_{Risk}$ premium has been shown to be 8.3 percent with a standard deviation of 2.3 percent(Keeley 1998, pp. 8-22).

$R_{Risk}$     = relative risk versus an average stock.

The $R_{Risk}$ risk factor is between 0.8 to 1.5 with technological enterprises at the high end.

As the debt and equity of an enterprise change, the cost of capital will change.

### 5.1.2 Debt and Other Financing

It is possible for a growing enterprise to deal with cash flow uncertainties by getting cash from receivables and inventories. This strategy only provides operating cash not growth capital. Most short term financing is used primarily to meet operating requirements and should not be used to grow the enterprise since it usually must be paid back before the financial growth produces sufficient returns.

Long-term debt can provide capital for a growing enterprise. In fact, long-term debt is the primary means for obtaining capital for growing an enterprise. Long-term debts with maturities over 10 years are difficult for small and intermediate sized enterprises to obtain. If this form of debt is available, it usually will require having it secured by long-term assets equal to approximately 1.25 times the amount of the debt. Growing technological enterprises may be able to obtain long-term loans through the small business investment corporations ("SBICs") (See Chapter 6 - Initial Enterprise Financing).

### 5.2 Managing Financial Growth

Managing the financial growth of the enterprise usually is the responsibility of the Chief Financial Officer ("CFO") of the enterprise. In the 1990s, the CFO position within the enterprise leadership team has become critical to the financial management success of the enterprise. The CFO must have (Skinner 1997):

- Strong internal fortitude to stand years of losses and research expenditures before seeing a balance sheet which is positive.
- Capacity to budget for rapid growth of 100 to 200 percent annually.
- Ability to command respect from the technological entrepreneur who may not be as interested in profit margins as he/she is in technology.

These CFO characteristics must be coupled with a sound grounding in financial management concepts and knowledge of the financing space.

### REFERENCES

Anthony, Robert N., John Dearden, and Norton M. Bedford. 1984. *Management Control Systems*. Homewood, IL: Richard D. Irwin, Inc.

Asim, Amy, and Charles E. Lucier. 1996. Toward a New Theory of Growth. *Strategy & Business* (2):10-16.

Bell, C. Gordon, and John E. McNamara. 1991. *High-Tech Ventures: The Guide for Entrepreneurial Success.* Reading, MA: Addison-Wesley Publishing Company, Inc.

Bendix, Reinhard. 1960. *Max Weber: An Intellectual Portrait.* New York, NY: Doubleday & Co., Inc.

Beyerlein, Michael M. , Susan T. Beyerlein, and Ann Jordan. 1997. Engineers Work in Teams: A Study of Collaborative Work Structures. Paper read at Portland International Conference on Management of Engineering and Technology - 1997, 97/7/27-31, at Portland, OR.

Bhide, Amar. 1996. The Question Every Entrepreneur Must Answer. *Harvard Business Review* (Nov-Dec):120-130.

Braudel, Fernand. 1979. *The Wheels of Commerce: Civilization and Capitalism 15th - 18th Century - Volume 2.* Translated by Reynolds, S. 2 vols. Vol. 2. New York, NY: Harper and Row, Publishers.

Burgelman, R. A. 1984. Designs for Corporate Entrepreneurship in Established Firms. *California Management Review* (Spring):154-166.

Carayannis, Elias G, and Jeffrey Alexander. 1998. Technology-Driven Strategic Alliances: Tools Exchange in a Positive-Sum World. In *The Technology Management Handbook*, edited by R. C. Dorf. New York, NY: CRC Press.

Cardullo, Mario W. 1996. *Introduction to Managing Technology.* Edited by J. A. Brandon. First ed. 5 vols. Vol. 4, *Engineering Management Series.* Baldock, Hertfordshire, England: Research Studies Press Ltd.

Cespedes, Frank C. 1996. The Marketing Gearbox: Integrating Products, Sales and Service. *Strategy & Business* (3):28-45.

Chung, Kam B. 1995. Technology Licensing for the Small Firm. Paper read at 1995 IEEE Annual International Engineering Management Conference, 95/6/28-30, at Singapore.

Cusumano, Michael A., and Richard W. Selby. 1995. *Microsoft Secrets: Company Creates Technology, Shapes Markets, and Manages People.* New York, NY: The Free Press.

de Geus, Arie. 1997. The Living Company. *Harvard Business Review* (March-April):51-59.

Drucker, Peter F. 1985. *Innovation and Entrepreneurship: Practice and Principles.* New York, NY: Harper and Row, Publishers.

Edosomwan, Johnson A. 1989. *Integrating Innovation and Technology Managment.* Edited by D. F. Kocaoglu, *Wiley Series on Engineering and technology Management.* New York, NY: John Wiley & Sons.

Ernst, Holger. 1997. The Patent Portfolio for Strategic R&D Planning. Paper read at Portland International Conference on Management of Engineering and Technology - 1997, 97/7/27-31, at Portland, OR.

Franco, Carlos A. 1997. Learning Organizations: A Key for Innovation and Competitiveness. Paper read at Portland International Conference on Management of Engineering and Technology - 1997, 97/7/27-31, at Portland, OR.

Fritz, Robert. 1996. *Corporate Tides: The Inescapable Laws of Organizational Structure.* San Francisco, CA: Berrett-Koehler Publishers.

382

Garvin, David A. 1992. *Operation Strategy: Text and Cases*. Englewood Cliffs, NJ: Prentice Hall.

Gates, Bill, Nathan Myhrvold, and Peter Rinearson. 1995. *The Road Ahead*. New York, NY: Viking, Penguin Group.

Gemünden, H. G., P. Heydebreck, and R. Heider. 1994. Technological Interweavement: A Means of Achieving Innovation Success. *IEEE Engineering Management Review* 22 (Summer):48 - 58.

Gerstner, Eitan, and Prasad Naik. 1998. Advertising High-Technology Products. In *The Technology Management Handbook*, edited by R. C. Dorf. New York, NY: CRC Press.

Goodman, Richard A., and Michael W. Lawless. 1994. *Technology and Strategy: Conceptual Models and Diagnostics*. New York, NY: Oxford University Press.

Grant, John H. 1994. Strategic Change: Managing Strategy Making Through Planning and Administrative Systems. In *The Portable MBA in Strategy*, edited by L. Fahey and R. M. Randall. New York, NY: John Wiley & Sons, Inc.

Grindley, Peter C., and David J. Teece. 1998. Managing Intellectual Capital: Licensing and Cross-Licensing in Semiconductors and Electronics. *IEEE Engineering Management Review* 26 (Summer):92-111.

Grove, Andrew S. 1996. *Only the Paranoid Survive: How to Exploit the Crisis Points that Challenge Every Company and Career*. New York, NY: Currency Doubleday.

Grzinich, John C., John H. Thompson, and Michael F. Sentovich. 1997. Implementation of an Integrated Product Development Process for Systems. Paper read at Portland International Conference on Management of Engineering and Technology, at Portland, OR.

Håkansson, H. , and Snehota. 1989. No business is an island. *Scandinavian Journal of Management* 5:187 - 200.

Hall, M. J. 1997. Designing for the Life Cycle. In *Concurrent Engineering - The Agenda for Success*, edited by S. Medhat. Taunton, UK: Research Studies Press, Ltd./John Wiley & Sons, Inc.

Hamel, Gary, and C. K. Prahalad. 1994. *Competing for the Future*. Boston, MA: Harvard Business School Press.

Harabi, Najib. 1996. Channels of R&D Spillones: An Empirical Investigation. Paper read at Fifth International Conference on Management of Technology, 96/2-3/27-1, at Miami, FL.

Henry, Shannon. 1998. Culture Club: Signing Up the High-Tech Workforce. *Techcapital*, 98/3-4, 42-51.

Herring. 1997. Hail to the Chiefs. *Red Herring*, 97/12, 66-69.

Hills, Gerald E. 1997. Market Opportunities and Marketing. In *The Portable MBA in Entrepreneurship*, edited by W. D. Bygrave. New York, NY: John Wiley & Sons, Inc.

Hisrick, Robert D., and Michael P. Peters. 1995. *Entrepreneurship: Starting, Developing, and Managing a New Enterprise*. Chicago, IL: Irwin.

Hitt, Michael A., R. Duane Ireland, and Robert E. Hoskisson. 1997. *Strategic Management: Competitiveness and Globalization - Concepts*. Second ed. Minneapolis/St. Paul, MN: West Publishing Company.

Iansiti, Marco. 1995. Technology Development and Integration: An Empirical Study of the Interaction Between Applied Science and Product Development. *IEEE Transactions in Engineering Management* 42 (August):259 - 269.

Keeley, Robert. 1998. Equity Financing. In *The Technology Management Handbook*, edited by R. C. Dorf. New York, NY: CRC Press.

Keller, Kevin Lane. 1998. Brand Equity. In *The Technology Management Handbook*, edited by R. C. Dorf. New York, NY: CRC Press.

Knott, David G. 1997. Vertical Integration: 80's Fuse or Health Care's Future? *Strategy & Business* (8):47-54.

Kurokawa, Susumu. 1997. Make-or-Buy Decisions in R&D: Small Technology Based Firms in the United States and Japan. *IEEE Transactions in Engineering Management* 44 (2):124-134.

Levy, Nino O. 1998. *Managing High Technology and Innovation.* Upper Saddle River, NJ: Prentice Hall.

Liker, Jeffrey K, Rajan R. Kamath, S. Nazli Wasti, and Mitsuo Nagamachi. 1995. Integrating Supplies into Fast-Cycle Product Development. In *Engneered in Japan: Japanese Technology - Management Practices*, edited by J. K. Liker, J. E. Ettle and J. C. Campbell. New York, NY: Oxford University Press.

Martin, Michael J. C. 1994. *Managing Innovation and Entrepreneurship in Technology - Based Firms.* Edited by D. F. Kocaoglu, *Engineering and Technology Management.* New York, NY: John Wiley and Sons.

Mather, John H. 1998. Marketing Segments. In *The Technology Management Handbook*, edited by R. C. Dorf. New York, NY: CRC Press.

Munter, Mary. 1995. Cross-Cultural Communication for Managers. *IEEE Engineering Management Review* 23 (Spring):60 - 68.

Nonaka, Ikujiro, and Hirotaha Takeuchi. 1995. *The Knowledge-Creating Company: How Japanese Companies Create the Dynamics of Innovation.* New York, NY: Oxford University Press.

Pearce II, John A., and Richard B. Robinson Jr. 1991. *Strategic Management: Formulation, Implementation and Control.* Fourth ed. Homewood, IL: Irwin.

Porter, Michael E. 1980. *Competitive Strategy: Techniques for Analyzing Industries and Competition.* New York, NY: The Free Press.

Prahalad, C. K., Liam Fahey, and Robert M. Randall. 1994. A Strategy for Growth: The Role of Core Competencies in the Corporation. In *The Portable MBA in Strategy*, edited by L. Fahey and R. M. Randall. New York, NY: John Wiley & Sons, Inc.

Pucik, Vladimir. 1994. Technology Transfer in Strategic Alliances: Competitive Collaboration and Organizational Learning. In *Technology Transfer in International Business*, edited by T. Agmon and M. A. von Glinow. New York, NY: Oxford University Press.

Ramanathan, K. 1996. Technology Acquisition: External Sourcing, Internal Generation and Alliances. Paper read at Fifth International Conference on Management of Technology, 96/2-3/27-1, at Miami, FL.

Roberts, Edward B. 1991. *Entrepreneurs in High Technology: Lessons from MIT and Beyond.* New York, NY: Oxford University Press.

Rogers, Everett M. 1995. *Diffusion of Innovation.* Fourth ed. New York, NY: The Free Press.

384

Selznick, Philip. 1948. Foundation of the Theory of Organization. *American Sociological Review* 13 (February):25-35.

Senge, Peter M. 1990. *The Fifth Discipline: The Art and Practice of The Learning Organization*. New York, NY: Currency Doubleday.

Shenhar, Aaaron. 1991. Management of Technology: a Morphological Taxonomy. Paper read at Portland Conference on Management of Engineering and Technology, 91/10/27-31, at Portland, OR.

Shenhar, Aaron J., and Dev Dvir. 1996. Managing Design, Uncertainty, and Risk in Product Development Projects: An Application of a Conceptual Framework. Paper read at Fifth International Conference on Management of Technology, 96/2-3/27-1, at Miami, FL.

Simon, Denis. 1994. International Business and the Transborder Movement of Technology: A Dialectic Perspective. In *Technology Transfer in International Business*, edited by T. Agmon and M. A. von Glinow. New York, NY: Oxford University Press.

Sioukas, Anastasios V. 1995. User Involvement for Effective Customization: An Empirical Study in Voice Networks. *IEEE Transactions in Engineering Management* 42 (1):39-49.

Sitkin, Sim B, Kathleen M. Sutcliffe, and Karl E. Weick. 1998. Organizational Learning. In *The Technology Management Handbook*, edited by R. C. Dorf. New York, NY: CRC Press.

Skinner, Ling. 1997. Behind the Curtain. *Techcapital*, 50-54.

Steele, Lowell W. 1989. *Managing Technology: The Strategic View*. Edited by M. K. Badawy, *McGraw-Hill Engineering and Technology Management*. New York, NY: McGraw-Hill Books Company.

Stevenson, Howard H., Michael J. Roberts, and H. Irving Grousbeck. 1994. *New Business Ventures and the Entrepreneur*. Fourth ed. Boston. MA: Irwin/McGraw-Hill.

Tapscott, Don, and Art Caston. 1993. *Paradigm Shift: The New Promise of Information Technology*. New York, NY: McGraw-Hill, Inc.

Tellis, Gerard J., and Peter N. Golder. 1996. First to Market, First to Fail? Real Causes of Enduring Market Leadership. *Sloan Management Review* 37 (2):65-75.

Thompson Jr., Arthur A., and A. J. Strickland III. 1996. *Strategic Management: Concepts and Cases*. Ninth ed. Boston, MA: Irwin/McGraw-Hill.

Tracy, Brian. 1995. *Advanced Selling Strategies*. New York, NY: Simon & Schuster.

Vanini, Sven. 1997. Half-life of technological knowledge: Measurement and implications for technology-planning. Paper read at The Sixth International Conference on Management of Technology MOT 97, 97/6/25-28, at Goteborg, Sweden.

Vasconcellos, Eduardo. 1994. Improving the R&D-Production Interface in Industrial Companies. *IEEE Transactions on Engineering Management* 41 (August):315 - 321.

von Glinow, Mary Ann, and Terri A. Scandura. 1998. Recruitment of High-Technology Workers: Today's Real Challengers and Keys to Success. In *The Technology Management Handbook*, edited by R. C. Dorf. New York, NY: CRC Press.

von Hipple, Eric. 1988. *The Sources of Innovation*. New York, Ny: Oxford University Press.

Werther, William B. 1997. Strategy-Driven Technology in International Competition. Paper read at The Sixth International Conference on Management of Technology MOT 97, 97/6/25-28, at Goteborg, Sweden.

Wheelwright, Steven C., and Kim B. Clark. 1992. *Revolutionizing Product Development: Quantum Leaps in Speed, Efficiency, and Quality.* New York, NY: The Free Press.

White, Donald E., and John R. Patton. 1991. Accelerating Time-To-Market: Methodology and Case Study Highlights. Paper read at Portland International Conference on Management of Engineering and Technology, 91/10/27-31, at Portland, OR.

Wilemon, David. 1995. Cross-Functional Teamwork in Technology-Based Organization. Paper read at 1995 IEEE Annual International Engineering Management Conference, 95/6/28-30, at Singapore.

Wyrick, David A. 1997. Leading Positive Change in Small Businesses: A Collaborative Approach. Paper read at Portland International Conference on Management of Engineering and Technology - 1997, 97/7/27-31, at Portland, OR.

Youngblood, Mark D. 1993. *Eating The Chocolate Elephant: Take Charge of Change Through Total Process Management.* Richardson, TX: Micrografx, Inc.

Zimmer, Thomas W., and Norman M Scarborough. 1996. *Entrepreneurship and New Venture Formation.* Upper Saddle River, NJ: Prentice Hall.

## DISCUSSION QUESTIONS

1. Discuss how globalization is affecting growing technological enterprises. Give examples of these impacts for five selected technological enterprises.

2. Using examples, discuss the four classifications of new technological venture, i.e., life-style, marginal, successful and growing, and high-growth. Use circles of varying size, to denote market share similar to that shown in Figure 7.2 of this chapter.

3. Plot for public technological enterprises the return on investment ("ROI") against growth rate similar to that shown in Figure 7.5 of this chapter. Discuss the reasons for why these enterprises may be in these quadrants.

4. Discuss how *killer applications* have influenced the growth of four technological enterprises.

5. Discuss the differences between external and internal acquisition of technology. Use examples to illustrate your discussion points.

6. Discuss the reasons why there exist technological marketing segments. Choose two technological products and illustrate how these segments influenced the growth of the enterprises involved.

7. Technological customization has served to accelerate the growth of such enterprises as Dell Computer. Discuss four other examples of technological customization and the impact on enterprise growth.

8. Strategic alliances are becoming an integral part of the technological landscape. Discuss how this concept has been used by Microsoft® Corporation to influence its growth. Similarly choose a new emerging technological enterprise and discuss how it has or has not used strategic alliances to impact growth.

9. Discuss why a technological enterprise would seek a presence in the international market space. Illustrate these reasons by referring to particular enterprises.

10. Discuss how an enterprise structure changes during growth. Choose two technological enterprises and show how their structures have changed during their growth.

11. Enterprise strategic leadership considerations require an individual to be multi-faceted. Discuss the leadership role in respect to these facets.

12. Discuss in detail how enterprise culture has influenced the growth of a selected enterprise.

13. Discuss how a technological enterprise can attract and retain human capital.

14. Using currently available data develop a graph of weighted cost of capital for a large public enterprise such as Sun Microsystems and similarly develop a graph for a technological enterprise which has recently had a public offering.

15. Discuss the financing options for a growing technological enterprise. Give advantages and disadvantages of each of the options.

# CHAPTER 8

# Next Entrepreneurial Step

*"To be or not to be, that is the question."*
**Hamlet, Act 3, Scene 1**
**William Shakespeare**
**1564–1616**

## 1.    INTRODUCTION

In many instances the future of the enterprise is associated with a series of financial crises relieved through infusion of capital from a myriad of sources other than the public markets.   At some point in the life of both the technological entrepreneur and the enterprise, a classic decision will have to be made.  This decision is how to *harvest* the large emotional and financial investments in the technological enterprise.  The *harvesting* is the strategy for achieving the terminal after-tax cash flows in the investments by the entrepreneur and other initial investors (Petty 1997).  This *harvesting* has many ramifications both for the entrepreneur and for the other stakeholders in the enterprise.

The decision to harvest investments is driven, in most cases, by the need for the enterprise to obtain growth capital from sources beyond those previously used to build and the grow the enterprise.  This point can come very close to the founding of the enterprise, as experienced by Netscape Communications, or ten or more years into the growth cycle as happened with MicroStrategy.  *Harvesting* is not the only reason mature enterprise choose financing strategies.  All enterprises must have capital to expand. This capital can come from internal or external sources (See Chapter 7 - Strategic Enterprise Growth).

There are a number of alternatives available to the technological entrepreneur and the enterprise leadership team both in providing a *harvesting* opportunity and in obtaining growth capital through the public

388

equity markets. The decision requires considering the best option for both the stakeholders and the enterprise.

In the 1960s, new technological entrepreneurs could easily access public capital through an initial public offering ("IPO") with access peaking in 1969 (Roberts 1991, pp. 140). However, this easy access is not always readily available to the technological entrepreneur as evidenced by subsequent peaks in 1983, 1986 and 1997. In much of the twentieth century, technological entrepreneurs have had to build a financially viable enterprise before seeking public funding and have had to cope with high cost even for very successful enterprises.

Thus at some point in the life of the enterprise, the technological entrepreneur will have to decide on a *harvest* strategy. It must be considered that many original investors at some point may want to *cash-out* their investments to *lock-in* their return.   *two extremes*

## 2.   HARVEST STRATEGY

All prospective investors will want to know before investing what will be the potential *harvest* or *exit* strategy. The *harvest* strategy can be driven by a number of reasons. These reasons include:

- Individual technological entrepreneur wants to exit.
- Original investors want to *harvest* their returns.
- Enterprise requires additional capital to grow the enterprise beyond the ability of former and current investment sources.
- Technological enterprise is in a rapidly growing technological and or market space and a merger and acquisition strategy have been chosen to maintain the enterprise's position in these spaces.

There are also a number of reasons that may work against a *harvesting* strategy. These include (Stevenson, Roberts, and Grousbeck 1994, pp. 31):

- Economic and market space cycles.
- Changes in the tax code.
- Actions of competitors.
- Regulatory and legal changes.
- Loss of trade secrets.
- Internal management and operational problems.

## 2.1 Technological Entrepreneurial Exit

A technological entrepreneur is not usually free to leave an enterprise without serious impact to the future of the enterprise. However, it is also possible that, due to enterprise financial reversals, the entrepreneur may be forced to leave the enterprise.

Regardless of the manner in which the entrepreneur *exits* the enterprise, a succession plan will be required (Zimmer and Scarborough 1996, pp. 525-530). This will require:

- Creating a method for bringing the future CEO up to date with the various aspects of the enterprise and the space in which it inhabits. This educating of the future CEO should not be hurried since the future of the enterprise will be in the *hands* of this chosen individual.
- Promoting an environment of trust and respect within the enterprise. This period should be no less than six months, but preferably a year before the entrepreneur's *exit*. During this period, the technological entrepreneur should empower the successor through a gradual delegation of responsibility. Various enterprise stakeholders, such as customers, creditors, suppliers and enterprise members can gradually develop confidence in the successor.
- *Exit* of the original technological entrepreneur might also have serious consequences for the entrepreneur. It will be important to consult professional tax counsel to deal with these implications.

## 2.2 Investor Harvest Strategy

The *harvesting* of enterprise value by the equity owners, both members of the enterprise and investors, is their strategy for achieving the terminal after-tax cash flows on their investment. The strategy will not necessarily require the technological entrepreneur to *exit* the enterprise. This *harvesting* can take many forms. These *harvesting* options include:

- Sale of the enterprise to third parties.
- Sale of the enterprise to management, known as a management buyout ("MBO").
- Sale of the enterprise to the employees of the enterprise, through creation of an employee stock ownership plan ("ESOP").

- Merger with another enterprise.
- Acquisition by another enterprise.
- Public offering of the enterprise's stock including the initial public offering ("IPO") and a secondary offering of shares held by vested owners including original investors.

## 2.3 Enterprise Sale

The enterprise can be sold to *insiders*, i.e., management and employees, or to *outsiders* including individuals and other enterprises. The sale of the enterprise to *outsiders* requires a valuation that represents the *value* of the enterprise.

Potential acquirers of the technological enterprise have certain motivations. Table 8.1 shows these motivations.

**Table 8.1**
Motivations of Potential Enterprise Acquirers

**Direct Competitors**
**Motivations**
- Gain additional market share.
- Eliminate potential competitor.
- Obtain technology, skills, other resources including production capacity, market space entrant, or distribution systems.
- Economies of scale and increased productivity by combining enterprises.
- Obtain tangible or intangible assets that cannot be easily duplicated such as patents, trademarks, and brand names.

**Non-Direct Competitors in Related Market Space**
**Motivations**
- Market space entry achieved through acquisition.
- Extension of technological products, processes or services.
- Technological knowledge acquisition to remove barriers to market space entry.

**Non-competitors**
**Motivations**
- Enterprise profitability makes it an attractive acquisition target.
- Enterprise technology and market space makes it an attractive acquisition target.
- Application of acquirer's management skills can possibly increase enterprise's profitability.
- Attractive opportunity-risk acquisition.

(Based on data contained in Zimmer and Scarborough 1996, pp. 531)

### 2.3.1 Insider Sale

There are a number of methods by which the entrepreneur and investors can *harvest* their investment by selling the enterprise to enterprise insiders. These methods include leverage buyouts, ESOP and cash buyouts.

#### Leverage Buyout ("LBO")

The LBO in one means for the members of the enterprise to purchase the enterprise. The LBO is primarily a cash transaction where the cash is borrowed from financial institutions using assets or cash flow of the acquired enterprise as collateral. This provides the technological entrepreneur and initial investors with an immediate return on their investment. The LBO is not limited to use by insiders but was quite prevalent in the 1980s for acquiring enterprises (PW 1997b, pp. 102). The LBOs in many instances are used by members of the enterprise leadership team, employees usually through ESOPs, former shareholders, investor groups and professional investors including *junk bond*[1] investors. Figure 8.1 shows the flow chart of the sequence of events for a LBO.

The LBO has a number of advantages and disadvantages for the technological entrepreneur and original investors. The advantages include:
- Immediate cash returns.
- Little risk of not obtaining return if it is a straight cash transaction.

The disadvantages include:
- Tax consequences of a straight cash transaction.
- Total relinquishing of enterprise control.

The LBO usually requires very little capital investment from the acquirers, thus making it an excellent vehicle for inside management and employees. The typical deal has 20 percent equity and 80 percent debt, i.e., four to one ratio (PW 1997a, pp. 102)

#### Employee Stock Ownership Plan ("ESOP")

The ESOP allows employees and or members of the enterprise leadership team to acquire the enterprise gradually (Zimmer and Scarborough 1996, pp. 533-536). The ESOP creates a market for the shares of the entrepreneur and original investors while enabling the technological investor to finance the growth of the enterprise. The ESOP usually is designed as a means to provide the employees with a retirement plan. This allows the employees to

---

[1] Junk bond is a corporate bond having a high yield and high risk.

392

invest primarily in their enterprise's stock (Petty 1997, pp. 431). Figure 8.2 illustrates the flow of events in an ESOP.

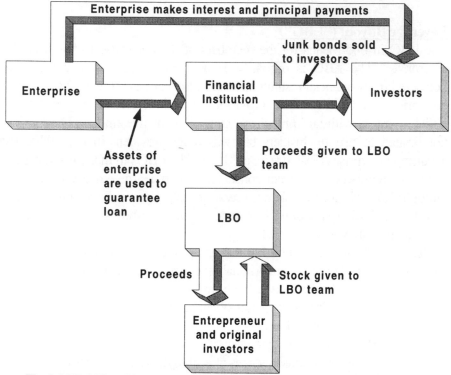

**Fig. 8.1** LBO Flow Chart (Adapted from Garner, Owen, and Conway 1992, pp. 282)

The use of an ESOP as a *harvesting* strategy provides a number of benefits to the selling entrepreneur and original investors including (Petty 1997, pp. 433):

- A market for selling stock.
- Opportunity for the enterprise to deduct both principal and interest payments on debt for the ESOP.
- A means for the entrepreneur and investors to avoid a capital gains tax if ownership by the ESOP is at least 30 percent and if the proceeds are used to purchase stock or bonds in another U.S. enterprise.
- Opportunity for lenders to the ESOP to pay only tax on 50 percent of the income received on the debt when ownership by the ESOP is at least 50 percent.

- Treatment of the dividends that the enterprise pays for the ESOP as a tax-deductible expense, i.e., an interest expense.

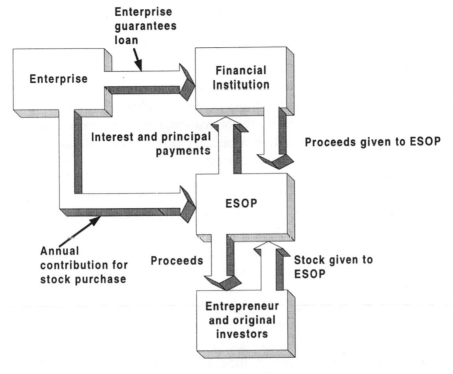

**Fig. 8.2** ESOP Flow Chart (Adapted from Garner, Owen, and Conway 1992, pp. 282)

However, there are certain disadvantages of an ESOP including:

- May make it difficult to sell the enterprise to outsiders or merge it with another enterprise.
- An ESOP must cover all employees and the entrepreneur is required to disclose certain information, such as performance, salaries and other sensitive information.
- An ESOP can place the employees in the position where both their position and retirement plans are at stake.

## Cash Buyout

This is the simplest *harvesting* strategy. It provides the technological entrepreneur and investors with immediate liquid assets. An example is the

1998 sale of Yurie Systems to Lucent Technologies, Inc. for more than one billion dollars, providing the CEO, Dr. Jeong Kim, with an immediate windfall of over five hundred million dollars. The principal disadvantage to this type of transaction is the potential capital gains tax if the transaction is not properly structured.

## 3.    INITIAL PUBLIC OFFERING

The initial public offering ("IPO") offers the enterprise the ability to access broader sources of capital and is a logical step in building the technological enterprise. However, the IPO is a major distraction for the entrepreneur and the enterprise leadership team (Rosenberg 1998). This distraction for a growing technological enterprise can be highly detrimental for a fast-growing, lightly staffed enterprise.

Before the late 1990s, IPOs had involved enterprises with experienced and committed leadership teams who had demonstrated a solid enterprise history, proven products, significant assets, strong earnings and a potential for substantial growth (Thornton 1996). However, in the late 1990s, many technological enterprises had IPOs with few or none of these factors. This market was driven primarily by stock market perceptions that these technological enterprises had a high potential. This was especially true for the rapidly expanding Internet market space that was becoming ubiquitous.

The IPO offers the entrepreneur and the other enterprise investors with an excellent opportunity to *harvest* their investment while providing the enterprise with growth capital and access to future capital. The ability to obtain growth capital is just one of the benefits of a public offering. Table 8.2 shows stages when technological enterprises have gone public.

**Table 8.2**
IPO and Stages of Financing

| Financing Stage | Percent of Enterprises Gone Public |
|---|---|
| Seed and Start-up | 7% |
| First and second | 40% |
| Third and mezzanine | 53% |

(Based on data contained in Roberts 1991, pp. 221)

While many technological enterprises may seek an IPO, there are also reasons why investors may want to invest in an enterprise's IPO. The principal reasons for investment in an enterprise's IPO include:

- Capital gains.
- Dividends.

However, the primary reason for investors to invest in technological enterprise IPOs is to participate in a potential rise in a stock's price after the IPO due to the perceived potential long-term growth opportunity of an enterprise. These potential IPO investors usually look for certain enterprise characteristics that include (CL 1997, pp. 1):

- Sound business plan.
- Strong enterprise management with depth, commitment and integrity.
- Strong enterprise growth potential with a sustainable competitive advantage.
- Growing enterprise technological and market spaces.
- Enterprise public perception and potential for a strong after-market stock value based on recent prior similar offerings.
- Use of proceeds directed in increasing the enterprise's market space position rather than provide a *windfall* exit strategy for the technological entrepreneur and initial investors.

In the 1990s, IPOs for investors have proven to be at best mediocre investments (Schwartz 1998).

While many Internet enterprises in the late 1990s had initial public offerings in their early stages of growth, this has not been the norm in the past and possibly will not be the norm in the future, i.e., this may have been an *exuberance* anomaly due to the excitement surrounding the Internet. As the marketing adage states, this exuberance was likely driven by *"sell the sizzle or sell the steak"* philosophy.

The market for initial public offerings is not continuous; in fact, it goes through almost a cyclic behavior. While 1969 was a year of many IPO offerings, 1970 saw a low point in IPO offerings. Similarly in the 1980s and 1990s windows of IPO opportunities have opened and closed. Therefore, while a technological entrepreneur and investors may want to enter the public market - *"timing is everything."*

The market for IPOs is very cyclical and coincides with the late stages of the so-called *bull markets*[2] as shown in Table 8.3(Batz 1990, pp. 86).

---

[2] Bull market is a market in which prices are on the rise.

**Table 8.3**
IPO or New Issues Market

| *Bull* IPO Market | Collapse |
|---|---|
| Late 1961 | May 1962 |
| 1968 - 1969 | May 1970 |
| 1983 - 1984 | October 1987 |
| 1996 - 1997 | June 1998 |

Table 8.4 shows the technological IPOs in the 1980 to 1997 period. During this period, 1134 technological enterprises had initial public offerings averaging $39.9 million. During this period, there were approximately 100,000 plus technological enterprises that may have sought an IPO. Thus, approximately one in one hundred technological enterprises had a probability of having a successful IPO.

The growth in the IPO market is characterized by (Batz 1990, pp. 87):

- Growth in new small underwriting enterprises that usually disappear when the new issue market goes into a decline.
- Relaxed standards from established underwriters due to the market *exuberance*.
- Underwriters actively seeking IPO's.
- Formation of new technological enterprises by *deal packagers* who actively seek to recruit technological professionals to establish these enterprises.

Figure 8.3 shows a ranking of the factors that IPO underwriters view as important in determining a stock offering. The growth prospects and the soundness of the leadership team are seen as the most important of these factors. Roberts' (Roberts 1991, pp. 227) also found that the historical growth in sales and price-earning ("P/E") ratio were not significant factors in determining the success of an IPO. Figure 8.4 shows the most important reasons that underwriters may not support an enterprise's IPO.

**Table 8.4**
Technological IPOs

| Year | IPOs | Total Proceeds ($ million) | Average Proceeds ($ million) |
|---|---|---|---|
| 1980 | 14 | 321 | 22.9 |
| 1981 | 31 | 565 | 18.2 |
| 1982 | 13 | 457 | 35.2 |
| 1983 | 85 | 249 | 29.3 |
| 1984 | 24 | 459 | 19.1 |
| 1985 | 12 | 203 | 16.9 |
| 1986 | 36 | 822 | 22.8 |
| 1987 | 33 | 832 | 25.2 |
| 1988 | 17 | 366 | 21.5 |
| 1989 | 29 | 858 | 29.6 |
| 1990 | 23 | 608 | 26.4 |
| 1991 | 49 | 1,761 | 35.9 |
| 1992 | 65 | 3,936 | 60.6 |
| 1993 | 96 | 3,015 | 31.4 |
| 1994 | 78 | 2,690 | 34.5 |
| 1995 | 142 | 7,071 | 49.8 |
| 1996 | 219 | 11,846 | 54.1 |
| 1997 | 168 | 6,988 | 41.6 |
| 1998 | 90 (est.) | 5,940 (est.) | 66 (est.) |

(Based on data contained in Greenberg 1999; Itoi 1998b)

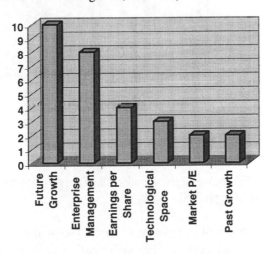

**Fig. 8.3** Factors Underwriters View as Important in IPO's (Based on data contained in Roberts 1991, pp. 327)

398

The technological entrepreneur and the enterprise leadership team need to understand the factors driving the public market before deciding on a public offering. These factors include (Petty 1997):

- IPOs tend to be under-priced relative to their market-trading price. In some instances, this undervaluing has been as much as one fourth to one fifth of the new issue price at the closing of the first day of trading. However, the average is ten to fifteen percent under-valuations.
- Timing for the initial public offering is important due to periods of high average initial returns and high volumes, known as *hot issue* markets.
- Technological enterprises who have had an IPO tend to under-perform the Standard and Poors ("S&P") 500 Index for up to five years after the IPO.

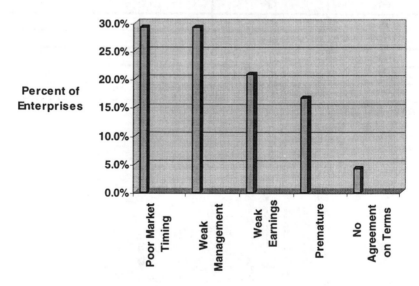

**Fig. 8.4** Factors Influencing Negative Underwriter Decision (Based on data contained in Roberts 1991, pp. 228)

There are a number of issues that the technological entrepreneur and the leadership team should consider before deciding to have an initial public offering including:

- Advantages and disadvantages of an IPO.

- The IPO process and the timing.
- Enterprise requirements.
- Legal requirements.
- Choosing an underwriter.
- Valuation of the offering.
- Enterprise operations as a public company.

The ownership of the equity or stock of the enterprise can take various forms based on the number and type of shareholders. Many technological enterprises are privately owned and as such are termed *closely held* enterprises and their stock is called *closely held stock*. When the equity ownership or stock is held by a large number of investors, the majority of which are not active in the management of the enterprise and the stock is publicly traded, the enterprise is termed a *publicly owned enterprise* and the stock is called *publicly held stock*.

## 3.1 Security Markets

The stock of most *publicly held enterprises* is traded on various stock exchanges[3]. The stocks of small publicly held enterprises are usually not listed on an exchange but are traded *over-the-counter* ("OTC") market a and are termed *"unlisted"*. These markets include the *pink sheets* and the OTC Bulletin Board (CL 1997, pp. 29).

There are three major security markets in the U.S.:

- New York Stock Exchange ("NYSE").
- American Stock Exchange ("AMEX").
- National Association of Securities Dealers Automated Quotation ("NASDAQ") Stock Market.

In 1998, AMEX and NASDAQ agreed to merge. The NYSE is also known as the *Big Board*. The NYSE and AMEX represent an *auction market* where the shares are auctioned on a trading floor by specialists responsible for all of a particular stock's activity. The specialist matches the stock transactions of buyers and sellers. The NASDAQ stock market includes the NASDAQ National Market and the NASDAQ Small Cap Market. The trading on the NASDAQ market is done electronically using computer and telephone transactions. The NASDAQ market provides a

---

[3] Stock Exchange is a market for the sale and purchase of securities of enterprises and municipalities, and, in some cases, of certificates representing commodities of trade. The stock exchanges have an important role in a capitalistic economy. Exchanges trace their history to the Amsterdam Stock Exchange in 1600s.

*liquid* market since it uses the combined capital of *market makers[4]* that use their capital and work together to make a market for the various stocks. Table 8.5 shows the listing criteria for the various security markets.

Stock market transactions can be divided into the following categories:

- Primary Market - Additional shares sold by publicly owned enterprises to raise new equity capital.
- Secondary Market - Trading in the outstanding shares of publicly owned enterprises. The enterprise does not receive any of the proceeds of the sale of the security.
- Initial Public Offering in Primary Market - The first time sale of enterprise securities to raise equity capital.

All stock market transactions are based upon:

- Bid price - The price at which the stock buyer will pay for the stock.
- Ask price - The price at which the stock seller will sell the stock
- *Spread* - The difference between the bid price and the ask price that provides the compensation above the commissions to those involved in the stock trade (PW 1997b, pp. 76). This spread varies between one-eight to one-half point of the stock value.

In May 1995, the European Association of Securities Dealers Automated Quotation ("EASDAQ") was formed to provide the European Union ("EU") with its own version of NASDAQ. The NASDAQ began trading stocks in November 1996. A similar stock exchange was also established in Germany, known as the Neuer Market (Itoi 1998a). The Neuer Market is an offshoot of the Frankfurt Stock Exchange and is designed especially for high-growth, small-cap enterprises. Another EU market similar to NASDAQ is Euro, NM located in Brussels, Belgium. The Nouveau Marché in Paris, France, Neuer Market and the NMAX in Amsterdam, Netherlands devised Euro, NM to link their exchanges electronically. These exchanges were in 1998 planning to standardize their requirements for listing and reporting, to allow cross-membership and to encourage joint promotion (Itoi 1998a).

---

[4] Market makers are individuals or enterprises that buy and inventory stock of a particular listed enterprise.

**Table 8.5**
Security Market Listing Criteria

| Criteria | NYSE | AMEX | NASDAQ National Market Listing 1 | NASDAQ National Market Listing 2 | NASDAQ National Market Listing 3 | NASDAQ SmallCap Market |
|---|---|---|---|---|---|---|
| Total Assets | N/A | N/A | N/A | N/A | $75 million | N/A |
| Pretax Income | $2.5 million for most recent year or $2 million for 2 years preceding or aggregate $6.5 million for last 3 years together with minimum in most recent years of $4.5 million (all 3 years must be profitable) | $750,000 | $1 million | N/A | N/A | $750,000 |
| Net Tangible Assets[5] | $18 million | $4 million | $6 million | $18 million | N/A | $4 million |
| Aggregate Market Value of Publicly Held Stocks | $18 million | $3 million | $6 million | $18 million | $20 million | $5 million |
| Public Shares Held | 1.1 million | 500,000 | 1.1 million | 1.1 million | 1.1 million | 1 million |
| Public Shareholders (Round-Lot holders[6]) | 2,000 | 800 | 400 | 400 | 400 | 300 |
| Minimum Price | N/A | Approximately $3 million | $5 | $5 | $5 | $4 |
| Number of Market Makers | N/A | N/A | 3 | 3 | 4 | 3 |
| Number of Outside Directors of the Board | 2 | 2 | N/A | N/A | N/A | N/A |

[5] Net tangible assets means total assets (excluding goodwill) minus total liabilities
[6] Round lot holders are considered holders of 100 shares or more.

While many EU enterprises are having IPOs on EU exchanges, Israeli enterprises in the late 1990s choose U.S. markets for their IPOs. In 1996, 19 Israeli most of which were technology enterprises had U.S. IPOs which equated to eight percent of all U.S. technological IPOs that year (Marcus and Mehta 1997). Table 8.6 shows the NASDAQ IPO distribution in 1996.

**Table 8.6**
Distribution of NASDAQ IPOs

| Enterprises | Total IPO Value ($ billion) |
|---|---|
| United States | 21.2 |
| Israel | 0.63 |
| Other Foreign | 2.28 |

(Based on data contained in Marcus and Mehta 1997)

## 3.2    IPO Advantages and Disadvantages

There are numerous advantages and disadvantages of an initial public offering. In the instances where the technological entrepreneur and the enterprise team have decided on an IPO, this is a financing decision to use issue equity to the public rather than obtain growth capital from other alternative sources.

### 3.2.1  IPO Advantages

There are numerous advantages to an initial public offering for the technological entrepreneur, the enterprise leadership team and other equity shareholders. These advantages are in the following areas:

- Access to capital.
- Market valuation.
- Harvest or exit strategy.
- Acquisition growth strategy.
- Financial strategy.
- Employee incentives.
- Glamour and prestige enhancement.

*Access to Capital* - An IPO provides access to capital from the public equity markets. This access to capital fills a need for cash and additional enterprise working capital. This capital is necessary to support enterprise growth, expand research and development, retire debt, acquire additional capital equipment, finance market programs and enable other enterprise growth initiatives. The public equity market can also be used in the future by the enterprise through secondary offerings to obtain additional capital if the equity market has confidence in the enterprise's progress.

*Market Valuation* - An IPO provides a means for valuing the enterprise that is in many instances acceptable to future investors. In the late 1990s, however, many Internet enterprises were valued in the billions of dollars without commensurate substantiating sales and income flows. These enterprises were valued on perceived market growth. A similar exuberant market valuation happened in the seventeenth century in the Netherlands in the valuation of tulip bulbs[7]. While high market valuations may in the short run increase wealth of certain technological entrepreneurs and their financial backers, the sustainability of these valuations is economically questionable.

*Harvest or Exit Strategy* - The IPO also provides a means for the technological entrepreneur and other initial investors to increase their liquidity. This increased liquidity can, within limitations of the security laws and practical market limitations, provide an exit whereby their equity is converted into cash (PW 1997b).

*Acquisition Growth Strategy* - The IPO provides market valuation of an enterprise's equity issues, i.e., stock which in some cases can enable acquisition of other enterprises. In the case of very high valuation enterprises, acquisition of other enterprises can be accomplished more easily and with less of an initial use of the enterprise's cash resources. Acquisitions of this type can be achieved through a tax-free exchange of stock.

*Financial Strategy* - An IPO becomes a means of obtaining capital with a lower dilution potential for existing equity stakeholders than the majority of other alternatives, such as with a private placement or venture capital. An IPO can also enhance the ability of the enterprise to obtain future debt capital since it gives the enterprise an improved debt-to-equity ratio. This also provides a means to increase net worth since capital obtained through an IPO does not have to be returned.

*Employee Incentives* - The availability of publicly traded stock can provide incentives to existing and new enterprise employees. When the availability of technological skills is limited, it provides an excellent means to

---

[7] In 1634 speculation in tulip bulbs reached new heights in the Netherlands, where one collector paid 1,000 pounds of cheese, four oxen, eight pigs, 12 sheep, a bed, and a suit of clothes for a single bulb of the Viceroy tulip. By 1637 tulip prices collapsed after years of speculation and hundreds were ruined as the bottom fell out of the tulip bulb market.

attract and retain scarce human resources. This allows the enterprise to have stock-based compensation plans that have market linked valuation.

*Glamour and Prestige Enhancement* - An IPO raises the enterprise's visibility by converting the enterprise from a private to a publicly held enterprise. This can possibly enhance the enterprise's image and brands with customers, suppliers, investors, and employees. This boosted image can enhance the enterprise's competitive position (Zimmer and Scarborough 1996, pp. 399). In addition, a public enterprise receives more media coverage than a private enterprise. An IPO not only increases the enterprise's visibility locally, but it also makes it more easy to allow for national expansion due to the nature of the public markets (PW 1997b, pp. 6).

### 3.2.2 IPO Disadvantages

While the advantages of an IPO may be very appealing to some technological enterprises, some entrepreneurs may believe the disadvantages serve as a negative stimulus. These disadvantages include:

- High cost.
- Dilution of ownership.
- Loss of control.
- Disclosure.
- Short term performance pressure.
- Management perquisites.
- Legal liabilities.
- Accounting practices.

*High Cost* - The IPO process is expensive and time consuming and results in costs that do not end with the IPO. A public enterprise must file quarterly and annual reports with the SEC and possibly state officials depending upon the state of incorporation. The SEC's periodic reporting requirements vary depending upon the number of shareholders and what major changes have occurred to the enterprise. These reports are available to the public, both shareholders and non-shareholders alike, through the Internet. Data are available through the Electronic Data Gathering, Analysis, and Retrieval ("EDGAR") system.

The cost of the IPO, for many small technological enterprises, represents twelve percent of the capital raised (Zimmer and Scarborough 1996, pp. 400). This cost can be divided between:

- Underwriter's compensation - Costs associated with a successful offering which are not deductible for income tax purposes. These expenses are considered a reduction of additional paid-in capital. However, if the IPO is not completed these can be expensed for income tax purposes.
- Direct cost - Costs associated with the offering whether or not the offering is completed and which are tax deductible.

The underwriter's compensation usually averages between seven and ten percent of the gross proceeds of the offering. Besides this percentage, the underwriter may be granted (Lybrand 1997, pp. 10):

- Warrants[8]
- Stock issued before the IPO at below the offering price.
- Right of first refusal on secondary enterprise stock offerings.

The direct expenses can include:

- Reimbursement of some of the underwriter's direct expenses.
- Legal fees.
- Accounting fees directly related to the IPO.
- Printing costs.
- Fees including SEC, NASDAQ, and state *blue-sky* filing fees, registrar and transfer agent fees, securities market's entry fees, and various miscellaneous fees.

There is also the annual expense associated with SEC and state reporting requirements.

*Dilution of Ownership* - The decrease in ownership by selling equity to the public can also be a disadvantage. This could eventually, depending on the amount of stock available to the public, cause the loss of management control. If more than fifty percent of the enterprise is sold, management may lose control if the shares held by the public are not widely distributed.

*Loss of Control* - The IPO and any secondary offerings will dilute existing shareholders' control. The enterprise leadership team must manage the enterprise to increase shareholder value or otherwise face serious consequences including stockholder litigation. The leadership team of a public company is much more vulnerable than a private enterprise. The

---

[8] Warrants are rights to purchase future shares at specific prices.

enterprise, when it is publicly held, is accountable to all stockholders, not just the technological entrepreneur and initial investors.

*Disclosure* - There are various disclosure requirements imposed on public enterprises by SEC regulations. These disclosures include profits, competitive position, executive compensation, employee benefits, and changes in enterprise circumstances. These requirements to disclose various enterprise conditions can provide existing and future competitors with important operational data. The requirements that the enterprise report the shares owned by officers, directors and major shareholders could also pose privacy issues. The reporting of profitability and other financial data of a public enterprise provides suppliers, customers, and competitors with important data for future negotiations.

*Short Term Performance Pressure* - The shareholders of a public enterprise expect a steady growth in sales, profits, market space, and technological innovations. Hence, the leadership team is constantly under pressure to meet short-term goals, sometimes to the detriment of long-term strategic objectives. This pressure in many instances is fueled by expectations publicized by market analysts. Not meeting these expectations can result in significant impacts on the enterprise's stock price and long term valuation. A report must also disclose the relationship between executive compensation and enterprise performance.

*Management Perquisites* - In a privately held enterprise management may have opportunities for various questionable but legal self-dealings (Brigham 1989, pp. 448). These may include compensation and benefit packages and related-party transactions that would not be either acceptable or legal for a publicly held enterprise.

*Legal Liabilities* - The SEC reporting requirements for transactions with officers, directors and large shareholders poses the threat of potential liability. Legal penalties can be imposed for failure to report these transactions adequately. In addition, *insider* trading is forbidden based on undisclosed information. Any *insider* gains realized in closed transactions within a six-month period can be recovered by the enterprise (Lybrand 1997, pp. 9).

*Accounting Practices* - The enterprise must follow both generally accepted accounting principles ("GAAP") and SEC accounting rules. These rules are usually different to those an entrepreneurial enterprise may use before an IPO. The cost of providing fully audited financial statements is also another IPO disincentive.

These disadvantages of an IPO can be daunting for the enterprise and must be carefully weighed against the advantages. Hence, many public enterprises have gone *private* in a LBO transaction in which the leadership team acquires debt to purchase the equity of the non-management stockholders.

## 3.3  IPO Preparations
Once the decision has been made to seek an initial public offering, there are a number of internal and external issues that must be addressed by the technological entrepreneur and the enterprise leadership team.

### 3.3.1  Internal Enterprise Issues
The pre-IPO internal enterprise issues include:
- Depth of management team.
- Enterprise performance and other metrics.
- Board of Directors membership.
- Enterprise image.
- Compensation plans.
- Corporate structure.

*Management Team* - An important element in achieving a successful IPO is the capabilities of the management team. It may be necessary to augment the existing leadership team in certain areas such as marketing, engineering, finance and other critical enterprise functions.

*Enterprise Performance* - The valuation of the enterprise will be based on past and projected growth in revenues and profits. This requires that the enterprise be able to forecast realistically the enterprise's future performance and is coupled with the SEC and exchange requirements to have audited financial statements. It is good practice for the enterprise to prepare realistic budgets and have audited financial statements from the beginning of the technological enterprise. While audited financial statements may be expensive for a new technological enterprise they will be easier and more cost effective to have available from the beginning than to try to accomplish them just before an IPO. The existence of audited financial information is also a means to increase the credibility of the enterprise.

*Board of Directors* - It is important to have a strong and knowledgeable board. Enterprises preparing for an IPO must have two outside directors within ninety days after the offering. However, having outside directors from almost the beginning of the enterprise can be of immense value.

Outside board members can help the enterprise during the IPO process, and their experience and skill can be a major asset to the enterprise following the IPO (PW 1997b, pp. 28). The board should form subcommittees before the IPO. These subcommittees usually cover audit, compensation and benefits.

*Enterprise Image* - Before an IPO, an enterprise must build its *brand* recognition. A positive image or *brand* for the enterprise will help to draw potential buyers of the enterprise's stock offering. This image or *branding* of the enterprise not only helps to enhance sales but also influences the financial analysts, stockbrokers, financial press, and industry publications so as to enhance the IPO. This image or brand building requires a professional approach from public relations firms who specialize in the technological market space.

*Incentive Compensation Plans* - Potential buyers of the enterprise's IPO will closely scrutinize the leadership team and the means of motivating them. Incentive compensation plans can tie the leadership team rewards to the growth of the enterprise and thus to a long-term commitment. It is important that the proper incentive compensation plans be established early in the enterprise's life cycle. Incentive compensation plans which grant equity, options and warrants within one year before an IPO can require the enterprise to expense an additional compensation charge (Lybrand 1997, pp. 17).

*Enterprise Structure and Agreements* - The existing structure and agreements of an enterprise may not prove beneficial to a publicly owned enterprise. Changes may be required to provide a proper legal structure to the enterprise including removing subsidiary enterprises to establish a single overall entity (PW 1997b, pp. 27). These changes should also dissolve or end shareholder control agreements that can prove onerous and remove any related entities that may have been used to shift taxable income. Needed changes should be made before an IPO since changes made post-IPO may require shareholder approval.

### 3.3.2 External Enterprise Issues

The external enterprise issues to be addressed following a decision to seek an IPO include:

- Choices of investment banker/underwriter, legal and accounting professionals.
- Type of securities to be issued.
- Type of underwriting.

- Offering price.

*Investment Banker/Underwriter* - The most critical decision that the technological entrepreneur and enterprise leadership team will have to make in the IPO process is the choice of the investment banker/underwriter. Investment bankers assist enterprises in the design of securities that are attractive to investors, purchase those securities from the enterprise, and then resell the securities to stock-buyers. The investment banker acts as a middle-person in the process of transferring capital from the stock-buyers to the enterprise and does this for a commission. The investment banker will serve as the managing underwriter and be the lead in forming the underwriting syndicate. The underwriter establishes the initial price for the enterprise's stock, supports the stock in the after-market to help stabilize its price and creates a following among stock analysts who are important in the continued performance of the stock.

The enterprise either can search for a potential investment banker or is *found* by them. In either case, the technological entrepreneur and the enterprise leadership team will have to make a major decision. The principal factor in selecting an underwriter is the reputation of the underwriter (Roberts 1991, pp. 225). Since the enterprise usually is not well known, the underwriter's *brand* must serve as the surrogate. The underwriter's *brand* will help *co-brand* the enterprise's stock and make a market for their equities. The underwriter's ability to distribute the stock is another important selection factor (Roberts 1991, pp. 225). The client base of the investment banker is an important element in its ability to distribute the stock. The client base is divided between institutional and individual investors; international or domestic; long-term or speculative; and local, regional or nationwide (Hisrick and Peters 1995, pp. 330).

The experience of the investment banker with technological underwriting is a third important factor that should be considered. While many of the major investment banks have multiple market space experience, some specialize in certain technological spaces such as biotechnology, telecommunications, software, hardware, etc.

The underwriter's ability to provide after-market support is also important. This support can consist of research on the enterprise and its technological and market space to keep the investor interested in the enterprise, making a market in the stock, and providing advice to the enterprise on matters such as dividends, new financing and mergers and acquisitions (Stevenson, Roberts, and Grousbeck 1994, pp. 549).

The decision on the choice of the underwriter will also depend on the compensation required by the investment banker. The underwriter's compensation usually is between seven and ten percent of the gross IPO proceeds. The National Association of Securities Dealers ("NASD") regulates the maximum compensation and direct costs of underwriters. The size of the offering, maturity of the enterprise, difficulty of the offering, type of security offered and type of underwriter commitment will determine the compensation (Lybrand 1997, pp. 10). The monetary compensation may be augmented by warrants to purchase future shares at specific prices, stock issued before the IPO and the right of first refusal on future offerings.

*External IPO Team (Excluding Underwriter)* - Besides an investment banker/underwriter, the enterprise will have to choose other members of its IPO team. These members include the enterprise's independent accountants, lawyers and principal investors all of whom are necessary to have a successful IPO. The independent accountants, besides being responsible for auditing the enterprise's financial structure, will also serve as an independent reviewer of the financial data, management's discussion and analysis, the use-of-proceeds, potential share dilution, capitalization and supplementary financial schedules included in the registration statement filed with the SEC. The independent accountants and legal counsel should be experienced in the IPO process and be totally familiar with SEC requirements. The enterprise's security counsel selection, since they have a lead role in guiding the enterprise through the registration process should be chosen carefully (Lybrand 1997, pp. 23).

*Types of Securities* - The initial public offering can sell common stock, preferred stock, warrants or a combination of financial instrumentalities. The usual offering for many technological enterprises is common stock.

*Type of Underwriting* - There are two types of underwriting that can be used by the investment banking firm, i.e., a firm commitment or a best efforts commitment. The firm commitment binds the managing underwriter to purchase all the securities being offered by the enterprise and by any selling shareholders at an agreed-upon price. This type of commitment ensures that the enterprise can raise the required capital by a certain date. The managing underwriter assumes all the risk in a firm commitment underwriting. For assuming this risk the underwriter will usually seek and obtain an over-allotment option for as much as fifteen percent of the total shares being offered. This over-allotment option is known as a *green shoe*. The firm commitment on the part of the managing underwriter is made just before the registration statement.

In a best efforts commitment, the managing underwriter agrees to use its best efforts to sell the enterprise's securities but is not obligated to purchase the unsold securities for their own account. This type of commitment has been rare in the 1990s of exuberant technological IPOs.

*Offering Price* - The managing underwriter is likely to provide the estimated offering price for the offering. The offering price is a negotiative issue between the underwriter and the enterprise that has many possible impacts. A low price estimate not only provides the enterprise with a lower amount of capital but also places an initial lower value on the enterprise. If the IPO produces a substantial price rise after the initial sale, the enterprise and the selling shareholders have not fully benefited, while the underwriters may in fact obtain substantial benefits. Similarly, a high price stock valuation may or may not provide benefits to the enterprise. A high price followed by a reduction in price after the initial sale can significantly damage the future capital plans of the enterprise. If the initial price is perceived to be too high by the investing public, a weak after-market may result causing the price of the shares to fall below the offering price (KPMG 1997, pp. 29). In theory the price should be set by estimating the enterprise's future earnings per share and then using industry price per earnings multiples to arrive at a per share value. These comparisons include (KPMG 1997, pp. 28):

- Leverage ratios - The debt to equity, number of times interest earned.
- Earnings ratios - The net earnings as a percentage of sales, net earnings to net worth, net earnings as a percent of assets.
- Efficiency ratios - The sales per employee.

However, the price per earnings multiple is a subjective judgment (Stevenson, Roberts, and Grousbeck 1994, pp. 577). The stock market conditions immediately before the offering will determine the offering price. The technological entrepreneur, initial investors and other enterprise stakeholders can only hope that the *stochastic resonance* is with them. The price of the IPO is usually set at ten to fifteen percent less than the anticipated after-market price (KPMG 1997, pp. 29).

Once the enterprise and the managing underwriter have agreed to have an IPO, the underwriter will issue a *letter of intent*. The issuance of the *letter of intent* by the managing underwriter begins what is called the *quiet period.*

412

The *letter of intent* is used as the basis for the underwriter agreement. The underwriting agreement is executed usually at the effective date of the registration but has been negotiated throughout the IPO process. The *quiet period* is the period before the IPO. In this period, the enterprise is subject to SEC guidelines regarding publication of information outside the *prospectus* (Lybrand 1997, pp. 31). The *letter of intent* will include (Lybrand 1997, pp. 22):

- Securities offered.
- Size and estimated total dollar value of the offering.
- Size and use of over-allotment options, known as a *green shoe*.
- Discount or commission to the underwriter.
- Price and number of warrants the underwriter may exercise.
- Underwriter expenses.
- Any underwriter restrictions on enterprise leadership team options or salaries.
- An agreement that prohibits principal investors from selling shares for a specific period of 120 to 180 days after the IPO. This type of an agreement is known as a *lock-up*.

## 3.4 IPO Process

The IPO process is based upon the registration statement that is filed with the SEC. The average time for the process ranges from 100 to 120 days of intense activity on the part of the IPO team. The registration statement covers a variety of forms that must be filed. The registration statement is a detailed and daunting document covering information about the proposed offering, enterprise's history, and existing and future conditions. The registration statement includes a *prospectus* that prospective stock buyers will use to make their investment decision. The final approved *prospectus* must be provided to all individuals purchasing the enterprise's stock for twenty-five days after the effective date of offering, or until the offering is sold or terminated. During this period, any material changes to the enterprise's conditions must also be distributed in the form of a *supplement* to the *prospectus*.

There are a number of filings that must be made to the SEC. The enterprise has a number of options depending on its size. The basic filing is the *S-1* form. All the SEC forms consist of two principal parts. *Part One* of the form contains the enterprise statements covering operations, financial conditions, leadership team and other information to be included in the *prospectus*. *Part Two* of the form contains all other data and information that will not be included in the *prospectus*, but will be available through the SEC for public inspection.

The SEC also provides for small enterprises with revenues less than $25 million and less than $25 million in publicly held securities registration forms *SB-1* and *SB-2*. Table 8.7 shows the requirements for an *S-1* and *SB-1/SB-2* filing.

The registration statements are available to the public as soon as they are filed with the SEC. This data is also available through the Internet using EDGAR SEC system. All filings to the SEC must also be prepared for incorporation into the EDGAR system. Figure 8.5 shows a schematic of the IPO registration process. Table 8.8 shows an average timeline for the IPO registration process.

**Table 8.7**
Comparison of *S-1* and *SB-1/SB-2* Filing Requirements

| Requirements | *S-1* Filing | *SB-1/SB-2* Filing |
|---|---|---|
| Income statement | 3 years | 2 years |
| Balance sheet | 2 years | 1 year |
| Earnings per share | 3 years | 2 years |
| Financial schedule | 3 years | Not required |
| Management discussion and analysis | Required | Required |
| Selected financial data | Required | Required |
| Pro forma financial statement | Required | Required |
| Financial statement of acquisitions | Required | Required |

(Based on information contained in Lybrand 1997, pp. 33)

### 3.4.1 Roadshow

The *roadshow* is the primary means of selling the IPO offering and as such is the critical element of an IPO. This effort usually takes approximately ten working days and is grueling and daunting. An example is the *roadshow* that preceded the MicroStrategy, Inc. IPO at the end of May and beginning of June of 1998 (Leibovich 1998). Michael Saylor (See Chapter 2 -

414

Technological Entrepreneurs), the CEO of MicroStrategy, Inc. and the Chief Financial Officer ("CFO"), Mark Lynch, spent eleven working days crossing the United States in a leased corporate jet to hold seventy meetings in eleven cities. The process consisted of meeting various institutional and other potential investors. While the process is both tiring and daunting, it is also exhilarating. When Michael Saylor and his team had finished the roadshow process, they had achieved an over subscription to their offering. The IPO was priced at $12 pr share, raising $48 million. The stock began trading on NASDAQ on June 11, 1998 and by the close of the trading day the stock closed above $20 per share; by July 13, 1998 it had risen to $44.50 per share, making Michael Saylor a stock-market billionaire (Leibovich 1998).

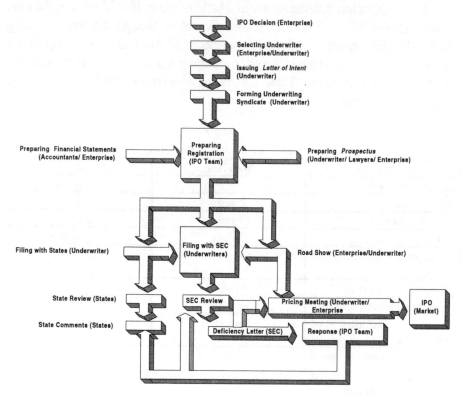

**Fig. 8.5** IPO Registration Process

**Table 8.8**
IPO Timeline

| Day | Activity | Enterprise | Selling Shareholders | Enterprise Counsel | Underwriter | Underwriter Counsel | Independent Accountants |
|---|---|---|---|---|---|---|---|
| < 3 years | Audited financial statements | X | | | | | X |
| <0 | Select underwriter | X | | | X | | |
| <0 | Letter of intent, quite period begins | X | | | X | | |
| 1 | Hold Board of Directors meeting to authorize issuing additional stock, preparing registration statement, negotiating underwriter agreement and hiring additional professionals | X | | | | | |
| 2 | Organizational meeting, also known as *all hands* meeting, to discuss parameters of offering, schedule, prospectus format and format of registration statement and due diligence | X | X | X | X | X | X |
| 3 | Begin due diligence process | | | | X | X | |
| 4 | Assign responsibilities and complete timetable | X | X | X | X | X | X |
| 5-30 | Begin drafting registration statement (S1) | X | | X | | | X |
| 12-30 | Prepare draft of underwriter agreement | X | | X | X | X | |
| 15-30 | Distribute questionnaires to directors, leadership team and selling shareholders related to registration statement | X | X | X | | X | |
| 20-30 | Complete review of corporate legal documents | X | | X | | | |
| 30-60 | Review first draft of registration statement (S-1) | X | X | X | X | X | X |
| 35-60 | Complete draft of financial statements for registration statement (S-1) | X | | | | | X |

| 45-70 | Review draft of registration including financial statements | X | X | X | X | X | X |
|---|---|---|---|---|---|---|---|
| 50-75 | Appoint stock transfer agent<br>Comfort letter requirements and procedure<br>Continue due diligence | X<br>X | | X | X<br>X<br><br>X | X | X<br>X |
| 50-70 | Drafting session<br>Review market conditions | X | X | X | X<br>X | X | X |
| 60-85 | Send draft registration statement (S-1) to printer | X | | | | | |
| 70-90 | Board of Directors meeting to approve and sign registration statement | X | | X | | | |
| 71-91 | File registration statement with SEC, NASD, and States<br>Distribute preliminary prospectus, (known as *Red Herring* ) to proposed underwriting syndicate<br>Send draft comfort letter to underwriter<br>Publish *tombstone* advertisement informing public of potential offering | X<br><br><br><br><br><br>X | | X<br><br>X<br><br><br><br><br>X | X | | X |
| 100-120 | Receive comment letter from SEC and States | X | | X | | | |
| 101-121 | Meeting to review comment letters | X | X | X | X | X | X |
| 105-125 | Prepare amendments to S-1 registration statement | X | X | X | X | X | X |
| 106-126 | Review printer proof of amendments | X | X | X | X | X | X |
| 108-128 | File amendments with SEC<br>Request acceleration of process | X<br>X | X | X<br>X | X | X | X |
| 113-133 | Resolve final SEC comments by telephone | X | | X | | X | |
| 114-134 | Hold due diligence meeting<br>Domestic roadshow<br>Notify stock exchange and NASD of effectiveness and start of trade | X<br>X | X | X<br><br>X | X<br>X | X | X |
| 115-135 | Finalize offering price | X | | | X | | |
| 116-136 | Deliver comfort letter to | | | | | | x |

| | | | | | | | |
|---|---|---|---|---|---|---|---|
| | underwriter<br>Sign underwriting agreement | X | | X | X | X | |
| 120-140 | Deliver second comfort letter to underwriter | | | | | | X |
| 120-140 | Complete *Blue Sky* and NASD filings | | | | X | | |
| | Begin stabilization reporting to SEC | | | | X | | |
| | Underwriter provides breakdown for stock certificates | | | | X | | |
| | Registrar and transfer agent authorized to deliver stock certificates for inspection | X | | | | | |
| | Preclosing | | | X | | X | |
| | Closing - complete settlement with underwriter, issue stock, collect proceeds and sign all final documents. | X | X | X | X | X | |
| | Issue press release | X | | | X | | |

(Based on data contained in KPMG 1997, pp. 32-33; Lybrand 1997, pp. 93-95)

### 3.4.2 Prospectus

The prospectus is the highly stylized narrative Part One of the *S-1* filing. This part of the *S-1* filing is the document that is given to the prospective buyers of the enterprise's stock. The prospectus format will be the responsibility of the enterprise and the underwriter but must contain the following sections and information:

- Prospectus summary.
- Risk factors associated with the offering.
- Use of proceeds.
- Dividend policy and restrictions.
- Dilution that is based on the difference between the IPO price and the net book value per share of tangible assets.
- Capital structures of the enterprise both prior to the offering and after the offering.
- Underwriting and distribution of securities
- Information about the enterprise business including the technological and market space factors.
- Financial information.
- Information about the enterprise's officers, directors, principal shareholders and their compensation.

- Management discussion and analysis of the enterprise's liquidity, capital resources, results of operations.
- Other discussions including any legal proceedings, interests of named experts, counsel, and relationships and related transactions.

A preliminary prospectus and a final prospectus are prepared. The final prospectus is prepared once approval of the SEC has been obtained. The printing costs for a prospectus can be $50,000 to $200,000 depending on its size and the number of revisions. This would also include the cost of preparing the documentation required for filing with the SEC via EDGAR.

## 4.    PUBLIC TECHNOLOGICAL ENTERPRISE

The life cycle of a technological enterprise does not cease with a successful initial public offering, but begins as public enterprise with all its benefits and associated issues. As a public enterprise, the enterprise leadership team will be under continuous scrutiny by the stockholders, financial analysts, and the SEC and as such must disclose how it operates. Each of these groups has a different objective.

- Stockholders are primarily concerned with the value of the stock and the growth of the enterprise.
- Financial analysts are primarily concerned with the present and future financial status of the enterprise in its technological and market space.
- SEC is concerned that the enterprise and those closely associated with the enterprise, such as the enterprise leadership team, directors and major shareholders, report what is happening to the enterprise through quarterly and annual filings.

### 4.1    Public and Investor Relations

The enthusiasm of the investment community must be maintained once the enterprise becomes a public enterprise. This enthusiasm will influence the market position of the enterprise's stock. Hence, it is important for the enterprise to retain the services of public relations professionals that are familiar with maintaining the public image of the enterprise.

In maintaining this enthusiasm, the leadership team of the enterprise is now faced with the problem of keeping long-term goals while providing short-term quarterly performance. In many instances these are conflicting goals, since short-term performance can in many instances be obtained by sacrificing long-term enterprise goals. The public technological enterprise must continuously demonstrate (Lybrand 1997, pp. 84):

- Sustained or increasing growth rates in both revenue and profitability. While in the late 1990s, investors in Internet stocks appeared to be interested more in potential growth of revenues than in actual profitability. This preoccupation with revenues instead of profits is an anomaly, that is of itself not sustainable.
- Innovative and committed enterprise leadership team that is flexible and capable of adapting to the rapidly changing technological landscape.

The financial and investor community requires that the enterprise maintain excellent lines of communication. This means that the enterprise should disclose both positive and negative information as rapidly as possible through press releases. Timely communication to the public, as in the case of the Intel Corporation with Pentium microprocessor defects in 1996, is vital. This communication must be forthright so that the enterprise's reputation can be maintained. It is also important from a legal viewpoint that investors have access to both positive and negative information to minimize the risk of shareholder litigation.

## 4.2 SEC Reporting Requirements

The U.S. security acts of 1934 require filings with the SEC. Table 8.9 shows the SEC reporting requirements. The technological enterprise should consult its legal counsel to confirm the SEC requirements for the filing of these and any other forms. These reporting requirements, while daunting, do help to build confidence in the enterprise. Current and prospective shareholders, stock analysts, current and potential customers and others use these reports to base their future decisions. These reports must be filed within the prescribed time limits, otherwise the enterprise can face serious financial and legal consequences. These reports are also available on the Internet through the EDGAR reporting system.

**Table 8.9**
SEC Reporting Requirements

| Form | Requirement | Timing |
|---|---|---|
| 10K & 10-KSB | Annual report to stockholders following SEC specifications | Within 90 days of end of fiscal year |
| 10Q & 10-QSB | Quarterly report includes financial data and information on significant events | Within 45 days of end of quarter |
| 8K | Report of significant events including acquisition/disposal of assets, change in control, bankruptcy, changes in independent accountants | Within 15 days of event |
| Proxy or Information Statements | Data furnished to shareholders to decide on assignments of their votes | Varying |
| 13D and 13-GB | Stockholders with five percent or more must file if there is any intent to change or affect control of the enterprise | Within 10 days after obtaining status |
| 3[9] | Stockholders with ten percent or more, officers or directors | Within 10 days after obtaining status |
| 4 | Subsequent changes to beneficial ownership | Within 10 days after the calendar month in which change occurred. |
| 5 | Stock transaction not previously reported in Form 3 or 4 | Within 45 days after the fiscal year-end |

## 5.    TECHNOLOGICAL ENTREPRENEUR'S NEXT STEP

The technological entrepreneur in many instances is not the individual who will always be with the enterprise.  It is important that the technological entrepreneur understand that there is a time and a place where the vision and drive of the entrepreneurial dream be replaced with professional managers who can grow the enterprise and bring it to maturity.  The life of a technological enterprise will in many instances exceed that of the technological entrepreneur.  The technological entrepreneur must always look to the future and build again.

---

[9] Holders filing Forms 3, 4 and 5 are required under Section 16(b) of the securities act require returning all profits made on trades with duration of six months or less regardless of whether or not there are any other losses on trading the enterprise stock.  The highest and lowest stock prices in the period are used to compute this profit.

# REFERENCES

Batz, Gordon B. 1990. *Entrepreneurship for the Nineties*. Englewood Cliffs, NJ: Prentice Hall.

Brigham, Eugene F. 1989. *Fundamentals of Financial Management*. Fifth ed. Chicago, IL: The Dryden Press.

CL. 1997. *A Guide to Going Public*. Second ed. New York, NY: Coopers & Lybrand.

Garner, Daniel R., Robert R. Owen, and Robert P. Conway. 1992. *The Ernst & Young Guide to Raising Capital*. New York, NY: John Wiley & Sons, Inc.

Greenberg, Julie. 1999. Burn Rate Olympics: 1998's IPOs. *Wired*, 99/01, 62.

Hisrick, Robert D., and Michael P. Peters. 1995. *Entrepreneurship: Starting, Developing, and Managing a New Enterprise*. Chicago, IL: Irwin.

Itoi, Nikki Goth. 1998a. Nothing comes easy. In *Going Public: Guide to Technology Finance 1998*. New York, NY: Red Herring.

Itoi, Nikki Goth. 1998b. Reality Check. In *Going Public: Guide to Technology Finance 1998*. New York, NY: Red Herring.

KPMG. 1997. Going Public: What the CEO Needs to Know. New York, NY: KPMG.

Leibovich, Mark. 1998. Journey Into the Secret Heart of Capitalism: Cross-Country "Roadshow" Makes a Young CEO's Stock-Market Debut. *The Washington Post*, 98/8/9, A1, A18-A19.

Lybrand, Coppers &. 1997. A Guide to Going Public. New York, NY: Coopers & Lybrand.

Marcus, Amy Dockster, and Stephani N. Mehta. 1997. Israel's High-Technology Push Stumbles; IPOs are Delayed. *The Wall Street Interactive Edition*, 97/6/10, http://interactive5.wsj.com/edition/current/articles/SB865898885733545500.htm.

Petty, William. 1997. Harvesting. In *The Portable MBA in Entrepreneurship*, edited by W. D. Bygrave. New York, NY: John Wiley & Sons, Inc.

PW. 1997a. The Buying and Selling a Company Handbook. New York, NY: Price Waterhouse.

PW. 1997b. The Going Public Handbook. New York, NY: Price Waterhouse.

Roberts, Edward B. 1991. *Entrepreneurs in High Technology: Lessons from MIT and Beyond*. New York, NY: Oxford University Press.

Rosenberg, Hilary. 1998. *A Cold Look at Going Public* [WWW]. Business Week Online, 1998 [cited 98/11/10 1998]. Available from http://www.businessweek.com/smallbiz/news/date/9811/e98111D.htm.

Schwartz, Nelson D. 1998. The Ugly Truth About IPOs. *Fortune*, 98/11/23, 190-196.

Stevenson, Howard H., Michael J. Roberts, and H. Irving Grousbeck. 1994. *New Business Ventures and the Entrepreneur*. Fourth ed. Boston. MA: Irwin/McGraw-Hill.

Thornton, Grant. 1996. Going Public: An Overview for Entrepreneurs. Burr Ridge, IL.

Zimmer, Thomas W., and Norman M Scarborough. 1996. *Entrepreneurship and New Venture Formation*. Upper Saddle River, NJ: Prentice Hall.

# DISCUSSION QUESTIONS

1. Discuss in detail the various harvest strategies available to the technological entrepreneur. Discuss in detail the advantages and disadvantages of these strategies. Give examples of these strategies from recent events.

422

2.  Choose a publicly held technological enterprise and trace its history. This history should include changes in senior management including the entrepreneur. Discuss the various harvest strategies that may have been employed by reviewing SEC filings.

3.  Discuss technological leverage buyouts including the related advantages and disadvantages. Where possible use examples of recent LBOs of technological enterprises.

4.  Employee Stock Option Plans ("ESOP") offer a means to harvest enterprise value. Discuss the advantages and disadvantages of an ESOP. Where possible use examples from recent LBOs of technological enterprises.

5.  Choose three technological enterprises that have had a recent initial public offering ("IPO"). Discuss in detail their prospectus including their technological and market space, pro forma financials, enterprise leadership team and directors.

6.  Obtain data on the technological enterprise IPOs over a twelve-month period and discuss in detail.

# INDEX

# F

432

# J

# K

# N

# O

# U

446

# X

# Y

# Z